CW00615961

TRAVEL G

Galápagos

2nd Edition

January 2014

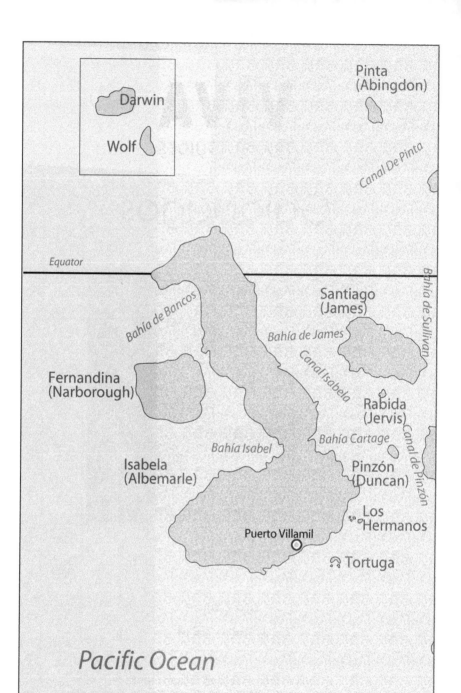

Pinta
(Abingdon)

Canal De Pinta

Bahía de Sullivan

Equator

Bahía de Bancos

Santiago
(James)

Bahía de James

Canal Isabela

Fernandina
(Narborough)

Rabida
(Jervis)

Canal de Pinzón

Bahía Cartage

Bahía Isabel

Isabela
(Albemarle)

Pinzón
(Duncan)

Los
Hermanos

Puerto Villamil

Tortuga

Darwin

Wolf

Pacific Ocean

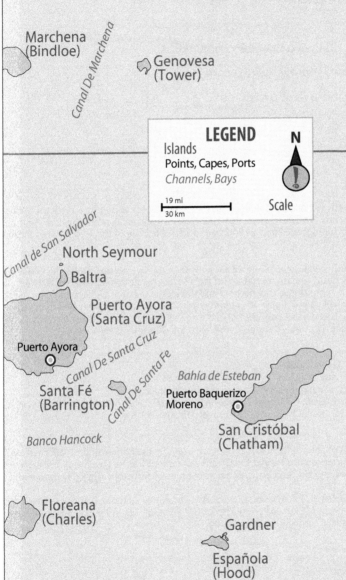

Pacific Ocean

Marchena
(Bindloe)

Canal De Marchena

Genovesa
(Tower)

LEGEND   N

Islands
Points, Capes, Ports
Channels, Bays

19 mi
30 km   Scale

Canal de San Salvador

North Seymour

Baltra

Puerto Ayora
(Santa Cruz)

Puerto Ayora

Canal De Santa Cruz

Canal De Santa Fe

Bahía de Esteban

Santa Fé
(Barrington)

Puerto Baquerizo
Moreno

Banco Hancock

San Cristóbal
(Chatham)

Floreana
(Charles)

Gardner

Española
(Hood)

V!VA Travel Guides Galápagos.

ISBN-10: 0-9825585-1-1

ISBN-13: 978-0-9825585-1-5

Copyright © 2014, Viva Publishing Network.

Website: www.vivatravelguides.com

Information: info@vivatravelguides.com

◇ Cover Design: Jason Halberstadt, 2013 ◇
◇ Cover Photo: "Baby Sea Lion" by Robin Slater, 2013 ◇
◇ Cover Photo: "Iguana and Hawk" by Jason Halberstadt, 2013 ◇
◇ Back Cover Photo: "Giant Galápagos Tortoise on Santa Cruz Island," by Jason Halberstadt, 2011 ◇
◇ Title Page Photo: "Small Lobo" by Christopher Minster, 2008 ◇

CONTENTS

INTRO & INFO

INTRO & INFO

Travelers' discussions. User reviews. Feedback. Photo contests. Book updates. Travel news. Apps. Writing contests. Give-aways.

V!VA TRAVEL GUIDES

Follow us online

www.facebook.com/VTGEcuador

www.vivatravelguides.com

Why reserve your hotel or hostel with V!VA ?

- Hand-picked recommendations on the best places to stay by V!VA's on-the-ground writers.

- Get a free e-book download for every reservation made.

- Get a 35% discount on book purchases when you reserve.

- Your reservation helps V!VA improve this guide.

www.vivatravelguides.com/hotels

ABOUT THE WRITER

INTRO & INFO

Christopher Minster, Ph.D. is from Rochester, NY, but lives in Ecuador. He is a professor at the San Francisco de Quito University and is an official resident of the Galápagos. He is also head writer at V!VA Travel Guides, and has collaborated on several V!VA guidebooks, including Ecuador, Peru, Argentina, Chile and Guatemala. Check out his Latin American History website at http://latinamericanhistory.about.com/. His wife, Maricarmen, is a certified Galápagos naturalist guide with nearly 20 years experience in the islands.

AUTHOR'S NOTE:

I wish to thank my wife **Maricarmen**, whose vast knowledge of everything Galápagos was crucial as I worked on this book. This book would not have been possible were it not for the support of the writers and staff of V!VA Travel Guides. I would like to particularly thank **Jason Halberstadt, Paula Newton, Karey Fuhs, Jena Davison** and **Lorraine Caputo**. Big thanks to Galápagos guides **Emma Ridley, Juan Carlos Avila, Fabio Iacoponi** and Lola Villacreses for their patience in answering my endless questions.

This guidebook is dedicated to my parents, Richard and Priscilla, who first took me to Galápagos over 20 years ago.

ABOUT THE EDITORS

INTRO & INFO

Christopher Klassen was the Managing Editor for this book. With parents that worked for the U.S. Foreign Service up until he graduated from high-school, Chris was raised to have the heart of a nomad throughout his life. He has resided in Honduras, Guatemala, Colombia, Panama and Ecuador throughout his years, and just recently spent the past four up in Canada finishing his Bachelor's Degree in Philosophy at the University of British Columbia.

Paula Newton has an MBA and a background in New Media, and was the organizing force behind the editorial team. With an insatiable thirst for off-the-beaten-track travel, Paula has traveled extensively, especially in Europe, Asia and Latin America, and has explored more than 30 countries. She currently lives in Quito.

Jena Davison was a former staff writer and editor at V!VA. Shortly after graduating from University of Wisconsin-Madison with a BA in Journalism and Mass Communication, Jena packed her backpack and headed across the equator to travel solo through South America. Born and raised in New Jersey, Jena's itch for travel has previously brought her to 20 countries, mostly in Europe and Latin America. She currently lives in Florida.

Jason Halberstadt is the founder of VIVA Travel Guides and VIVA's parent company MetaMorf. He has lived in Ecuador since the mid 1990's and has traveled extensively in the Galapagos, and throughout Ecuador. He has trained writers and editors in VIVA's Travel Writing Boot Camps throughout Latin America and currently runs Metamorf's Silicon Valley office.

MANY THANKS TO:

Cristián Ávila, the programming mastermind who keeps www.vivatravelguides.com running smoothly and is always willing to lend a hand to the not-so-computer-savvy staff; and to the whole **Metamorf** team for their support.

INTRO & INFO

About VIVA Travel Guides

VIVA Travel Guides pioneers a new approach to travel guides. We have taken the travel guide and re-designed it from the ground up using the Internet, geographic databases, community participation, and the latest in printing technology, which allows us to print our guidebooks one at a time when they are ordered. Reversing the general progression, we have started with a website, gathered user ratings and reviews, and then compiled the community's favorites into a book. Every time you see the V!VA insignia you know that the location is a favorite of the V!VA Travel Community. For you, the reader, this means more accurate and up-to-date travel information and more ratings by travelers like yourself.

Community and Free Membership:

The accuracy and quality of the information in this book is largely thanks to our online community of travelers. If you would like to join them, go to www.vivatravelguides.com/members/ to get more information and to sign up for free.

Your Opinions, Experiences and Travels:

Did you love a place? Will you never return to another? Every destination in this guidebook is listed on our web site with space for user ratings and reviews. Share your experiences, help out other travelers and let the world know what you think.

Corrections & Suggestions:

We are committed to bringing you the most accurate and up-to-date information. However, places convert, prices rise, businesses close down, and information, no matter how accurate it once was, inevitably changes. Thus we ask for your help: If you find an error in this book or something that has changed, go to www.vivatravelguides.com/corrections and report them (oh, and unlike the other guidebooks, we'll incorporate them into our information within a few days).

If you think we have missed something, or want to see something in our next book go to www.vivatravelguides.com/suggestions and let us know. As a small token of our thanks for correcting an error or submitting a suggestion we'll send you a coupon for 50 percent off any of our E-books or 20 percent off any of our printed books.

Coming soon on www.vivatravelguides.com

This is just the beginning. We're busy adding new features that our users have requested to our books and website. A few coming attractions to improve community functions include the ability to: join specialized groups, find travel partners, participate in forum discussions, write travel blogs, add maps, and much more!

How to Use This Book:

This book is a best-of Galapagos taken straight from our website. You can check out www.vivatravelguides.com to read user reviews, rate your favorite hotels and restaurants, and add information you think we are missing. The book also features highlighted sections on Ecuador, Quito and Guayaquil.

About this Book

At V!VA, we believe that you shouldn't have to settle for an outdated guidebook. You can rest assured that in your hands is the most up-to-date guidebook available on Galápagos because:

-- The final research for this book was completed on August 1, 2013
-- Each entry is "time stamped" with the date it was last updated
-- V!VA's hyper-efficient web-to-book publishing process brings books to press in days or weeks, not months or years like our competitors
-- V!VA's country guides are updated at least once per year.

When you buy a V!VA Guide, here's what you're getting:

-- The expertise of professional travel writers, local experts and real travelers in-country bringing you first-hand, unbiased recommendations to make the most out of your trip
-- The wisdom of editors who actually live in Latin America, not New York, Melbourne, or London like other guidebook companies
-- Advice on how to escape the overly-trodden gringo trail, meet locals and understand the culture
-- The knowledge you'll need to travel responsibly while getting more for your money

Contribute to V!VA

V!VA is an online community of travelers, and we rely on the advice and opinions of vagabonders like yourself to continuously keep the books accurate and useful.

Take a part in this ongoing effort by reviewing the places you have been on the website, www.vivatravelguides.com.

Other travelers want to know about that rarely visited town you stumbled upon, about that bus company you will never take again, about that meal you just can't stop thinking about.

Together, we can help enhace each other's travel experiences and share in our love and passion for exploring Latin America.

Go ahead! Log on and create a free user account to help make the best guidebook series to LatinAmerica even better.

Introduction

Ecuador might be the smallest of the Andean countries, but size is a hardly a factor in light of what it contains. The entire country covers the Coast, Andean Highlands and the Amazon Basin - all packed into its small surface area. Not to mention, there's the Galapagos Islands sitting 1000 km. off the coast. As a result of this, Ecuador - in many ways - boasts a little bit of everything that South America has to offer, and its relatively small size and wide diversity ultimately become its most enticing qualities.

Get stoked, and plunge right into the sparkling blue waters of the Galapagos Islands where playful sea lions swim through your legs and hammerhead sharks slither by without even a glance in your direction.

Relax, and sip a cappuccino in the capital's historic colonial center while taking in the beauty of Spanish cathedrals built over the ruins of the Inca Empire - all of which is set against the majestic backdrop of the Andes.

Finally, awe yourself, and pull up to a remote jungle lodge in a dugout canoe - carved out using the same techniques that Amazon tribes have used for thousands of years - and allow yourself to be lulled to sleep by the sounds of toucans, parrots and howler monkeys that inhabit the dense forest surrounding you.

Hard to believe, but it's all possible here in Ecuador.

It's so enticing that , in recent years, Ecuador has become a hotspot for expats and retirees from all over the world to come and establish new roots in. The country itself is still incredibly cheap to reside in, and you'll find that an abundance of affordable travel services - along with luxury travel options - are readily available.

However, the country still remains largely undiscovered and there are still plenty of opportunities for remote adventure travel. Some of the most popular activities in Ecuador include birdwatching, mountain biking, kayaking and hiking. remote adventure travel. Some of the most popular activities in Ecuador include birdwatching, mountain biking, kayaking and hiking.

Other travelers come to volunteer, often as language teachers; either to help with reforestation (the rainforest is being stripped at an alarming rate) or to work with one of the many NGOs operating in Ecuador. Many also choose to spend a few weeks studying Spanish in Quito - currently the biggest language-learning center in South America.

But whatever it is you're in search of throughout Latin America, this might very well be the place to find it.

Geography of Ecuador

At 283,560 square kilometers (176,196 sq mi), Ecuador is about the size of the US state of Nebraska and slightly larger than the United Kingdom. Bordered by Peru to the south and Colombia to the north, the nation forms a small bulge off the Pacific northwestern coast of South America, with the equator cutting across the northern part of the country.

Ecuador is divided into four distinctive regions, making it one of the most varied countries in the world for its small size. Pacific coastal lowlands lie to the west, the extremely bio-diverse jungles of the Amazon basin form the east, and the arresting peaks of the Andes cut down through the center of the country and constitute the central highland region. The country also holds the unique archipelago of the Galápagos Islands some 1,000 kilometers (621 mi) off-shore to the west.

Almost all rivers east of the Andes in Ecuador drain to the Amazon. The major waterways are: the Napo, Pastaza and Putumaçyo, which all drain to the east; and Daule-Guayas and Guayllabamba-Esmeraldas, which flow into the Pacific Ocean.
Updated: Sep 03, 2012.

Weather and Climate

Ecuador has two seasons, wet and dry, which have much to do with the part of the country you are in. Generally speaking, the temperature is dictated by altitude. **Quito** and the Andes enjoy spring-like weather year-round, with highs of around 20-25° C (68-77°F) and lows of about 8-10°C (45-50°F). Weather in the **Galápagos** varies between misty and cool, and steamy and sunny. The Amazon region is generally either hot and humid, or hot and rainy.

The wet season or *invierno* (winter) in the highlands is from October until April (with a short dry period from mid-November to the end of December known as *veranillo*, or small summer).

The dry season, *verano* (summer), lasts from June until September. However, no matter what season it is said to be, the weather is ultimately unpredictable. Warm sunny mornings can often lead to bone-chilling, rainy afternoons, hence the *sierra's* adage "four seasons in one day."

The Pacific Coast is at its coolest from June to November, when it is often cloaked in *garúa*, a thick, foggy mist. Generally, the region is warm and humid year round, with temperatures averaging 25-31°C (77-90°F). The rainy season—from December to May—is warm and muggy. The dry season is less humid, but by no means any drier. It actually tends to be wettest in the north (Esmeraldas) and driest in the South as you get near the Peruvian border.

Temperatures in the Oriente (Amazon) hover around the high 20s to low 30°sC (high 80s to low 90s°F). It rains most days in this area, but the wettest months are April to September, which can provide a nice bit of respite from the inescapable heat. Some secondary roads may be closed due to flooding at this time, which can put off a trip if it involves road travel off the main roads. Many of the lodges in the Oriente are reached by canoe.

During the dry months, especially December to February, many of the subsidiary rivers completely dry up and lodges are reached by foot instead of canoe. This provides a completely different experience and you may want to check with your tour operator before lugging your bags along the dried-up river bottom.

In the Galápagos there is a rainy season, a dry season and a transition season. The months of June to December tend to be characterized by cool garúa (mist) and temperatures averaging 22°C (72°F). From January to May, the climate is more typically tropical: hot air temperatures, wide stretches of blue sky, and occasional brief downpours. Because many of the islands are covered in black (bare) lava rock, you may feel yourself baking (and burning) in the heat as a result of the heat that they tend to absord.
Updated: Aug 06, 2012.

Flora and Fauna in Ecuador

Nature lovers from around the world are drawn to the rainforests, jungles, cloud forests, deserts, islands, volcanoes and snow-capped peaks of Ecuador, one of the world's most bio-diverse nations. This tiny country holds 46 different ecosystems. Many private and public organizations work to protect Ecuador's biodiversity, which includes 44 national parks and reserves, and several UNESCO Natural Heritage sites. The most notable of these regions are Ecuador's portion of the Amazon Rainforest and the enchanted Galápagos Islands.

Whether you are interested in seeing some of the 2,725 orchid species growing in the wild in the Andes, or the 25,000 different species of trees in the northeastern Amazon Rainforest, Ecuador has what you're looking for. The Amazon is particularly rich in flora, partially because of its geographical advantage; the Andes sharply drop off into the Amazon River basin, feeding rich nutrients right into the rainforest basin. The Andes feature cloud forests rich in orchids, bromeliads and tropical plants and trees. In total, the Andes have an estimated 8,200 plant and vegetable species. Although the Galápagos Islands were volcanically formed and are largely barren, they are home to over 600 native plant species, and many more have been introduced.

The small country is also home to more bird species than exist in North America and Europe combined: a total of 18 percent of the world's birds and 15 percent of its endemic bird species can be found in Ecuador. A million species of insects, 4,500 species of butterflies, 350 reptiles, 375 amphibians, 800 fresh water fish, 450 salt water fish species, and 1,550 mammal species crawl, climb, fly and swim throughout this bio-diverse wonderland.
Updated: Sep 03, 2012.

Regions of Ecuador
QUITO

Quito, the bustling capital of Ecuador, is more than just a place to pass through *en-route* to other spectacular sites. Most visitors to Quito are struck by how the modern and the traditional exist side by side: The city has everything from Baroque cathedrals to TGI Friday's. The colonial city center, named by UNESCO as the first World Heritage site because of its well-preserved, beautiful architecture, is a great place to take a stroll or even spend the night if you don't mind a little more noise. A downtown highlight is La Compañia church: the interior is one of the most striking in the world, as there is a vast amount of gold leaf covering all of the intricate woodwork on the walls and ceiling.

You'll want to visit the Panecillo, a small hill near colonial Quito where an impressive statue of an angel overlooks the city. The view is fantastic.

The Mariscal district, beloved by international visitors, is where you'll find all of the *chévere* (cool) places: nightclubs, bars, internet cafes, bookstores and hip restaurants. Shoppers won't want to miss the artisan markets in and around El Ejido park: they're the best place to find a bargain south of Otavalo. Visitors of all ages will want to visit Quito's highest attraction, the Telefériqo, a gondola-style cable car that whisks visitors from Quito to the top of the Pichincha volcano, climbing several hundred meters in the process—the complex also features an amusement park at the base, with restaurants and shops and the top and bottom.

Quito is the cultural and artistic heart of Ecuador—here is where you'll find all of the best museums, restaurants and upscale shops. Visitors can see shows and concerts at the elegant and newly restored Teatro Sucre or catch the world-famous Jacchigua national folkloric ballet. No visit to Quito is complete without a stop at Mitad del Mundo, a small "village" for tourists about twenty minutes north of the city where the equatorial line is marked by an impressive monument. Take your photo with one foot in each hemisphere, then enjoy local cuisine at the restaurants in the complex as you listen to impromptu concerts by Andean bands.

THE ANDES

The majestic Andes mountains bisect Ecuador along a north-south line, effectively dividing mainland Ecuador into three zones: the rainforest, the highlands, and the coast. The Andes region is home to several of the most interesting places to visit in Ecuador, including the country's most charming cities, one of the best markets in the Americas, several volcanoes and plenty of opportunities for adventure travel, such as rafting and hiking.

The famous indigenous crafts market at Otavalo is located about two hours north of Quito. South of Quito, the mellow tourist town of Baños attracts visitors from around the world who want to enjoy the thermal baths, which supposedly have divine healing powers.

Most travelers try to find time to fit in at least a day trip to Cotopaxi, one of the highest active volcanoes on earth. On a clear day, it can be seen towering over Quito. If remote is your thing, head to the Quilotoa Loop where you will find a spectactular crater lake and opportunities to observe rural life. The city of Cuenca should not be missed with its well-preserved colonial center and opportunities for hiking and shopping in the surrounding area. If you have the time, head very far south to Vilcabamba—you will quickly see why its inhabitants claim to live long lives—the pace of life is sublimely relaxed.

THE AMAZON BASIN

Much of the water that flows eastward through South America along the Amazon river and its tributaries originates in the mountains of Ecuador. The Ecuadorian Amazon Basin is a fantastic place to visit—you can expect to see monkeys, birds, caimans, butterflies and more on a trip to the jungle. Most visitors to the rainforest take advantage of the services offered by the various jungle lodges, who arrange everything from transportation to guides and food. If you want to see lots of wildlife, head deep into the primary rainforest to one of the outlying lodges.

THE COAST

Ecuador's Pacific coast is long, largely undeveloped (apart from major ports at Esmeraldas, Manta and Guayaquil), and dotted with many excellent beaches.

One of the routes to the beach passes through the small town of Mindo, located in the tropical cloud forest. Mindo is a prime destination for birdwatchers, who can expect to see hundreds of species in a very small area. Mindo is also known for rafting and adventure travel. Ecuador's biggest city, Guayaquil, is located in the coastal region as well.

While the northern coastline is lined with greenery, the southern coast is typified by countless shrimp farms and drier scrubland. Banana plantations and swampy mangroves are found along pretty much the entire length of the coast. Coastal highlights include the beach towns of Esmeraldas province, which have good nightlife, but can get overrun on weekends and public holidays with quiteños escaping the city; the laid-back surfing town of Montañita, and the stretch of beach in between known as La Ruta Del Sol—the route of the sun.

Ecuadorian History
PRE-INCA TIMES

Although the earliest evidence of man in Ecuador can be traced back to 10,000 BC, there are few concrete facts about the country's history before the invasion of the Inca in the mid-15th century. Research is ongoing, and the **Museo Nacional** in Quito has some fascinating artifacts that are laid out to chart the probable development of the country before the Inca, from the age of hunter-gatherers to the dawn of pottery and ceramics, agriculture and fixed settlements. By 1480, dominant indigenous groups included Imbayas, Shyris, Quitus, Puruhaes and Cañaris in the highlands; and the Caras, Manteños and Huancavilcas along the coast.

THE INCA INVASION

The Inca began dominating present-day Peru in the early 13th century, but it was not until the mid-15th-century that they began to expand into what is now Ecuador. Pachacútec led the invasion with his son Túpac Yupanqui. Native resistance was fierce, particularly in the north, but they eventually arranged peace terms with one dominant group in the south, the Cañari.

Túpac Yupanqui extended the empire further after the death of his father, establishing himself at Ingapirca before conquering the Quitu-Caras nation at present-day Quito. He then built an impressive network of roads stretching the length of his empire from Cusco in southern Peru all the way up north to Quito. Some of these roads survive today and are popular with hikers.

Túmac Yupanqui was succeeded by his son, Huayna Cápac, who had been born at Tomebamba (also called Tumipampa; modern-day Cuenca), who established another administrative seat at Quito, where his son Atahualpa was born. Problems arose when Huayna Cápac died, setting off a war of succession between two of his sons, Huáscar and Atahualpa. Huáscar, Huayna Cápac's eldest son, was based at Cusco, while Atahualpa, Huáscar's younger brother, governed his half of the empire from Quito. Both brothers were power hungry, and soon after their father's death civil war broke out. In 1532, Atahualpa secured victory over his brother.

THE SPANISH INVASION AND CONQUEST

The Inca ruler Atahualpa governed for less than a year before the Spanish arrived, led by Francisco Pizarro. Atahualpa—foolishly as it turns out—thought of Pizarro and his band as an innocent bunch of foreigners. He welcomed them into his empire and befriended them, only to be captured and held hostage by them. Fearing for his life, Atahualpa offered a huge ransom of gold and silver in return for his release. Pizarro accepted, then beheaded the leader anyway. Knowing that the Spanish had assassinated Atahualpa, the Inca, led by General Rumiñahui, chose to destroy Quito rather than leave it in the hands of the Conquistadores. Within one bloody year, hundreds of thousands of Incas had been slaughtered and the whole empire had fallen to the Spanish.

Pizarro founded his capital at Lima, Peru, while his lieutenants Sebastián de Benalcázar and Diego de Almagro founded **San Francisco de Quito** in 1534, on the charred remains of the Inca city. Following a local legend of great riches in the lands to the east, Pizarro sent an expedition down into the Amazon Basin in 1540. Pizarro placed his brother, Gonzalo, in charge of the expedition, which departed from Quito. Having found nothing after several months, and running out of food, Gonzalo Pizarro sent Francisco de Orellana ahead to see what might be found. Orellana never returned. Instead he had floated down the entire Amazon River, through Brazil, out to the Atlantic Ocean. This marked the first crossing of the continent by a white man in a canoe, and the event is still celebrated in Ecuador today.

Meanwhile, the Spanish had been busy dividing up Ecuador's land among themselves. The *encomienda* system was established by the Spanish crown to reward conquistadores by granting them huge estates upon which they could force the indigenous people who happened to occupy the land into slavery. In exchange for their back-breaking labor, the slaves were given room, board and religious instruction. The food was so meager and the work so hard that many starved to death or died from diseases. As a result, the

Manuela Saenz

Born in Quito in 1793 as the illegitimate daughter of a married Spanish nobleman, Manuela Saenz led one of the most fascinating lives in the history of Latin America. Forced into a convent because of her illegitimate status, she was kicked out at the age of seventeen when it was discovered that she was carrying on an affair with a Spanish military officer. Her father arranged for her to marry James Thorne, a wealthy Englishman who was much older than she. They moved to Peru, where Manuela lived as an aristocrat and became involved in the planning of the independence movement.

In 1822, she left her husband and moved back to Quito, where she met Simón Bolívar, the hero of South American independence, and they began a torrid affair. Although she lived with Bolívar for a short while, they spent most of their time apart as he traveled a great deal in pursuit of independence.

Manuela herself was an important heroine of independence. She was a skilled horse-woman who fought at the Battles of Pichincha and Junin and was eventually given a cavalry command. She was promoted to Colonel on the recommendation of Antonio José de Sucre, Bolívar's second-in-command.

On September 25, 1828, she saved Bolívar's life by helping him escape an assassination attempt. Bolívar died two years later of tuberculosis. After his death, anti-Bolívar factions in Peru and Ecuador conspired to exclude her from any position of influence, and she wound up living in Jamaica for some time. She moved to a small town in northern Peru, where she lived by selling tobacco and translating letters that North American whalers wrote to their lovers in various ports of Latin America. She died penniless in 1856.

Today, Ecuadorians (and Quiteños in particular) have embraced Manuela Saenz as one of their own. She is considered a national heroine and is the subject of the first ever Ecuadorian opera, which premiered in 2007 to rave reviews. You can visit the Manuela Saenz Museum in Quito: Barrio San Marcos, Centro Histórico: Phone 593-2-295-8321. Monday – Friday 8:30 – 5:30. Entrance: $1.

indigenous population decreased dramatically. About half of Ecuador's Indian population was forced to live in this manner for centuries.

Although the encomienda system was theoretically outlawed in the 17th century, in practice, the oppression of the indigenous population continued under various guises until 1964 when the Agrarian Reform Law was passed.

Two sectors of the indigenous population escaped the encomienda system. Some were rounded up to live in specially constructed indigenous towns and forced to work in textiles or agriculture (it is for this reason that **Otavalo** became so famous for its weaving), or lived so deep in the Amazonian lowlands that they completely escaped all the implications of Spanish rule, both good and bad. One positive legacy of this troubled time is Ecuador's beautiful haciendas, elaborate country mansions built by the wealthy

Spaniards. Today, many of these haciendas have been converted into some of Ecuador's most memorable and unique hotels.

INDEPENDENCE FROM SPAIN

Spanish rule continued with relative peace until the late 18th century, when creole (Spanish born in the New World) leaders started to resent Spain for its constant interference and its demand of high taxes. The creoles began working toward independence. When Napoleon placed his brother Joseph on the throne of Spain in 1807, many creoles saw it as the opportunity for independence they had been waiting for. After a couple of failed attempts to defeat the Spanish armies, the first real victory was won at Guayaquil, which gained independence in October 1820. At this point an urgent request for backup was sent to the South American liberator, Simón Bolívar.

To help prevent the Spanish from regaining power, Bolívar swept into action by sending his best general, Antonio José de Sucre, to take command of the rebel army based in Quito. Sucre and his forces won the pivotal battle of Pichincha on May 24, 1822, ending Spanish rule in Ecuador. Bolívar declared Quito the southern capital of a huge new nation, Gran Colombia, which included present-day Ecuador, Colombia, Panama and Venezuela. His dream was to make the whole continent into a single, independent nation; but this idea went down badly with the residents, and in 1830 the Quito representatives won independence for their own republic, calling it Ecuador because of its location.

CIVIL WAR AND COAST-SIERRA RIVALRY
Fresh disputes emerged between the conservative residents of the highlands, who were content with Spanish rule, and the liberal costeños, who wanted complete independence. To some extent this rivalry still continues, albeit in the form of lighthearted teasing: The coastal residents call the highlanders boring and backward, and the highlanders call their coastal counterparts *monos* (monkeys) and tease them for being loud and obnoxious. In the mid-1800s, different cities and areas attempted to declare their own set of rules. Guayaquil gave itself over to Peruvian rule, and much of Ecuador was close to being taken over by Colombia. However, in 1861, Gabriel García Moreno, a fearless leader and devout Catholic, became president. The most significant legacy of his rule was to turn Ecuador into a Catholic republic and force his beliefs on all of its residents by denying official citizenship to those who rejected Catholicism.

Moreno was assassinated in the streets of Quito by political rivals in 1875. After Moreno's death, the equally fearsome but liberal president, Eloy Alfaro, took over and immediately started undoing Moreno's work by secularizing the state and education. His decades-long reign came to a bitter end in 1911, when he was overthrown by the military. The following year, while leading a revolt, he was captured found guilty of treason. His body was dragged through the streets of Quito and publicly burned. This event marked the beginning of a 50-year battle for power between the liberals and conservatives, which cost the country thousands of lives and numerous presidents (some of whom lasted only days). Taking advantage of Ecuador's weakened state, Peru challenged Ecuador in a border dispute from 1941 to 1942, which resulted in Ecuador losing almost half of its land to Peru in a 1948 treaty.

BANANAS AND OIL
Ecuador went through a relatively peaceful period in the 1950s and 60s, helped by both the popular president, Galo Plaza Lasso, and the beginning of the banana boom, which created thousands of jobs and had a positive impact on the economy. It was during this period that the Agrarian Reform Law put a halt on the virtual slavery that the indigenous people had been subjected to since the 16th century. Unfortunately, in the 1960s, banana exportation was abruptly nullified by a fungal disease that affected the country's entire crop, evoking a short period of economic decline in Ecuador.

This decline ended when large oil reserves were found in the Oriente in 1967 by Texaco, an U.S. oil company. The Ecuadorian military, led by General Guillermo Rodríguez Lara, managed to block the swarms of money-hungry oil companies waiting to pounce on the land and negotiated fair contracts for oil extraction. Though at the cost of ghastly damage committed on the environment, the economy began to prosper and new wealth was being pumped into education, health care, urbanization and transport. Even with the new oil money, Ecuador was unable to pay off its enormous debts, and foolish decisions by Lara to overcome this problem (such as raising taxes to absurd levels) resulted in his overthrow in 1976. A stable democracy was reinstated soon after.

ECUADORIAN-PERUVIAN BORDER DISPUTE
The border dispute between Ecuador and Peru lasted over 160 years and was the longest armed conflict in the Western Hemisphere. Amazonian land was the source of the conflict.

After Simón Bolívar liberated Gran Colombia (present-day Colombia, Venezuela, Panama and Ecuador) in 1819, he had the bold ambition to unite all of South America into the republic. However, Peruvian president José de la Mar wanted to be the sole ruler of Peru. De la Mar incited anti-Colombian sentiment within Peru and Bolivia and the Colombian army was expelled in 1828. De la Mar went even further by invading southern Ecuador. This caused the Gran Colombian-Peruvian War. Peru officially lost Guayaquil to Gran Colombia. The two countries agreed to recognize the viceroyalty-era boundaries between them, delineated by the Marañón and Amazon rivers.

In 1830, Ecuador succeeded from Gran Colombia. In 1857, Ecuador planned to repay
its debt with British creditors, which it had
accumulated from the war for independence,
by giving Britain land in the Amazon. Peru
claimed this land as its own and this set off
the Ecuadorian-Peruvian War of 1859. The
Peruvian navy blockaded Guayaquil until
Ecuador signed a treaty to agree not to sell
the Amazonian land to Britain. Still, it was
debatable what country owned the land.

From 1860 to 1941, a number of treaties
were signed to settle the territorial dispute,
but the two countries took up arms again
in 1941. Peru claims Ecuador invaded its
Zarumilla Province, while Ecuador claims
Peru launched attacks on Ecuadorian troops
around the border. The war lasted less than
a month until Ecuador requested a cease fire
and Peruvian forces withdrew from Ecuador's El Oro Province. The Protocol of Rio de
Janeiro of 1942 ended the war, and Ecuador
lost nearly half of its Amazonian holdings,
an area rich petroleum, gold, uranium and
other minerals.

In 1960, Ecuador's President José María
Velasco Ibarra stated that the 1942 protocol was null, as Ecuador had been forced to
sign under duress. Tensions flared again in
the Cordillera del Cóndor region, briefly in
1981 and again in 1994-1995. This later conflict also involved the headwaters of the Río
Cenepa. The conflict came to an end February 28, 1992, with the signing of the Mon-
tevideo Declaration and the later Itamaraty
Peace Declaration, which reaffirmed the Rio
Protocol.

Finally, on October 26, 1998, the two nations
signed a comprehensive border agreement,
which was ratified by both nations' congress.
Ecuador and Peru established Parque Bina-
cional El Cóndor in the Cordillera del Cóndor. Today the borders are clearly defined,
but there is still bitterness between the two
countries. Updated: Sep 11, 2012.

DOLLARIZATION AND BEYOND

From 1979 until 1996 a string of govern-
ments attempted (and failed) to stabilize the
delicate economy—which swung dramatically back-and-forth due to fluctuating oil prices and severe debt. The perilous state of the
economy provoked the indigenous people to
rise up against the government through their
new organization, Confederación de Nacio-
nalidades Indígenas del Ecuador (CONAIE).

In 1998, the situation worsened. Ecuador
suffered its most severe economic crisis;
the GDP shrank dramatically, inflation rose
and banks collapsed. The citizens of Ecuador
were furious with their leaders, whose cor-
ruption and ineptitude had contributed to
the crisis. Roads were blockaded and virtually the entire country went on strike.

In 1999, then-President Jamil Mahuad decided nothing could be done to protect the
national currency, the sucre, from failing
completely, and he concluded that the only
answer was to transfer to the U.S. dollar. Although this move had the immediate desired
effect of stabilizing the economy, it brought
numerous other problems for the Ecuadorian people. The cost of living skyrock-
eted and poverty worsened. The indigenous
population suffered greatly, and in 2000,
thousands of protesters stormed Congress,
backed by the military, and ousted Mahuad
from office in just three hours.

He was replaced immediately by his vice-
president, Gustavo Noboa, under whom the
economy slowly started to recover. On April
20, 2005, President, Lucio Gutiérrez, elected
in 2002, was overthrown by popular protest
and a vote in Congress, and was replaced by
his vice-president, Dr. Alfredo Palacio.
Updated: Apr 23, 2013.

Politics

Ecuador has been a constitutional republic
with a democratic government since 1976.
The government consists of three main
branches: executive, headed by the president, currently Rafael Correa Delgado (since
January 2007); legislative, the National Assembly, with representatives from dozens
of political parties that are constantly inter-
changing; and judicial.

Between 1996 and 2007, political instability
plagued Ecuador once again. The country
witnessed a procession of incompetent and/
or corrupt leaders. Eight different presidents
rose to and fell from power in that decade,
three of them elected and subsequently
overthrown. Ecuadorians were generally
frustrated with their politicians, as was often
demonstrated in numerous street protests
throughout the country. In April 2005,
popular protests against unconstitutional
actions by former President Lucio Gutiérrez
reached their peak and brought an early end
abrupt end to his term.

Then Vice President Dr. Alfredo Palacio took over shortly after congress voted to remove Gutiérrez from office. U.S.-trained economist Rafael Correa was elected president in November 2006 and sworn-in to replace Palacio as president in January of 2007. Later that year, several elected members of Congress were charged with violating campaign laws and were subsequently thrown out.

In September 2007, a constitutional assembly was voted into power and drafted a new constitution—Ecuador's 20th since gaining independence—which was then approved by voters in September 2008. The new constitution grants the executive branch more control, and allows two consecutive four-year terms for the president, vice president and National Assembly members. While supporters welcome the idea of a more stable government with longer elected terms, opponents fear the president's increase in power could lead to autocracy.

The new constitution also includes a world first: a bill of rights extending unalienable rights to nature using a cap-and-trade strategy. Although this could certainly benefit the biologically diverse and dense country, some skeptics wonder how successful the government will be in terms of implementing this unprecedented concept.

Correa led congress to rewrite the constitution to reflect the progress of Ecuador in 2009, which includes free education through university and provides social security to stay-at-home mothers, as well as extends the rights of the president. It also pioneered an "eco-constitution," extending inalienable rights to nature.

As a result, the Ecuadorian government has been working toward an initiative to keep underground billions of barrels of oil in order to collect monetary benefits from developed countries using a cap-and-trade policy, of which is intended for innovation in renewable energy sources. It is questionable whether or not this initiative holds enough strength to be sustained.

Political disputes over oil exploration in the Amazon continue to persist, honing in on the Yasuni rainforest in recent years and continuing to seek payment of $18.2 billion courts have ruled Chevron owes for environmental damages incurred.
Updated: Aug 22, 2012.

Ecuador's Economy

Ecuador's economy is based on exports from the agricultural industries, such as bananas and shrimp; money transfers from native employed abroad; and petroleum production, which accounts for 40 percent of export earnings and one-third of the central government budget revenues.

The economy delved into a frightening free-fall in the late 1990s when the nation suffered the natural disasters of El Niño and the eruption of Pichincha volcano, in addition to a sharp decline in world petroleum prices. Poverty worsened (over half the population lived below the poverty level) and the banking system collapsed.

Bankers fled the country in 1999 without honoring their clients' accounts. When the sucre—the nation's currency—depreciated by about 70 percent in the same decade, then-President Jamil Mahuad made the wildly unpopular announcement that he would adopt the U.S. dollar as the national currency. A military coup in January 2000 ousted Mahuad. With few alternatives to save the struggling economy, Congress went on to approve the adoption of the U.S. dollar in March of that year.

Since then the nation's economy has been relatively solid. Economic growth reached 7.2 percent in 2008, but dropped to 0.4 percent in 2009 due to the global financial crisis. Soon it rebounded, achieving 6.5 percent growth in 2011. An estimated 28.6 percent of the population still lives below the poverty line (2011).

At the start of Correa's term, the President was outspoken about his reluctance to getting involved with Free Trade Agreement talks with the U.S., and stated that Ecuador will acknowledge its external debt—and only what it deemed to be "legitimate debt"—only after successfully funding domestic social programs. The government implemented income transfers to the poor and announced plans to increase spending on health and education across the country.

Talks have resumed between Correa and the European Union over fair trade development in recent months, which Correa has publicly stated does not have anything to do with the Free Trade Agreement, and still adamantly opposes arriving at any agreement over the official act itself .

In 2009, Ecuador joined the Alianza Bolivariana para las Américas (ALBA), an alliance of the leftist South American countries that promotes fairer trading and other relationships between nations.

- Unemployment: 4.1 percent (as of 2012)

- Underemployment: 44.8 percent (as of 2013)

- GDP Per Capita: $8,800 (as of 2012)

- Public debt: 23.3 percent of GDP (as of 2012)

Chief agricultural exports: flowers, bananas, coffee, cocoa, rice, potatoes, manioc (yucca / cassava and tapioca), plantains, sugarcane; cattle, sheep, pigs, beef, pork, dairy products; balsa wood; fish, shrimp.

Export commodities: petroleum, bananas, cut flowers, shrimp.

Main industries: petroleum, food processing, textiles, wood products, chemicals.
Updated: Aug 22, 2012.

Population of Ecuador

The estimated population of Ecuador is 15 million (2011). Annual population growth is currently two percent (2012). Half of Ecuador's population is under 25 years and over 30 percent under 14 years. Because many Ecuadorians do not know their precise ethnic heritage, the 2010 national census asked Ecuadorians with which culture or customs they related. Almost 72 percent stated mestizo (European-indigenous mix), and 6.1 percent as white. Afro-Ecuadorians, who reside mostly in Esmeraldas Province, but also in the Valle del Chota in the northern Andes, constituted 7.2 percent of the respondents.

For the first time ever, Ecuadorians could choose to identify themselves as *montubio* - a mestizo ethnic-cultural group of the coastal mountains of Manabí, Los Ríos and Loja provinces; 7.4 percent of chose this classification. Approximately seven percent of the population is indigenous, almost two-thirds of whom live in Chimborazo and Imbabura provinces. Morona Santiago, Pastaza and Napo provinces also have large indigenous populations. Other ethnicities constitute less than half-percent of the population.
Updated: Sep 03, 2012.

Ecuador's Languages

The 2008 Constitution establishes Spanish (castellano) as the official language of Ecuador, with Kichwa and Shuar as additional official languages for intercultural relations. Other ancestral, indigenous languages may be used as the official and legal language in areas where they are spoken.

Almost all Ecuadorians speak Spanish as either a first or second language. Ecuadorian Spanish varies according to each region. On the coast, the Spanish is slurred and final consonants are dropped. In the Andes, the Spanish is slower and clearer-making it one of the easiest places to learn the language.

Quichua (Kichwa) is the most common indigenous language, with almost 600,000 speakers; most live in the sierra, and about one percent in the jungle. The most common Amazonian languages are Shuar, with over 79,000 native speakers, and Achuar, with over 7,000. Of the 15 languages spoken in modern-day Ecuador, three have fewer than 700 speakers.

English is taught from an early age in schools, but is not taught well. Most Ecuadorians understand much more English than one would imagine, but relatively few are fluent.
Updated: Sep 03, 2012.

Religion in Ecuador

Indigenous groups once practiced different religions across Ecuador, but the arrival of the Spanish wiped out much of this diversity. Using fear, intimidation and bribery, the country was almost completely converted to Catholicism. Today, even those Amazon villages that have never seen a car have Catholic churches. Many rural villages that once practiced other religions still blend old traditions with the practice of Catholicism. Native religious celebrations are still occasionally held at Ingapirca, the most important Inca site in Ecuador. Other Christian denominations with temples in Ecuador are Eastern Orthodox, Anglican, Episcopalian, Methodist, Lutheran, Presbyterian, Mennonite, Baptist and Mormon, as well as a number of evangelical and Pentecostal churches. Other faiths represented in Ecuador are Judaism, Islam, Buddhist, Hinduism and Spiritualism.

In 2012, the Instituto Ecuatoriano de Estadística y Censos (INEC) conducted a study that revealed that 80.4 percent of

Ecuadorians are Catholic, and 19.6 percent of the population belong to another religion, or is atheist or agnostic.
Updated: Sep 03, 2012.

Culture in Ecuador

Elements of *cultura* (culture) are everywhere you go in Ecuador. From the gilded, glittering 19th-century theaters of Quito to the raucous parades and dancing in the streets of tiny Andean towns, Ecuadorians across the nation love to celebrate their heritage and traditions.

Ecuador brandishes a rainbow of cultures: the native inhabitants had a well-developed sense of cultural identity before the arrival of the Spanish, who added their own traditions to the mix. Later, Africans came to the region—primarily the coast—and brought with them their own unique culture. Today, Ecuador has even embraced international traditions, such as Halloween.

Ecuador's culture ranges from upscale (opera at Teatro Sucre in Quito) to low-key (cockfights in rural towns), and from very old (religious processions for Holy Week) to new (*chivas*—party buses with a loud band on top—driving through the streets of Quito). No matter what aspects of Ecuadorian culture you choose to explore, you can be sure that it will be colorful, boisterous and lots of fun. Ecuador takes its art and music very seriously, so be sure to keep your eyes curious and open for what's around.
The nation—and Quito in particular—was a thriving artistic center during the colonial period, and the people of Ecuador developed a love for art that continues to this day. Quito's museums and galleries should not be missed if you are an art aficionado. Music is also important to Ecuadorians: you won't go anywhere in Ecuador without seeing a small Andean band playing traditional tunes, hoping to sell a CD to tourists.

Ecuador has the wonderful Casa de la Cultura Ecuatoriana (URL:www.cce.org.ec) that promotes the visual and performance artists of the country. The main complex is in Quito; but every provincial capital has a *nucleo*, or a branch, where regional artists are highlighted. The casas host literary readings, concerts, art exhibits, films and other cultural events—many of them free. Many also have shops where books and recordings may be purchased.

Keep your eyes and mind open: there are opportunities everywhere in Ecuador to sample local culture. The people of Ecuador are excited when a foreigner wants to participate in a town festival or other local celebrations: let the locals be your guides and enjoy!
Updated: Sep 13, 2012.

ECUADORIAN LITERATURE

Before the Spanish conquest, literature was an oral affair in Ecuador. During the colonial period, the written tradition began. One notable works of that era is *Elegía a la muerte de Atahualpa*, written in Quichua and attributed to *cacique* Jacinto Collahuazo (18th century).

In the years leading up to Independence, several important writers emerged on the scene: **Eugenio Espejo** (1747-1795), the country's first journalist, and poet **José Joaquín de Olmedo** (1780-1847), who wrote *Canto a Bolívar* and *Canción del 9 de octubre*, which would become Guayaquil's anthem.

In the mid-19th century emerged two of Ecuador's most important writers: **Juan Montalvo** (1832-89) and **Juan León Mera** (1832-94). Montalvo was principally an essayist who wrote about social, political, historical and cultural issues. His works include *Cosmopolita*, *Geometría moral*, *Las Catilinarias* and his masterpiece, *Siete Tratados*. A collection of his oeuvre, published by Arizona State University, is available in English. Mera is credited with writing the first Ecuadorian novel, *Cumandá* (1879), a Romantic genre story set in Ecuador's jungle. This writer was also a musician, and composed the lyrics for Ecuador's national anthem.

The next important Ecuadorian novel was written by **Luis A. Martínez** (1869-1909). His work, *A la costa*, launched the Realism movement in the Andean country. This novel vividly displays the social changes Ecuador experienced at the end of the 19th century. Of the same genre is *Plata y bronce* (1927) by **Fernando Chávez**, which examines race and social class relations between the Indigenous and whites.

Chavez' work ushered in Ecuador's next literary movement, Social Realism. Its most famous representative is **Jorge Icaza** (1906-79), who penned *Huasipungo (in English,The Villagers*, 1934). This controversial Indigenismo novel portrays the Indigenous struggle against exploitation. It is widely acclaimed as one of the most significant works in contemporary Latin American literature.

Another noteworthy work of this period is *Los que se van* (1930) by **Joaquin Gallegos Lara** (1911-1947), **Demetrio Aguilera Malta** (1909-1981) and **Enrique Gil Gilbert** (1912-1973). This collection of stories focuses on the social reality of Ecuador's Indigenous and Montubio peoples. These three writers, along with **José de la Cuadra** (1903-1941) and **Alfredo Pareja Diezcanseco** (1908-1993), formed the Guayaquil Group. All became famous in their right.

Contemporary Ecuadorian writers continue to focus on social and political issues. **Jorge Carrera Andrade** (1903-1978) is considered to be one of Latin America's most important 20th-century poets; most of his works have been published in English. **Jorge Enrique Adoum** (1926-2009) wrote *Entre Marx y una Mujer Desnuda* (1976), which is not yet available in English; it was turned into a movie by Camilo Luzuriaga in 1995. An English collection of Adoum's poetry, *Disinterred Love*, was released in 2012 by Salt Publishing. **Demetrio Aguilera Malta** is widely translated into English. His magisurrealist novels include: *Don Goyo* (1980), *Seven Serpents and Seven Moons* (1981) and *Babelandia* (1985).

Influential Afro-Ecuadorian writers are Nelson Estupiñán Bass, (1912-2002), Antonio Preciado (1944-) and Adalberto Ortiz (1914-2003), who wrote *Juyungo* (1942) which appears in English. Other 20th and 21st century wordsmiths from this Andean nation to check out are: Abdón Ubidia, Alicia Yánez Cossío, Eliécer Cárdenas, Enrique Gil Gilber, Mariana Falconí, Nuria Rengifo and Raúl Pérez Torres. The books of these and many others may be purchased at the bookstores of the Casa de la Cultura Ecuatoriana, which has branches throughout the country. Updated: Oct 03, 2012.

Art and Painting in Ecuador

Ecuador has always been a nation of painters and artists. During the colonial era, Quito built a solid reputation as a center for religious art in the New World, and has never looked back. Today, Ecuador is still one of the best places in the world to appreciate and purchase beautiful works of art.

THE QUITO SCHOOL OF ART

Within a few years of arrival in Quito, the Catholic Church began constructing houses of worship—from small chapels to huge cathedrals. These churches, emulating their European counterparts, featured elaborate, impressive interiors with hand-carved decorations and pillars, paintings and arches. Rather than import artistic works such as crucifixes, paintings and statues of saints from Europe, the priests began training local artists to produce them.

For the first hundred years or so, the copies of European art made by Ecuadorians were skilled and workman-like, if uninspiring in nature. But then, something happened that the priests did not foresee: The local artists began to develop their own techniques and styles. Their art became more visceral and detailed than the European works they copied. The crucifixes, which had previously portrayed a stoic Christ on the cross with a single wound over his heart, now were of a Christ in agony; his flesh shredded, his ribs showing, his skin flayed. Few who view crucifixes from this period can resist an involuntary shudder as they see Christ's pain and torment—the pain and torment of the conquered, enslaved native people who produced the crucifix.

The Quito (Quiteño) school is also known for highly detailed statues. The saints and other religious figures that were depicted were made from finely carved local wood, painstakingly whittled into shape before being painted with incredible attention to detail. The cheeks of the saints were given a rosy glow, and fake glass eyes were included to improve the sense of realism. Some even had real hair, and many had robes of fine local cloth.

The Quito style of art became well-known in the region and in the world, and by the middle of the 18th century, there were more than 30 art guilds operating in Quito, producing art full-time. With the advent of independence and the resulting loosening of the Catholic Church's stranglehold on art and culture, the Quito school of art began exploring their roots, blending what they learned and blending it with their own culture.

From this period come the distinguished paintings of Christ wearing Andean clothes and even eating *cuy* (guinea pig) at the last supper.

INDIGENOUS MOVEMENT

In the early twentieth century, a new artistic movement swept the country: the indigenous movement. Inspired by the Quito School of Art as well as by the suffering of native peoples in the Americas, artists from Ecuador began producing works which reflected the sorry state of native populations in South America. Artists such as Oswaldo Guayasamín, Eduardo Kingman and Camilo Egas gained world-wide fame with their portrayals of the trials and tribulations of native life, contact between natives and Spaniards and pressures of modern life. Their works can be seen in Quito at the Casa de la Cultura and the museums dedicated to Guayasamín, Egas and Kingman. See the museums section for locations and hours.

TODAY'S ART SCENE IN ECUADOR

Today, Ecuador—and Quito in particular—is home to a vibrant art scene. Several impressive art galleries in Quito feature work by local artists. The capital's Centro Cultural Metropolitano and Centro de Arte Contemporáneo hold special exhibits. The annual salon, Mariano Aguilera, is the national art competition. A neat place to see local artists showcasing their work is Ejido Park (across from the Hilton Colón) on Sunday morning, when dozens of local artists unpack their canvases for everyone to see and (hopefully) purchase.

If you're interested in other forms of art, such as tapestries, check out the fancy boutiques on Amazonas and Juan León Mera. The few art galleries in Mitad del Mundo offer touristy paintings. There are several galleries (the term is used loosely: some are converted family living rooms) in Otavalo. On that town's market day (Saturday), you can choose from a wide array of local art, mostly watercolors. Prices are reasonable, but be persistent in your bargaining. Art sellers in Otavalo tend to jack up their initial prices relatively more than other merchants. You may find yourself paying less than half the original price for a piece of art if you bargain well.

One local form of art that is popular with visitors is the Tigua painting. Tigua is a tiny town high in the Andes known for small, colorful paintings made on stretched sheepskin. The paintings usually feature tiny figures of Andeans about their daily life herding llamas, attending local fairs and the like. Some feature mythological elements, such as condors, faces in the mountains, and volcanoes. Be sure to ask the vendor (who is often also the artist) about any element in the painting that you don't understand: often, the artist offers and interesting explanation. Tigua paintings are available almost everywhere: you'll see them in any market you visit. Updated: Sep 03, 2012.

Music in Ecuador

Ecuadorians love music. On the streets, in homes, at parties, and on buses—if you're traveling in Ecuador, you're going to hear plenty of sound. In tourist areas such as Otavalo or Baños, you're bound to encounter a native band (called a *grupo* or *conjunto*) composed of anywhere from four to 10 Ecuadorians, often dressed in native clothing, playing folkloric songs on traditional instruments. The group is bound to have at least one guitarist, a drummer and at least one musician producing a haunting melody on a panflute, a traditional Andean instrument composed of varying lengths of bamboo lashed together.

In towns like Baños, the groups make the rounds of the more expensive tourist restaurants, stopping by and playing three or four songs, then passing the hat for tips and selling CDs of their music. Some fancier places, such as haciendas that have been converted into hotels, have their own native bands that play for guests in the evening and during dinner (they'll probably have CDs, too).

If you're lucky enough to get invited to a private party or make it to a local festival, you may see a *banda del pueblo*. These bands are composed of locals who get together on special occasions to play mostly traditional music.

Their instruments are often old and fairly beat up, and occasionally the musical talent is questionable, but whatever they may lack in skill or instruments they more than make up for in exuberance and volume. The crowd ocassionally joins in to sing (if there's been enough liquor passed around).

Ecuadorians also perform modern genres, like cumbia, reggaetón and salsa. Paulina Aguirre and her producer-husband Pablo Aguirre were the first musicians of this Andean nation to win a Latin Grammy, in 2009 for Best Christian Album.

Oswaldo Guayasamín

Born in 1919 to humble, indigenous parents, Oswaldo Guayasamín would later mature into Ecuador's most famous artist. His striking art portrays the humanity and suffering of the repressed classes and people of the Americas. Considered an expressionist, Guayasamín used bright colors, symbolism and images of pain and torment to create truly unique and memorable works.

By the time he was middle aged, Guayasamín was awarded numerous artististic and humanitarian honors and his art had been exhibited all over the world, including in the U.S.A., Italy, Spain, France, Brazil, the Soviet Union, Cuba and China. Some of these exhibitions were in prestigious locations, such as the Palais de Luxembourg (Paris, 1992) and the L'Hermitage Museum (Saint Petersburg, 1982). In 1978 he was named to the Royal Academy of Fine Arts of Spain and in 1979 he was named to the Academy of Italian Arts. The United Nations Educational, Scientific and Cultural Organization gave him a prize for "an entire life of work for peace."

In spite of these lofty awards, Guayasamín never lost his connection with the common people of Ecuador who adored him. Toward the end of his life he began work on "la Capilla del Hombre" ("The Chapel of Man"), which he dedicated to the races of Latin America, although he never lived to see it finished. He passed away in 1999 and the chapel has since been completed.

Guayasamín never lost his artistic edge. Commissioned to do a series of murals for the Ecuadorian Congress in 1988, he painted 23 panels depicting his nation's history. One of the panels features a black-and-white painting of a horrid, skeletal face wearing a Nazi-style helmet with the letters CIA on it. The painting caused an international incident between Ecuador and the United States. The artist held firm and the painting remains.

Today, Guayasamín is still very popular. His works are on display in his museum and at the Capilla del Hombre. If you go shopping in the Mariscal area, you're likely to see many knockoffs of his works for sale in a variety of mediums. His works are easy to spot: they are colorful and feature people with distinctive twisted hands and faces.

Capilla del Hombre: Mariano Calvache and Lorenzo Chávez, Bellavista. Tuesday – Sunday, 10 a.m. – 5 p.m. Admission $3.

Guayasamín Museum: José Bosmediano 543 and José Carbo, Tel: 593-2-244-6455. Monday - Friday, 10 a.m – 5.30 p.m.

Ecuadorians have diverse musical tastes in regards to international music. If you spin the dial on a radio in Quito, you'll find different stations playing salsa, rap, Spanish oldies, elevator music, pop, rock, reggaetón and everything in between. Some stations consider "music in English" to be its own genre, which means that the same station plays music that would never be played together in the U.S., like Britney Spears, Eminem, Korn and the Bee Gees. It's rather confusing, but Ecuadorians seem to enjoy it.

International Spanish-language music is widely popular in Ecuador. Salsa, merengue and cumbia—all different forms of dance music from Latin America—can be heard around the nation. Each is a different genre of music that requires different dance moves, but to the untrained ear they can be difficult to tell apart. If you plan on visiting a *salsateca* (salsa dance club) while in Ecuador (and you should, they're a lot of fun) you may want to take a dance class or two first. The Mariscal area in Quito (see Quito section) is full of dance schools. Alternatively, check out a dance show if you can. They're hyped up by the tour companies for a reason. You should also see what is happening at major cultural centers such as the Casa de la Cultura and Teatro Sucre, as they often have special events and shows.

Dance, Theater and Comedy

Ecuador's deeply rooted history, variety of cultures and geography has treated its artistic expressions no differently: The evolution of dance, theater and comedy has taken many forms. All these can easily be combined, because dance often takes the form of theater and vice-versa, and comedy is a great artistic expression.

DANCE

Marimba, the official dance of Ecuador, was created and popularized by the Afro-Ecuadorian population. The *currulao* portion of the dance performance corresponds with the rhythm of the marimba instrument, which resembles a xylophone, and has strong roots in West African Bantu and Mande heritage. The dance signifies freedom from colonizers.

Photo by: Antonio

Afro-Ecuadorians were able to fend off the Spaniards in the coastal city of Esmeraldas until the mestizo encroached on their land in search of mineral resources. The mestizos regulated the Afro-Ecuadorians' use of *currulao* dance, prohibiting them from performing unless they possessed a specific license. But in the 1970s the Afro-Ecuadorians reclaimed their power and formed dance troupes, in order to spread and preserve the knowledge and technique of their music and dance to new generations. Often this music and dance is combined with theater to tell the rich history of the Afro-Ecuadorian.

Ballet has swept into Ecuador in colossal form, especially in the capital city of Quito. One of Ecuador's ballet companies, Ballet Folklórico Ecuatoriano de Virginia Rosero has, in recent years, traveled around the world representing the indigenous culture of Ecuador.

Ballet companies usually encompass folkloric dances portraying all traditions, including Inti Raymi, Amazonian dance, mestizo dance, and bombas from Chota.

In larger towns and cities salsa has become the modern dance of choice. Salsa is usually performed by partners, moving to a brisk beat.

THEATER

Ecuador's history of theater and modern productions offers insight into its true culture. During the pre-Columbian period, plays were once pure creations of improvisation. Theater was banned by the Spanish colonists because the leaders deemed the artistic expression to pose too much a threat to their succinct society. But through it all, theater has helped preserve the perils and hardships the country has had to face, and expresses it in all its beauty.

In the past couple of decades, theaters have experienced cutbacks in funding, hindering their ability to function at a high level. This could be due to the rising trend in film production or a simple lack of interest, but there is an esoteric triumph of individuals working to keep the tradition very alive. An example of this is "Malayerba," a politically and economically independent theater group. For more than 30 years, it has traveled, addressing relationships between men and women and domestic violence.

A lot of great theater houses and productions can be found in cities, especially in Cuenca, the cultural capital of Ecuador.

COMEDY

Comedy in the form of theater, stand-up and performances have not made too large of a break in Ecuador. Comedy Central is now an Ecuadorian channel, however.

Special Events in Ecuador

Holidays and Fiestas

CARNAVAL

Carnaval, which is celebrated each year in February or March the week before Lent, is Latin America's version of Mardi Gras. The celebrations that take place in Ecuador the four days preceding Ash Wednesday may not be as crazy as some countries, but if you happen to be in the area during this holiday it is worth checking out.

During the four days before Ash Wednesday, Quito is almost a ghost town. Many of its residents head to the coast to soak up the sun. Atacames is particularly busy. Children run around at all hours of the night, spraying the random passerby with foam in a can while their parents are busy dancing in one of the many bars along the beach. The main component of any carnaval celebration in Ecuador is abundant water, used for soaking people.

Beware, foreigner, as you are a very attractive target. Without a doubt you will be drenched with water and silly string by hoards of children. Quito is no exception. It can be vexing, but try to accept that it is simply their way of celebrating this holiday.

If you prefer a bit dryer holiday weekend, head to Ambato, where water throwing is prohibited. Here, the huge festival is called Fiesta de la Fruta y de las Flores. This event is filled with colorful parades, bullfights and handicraft exhibits.

Another town that has an impressive carnaval celebration is the town of Guaranda, located in the central Andes. Usually this is your average sleepy Ecuadorian town, nothing remarkable for a tourist. However, carnaval transforms it into a four day non-stop party, filled with parades, music and fun.

Also the locals tend to be very hospitable, many prepare large feasts and invite anyone on the street into their homes to celebrate with them.
Updated: Sep 03, 2012.

GOOD FRIDAY
One of the most grandiose events for Quito's religious community, the great procession of Santo Viernes (Good Friday) follows the morning *Via Crucis* prayer on the final Friday of Holy Week, observing to the crucifixion of Jesus Christ.

Tens of thousands—many donning purple robes and coned hoods reminiscent of the Ku Klux Klan—flock to the city's historic center and wind through the streets in a solemn procession. It's a colorful scene definitely not to be missed. Watch it from a balcony or join the masses walking through the streets.

The procession begins at midday at Iglesia San Francisco, making its way through the Centro Histórico to the Basílica and back to San Francisco. Traditional purple-hooded *cucuruchos* (penitents, many donning thorny headpieces, massive crosses and chains around their feet demonstrating their will to change) and robed *Verónicas* (also

wearing purple dresses and black shrouds as they pay tribute to the woman who wiped the sweat and blood from Jesus' face as he was carried on the cross) encircle a figure of Jesus and the Virgen Dolorosa (Our Lady of Sorrows), further surrounded by the solemn masses.

The procession ends at 3 p.m.—the hour of Jesus' death—and is followed by a ceremony reenacting the Descent from the Cross at six in the evening. Some Quito churches make quite an ordeal of this, with the priest recounting the story of the apostles performing the sepulcher of Christ from his pulpit. Finally, designated men remove the nails from the crucified Christ, passing the body along to a group of women who lay him to rest in a white tunic and flowers.

In addition to watching the procession, Quiteños typically go to church on the morning of Good Friday and spend the rest of the day at home, perhaps watching religious movies about Jesus. In the evening, the extended family gets together for dinner, where *fanesca*, a traditional Easter-time soup made with twelve grains and fish, is usually served.

Many families also go to the coast for Good Friday and Semana Santa because children have off school and adults have time off work.
Updated: Aug 23, 2012.

THE DAY OF THE DEAD IN ECUADOR
Celebrated throughout Latin America as a result of the combination between indigenous beliefs and Catholic religion, the Day of the Dead (Día de los Muertos) takes place on November 2 around the continent.

In Ecuador the holiday is interpreted as a day to "catch up" with the ones who are no longer with us but have a life in a different world. People pack lunches of traditional food, flowers and offerings and head for the cemeteries where they spend the day as a family talking, eating and performing routine maintenance on the grave site.

The staple food of the season is the famous *colada morada*, a thick purple drink, and *guaguas de pan*, sweet bread in the shape of dolls. Weeks before the holiday, supermarkets and bakeries begin selling the ingredients and store-made versions of the drink and breads. Colada morada is made out of black corn flour, blackberries, cinnamon, and pineapple, among other ingredients that are cooked together and served hot or cold with the sweet bread. To some people, the reddish-purple drink symbolizes blood, which in turn symbolizes life of the ones who have moved on from this existence.

There are as many versions of colada morada and guaguas de pan recipes as there are households, because whether a family visits their long-time gone relatives at cemeteries or not, the great majority of Ecuadorians will taste their version of the traditional food.

The tradition of spending the day at cemeteries has declined in urban areas of Ecuador. However, once you leave the city behind it is easy to find entire communities mingling at the local cemetery for the occasion.

It is probably best to catch this holiday in the southern provinces of the Sierra, since November 3 marks the Independence of Cuenca and colorful festivities of the two consecutive holidays can be enjoyed in the area.
Updated: Sep 10, 2012.

FIESTAS DE QUITO

If you are in Quito during the last days of November and during the run-up to December 6, you cannot fail to notice a distinctly fiesta-ish atmosphere in the city. During these days, Quiteños let their hair down to commemorate the Spanish founding of the city on the same date in 1534.

Fiestas de Quito celebrate Ecuador's Spanish roots, so traditional Spanish culture is appreciated and enjoyed during these days. Traditional food like *fritadas* (fried, chopped pork) and *llapingachos* (potato pancakes with cheese), as well as copious amounts of wine, are commonly consumed.

Pasillos, or traditional Spanish music,is widespread and games like *trompos* (spinning of tops) and *carros de madera* (wooden car racing) are played. Joke-telling in theaters and *cuarenta* card game competitions are two other traditions during the festivities.

For the ten days running up to - and including December 6 - there are also bull fights that are held at the Plaza de Toros; the only time during the year when the bull ring is actually used for bull fighting. The fights are considered by most to be a high-class social event, and Quito's elite flock to the fights,

dressed in their finest smart-casual wear, donning cowboy or panama hats to keep the sun off.

Many also have *botas* (wineskins). Those who can't afford to go inside linger outside and in the surrounding streets in groups drinking beer and whiskey and dancing in makeshift discos.

In late November, the festivities start with the election of the Queen of Quito. From this point onwards, in the streets you can see *chivas*, or colorful open-topped buses driving through the streets, carrying as many as 50 people who may be dancing to the *banda del pueblo* (town band) which play on the top, or drinking *canelazo*, a potent alcoholic drink with a sugar cane alcohol and cinnamon base. This happens night and day, and chivas are reserved well ahead of time for the early days of December.

On the night of December 5, the partying reaches a climax and there are street parties all over Quito. The Mariscal district is more alive and crowded than usual as bars and clubs overflow with revelers. Large parties in haciendas in the surrounding valleys are also common occurrences. A good place to head is Carolina Park, where there will often be open-air concerts and fireworks.

In some of Quito's traditional neighborhoods, like the Centro Histórico, roads are closed for dancing and candelazo drinking as *vacas locas* (crazy cows), or cows made out of fireworks, spark in the streets. If street parties are your thing, head to Vancouver and Polonia streets (located behind the Petrocomerical gas station on Amazonas), where there is usually a DJ, decent music and plenty of dancing to be enjoyed.

Those with leftover stamina will continue to party throughout the day and night of December 6 into the morning of December 7. Street parties persist throughout the city and in the valleys as more dancing and drinking takes place. Some bars and clubs even serve breakfast on the morning of December 7 for a small cover, so those who stay up all night can enjoy some food with friends as a farewell to the year's festivities. However, for many, December 6 itself can end up being a fairly quiet day, as many Quiteños and foreigners simply choose to sleep off their hangovers indoors.
Updated: Sep 10, 2012.

NEW YEAR'S EVE

A New Year's Eve, or *Año Viejo*, spent in Ecuador provides a fascinating insight into local culture and folklore. During the week or so preceding the day itself, you will see effigies for sale in the streets, made from wood, paper, cloth and firecrackers. These effigies will usually represent international political figures that are hated, locally despised politicians, or icons from popular music or culture, from the old year. These figures are dressed up in the family's clothing and with masks of the personalities they seek to depict. They are then burned on New Year's Eve to banish the bad and welcome in the new.

In Quito, Avenida Amazonas is the place to head early in the evening to check out the stalls and the open-air entertainment. Themed effigy displays line the road along with live music and street food. You may see effigies being burned here and you will certainly see fireworks. Outside of Quito, the coastal town of Salinas is a popular Ecuadorian New Year's Eve haunt. In the countryside, many people light fires in the street, upon which they burn the effigies. This happens in Quito too, but more frequently in the suburbs.

Similar to Halloween in the States, New Year's Eve is a day when children and adults alike dress up in costumes, wigs and masks. Throughout the country, a popular pursuit is for men to dress up as women—the *viudas alegres*, or merry widows —and beg for money. Also, outside of the main cities, especially on roads to the smaller countryside towns, you may come across children holding string across the roads. They are trying to stop the traffic with the aim of relieving you of your small change.

Midnight tends to be a family affair, indulging in a meal served at home with relatives. A local tradition is to eat twelve grapes (*uvas*) at the stroke of midnight, which is supposed to bring luck throughout the year. An even more radical tradition involves filling up an entire suitcase with your valuables and running around the entire block once, all of it to guarantee a year full of travels.

The streets become ablaze with little fires as each family burns its own effigy, along with the loud resounding noise of fireworks going off across the city. After dinner, younger people head off to clubs or parties to see in the New Year with style.

Social and Environmental Issues

There are a number of social and environmental challenges facing Ecuador today as the nation tries to balance conflicting requirements of repaying international debt, developing industry and keeping the poorest sectors of society alive. Currently, the most pressing issues are: oil exploitation, the development of sustainable tourism and indigenous rights.

OIL EXPLOITATION

Oil was discovered in Ecuador in the late 1960s and large-scale production began in the 1970s. Oil has been a huge boost to the nation's economy. However, development has not been sustainable, the effects have not been felt at community level and there have been negative consequences for both public health and the environment.

Oil cexploitation is a serious threat to the rainforest today. Even at lodges deep in the jungle, plumes of smoke coming from oil refineries smudge the otherwise untouched horizon. The Ecuadorian Amazon is one of the most biodiverse regions on the planet, and the exploitation of oil has been particularly detrimental to the region's fragile ecosystems and vulnerable indigenous populations.

Additionally, the development of oil has not generally benefited the development of infrastructure and basic services for local indigenous populations. There have been instances of drilling on ancestral land, notably in 1999, when the government sold exploration rights in two areas of the jungle, known as Blocks 23 and 24, without consulting the indigenous communities to whom those areas were considered ancestral.

However, the general government response to the situation in the Oriente has not gone far enough to limit environmental damage, impacts on health of the local people or the negative consequences for community life. Experts argue for a more inclusive approach with Amazon communities, including partnerships between indigenous bodies and the oil companies.

It is undeniable that a detailed environmental impact analysis, a plan to repair the destruction that has already taken place, and a series of environmental controls and planning for future development to minimize the impact are urgently needed.

SUSTAINABLE TOURISM

Ecuador suffered a severe economic crisis in the late 1990s and currently has a poverty rate of 41 percent, which has led to high levels of migration to cities and foreign countries. Tourism is an important source of income for Ecuador, bringing in over $710 million of annual revenues to the country, contributing 1.8 percent to the GDP (World Tourism and Travel Council, 2007). The tourism and travel industry was expected to provide 361,000 jobs in 2007, representing 6.7 percent of total employment. Thus, tourism has the ability to decrease poverty in Ecuador in a manner that is potentially less damaging to the environment and more sustainable than other revenue-generating enterprises such as export agriculture and petroleum extraction.

Many of the tourist operations in the Andean region of Ecuador promote the beauty and indigenous culture of the area, yet only a handful classify themselves as ecological and try to meaningfully engage in conservation and community awareness. Key factors determining the success of pioneering eco-lodges are conservation and community development. Most tourist operations recognize the importance of sustainable practices but lack sufficient technological or financial resources to actively engage in them.

There are a number of ways you can leave a positive mark on the places you visit. Practicing responsible tourism and using companies that have received ecotourism certification are two of the most important measures to ensure the country and its people benefit from your travels as much as you do.

THE INDIGENOUS MOVEMENT
IN ECUADOR

Over the past 20 years or so, a strong and largely united indigenous movement has been developing in Ecuador, and it is considered to be among the most persuasive in all of Latin America at the moment. Indigenous political groups here wield significant power in Ecuador and have a voice that is much louder than in other nations. In the 1980s the Amazonian and highland federation CONAIE (Confederation of Indigenous Nationalities of Ecuador) was formed, bringing together the 11 ethnic groups (approximately 3.5 million people) in Ecuador with a united purpose.

This was no easy feat, considering all the different needs of the ethnically and culturally diverse indigenous groups. The group focuses on high-level key aims for all of its member groups such as human rights, consolidation of territory and education.

It is unclear what the future holds, however. A certainty is that the indigenous movement is here to stay and now wields significant power within Ecuadorian politics and is gaining more and more traction by the year.

Indigenous groups currently face the arduous task of taking a clear stand on primary issues facing their communities. The free trade agreement, and water, agriculture and natural resource management are among the most polemic matters on the table. Recent protests against oil exploitation in the Amazon have been smaller but frequent as local residents urge their government to leave oil in the ground throughout the environmentally sensitive areas.

Additional Basic Facts

TIME
Mainland Time = GMT minus 5; Galápagos Time = GMT minus 6.

ELECTRICITY
Ecuador's electrical current is 110 volts 60 cycles, the same as North America, so adapters for North American equipment are not needed. However, plug converters are necessary in older buildings.

Generally speaking, European electrical equipment, such as portable computers and digital cameras, will have variable power blocks that work on both 110-240v currents, so all you need is a plug adapter to use the appliance in Ecuador. Cheaper appliances that demand much higher voltages, such as hairdryers, will probably require a power adapter (as well as a

ECUADOR INTRO

plug adapter) to make them suitable. It's rather hit and miss to be able to find an adapter in the city, so it's advised to order one online before leaving home if you can.

Getting To and Away From Ecuador
BY PLANE

There are two international airports in Ecuador. The majority of international flights leave from the **Mariscal Sucre International Airport (UIO)**, located about 19 km (12 mi) east of Quito. It takes approximately 1 hour to get to the city from the airport.

Some airlines offer service to the southern coastal city of Guayaquil. Flights to Guayaquil touch down at the **Aeropuerto Internacional José Joaquín de Olmedo (GYE)**. Formerly known as Simón Bolívar International Airport, it was renamed in 2006 to honor the former Ecuadorian president, poet and first mayor of Guayaquil. The following airlines offers international flights to Quito and Guayaquil:

- Aerogal
- Copa Airlines
- American Airlines
- Avianca
- Continental
- Delta Airlines
- Iberia
- KLM
- LAN
- TACA
- Tame
- United Airlines

For information on flights to the Galapagos, please consult our Getting To and Away from the Galapagos section on page 45.

BY LAND

Ecuador may be reached by land from Colombia and Peru. Taking a reputable international bus company is ideal because it eliminates the potential complications that can occur at border crossings. Some of these companies also have service to other Latin American capitals. The borders are also open to private vehicles for those who are crossing the border by bicycle, motorcycle or car.

Getting to Ecuador from Colombia

At present, only two border crossings are open to international travelers. The most commonly used one is Rumichaca, on the Pan-American Highway, connecting **Tulcán**, Ecuador to Ipiales, Colombia. The second option is through the jungle, at San Miguel. This journey begins in **Lago Agrio**, Ecuador, and ends at Mocoa, Colombia.

Getting to Ecuador from Peru

Three major border crossings exist between Ecuador and its southern neighbor, Peru. The fastest option is Huaquillas, Ecuador, a coastal city south of Machala by the Río Zarumilla to Aguas Verdes, Peru. Another popular route—and the safest—is at La Tina, south of Macará, Ecuador. Both borders are open 24 hours and have international bus service. The third choice is a beautiful, several-day journey through jungle mountains from **Vilcabamba** to the La Balsa border south of Zumba.

International Buses

Taking a reputable international bus company to and away from Ecuador is ideal because it eliminates potential complications, like excess fees and rip-off money changers, that can occur at border crossings. Buses will stop at the border and wait for passengers to complete immigration procedures.

Rutas de America (URL:www.rutas-america.com) offers direct service between Quito or Guayaquil and Lima, Peru (24 hr, $50-60). It also has direct trips to: Colombia (Bogotá, $60; Cali, $30) and Venezuela (Caracas, $90), and indirect trips to: Bolivia (La Paz, $145), Chile (Santiago, $160), Argentina (Buenos Aires, $200), Brazil (Río de Janeiro, $300). The company has two Quito offices in Quito (Selva Alegre OE1-72 and Av. 10 de Agosto. Tel: 593-2-254-8142, E-mail:quito@rutasamerica.com). In Guayaquil, the office is at La Garzota 3, Manzana 84, Villa 1 (Tel: 593-4-223-8673, E-mail:guayaquil@rutas-america.com).

Panamericana Internacional also provides direct service between Ecuador and Caracas, Venezuela, and indirect services to Colombia (Bogotá, Cali), Peru (Lima), Chile (Santiago) and Argentina (Buenos Aires). The company's Quito office is in the La Mariscal neighborhood (Av. Colón 852 and Reina Victoria. Tel: 593-2-255-7133).

Expresso Internacional Ormeño (URL:www.grupo-ormeno.com.pe) operates buses to Colombia (Cali, Bogotá, Cúcuta) and Venezuela (Caracas). Southern destinations are Peru (Lima, Cusco, Puerto Maldonado),

Brazil (Rio Branco, São Paulo), Bolivia (La Paz), Chile (Santiago), Argentina (Mendoza, Buenos Aires). Its Quito office is near Parque Carolina (Av. Los Shyris 34432 and Portugal, Centro Comercial La Carolina. Tel.: 593-4-213-0847, E-mail:adm.quito@grupo-ormeno.com.pe). In Guayaquil, Ormeño's offices are near the Terminal Terrestre (Av. de Las Américas, C.C. El Terminal, Bloque C, Oficina C-34. Tel.: 59 3-4-214-0487, E-mail:adm.guayaquil@grupo-ormeno.com.pe).

Loja Internacional (cooperativaloja.com) has several buses per day from **Loja** to Piura, Peru.

Other companies that offer service from Guayaquil and Machala to Tumbes, Máncora and other destinations on Peru's northern coast, via the Huaquillas / Aguas Verdes border crossing are: **CIFA Internacional** (URL:www.cifainternacional.com), **Civa** (URL:www.civa.com.pe) and **Cruz del Sur** (URL:www.cruzdelsur.com.pe).

BY BOAT

Traveling to and away from Ecuador by boat can be both expensive and inconvenient, but is inarguably the most adventurous method of transportation.

To Peru

The river crossing from Ecuador to Peru on the Río Napo is becoming popular once more. The trip goes from **Coca** (Francisco de Orellana) to Nuevo Rocafuerte and then to Pantoja and Iquitos, Peru.

To Colombia

Presently, the river journey up the Rio Putumayo into Colombia is not recommended, as it passes through the red zone of Colombia's civil war. By sea, a cargo-passenger service ploughs the waters between **Esmeraldas** and Tumaco, Colombia.
Updated: Aug 31, 2012.

Ecuador Border Crossings

The two border crossings from Ecuador to Peru are at Huaquillas, by the Rio Zarumilla, and Macará. The border at Tulcán/Rumicacha is the best place to cross into or out of Colombia.

The Ecuadorian town of Rumichaca is where the border patrol will stamp your passport and Ipiales is the border town six kilometers away on the Colombian side. Change money in a large Ecuadorian city before crossing any border. The money -changers at the border often pass false bills and will rip you off on the exchange rate, so it's best not to take any chances.

At each border post you will need to show your passport in order to be given an entry stamp, which will state the number of days you are allowed to stay in Ecuador. Most foreigners receive 90 days free, whereas citizens of the Andino Pact countries receive up to six months. See Ecuador Visa Information for more information on entry requirements.

Border crossings are generally only open 6 a.m.-8 p.m., so plan accordingly if traveling with local transportation. The major border crossings—at **Huaquillas / Aguas Verde** and **La Tina**—are open 24 hours for international buses only.

Upon arriving at the border, locals may offer to assist you with forms, taxes and other border paperwork. They will charge a fee for their services. It is best to avoid these unnecessary costs, and deal only with verifiable immigration and border officials. Change money only at banks or legitimate *casas de cambios* (exchange houses).
Updated: Apr 22, 2013.

Visa Information

NOTE: The following information should be confirmed with the Ecuadorian Embassy or Consulate in your own country, or the Ministerio de Relaciones Exteriores (Ministry of Foreign Affairs) website (www.mmrree.gob.ec/eng/services/visas.asp). Visa policies and regulations change frequently, and can vary from one office to another. Sometimes the best sources are other travelers who have gone through the process themselves.

The Ministry of Foreign Affairs is located in Quito, at Carrión E1-76 y Av. 10 de Agosto (Tel: 593-2-299-3200).

U.S. citizens need to have passports that are valid for at least six months prior to departing Ecuador as well. This only applies if you have an international stopover, though. If your flight is direct to the United States, departure will not be denied in the instance of less than six months validity.

TOURIST VISAS

Most travelers to Ecuador will not need to obtain a visa before departure.

Citizens of Afghanistan, Bangladesh, Eritrea, Ethiopia, Kenya, Nepal, Nigeria, Pakistan, the People's Republic of China and Somalia require a visa to enter Ecuador. As of August 2011, visitors need to have at least six months valid on their passport prior to travel in order to enter the country. When you arrive, the migration officials will stamp a tourist visa valid up to 90 days. If you plan to stay the entire 90 days, be sure to request the full visa limit as migration officials will sometimes give a visa for less time. They will also give you give you an embarkation card. Save this. You will need to present it when you leave the country.

If you come from a country that requires a tourist visa, you will need to apply for a 12-X visa. The fee for this visa is $30, plus a processing charge of $30 which you have to present at the Ministerio de Relaciones Exteriores, along with: two copies of the completed *formulario de solicitud de visa de no inmigrante* (non-immigrant visa application form; print off from the Ministry's website), two passport photos (in color, with white background), an economic guarantee (print-out of your bank account), your original passport with at least six months validity, a photocopy of your passport, a photocopy of your round-trip plane ticket and a *solicitud de visa* (an explanation of why you want to extend your stay, in Spanish).

Extending Your Tourist Visa

Your 90 day visa can be extended for a further 90 days by applying for a 12-IX visa, the Commercial Activities Visa. It is valid for up to six months and allows you to change your visa status. It allows the foreigner to engage in tourism, sports, health, education, science, art or commercial transactions. The fee for this visa is $200, plus $30 processing charge. The paperwork entails: two copies of the completed *formulario de solicitud de visa de no inmigrante* (non-immigrant visa application form; print off from the Ministry's website), two passport photos (in color, with white background), an economic guarantee (print-out of your bank account), your original passport with at least six months validity, a photocopy of your passport, a photocopy of your plane ticket and a *solicitud de visa* (an explanation of why you want to extend your stay, in Spanish).

WORK, STUDY AND OTHER NON-RESIDENT VISAS

If you want to work, study (long-term) or just travel for more than 180 days, you will need to look into a different visa. There are two main types of visas: resident and non-resident (referred to as immigrant and non-immigrant on the Ecuadorian government website).

Student visas, work visas, volunteer and religious work visas, cultural exchanges and tourist visas all fall under the category of non-resident and will set you back between $50 and $200, plus $30 processing fee. All of these visas have to be applied for before you arrive in Ecuador at the consulates in you native country.

Work visas are extremely hard to obtain and are much more complicated than tourist visas and are best arranged with your employer. Student visas on the other hand are much less complicated but are also best obtained with the help of your school or study program, which will undoubtedly have experience in jumping through the necessary bureaucratic hoops.

NOTE: All non-resident visas, except for the 12-X Tourist, that were applied for overseas must be registered at the Dirección de la Extranjería (Av 6 de Diciembre, between Colón and La Niña) within the first 30 days of arrival. Failure to do so will result in a hefty $200-2,000 fine. If you applied for it in Ecuador, you do not need to register it.

Censos are no longer issued to foreigners. Instead you are supposed to carry your passport at all times. A photocopy of the photo, visa page and visa registration pages may suffice in most circumstances.

Getting Around Ecuador
BY PLANE

Four carriers provide domestic air service in Ecuador.

Tame (URL:www.tame.com.ec) has the most extensive schedule. From Quito, it flies to Baltra (Galápagos), Coca, Cuenca, Cumbaratza, Esmeraldas, Guayaquil, Lago Agrio, Macas, Manta, San Cristóbal (Galápagos), Santa Rosa, Tena and Tulcán. From Guayaquil, Tame has flights to Cuenca, Esmeraldas, Loja, Latacunga and Quito, as well as Galápagos.

Aerogal (URL:www.aerogal.com.ec), flies from Quito to Baltra (Galápagos), Coca, Cuenca, Guayaquil, Manta and San Cristóbal (Galápagos); and from Guayaquil, to Quito and the two Galápagos airports.
Lan Ecuador (URL: www.lan.com) offers services from Quito to Baltra (Galápagos), Cuenca, Guayaquil and San Cristóbal (Galápagos). From Guayaquil, it flies to Quito and the Galápagos.

Saereo (URL:www.saereo.com) has flights from Quito to Lago Agrio and Macas, and offers inter-island flights in the Galápagos Islands (Isabela, Baltra, San Cristóbal).

For more information on flights to the Galapagos, please consult our Getting To and Away from the Galapagos section on page 45.

Flying within Ecuador is not always cheap considering the short distance from point-to-point, but it can save you hours of travel time. For example, a flight from Quito to Guayaquil takes about 50 minutes and costs $110-200 round trip, while the bus takes over 10 hours (each way) and costs about $24 round trip. A flight from Quito to Lago Agrio, the jump-off point to the Cuyabeno National Reserve in the Amazon, takes 30 minutes and costs $110-130 round trip as opposed to the six- to eight-hour bus ride on shoddy roads that costs $20 round trip. There are also only very specific times this flight is available.

Student and senior discounts may apply for both land and air travel, so be sure to ask. It is easiest to stop at a travel agency to book your flight, but be sure to call the airline to confirm a couple of days before you travel.

BY BUS

Traveling by bus is the most common method of transportation for Ecuadorians as well as the cheapest and often the most convenient. Long-distance buses charge $1 per hour on average, slightly more for the Ejecutivo or First-Class buses. Bus drivers, especially in the sierra, are fearless. If you have a queasy stomach, sit near the front, but you may not want to sit at the very front where you can see exactly what the driver is doing. Sometimes it is better not to know! Most long-distance buses are equipped with DVD players and TVs so you can enjoy Jean Claude Van Damme, Arnold Schwarzenegger and many more action stars dubbed in Spanish as you

speed around curvaceous two-lane mountain roads. Ecuadorian bus drivers tend to like action flicks, so don't get your hopes up for anything along the lines of sappy dramas or romantic comedies. They also tend to blast the volume, so take ear-plugs.

BY TRAIN

The construction of a railway from the sierra to the coast in 1873 was initiated by President Gabriel García Moreno. The 461-kilometer (288-mi) line from Durán on the coast to Quito, which took 35 years to complete, was essential for commerce and trade within the country.

The El Niño phenomenon of 1993 destroyed the Riobamba-Durán line at Río Chanchán, near Aluasí. In 2008, the federal government initiated an intense program to bring the Quito-Durán and Otavalo-San Lorenzo trains back on line. At present, 10 tourist routes operate, some using steam locomotives and other *ferrobuses*.

The most popular thrill ride is the El Nariz del Diablo (the Devil's Nose), a 12-kilometer (7-mi) series of switch back rails between Alausi and Sibambe. Ferrocarriles del Ecuador lists the timetables and prices for these trips on its website (Tel: 1-800-873-637; URL:www.ferrocarrilesdelecuador.gob.ec).

BY TAXI

In Quito and Guayaquil, taxis will be an important way for you to get around. They are quite cheap, reliable and safe. There are a few rules and tips you need to familiarize yourself with first, however. Before you get in the cab, you should agree on the price for your destination.

Never simply get in and ask how much the ride costs once you get to your destination. The rate will go up if you're sitting in the back seat when you begin to negotiate. City buses stop running about 8 p.m. or so, and after that it is safest to travel in taxis, even for very short distances.

HITCHHIKING

In a country full of pickup trucks, hitchhiking is a fairly common way to get around, especially in small towns and the jungle where there is no established bus system. Some drivers, especially those with the larger pickup trucks that have seats and wooden walls to block the wind in the back, will go ahead and charge a small fee.

The Devil's Nose

Thirty kilometers into the ascent of Ecuador's towering western range, a railway snakes up a mountain known as La Nariz del Diablo (The Devil's Nose). This nearly vertical wall of rock was the greatest natural obstacle engineers encountered during construction of the country's train system, and the decision to go up it instead of around was one of a string of blunders that nearly smothered the dream of connecting Ecuador's two largest cities, Guayaquil and Quito, by rail.

Today, the Devil's Nose is the highlight of a fantastic rail trip that meanders through the rich tapestry of cultivated fields and rugged highland spread across the southern half of Ecuador's 400-kilometer long Central Valley, aptly christened "The Avenue of the Volcanoes" in 1802 by the German explorer Alexander Von Humboldt.

The journey begins in the picturesque city of Alausí. Like many cities in Ecuador, Alausí sits near the giant volcano, Chimborazo, which at 6,310 meters (approximately 20,702 feet) enjoys the dual distinctions of being Ecuador's highest peak and the furthest point from the center of the earth, thanks to the bulge at the equator. The train travels south from Alausí through a few small towns and large expanses of open country before arriving at the "most difficult railway in the world," where it begins a hair-raising descent up the Devil's Nose. It's here that passengers will experience the engineers' ingenious solution of carving a series of tight zigzags into the side of the mountain, which allow the train to climb a gradient of 1-in-18 from 1,800 to 2,600 meters, by going forwards then backwards up the tracks.

A hundred years after it was constructed, the steep grade of the Devil's Nose stretch of track precludes its use as a freight or efficient passenger line, but affords the perfect means for present-day explorers who want to discover the rugged and breathtaking Ecuadorian countryside.

You should always ask about price before hopping in. Although hitchhiking is more common in Ecuador than in many other countries, it is still not guaranteed to be safe. Use common sense, especially if you are a woman or traveling alone.

BY CAR AND MOTORCYCLE

The general philosophy of drivers in Ecuador is, "I have the right of way." In practice, whoever is bigger goes first. As a result, you will hear lots of horns blaring, brakes screeching, insults flying and pedestrians running for their lives. That said, renting a car while you are traveling in Ecuador has its advantages. There are many spots where buses dare not venture and can only be reached by four-wheel drive, on bicycle or by foot.

In order to legally drive in Ecuador, you need an international driver's license used in conjunction with a driver's license from your home country. It's a good idea to also have good insurance coverage. Four car rental companies operate in Ecuador, including:

Avis: www.avis.com.ec
Budget: www.budget-ec.com
Hertz: www.hertz.com
Localiza: www.localiza.com

You'll need to rent a car in one of the larger cities in Ecuador: Cuenca, Guayaquil or Quito.

Adventure Travel in Ecuador

Ecuador is a great destination for adventurous visitors itching to get off the tourist track. This country features a fairly well developed infrastructure for activities like climbing, hiking, mountain biking, rafting, horseback riding, surfing, scuba diving and birdwatching. Whether you decide to ramble out on your own or hook up with a local guide service, the logistics of planning excursions in Ecuador are simpler and the planning time shorter than in other, more remote areas of the world.

ECUADOR HIKING

There are a number of excellent trips through the Andean páramo (grassland) which features spectacular views of Ecuador's volcanic peaks. The most popular, longer treks are the Trek de Condor, which passes the often cloud-shrouded Antisana and ends at the Cotopaxi Volcano; and the Ingapirca Trek which takes you along an old Incan trail to Ecuador's most important Inca site. For the intrepid trekker there are several multi-day Andes-to-Amazon hikes that take you from the grassy plains of the high altitude páramo, through cloud forest, and finally to lowland rainforest. During your descent, as you pass through one ecosystem to another, you'll see dramatic changes in the flora and fauna while you are peeling off layer after layer of clothing. Rainforest hikes are also possible, but it's a good idea to hire a local guide to ensure you don't become lost. There are some great hikes from lodges along the Napo River in the Amazon.

ECUADOR RAFTING AND KAYAKING

Ecuador is considered one of the best destinations in the world for whitewater sports due to the steep drop-offs from snow-capped peaks to rich lowland areas connected by one of the highest concentrations of rushing rivers per square kilometer. In addition, its tropical location provides for year-round water sports. Whether you are interested in whitewater rafting or kayaking, Ecuador has the tours, isolated destinations and heart-racing rapids.

Where to Go

Tena is the biggest kayak and rafting destination in Ecuador; some say it offers the best kayaking rapids in Latin America. Many travelers choose to start in Quito and shop around the dozens of tour operators that base their operations in the capital before heading out. Santo Domingo also has a developed whitewater community, and offers warmer water than mountain rivers at higher altitudes. For something a bit more low-key, head down to Baños and give rafting a go on the Río Pastaza.

Packing List

Swimsuit, tennis shoes or Teva-like sandals with secure ankle straps, T-shirt (quick-drying material is best), easy-dry shorts or running tights, safety strap if wearing glasses, and waterproof cameras are all suggested. Don't forget a waterproof bag for anything you want to keep dry during your trip and a dry change of clothes for the trip back to Quito. Updated: Sep 10, 2012.

ECUADOR MOUNTAIN CLIMBING

Ecuador offers an incredible diversity of mountains to explore. Within a day's drive from Quito are glaciated peaks which rise over 5,000 meters (16,400 ft) and one over 6,000 meters (19,680 feet), all of which are volcanoes. The highest Andean summits in Ecuador are located primarily along the Avenida de los Volcanes (Avenue of the Volcanoes), a fertile central valley just south of Quito, which is buttressed by two mountain ranges, the Eastern and the Western Cordilleras. Some of the summits are young, cone-shaped volcanoes like Cotopaxi (5,897 m / 19,342 ft) with technically straightforward climbs offering the novice a chance to get near to or above high altitudes. Others are deeply eroded, older volcanoes with challenging rock and ice routes, such as the glorious ring of peaks on El Altar (5,319 m / 17,446 ft).

ECUADOR MOUNTAIN BIKING

Ecuador offers the cyclist seemingly endless back roads and trails to explore. The Incas, who were legendary road builders, and their living descendants have been carving scenic paths for centuries. Today, mountain bikes are used by rural communities as a major form of transportation in many areas.

The Andes create a playground of huge vertical descents and lung-bursting climbs where the snow line and the equator meet. For most people, the extreme cycling environment of the Andes is best enjoyed going downhill. Descents of 3,000 meters (10,000 ft) in a single day can be done in several areas of the country. The world-class descent directly down the slopes of Cotopaxi Volcano, the technical descent down Pichincha Volcano and trips that take riders from the heights of the Andes to the Amazon Basin are all highly recommended.

Biker-friendly buses and pickup truck taxis, plus readily available lodging and food in most rural areas make cross-country independent bicycle travel in Ecuador extremely appealing, but careful planning is essential. The lesser-traveled back roads make the best routes.

Bike rental is available in Quito and Baños, but quality varies widely. Check your bike carefully before heading out. Shocks and strong aluminum rims are essential as the high-speed descents on potted terrain will otherwise lead to unwanted bent wheels.
Updated: Sep 05, 2012.

ECUADOR HORSEBACK RIDING AND TOURS

Ecuador provides riding enthusiasts with a surprising range of excellent opportunities. You can jaunt high in the Andes through the *páramo* grasslands and plains with snow-capped volcanoes as a backdrop; through lowland tropical rain forest; or even through the many unique ecosystems of the Galápagos Islands. Ecuador's extensive hacienda system makes it possible to ride through quilted pasture land from one hacienda to another, many of which now operate as country inns and send riders out with scrumptious picnics.

Ecuador has a number of stables that rent good horses, and if you know where to look you can find pure Peruvian Pasos, Andalusians and Arabs. Beginning riders are advised to hire the tough, mixed-blood Criollo horses. Be forewarned: even healthy horses will generally look thin in the Sierra. At these altitudes, the horses cannot afford to carry extra weight-so you will rarely find well-padded mounts.

When to Ride

In Ecuador you can ride year-round, although some months are better than others for certain areas. The coastal areas and semi-tropical Baños have a tendency to be muggy. In the Sierra north of Quito, the month of May can be rather wet. During the rest of the year it typically rains only in the late afternoons and by this time the horses are back in the stables and you are fireside enjoying a pre-dinner cocktail.
Updated: Sep 04, 2012.

BIRDWATCHING IN ECUADOR

Ecuador is a popular destination for bird watching. With upward of 1,500 species, it has as many species as in Europe and North America combined. Ecuador's top birding spots are in the Oriente region, with over 600 species, and the Galápagos with its abundant endemic species. However, other regions birders may wish to explore include the bird-rich cloud forest area surrounding Mindo. Many unusual species can also be found in the páramo region. Because Ecuador is small and has a decent infrastructure, it is possible to access many of these areas fairly easily. It is recommended to hire the services of local guides for the best birding experiences, as they have good local knowledge and know exactly where to look in the undergrowth to locate that rare bird. Don't forget your binoculars!

Birdwatching in the Amazon

To spot the widest variety of species of birds in the Amazon, it is worth heading there during the transitions between the dry and wet months. The worst time is during the dry months (December, January and August). Species to be spotted in the Amazon include the Rufous-headed Woodpecker, Fiery Topaz, Harpy Eagle and Zigzag Heron, as well as various species of tanagers, toucans and parrots and antbirds, to mention just a few.

The best birdwatching opportunities in the Amazon region are found by staying at one of the many jungle lodges. Be sure to select one with an observation tower: these are built around the tall kapok trees and allow climbing above the forest canopy to spot a great variety of species, as well as appreciate and admire the never insurmountable vistas of the forests and jungle.

Sacha Lodge is unique for its 40-meter (131-ft) tower, from which it is possible to spot many species. From the tower, a wild cacophony greets you as you spot a wide variety of colorful birds, including parrots and macaws. Sacha boasts that it is possible for a guide to spot as many as 80 species in a single morning from this tower. With 500 recorded species in the area, this could be true. For an alternative birding experience, take a motorized canoe for one and a half hours to the Yasuní Parrot Lick. Here, in a colorful spectacle, several species of parrots gather in the early morning to eat the exposed salty clay, which is vital for their digestion. Hope for a dry, sunny day; you'll see more parrots.

Kapawi Lodge is another alternative for great birding. In a stay of ten days, it is possible for a keen and dedicated spotter to see up to an astounding 400 species. The building of the lodge was one of the biggest community-based projects in Ecuador and there is a wish to provide genuine ecotourism. River islands close to Kapawi are home to Horned Screamers, Orinoco Geese and Muscovy Ducks. Other birds in the locality include Brown Jacamars, Plumbeous Antbird, Buckley's Forest Falcon and the Blue-winged Parrotlet, to name just a few. It is possible to observe species here that cannot be found at other lodges.

At **La Selva**, native birding experts are hired to assist those interested in birdwatching. While their English is not great, their birding skills more than make up for this. Close to the lodge it is possible to see many varieties of birds just by walking around. However, for a great view, La Selva offers an observation tree tower. La Selva is also close to parrot salt licks, and it is a great place for spotting the Cocha Antshrike and the Zigzag Heron.

Birdwatching in the Páramo

Above the cloud forest region sits the páramo, the barren zone above the tree line, (3,100-4,700 meters / 10,170-15,419 ft a.s.l.). Birds here are easy to spot due to the lack of vegetation. Ecuador's national symbol, the Andean Condor, can be found here, along with the Tawny Antpitta and the Andean Snipe. Condors can also be spotted on the road to Papallacta from Quito. Areas of the páramo worth visiting include the national parks of El Ángel, Cajas and the highland areas of Cotacatchi-Cayapas and Cayambe-Coca. **Parque Nacional Cajas** is home to 125 species, including the condor and Violet-tailed Metaltail, an endemic hummingbird. **Parque Nacional Cotapaxi** is also a good place for páramo birding, with 90 species to spot, including the Black-chested Hawk-eagle, Andean Coot, Andean Lapwing and Páramo Pipit. Other birds that make their home in the páramo include the Rufous-bellied Seed Snipe and Stout-billed Cinclodes. Updated: Sep 07, 2012.

)))))

Galápagos

Leaving behind the smog, traffic and fast food of Quito, an airplane flies two hours west and eons backward in time. The Galápagos Islands are a land that time forgot, a rugged and unforgiving paradise where the air, land and sea are home to species found nowhere else on earth. It is a zoo without cages: each island is its own harsh laboratory of evolution, adaptation and competition. The marine iguanas understand this—stoic black dragons that seem to have crawled out of the volcanic rock itself, they share the lordship of these islands with the birds, tortoises and sea lions. They were here first, and they will permit you to visit, but they know that you couldn't stay even if you wanted to. You're not tough enough to share their rocky bit of paradise.

Fun and sun? Surf and sand? Forget it. If that's what you're looking for, go to Cozumel. A visit to Galápagos is an expedition, a chance to walk in the footprints of Charles Darwin. It's not about the beach; it's about the birds, fish and animals, and simply put, there is no better place to see them than here.

In a sense, there are no species that are purely native to the islands. The islands were never connected to any continent— every resident reptile, mammal, bird and fish arrived after the islands were born of thunderous volcanic upheavals in the deep crevasses of the Pacific Ocean. Once these animals found themselves on these rock-strewn, desolate islands, survival dictated the long process of adaptation. Ages later, the island species no longer even resemble their cousins on the continent.

There are dozens of species on Galápagos, animals that can be found nowhere else on earth. Not counting Lonesome George, there are 10 surviving species of giant Galápagos Tortoise: four more have gone extinct. The Galápagos Penguin is the only penguin to live north of the equator. The Flightless Cormorant has lost its wings to evolution—there are few predators to flee. The iguanas are marvels of adaptation—the land iguanas eat spiny cacti with ease, while the marine iguanas can survive a 15 degree drop in body temperature while they eat underwater algae. Even the nondescript little finches have their share of the fame: Darwin used the 13 different

endemic species of finch as an example to prove his theories (one variety can suck blood!). Even many marine species are endemic: the Galápagos Shark is a gray reef shark only found in the islands.

Young Sea Lions, Española

For all the rugged vistas and parched, rocky trails, Galápagos is actually a very fragile ecosystem. The first settlers released goats and pigs into the wild. This did provide food in the short term, but now they're considered an ecological disaster: they destroy the vegetation and ruin the habitat of other native animals; the tortoises and iguanas in particular have been badly affected. Introduced plants such as the sour apple and blackberry have taken over acres of park area, forcing out native plants in the process. Domestic dogs and cats that escape and breed in the wild are considered a serious problem as well. Efforts to control these animals and plants have met with mixed success: for example, goats have been successfully eradicated from some of the islands.

There is hope—concerted efforts of park staff, international organizations and tourism operators have helped greatly in recent years to protect the islands and the animals that live there. And don't let the gloomy human record in the islands discourage you from a visit; as long as you closely follow the instructions your specially trained naturalist guide gives you, you'll not cause any damage.

There is a reason why the Galápagos Islands are one of the top three visitor destinations in South America on any list you check: they're magnificent. Enjoy the white sand beaches, lounge on a luxurious cruise ship, but bring extra rolls of film or digital memory cards for the real stars of the islands—the flora and fauna of one of the last original places in the world!

GALÁPAGOS INTRO

Planning Your Galápagos Trip

A visit to the Galápagos is the trip of a lifetime, and it needs to be planned accordingly! There are a limited number of visitors who are allowed to go to the islands every year and the cruise ships tend to fill up at certain times of the year in particular. You'll want to start planning long before your actual trip if you can. Here are some of the questions you need to ask yourself while still in the early planning stages.

WHEN TO GO?

Galápagos is always nice, but there are other factors such as animal life cycles and high/low tourism seasons to consider. See the following section for details.

HOW MUCH CAN I AFFORD TO SPEND?

Unless you have a minimum of about $1500 for a five-day trip, not counting airfare from wherever you are to Ecuador, you will not be able to afford a cruise and will have to see the islands while staying in Puerto Ayora or one of the other towns. That's not necessarily a bad thing; many people choose to see them this way. Just bear in mind that Galápagos is expensive. Even if you're already in Quito, it will cost you some $600 for the flight and park entrance taxes...just to set foot in Galápagos!

If you can afford a little more, services improve greatly the more you spend, and you're more likely to have a memorable time.

WHAT DO I WANT TO DO WHILE I'M THERE?

Do you want to spend a day SCUBA diving? Then you'll need to stay in one of the towns for a while. Do you want to shop for souvenirs? You'll want to go to Puerto Ayora or Puerto Baquerizo Moreno. Want to try some local food? Puerto Ayora is your best bet. Need a few days on the beach? Head for Isabela Island.

This goes for the animals, too. Do you want to see a Galápagos Penguin? They are only at certain visitor sites. Same goes for the albatrosses, cormorants, tortoises and land iguanas. If you desperately want to see one of these species, look closely at our Wildlife and Visitor Sites sections while planning your trip, and only go on a cruise that visits those sites.

WHO DO I BOOK WITH?

There are countless tour agencies and travel agents that offer trips to Galápagos. Your friendly hometown travel agency can help, but if you want someone with a little more experience in the islands, I personally recommend the following:

Haugan Cruises: Haugan Cruises operates the catamarans Ocean Spray and Cormorant, two of the nicer ships in Galápagos. They can also set you up on other cruises and get last-minute deals if that's what you're looking for. Reliable, responsible and professional, Haugan cruises is a big step up from the places in Mariscal. URL: www.haugancruises.com.

Opuntia Eco Journeys: Contrary to all the hype and fuss over cruises, Opuntia aims to organize a well-rounded experience that's based around taking in the wildlife, nature and adventure that's to be found in land-based tours of the islands. The moments you do spend in the water will only involve either going from island to island quickly or checking out the wildlife below with snorkeling, rather than spending it on a cruise. As added karma, Opuntia is also recognized by the Rainforest Alliance as a sustainable tour operator. Their guides are top-notch and the tours are meant to give you a thorough experience of the Galápagos islands and its highlights, rather than just a passing visit which cruise-based tours are prone to giving. Manuel Sotomayor E17-105 and Flores Jijón Tel: 1-800-217-9414, URL: www.opuntia-galapagostours.com.

Andean Discovery: Experts in putting together your Andean "dream trip," Andean Discovery sets out to take care of all the logistics involved in arranging an itinerary for you and filling your time in Ecuador (or even Peru). Their interest and devotion in taking you off the beaten path is what makes them quite exceptional, showing you places many others rarely get to see. Their itineraries can also convert just about any set of variables (budget, interests, schedule, group size, etc.) into an unforgettable and solid experience. The guides are well-trained English speakers and will be there to offer you a safe and memorable experience as well. Tel: 1-800-893-0916, E-mail: info@andeandiscovery.com, URL: www.andeandiscovery.com.

Columbus Travel: Based in Quito, Columbus specializes in Galápagos and trips to mainland Ecuador. They are experienced and professional and have a long track record of satisfied clients. Columbus is best if you know you want to go to Ecuador and Galápagos but don't know exactly what you want to do: their staff will patiently talk you through any questions you may have and find the right cruise/tour/ itinerary for you. They know all of the ships, and therefore any budget level is welcome to book with them. URL: http://www. galapagosisland.net.

Metropolitan Touring: Metropolitan is an Ecuadorian agency which has been working in Galápagos for decades. They have international offices and agents and can combine your Galápagos tour with visits to mainland Ecuador, Peru (Machu Picchu!), Argentina or other South American points of interest. Metropolitan is best for those with a little more money to spend who want to hire one of the top local agencies to make sure there is always someone to meet them at the airport, make sure their tour van is ready to go, etc. URL: http://www.metropolitan-touring.com/

Come to Galápagos: Based in Puerto Baquerizo Moreno (San Cristóbal Island), Come to Galápagos is run by an American/ Ecuadorian couple who are residents of the islands and therefore have local knowledge other agencies lack. They specialize in land-based tours (as opposed to cruises) and pride themselves on individual attention. They also sponsored the first ever Galápagos marathon! Best for those who want a land-based tour or who prioritize helping local communities, a foundation of Come to Galápagos. URL: http://www.cometogalapagos.com/

Galápagos Travel Center: GTC is a reliable operator with an office near the corner of Foch and Reina Victoria in Mariscal. They specialize in personalized service and good prices. They do all things Galápagos: land tours, diving, cruises - you name it. Combination tours with mainland attractions are also possible. URL: www.galapagosislands. com.

Galápagos Travel Line is run by Rodrigo Miño (formerly of Columbus Travel) who has a great many years of experience in the industry and contacts with boats and operators. Miño and his team are friendly, helpful and accommodating in finding you a trip to suit your needs and budget. URL: http:// www.galapagostraveline.com.
Updated: July 31, 2013

When to Go to the Galápagos
There is no bad time to visit the Galápagos Islands. There is always something interesting to see and the weather is usually great. Still, there are a few variables you may want to consider.

WEATHER
The Equator passes through the islands, so it's never frigid, but there are significant seasonal variations. From June to November, currents bring cool water and air to the islands. The islands are cooler, there is often rain or mist (garúa), and water temperatures are cool enough that you may want a wetsuit while snorkeling. From December to May, the islands get hotter (sometimes it's quite brutal) and there is more rain. The highlands of San Cristobal and Santa Cruz can get cool any time of year.

WILDLIFE
There are cycles and patterns to the wildlife as well, and you should bear this in mind if seeing a particular type of animal or behavior is important to you. For example, the tortoises migrate into and out of the highlands; if you want to see them in their natural habitat, it's best to go between January and June. If you want to see a Waved Albatross, don't go from January to April, because they won't be there. If you want to see a specific animal, your tour company should be able to tell you or see our wildlife section.

TOURISM
If it's your plan to go to the islands and either island hop or try to find a good last minute deal, you'll want to do so during low tourist season. Try May-early June or late September-October. Early December is also a good time to go. If you go during high season, hotels and last minute deals will be much harder to find.

Galápagos Budgeting and Costs
Once you've paid for your Galápagos tour and flights, you don't need any more money, right? Wrong! There are still some costs you'll need to consider.

OFFICIAL FEES AND TAXES
All adult foreigners must pay a $100 entry fee to Galápagos. The majority of this income (over 95%) goes to the maintenance and conservation of the Galápagos National Park. The Instituto Nacional Galápagos is now charging visitors an additional $10 fee

for the issue of "Transit Control Cards." The new cards will keep better track of tourist numbers on the islands and monitor both arrival and departure dates. You get your card in the airport in Quito or Guayaquil.

Leaving the pier on Isabela Island (on a ferry to Puerto Ayora) will cost you $10.

EXPENSES ON CRUISE SHIPS

If you're on a cruise ship, most of your expenses will be paid for. Most likely you'll only be paying for drinks such as alcohol or soda. There may in some cases be a small fee to rent gear such as fins or wetsuits. Most of the larger ships have gift shops with T-shirts, playing cards, etc. There has been some talk of charging cruise-going visitors an additional $100, but this fee has not yet been implemented. Recently, a "fuel surcharge" has been added to cruise costs, but it's generally just factored in when you pay.

TIPPING YOUR GALÁPAGOS GUIDE AND CREWS

Tipping guides and ship crews is customary in Galápagos. This is always a delicate subject, since tips are generally meant to be a reflection of services rendered and not an obligation.

Some people recommend giving the crew between $20 and $50 per passenger per week, and giving the guide as much as half of that amount. Others suggest tipping as much as $10 per passenger per day, which can add up. Each boat has its own system for accepting tips—two envelopes, a communal tip box, the honor system—but the crew, not the tourist, is responsible for dividing the tip money among the individual members.

If any of the crew members were exceptional, feel free to give them an individual display of gratitude, monetary or verbal.

Guides, staff and crew can make or break your Galápagos cruise experience!

SHOPPING IN GALÁPAGOS TOWNS

When you are in Puerto Ayora or Puerto Baquerizo Moreno the potential for spending money is high. A tourist's necessity items—camera supplies and sunscreen, to mention a few—are two to three times more expensive in Galápagos than in the United States, or even on the mainland, so stock up before you come.

Souvenir shops abound in both major towns. Visitors can select from Galápagos T-shirts, coffee mugs, hats, playing cards, posters and much more. Prices for these tend to run relatively high; figure on $12-20 for a T-shirt, three postcards for a dollar, etc. Selection is pretty good, so getting little gifts for friends back home is easy. Savvy Galápagos souvenir shoppers may want to check out the little stuffed boobies, sea lions and other animals; some of these are actually made in Galápagos out of recycled material and make great gifts.

Major credit cards are accepted in many of the nicer hotels, restaurants, gift shops and tour centers, but they often charge for use of this particular service.

There is one bank in Puerto Ayora, the Banco del Pacífico, which gives cash advances on MasterCards, changes traveler's checks (with a minimal surcharge), and has a MasterCard and Cirrus-compatible ATM. The bank is open from Monday to Friday (8 a.m.-3:30 p.m.) and Saturday (9:30 a.m.-12:30 p.m.). There are also some stores on Avenida Charles Darwin that will change your traveler's checks for you. Make sure before you come that you will have the ability to withdraw money; otherwise, bring more cash than you think you will need—small bills are preferred. You are more likely to spend all of your cash than have it stolen!

There are also ATMs in Puerto Baquerizo Moreno (San Cristóbal Island), but note that **there is no ATM on Isabela**. There isn't much to buy there, as there are no souvenir stores, but you'll want to bring enough cash with you to cover your hotel, food, tours, etc.

STAYING IN GALÁPAGOS

If you're staying in the cities instead of on a cruise ship, your budget can vary greatly. Hotels run from as little as $10 per night on up into the thousands of dollars. Restaurants are similar: it's possible to eat dinner for anywhere from $4 to $30. In general, it's tough to economize in Galápagos. As a bare minimum, plan on spending $50 per day in Galápagos, including the most basic hotels and food and a day trip to a snorkeling spot, beach or nature trail with guide. Some of the best visitor sites are free: if you're saving, look for those!

DAY TRIPS

Packaged tours may offer any combination of trips to local visitor sites. You can book individually (with one or a few companies) or you can book a weekly tour package comprised of a series of day trips, which can include land sites, snorkeling/dive sites, surf sites, or all three.

Daily tours to island sites range in price from $30 to $115 per person per day when booked individually, depending on the

Top Ten Questions Asked by Galapagos Tourists

Poor guides. They sometimes have to put up with a great deal. Every now and then, passengers come along who are clueless, rude, ignorant and/or unwilling to follow the strict rules of Galapagos, but the guides must be patient and pleasant nevertheless. It's not all bad, though: sometimes tourists say the darndest things. I asked several of my guide friends what were some of the best (worst?) questions that tourists have ever asked them. Here, in top ten format, are the best tourist questions, as chosen by veteran Galapagos guides.

10. "Do you feed the birds every day?"
9. "Where do the fish live?"
8. "Do the sharks come into the boats very often?"
7. (to a cruise guide on a ship) "How do you get home every night when you're working here?"
6. "Do the sea lions lay eggs?"
5. (asked in a zodiac, going from the ship to an island) "How far above sea level are we?
4. "Yesterday we were on the Pacific Ocean, what ocean are we on today?"
3. "Do the sea lions fly?" (upon seeing a sea lion perched high up on some craggy rocks)
2. "Are we going to meet Charles Darwin today?"
and #1... "How do you say piña colada in Spanish?"

services provided by the tour company and the sites visited. Daily tours to dive sites have less variable prices; most dive centers charge a standard $100 to $150 per person per day, according to the site. The price of combination tour packages range from $800 to $1,200 per week, including guided trips, hotel and meals. You can arrange these types of trips from your home country or from the mainland, following the same guidelines outlined for navigable tours.

For some companies that offer land-based or snorkeling tours, visit our Galápagos Tours page for an overview and list of operators.

A typical island day trip begins at dawn, with a walk to the dock or a bus trip to the canal, where you meet the boat that will take you to your destination. You spend a short time sailing to the predetermined visitor site. Once there you will spend the majority of the day touring the island with a naturalist guide, eating lunch, and (if available at the island site) swimming and snorkeling from the beach. You return to town via the same route in the early afternoon.

There are plenty of day trip operators in Puerto Ayora (fewer in Puerto Baquerizo Moreno) who will accept reservations until the day preceding the excursion. Day boats can vary in quality and comfort, but since most island sites are close and you spend a relatively longer period of time on-site, it is probably more important to shop for day trips by destination. Most day trip destinations from Puerto Ayora include visitor sites on the central islands of Santa Cruz, Santa Fé, North Seymour, South Plazas and Bartolomé. Different boats visit different islands on different days, so plan accordingly.

DIVE DAY TRIPS

Galápagos is a world famous dive destination and many visitors will want to spend a day or more diving. This is easily done with one of the many dive shops in both major towns. Visit our Galápagos Diving section for more information.

LAND-BASED VS. CRUISE TOURS

There are certain benefits associated with land-based tours, the most important of which is the comfort of stationary hotel accommodations versus mobile staterooms. You are not limited to on-board facilities and services, gaining access to a wider variety of port town restaurants, nightlife and shops. Finally, your community and associated social outlets extend to town visitors and residents, not just the other passengers on your boat. You can also pick and choose where you want to go instead of being tied to an itinerary mandated by the national park.

There are downsides to land-based tours relative to navigable tours. A considerable time is spent sailing back and forth to visitor sites; you are limited to visiting the close, central islands; only one (versus two) site is visited per day; and there is no chance of visiting sites either very early or late in the day.

Galápagos Packing List

Most things travelers need are available in Galápagos, but at a much higher price than on the mainland. You should plan on bringing what you'll need.

CLOTHES

There is no dress code on most boats or in island towns, so pack casual yet comfortable clothing. Bring lightweight, breathable items for day hikes and a sweater or jacket for cool evenings on the boat. Terrain on some islands is rough and rocky, so bring comfortable sneakers or hiking boots with good traction. Tevas, Chacos or any other types of sandal with a security strap are great for beach sites and less rugged trails. On the boat, you will keep your shoes in a communal bin and either walk barefoot or in flip-flops. A good hat, preferably with a wide brim, is a must.

LUGGAGE

If you are on a cruise tour, it is a good idea to pack as lightly and compactly as possible, since there is only a finite amount of space in your cabin and on board. Backpacks are the most portable through all of the required land-water transfers, but suitcases and duffel bags are fine.

Snorkeling is a Galapagos highlight

Your boat will send representatives from the crew to meet you at the airport, collect your bags, deliver them to the boat, and ultimately place them in your cabin. So if you have bulky or awkward pieces of luggage, the burden of transporting them will fall upon the helpful and gracious members of the crew.

Because you will have day excursions on the islands, it is essential that you bring a day pack or fanny pack so that you can have water, sun protection, photographic equipment, rain gear and any other items you may need with you at all times.

SWIMMING/SNORKELING GEAR

You will have a number of opportunities to swim, snorkel or scuba dive in Galápagos, oftentimes more than once a day. As such, you should bring a swimsuit, a towel (most ships provide beach towels but the cheap ones might not), and beach attire (a sarong or beach wrap is perfect for women).

Because you can get cold and sunburned very easily in Galápagos waters, it is also a good idea to bring a lightweight neoprene wetsuit or dive skin, if you have one, or some other quick-dry outfit that you don't mind wearing in the ocean. Wetsuits are available for rental on most of the reputable cruise ships— check once you've booked. If not, you can rent one in Puerto Ayora or Puerto Baquerizo Moreno.

Many boats have their own snorkeling equipment, which is complimentary or available for rent, but the quality and maintenance may be sub-par and the sizes available may be limited. If you are on a boat with scuba diving capability, you will probably have more luck, but you should still bring your own if you have it.

SCUBA DIVING EQUIPMENT

If you plan on scuba diving and have your own equipment, bring it. You will need at least a 6mm wetsuit, boots, gloves and possibly a hood, in addition to a regulator, BCD, computer, fins and mask. All of the dive shops will include equipment in the price of their packages, but the quality and size availability vary from place to place. Some dive shops replace their equipment every year, keep a variety of sizes and styles and maintain their gear in stellar condition. Others have older, worn-out equipment— a sticky regulator, a leaky BCD, ill-fitting apparel, etc.—that is still usable but less desirable for many recreational divers. The conditions in Galápagos can be challenging for many divers, so if you are at all nervous about your abilities, ease some of your worries by bringing your own gear.

MEDICAL

If you use any prescription medications, be sure to bring plenty, as they can be tough to find in the islands. You'll also want seasickness tablets if you tend to suffer from it, as well as aspirin, anti-diarrheal medicine such as Lomotil, and other basics. You'll definitely want sun protection: sunscreen, hats, sunglasses, after-sun lotion, etc.

PHOTOGRAPHY

Galápagos is an excellent place—even for novices—to take magazine-quality photographs and to make exciting home videos. Because much of the wildlife in Galápagos is close to the trails, you can get very good results with even the most basic cameras. Although you probably don't need anything larger than a standard lens, you can get some stunning close-up results if you bring a zoom lens.

Make sure you have plenty of memory space; you'll be taking a lot of photos. Bring a memory stick as well, to help with sharing photos with fellow guests and new-found friends. If you know you will be making a stop in Puerto Ayora during your cruise, you can plan to download photos from your memory card onto a CD at any of the internet cafés in town. Some cruise ships offer this service as well. Back up your favorite photos: more than one camera has accidentally found its way to the bottom of Galapagos waters!

You should also bring an underwater casing for your camera (if you have one) or an underwater camera. Although capturing the

underwater landscape and bigger creatures is best with a video camera or a camera with a strobe, the smaller digital cameras with flash are great for macro shots of fish, seascapes or coral.

If you own binoculars, this is the time to bring them.

In Summary ... A basic packing list of the essentials in Galápagos:

- Sunhat
- sunglasses
- sandals (for the boat)
- sneakers (for dry landings and rocky shores) Teva-style sandals (for wet landings)
- swimsuit
- umbrella (for sun protection during island hikes or the occasional downpour)
- high factor, waterproof sunscreen
- binoculars
- flashlight or head lamp
- water bottle
- plastic Ziploc bags to keep things from getting wet
- snorkel and mask if you aren't renting
- beach towel and bath towel
- wind resistant jacket
- light sweater or sweatshirt (nights can get rather cool and you don't want to miss stargazing on deck)
- twice as much film or memory cards as you think you will need
- extra batteries
- underwater camera
- motion sickness pills
- Water can be very cold so you may want to bring a dive skin or wetsuit

WHAT NOT TO BRING:

Although there are mosquitoes in Galápagos, none of them are carriers of malaria or dengue fever, so you don't have to worry about bringing medicine. Parts of mainland Ecuador are risky for malaria and other ailments, so if your trip will take you to other parts of Ecuador, you may want medicine.

Galápagos Health and Safety

Touring Galápagos can be a mentally and physically exhausting vacation. The long flights, extended periods of time on a moving boat and drastic changes between land and sea temperatures can all take their toll on the body. Here are some tips for keeping healthy.

Lava formations, Fernandina

COMMON MEDICAL PROBLEMS

The two most common ailments for Galápagos visitors are overexposure to the sun and seasickness. Sunscreen and motion sickness medicines are available in Puerto Ayora or Puerto Baquerizo Moreno, but it's better to bring your own.

MEDICAL FACILITIES IN GALÁPAGOS

Medical facilities and pharmacies on Puerto Ayora are decent. The town's hospital offers basic medical services, but it is not very modern or well-stocked. There is a 24-hour clinic on San Cristóbal and a small clinic on Isabela as well. You can usually find an English-speaking doctor at the hospitals.

The hyperbaric chamber/clinic in Puerto Ayora offers 24-hour care for diving emergencies and serious burns. Dr. Gabriel Idrovo and Dr. Ramiro López specialize in hyperbaric medicine, but they also provide general medical consultations during their regular office hours (9:30 a.m.-1:30 p.m. and 3:30-7:30 p.m.). Since it is a private facility that counts on only a small percentage of its funding from local scuba-diving operators, they may ask tourists that use the clinic to give a small contribution in addition to the $20-30 consultation fee.

SAFETY IN GALÁPAGOS

Mainland Ecuador has its share of problems with crime and poverty. Fortunately, Galápagos is a different matter. You really only need to be watchful of unattended things—do not leave valuables behind at public beaches or snorkeling sites, or purses or cameras unattended on restaurant tables. Belongings left behind in hotel rooms will usually be pretty safe, but lock them up if there is a strongbox in your room. Cruises are generally safe in terms of things stolen from rooms, but if you're on a budget cruise, keep an eye on your stuff.

Galápagos Transportation

Transportation on Galápagos is mainly based on boats and planes. In the two main towns, there are some cars and taxis. Transportation to the islands from mainland Ecuador is only by plane, given no boats offer transportation. All flights to the islands leave from Quito or Guayaquil. Once you are on the islands, most visitor sites are reached by boat. We have divided this section into: "transportation to and from Puerto Ayora," "transportation around Puerto Ayora" and "transportation around the Galápagos Islands."

Transportation To and From the Galápagos Islands

Flights to the main Galápagos airports in San Cristóbal and Baltra depart from Quito and generally stop en route in Guayaquil. The Quito-Guayaquil flight lasts about 40 minutes, and the Guayaquil-Galápagos flight takes just under two hours.

The archipelago is one hour behind mainland Ecuador. Three airlines, LAN, TAME and Aerogal, service the Galápagos Islands. Children and infants do receive a discount. According to TAME, the low tourist season is from May 1 to June 14 and from September 15 to October 31. Times vary and change in different seasons, but the prices are fixed, so there's no need to comparison shop.

If you book a cruise, the travel agency generally arranges your flight for you. Even though there is usually some availability on flights to the Galápagos, it is a good idea to make independent flight reservations at least a few days in advance.

Travel agencies will block seats for their all-inclusive tours, but then release them on the day of the flight if there are cancellations or unsold tour spaces. So if you are desperate to get to (or return from) the Enchanted Islands, in all likeliness you should be able to find spaces last-minute, especially during low-season.

Since flight prices are fixed, you can usually change the date of your ticket after purchasing it without penalty.

This policy can come in handy if you—like many other tourists—get caught up in the small-town charm of Puerto Ayora and decide to extend your stay; just stop by the TAME office anytime before your flight to make alternative arrangements.

Furthermore, if you decide after sunbathing for a week that you want to spend more time in coastal climes, you can easily change your final destination to Guayaquil. This requires simply checking your luggage to Guayaquil; no ticket change is needed.

It is not feasible to take a boat from mainland Ecuador to the Galápagos: it is a three-day trip over rough waters and there are currently no ships or agencies selling this service.

Going to Galápagos: Inside the Quito Airport

Because Galápagos is a very special destination, it's necessary to do a couple more steps in the airport than you would normally need. For information on getting to the airport, see our Getting To and Away From Quito section at the back of this book.

Here are the steps you'll need to follow to get through the airport when your there:

1. The taxi or bus will drop you off on a crowded curb. If you have loads of luggage, there should be a fellow nearby with a cart. Go to the right of the main doors, where you will see some metal railings and a door.

2. Just to the right of the main entrance is the Galápagos tourism and luggage inspection area. Prior to walking through the screening area you'll have to purchase your $10 tourism card.

3. After acquiring your tourism card, walk through with your stuff and they'll x-ray it and might open it. They're looking for fruit, vegetables, seeds and other things forbidden in Galápagos. They'll put a little tag on your luggage that says it has been inspected.

4. Now go to the airline counter and check in. If you're on a cruise, there will probably be someone there to help you.

5. Pass through security (it's just a bored guard at a gap in the metal railing right inside the airport). Show your boarding pass and they'll let you through.

6. Pass through security (carry-on checkpoint) and into the waiting area. There are screens with flight information and your flight will be announced.

7. Once you arrive in Galápagos, you must first pass through a migration checkpoint. There are usually three lines: foreigners, Ecuadorians and Galapagueños. Foreigners will have their papers checked and must pay their $100 park fee here. Remember, cash only, and have it handy!

If you're with a tour, they'll probably pick up your luggage for you. If you're by yourself, you'll have to wait at the little counter until they bring the luggage in. It can get hectic, but there's no real rush, so just be patient and you will get your bags. Stealing luggage in either airport is unheard of, so don't worry about pushing your way to the front of the line.

MORE USEFUL INFORMATION:
At the Quito airport, there is an ATM on the main floor. It's not far from where the taxis and buses drop you off. There are no ATMs at the airports in Baltra and San Cristóbal, so make sure to have your $110 for park fees and tourism cards with you!

Inside the waiting area, there is a small café which sells sandwiches, coffee and other snacks.

The same restrictions apply on Galápagos flights as any other in terms of what you can have in your carry-on: so pack away the liquids, nail clippers, scissors and other forbidden stuff in your checked luggage.

Transportation To and From Puerto Ayora or Puerto Baquerizo Moreno

After you deplane in Baltra, you will either meet the naturalist guide leading your pre-arranged tour or you will head off individually to Puerto Ayora. If you have an organized cruise tour, you will go with your guide and boat-mates on a five-minute TAME or Aerogal bus ride to the *muelle*, or dock, where your boat is anchored. These same buses are offered to those without guides, too.

If you are on your own and heading to Puerto Ayora, you can ride the same TAME or Aerogal bus to the canal (for free) and take the same ferry to Santa Cruz ($1 one-way). Once you get across the channel to Santa Cruz, you can either catch a taxi (about $20 per truck, so try to share) or public bus ($3) to take you the final leg to Puerto Ayora. Ideally, the ferries and buses are scheduled to coincide with flights landing and taking off, so you should not have to wait long. The taxi or bus will drop you off in any of the most frequented central spots—like the main pier or boardwalk—or the hotel you specify to the driver.

If your point of arrival is Puerto Baquerizo Moreno (San Cristóbal) it's not nearly as complicated. The airport is right on the edge of town. There are plenty of taxis there to take you to your hotel and the ride should cost less than $2.

Transportation Between Islands

Inter-island transportation is relatively straightforward. You can travel between Santa Cruz and the other main islands of San Cristóbal and Isabela either by plane, ferry or private boat. Itineraries and prices can change. The small airline, EMETEBE, flies a small plane between the main islands every day, if there are passengers. Tickets can be purchased at any of the airports or at the EMETEBE office near the port supermarket in Puerto Ayora (hours: 7:15-10:45 a.m., 2-6 p.m.; telephone: 05-252-6177). The flight costs about $160 one-way and lasts about 30 minutes.

Most people simply use the ferry. Every day, a handful of private ferries will leave Puerto Ayora for Isabela or San Cristóbal and vice versa. Some are better than others, so book your ferry ahead of time with a tour agency in town. You'll see signs on the travel agencies that say "Ferry Isabela San Cristóbal" or something similar. Stay away from the cheesy little hole-in-the-wall agencies near the dock and **never** buy a ferry ticket from a "tour operator" in the street. It's possible to buy a return ticket when you book your ferry, but it's not necessary.

The "system" of ferries is a little hectic. There are several small boats that go between the islands, and some are better than others. Some are quicker, and some have less fumes or have more comfortable seats. There is a co-operative of these ferries loosely overseen by the Galápagos park service.

Here are the steps you must take:

• Decide when you want to travel. You can buy your ferry tickets a couple of days in advance.

• Purchase your ticket. They cost $30, or sometimes a little less. There are several places to buy them; many little tour agencies will have signs out front that say "Tickets San Cristóbal & Isabela" or something similar. Do not buy them on the street, or from the cheesy little tour agencies close

to the pier. Many hotels will help you: if your hotel has this service, use it.

• You do not need to purchase your return ticket when you buy your departure ticket. You can, but it's just as easy to get it in Puerto Villamil or Puerto Baquerizo Moreno, and in fact may save you some hassle.

• To get back to Santa Cruz from Isabela, book a return ticket at the ferry co-op office on the main square. In San Cristóbal, any tour agency can sell you a return ticket.

• The tour operators know which are the better boats, and a good vendor will help you get on one of the more comfortable ones.

• You'll need to arrive at the old tourist pier (next to the Proinsular supermarket) by 1:30 p.m. on the day of your departure, because the park service must inspect your bags before you board. Stand in the "line" and wait your turn: when the park official determines that you are not smuggling illegal plants from one island to the other he or she will put a little tag on your bag.

• Find your ferry. The vendor might have told you which one to look for, or it might say on your ticket. Sometimes, the vendors will accompany you to the pier and help you find the right one.

• Get comfortable for the two-hour ride!

TIPS FOR THE FERRY RIDE:

The water can get quite rough on the two-hour ferry ride, especially during the colder months of June-October. If you are prone to motion sickness, don't eat anything after 10:00 a.m. or so and take a motion sickness pill about 45 minutes before the ferry leaves. Motion sickness pills are called "mareol" in Ecuador and are available at any pharmacy.

On the bright side, you'll know quickly how bad the waves will be: within 15 minutes of leaving port you'll be in open water and you'll know how rough it will be for the rest of the trip.

Also, if you get motion sick, sit near the back of the boat, as it moves less, or you can also ask to be placed on top before you leave the port. Sometimes, the water is not your worst enemy. Many of the ferries are small and covered and quickly fill up with fumes from the engines. If you feel yourself getting light-headed, sit where you can get some air.

Ferry times: Puerto Ayora-San Cristóbal: Daily, 2 p.m.

San Cristóbal-Puerto Ayora: Daily, 6:30 a.m.
Puerto Ayora-Isabela: Daily, 2 p.m.
Isabela-Puerto Ayora: Daily, 6 a.m.

All ferries leave from the municipal docks and cost $30 one-way.

If you are in a hurry or cannot acquire a space on the ferry, you can contract a private boat in any of the port towns. Private transportation will be more expensive. Prices are negotiable, but you should expect to pay between $80 and $100 one-way to either San Cristóbal or Isabela.

However, this latter option will be much faster and most certainly guided, since local boat-owners love to share their knowledge with tourists along the way. The capitanía, or port captain, should also be able to tell you which boats are going to these islands as well as their expected departure times. Otherwise, just ask around the area.

Galápagos Work and Volunteer Opportunities

Since Puerto Ayora is a magnet for English-speaking tourists, there are a variety of tour operators looking for people who have language capacities (Spanish-English) and can work for cheap. Many travelers have found work in exchange for courses, dives, or accommodation. Although migration policies are strict and usually limit tourist visas to three months, there are project-based opportunities that may allow you to stay for a longer period of time.

The easiest way to get a job or volunteer position in Galápagos, especially if you are a certified diver (or better yet, dive-master) and speak English, is to contact scuba-diving operators directly. Some dive centers will accept volunteers as office contacts and helpers in exchange for certification courses.

Students of environmental science and/or conservation may have luck finding volunteer or research opportunities with the Charles Darwin Research Station, but the application process is rigorous and competitive. CDRS is

usually looking for well-qualified volunteers, usually graduate students, who can give at least six months of their time. You can apply directly through the Charles Darwin Foundation website (www.darwinfoundation.org) or by contacting scientists collaborating with the station, a list of which is included in its annual publication.

If you have some teaching qualifications, you may be able to find a job teaching English on the islands. Most schools work with specific work-abroad or study-abroad organizations, like World Teach, AmeriSpan, or the Alliance Abroad Group, but qualified teachers may find opportunities with specific schools, like the Galápagos Academic Institute for the Arts and Sciences (GAIAS).

Note one important Galápagos policy—volunteers must have their paperwork completed BEFORE arriving in the islands. In other words, you can't just show up in Galápagos and get a volunteering gig. Even if you get one, you would have to leave the islands and re-enter.

Volunteering at Jatun Sacha's Galápagos Biological Research Station

The Jatun Sacha Foundation—which in Quechua means "Great Wilderness"—is an environmental conservation organization with eight biological stations in Ecuador, spread between the coast, the Andes, the jungle and Galápagos. "The San Cristóbal-Galápagos Biological Research Station" opened in 2003 to begin reforestation work replacing exotic plants with Galápagos endemic ones. The station is also developing a greenhouse that will grow Galápagos varieties of organic fruits and vegetables.

Volunteers pay $700 a month for the program, which includes room and board, plus an application fee of $60. They must also commit to a minimum of 14 days at the station. For more information about volunteering visit Jatun Sacha's website (www. jatunsacha.org).

Hacienda Tranquila Bio Station

At Hacienda Tranquila, volunteers work in a controlled plot of land to eliminate introduced/invasive plant species and to restore native and endemic species, growing the plants first in a greenhouse, and then transplanting them to their permanent locations.

Volunteers also assist in community projects, such as burying a new water pipeline for the local community. In addition, they mentor children from INFA, working with them in hippo-therapy, gardening, environmental education and fieldtrips to the Hacienda Bio station. This is the only project in the Galápagos islands that works in environmental, community and social work.

Since its inception, the station field house and a nursery have worked in the development of reforestation, habitat recomposition and agro forestry activities. In virtue of this, one of the objectives of this station is to develop methodological practices for natural system reconstruction that will serve as a model for similar projects in other reserves. Hacienda team members are always on hand for assistance and guidance in volunteer projects. Geovanny Sarigu, La casa verde. Tel: 593-5-252-1732, Email: haciendatranquila@gmail.com, URL: www.haciendatranquila.com.

Galápagos Ecology and Ecotourism

The Galápagos Islands may look rough and harsh, but the numerous ecosystems found on each of the islands are, in fact, very fragile. Inadvertent damage or the introduction of a new species can devastate a timeless island environment. Because the islands get over 100,000 visitors every year, some steps have been taken to preserve the islands.

How are the Galápagos Islands Being Protected?

97% of the 7,800 square kilometers total land area of the archipelago has been protected as the Galápagos National Park (GNP) since 1959 and managed by the Galápagos National Park Service, a specialized governmental arm of the national forestry, protected areas and wildlife agencies created in 1968. Legal protection was extended to the water in 1986 with the declaration of the islands' adjacent waters as the Galápagos Marine Resource Reserve.

Since the passing of the Special Law of the Galápagos in 1998, the area extending 40 miles beyond island territory has also been protected, patrolled and managed by the Galápagos National Park Service.

Population size on the four colonized islands—Santa Cruz, Isabela, San Cristóbal, and Floreana—is controlled through strict migration policies regulating the number of permanent residents and limiting the stay of temporary residents (tourists, volunteers and workers from mainland Ecuador and abroad) to six months. Mandates for protection of the Galápagos Marine Resource Reserve place limits on the size, number and location of fish captured by local fishermen. Foreign fishermen (and even Ecuadorians from the mainland) are not allowed to fish in Galápagos.

Has the International Community gotten involved in the preservation of Galápagos?

The importance of preserving the ecological dynamics of the Galápagos Islands has also been prioritized and supported on the international scale. Galápagos was declared the world's first Natural World Heritage Site in 1978 and a UNESCO Biosphere Reserve in 1984. The Galápagos Marine Resources Reserve is now the second largest marine reserve in the world, after the Great Barrier Reef National Park in Australia.

Are these steps working to protect the Galápagos environment?

Unfortunately, despite progressive legislation, the impact of human populations and illegal fishing—especially sea cucumber and shark-fin harvesting for lucrative Asian markets—continues to be a significant challenge to conservation.

How will these measures impact my Galápagos trip?

The regulations mean some inconveniences for Galápagos travelers. The restrictions aren't major, and hopefully they'll help keep the islands pristine for future generations.

Visitation to the islands' National Park territory is limited to about 50 total sites, available only during daylight hours (6 a.m.-6 p.m.) and subject to park rules and guidelines. The park service charges foreign visitors $100 to enter the Galápagos. This money goes towards conservation efforts and park service costs. Navigable and day cruise ships may not deviate from the itineraries specifically approved for them by the National Park Service.

Park rangers and naturalist guides will insist that tourists refrain from eating, drinking alcoholic beverages and smoking on the islands; touching, feeding, chasing, and/or photographing animals with flash, removing any item—living or dead—from the islands, and venturing off the trail or away from the tour group. Water-skiing and jet-skiing are also prohibited around the islands due to their considerable environmental impacts, and recreational fishing is restricted to those boats that have legally purchased catch permits from operational artisanal fishermen.

What role does tourism play in the management of the Galápagos Ecosystem?

By following the guidelines established by the GNP, visitors will promote a standard of nature tourism that maintains the majestic appearance and wildlife abundance—as well as the overall ecological integrity—of the sites visited, which are among the most spectacular within the archipelago.

Visitors serve as an important link in the conservation strategy of Galápagos: tourism promotes income generation in an environmentally benign way and generates sustainable ecological consciousness and understanding. Educating tourists about natural history and the interconnectedness of humans and the environment in Galápagos spreads a localized message of conservation that can be promoted on a larger scale.

Are the new laws and controls working?

The efforts to save Galápagos are paying off. The damage to the islands has been significantly slowed and in some cases reversed.

Invasive rats were eradicated from North Seymour Island in 2008. Feral goats, once considered the worst of the introduced species, have been eradicated on Santiago, Española, Floreana, Northern Isabela and other islands. The boundaries of the park are closely monitored to prevent settlers from encroaching on park land. The Floreana mockingbird became extinct on Floreana Island itself and only survives on two offshore islets, but there are plans to remove the factors that destroyed the original population and reintroduce it to Floreana.

There have been many other success stories, but the park authorities must maintain constant vigilance to prevent further damage to the island ecosystems. Be sure to do your part!

Galápagos History

NATURAL/GEOLOGICAL HISTORY OF GALÁPAGOS

The Galápagos Islands were formed ages ago by what geologists call a "hot spot." Basically, a hot spot is a place on the earth that is hotter than normal. As the earth's crust moves over this spot, it burns holes in it which form volcanoes. If the hot spot is far out to sea, these volcanoes form islands. Hawaii was formed in a similar fashion. Because the earth's crust moves from west to east over the Galapagos hot spot, the oldest islands are the ones on the eastern side of the archipelago, such as Española and Genovesa. There were once other Galápagos islands to the east of Española, but they have been reclaimed by the sea. The western islands of Isabela and Fernandina are the youngest islands, and they are also the ones that are still volcanically active, as they are still over the hot spot.

> The inhabitants, although complaining of poverty, obtain, without much trouble, the means of subsistence. In the woods there are many wild pigs and goats; but the staple article of animal food is supplied by the tortoises. Their numbers have of course been greatly reduced in this Galápagos islands, but the people yet count on two days' hunting giving them food for the rest of the week. It is said that formerly single vessels have taken away as many as seven hundred, and that the ship's company of a frigate some years since brought down in one day two hundred tortoises to the beach.
>
> *Charles Darwin, from The Voyage of the Beagle*

These rocky, hot volcanic islands far out in the ocean are inhospitable to life, as fresh water is very scarce. Nevertheless, life on earth is nothing if not rugged, and over time, plant and animal species found their way to the islands, colonizing them.

Most if not all of the plants and animals in Galápagos came from the mainland. Sudden storms would wash a clump of vegetation out to the islands, perhaps with an iguana, tortoise or rat clinging to it; when it arrived, the plants and animals just might thrive and reproduce. Because the islands are so remote, island life has been dominated by birds and reptiles, which had a far better chance of getting there in the first place.

Over time, these plants and animals evolved, filling in all the available spots in different ecological niches. Over the course of thousands of years, they became new species, endemic to the islands. Some of them died off naturally, but many of them are still there to this day.

The arrival of man to the islands had a disastrous effect, as they introduced new species into the mix, such as cats, dogs and goats, in addition to the even-harder-to-eradicate plants. Scientists and park service staff are trying to reverse this damage with encouraging results.

HUMAN HISTORY OF GALÁPAGOS

In 1535, Tomás de Berlanga, the Bishop of Panama, set sail for Peru to help settle a dispute between conquistador Francisco Pizarro and his lieutenants. Along the way, strong winds and currents forced the ship off course, and for a while things looked grim. The sailors were running low on provisions, particularly water. Unwittingly, they stumbled upon the archipelago and were at first relieved, then distressed when they found out how barren and harsh it was. It inspired Berlanga's famous quote, which appeared in a letter to the king of Spain:

"The abrupt landscape is desolate and mysterious, with no signs of human presence; the rocks are sterile, and there is nothing but seals, and turtles and such big tortoises that each could carry a man on their back, and many iguanas that are like serpents. Great masses of volcanic rocks cover the beaches, as if God had rained stones all over!"

The Bishop's report included some description of the Giant Tortoises, and in 1574 a Flemish Atlas was published with the islands on it, named "Insulae de los Galopegos," or "islands of the saddle-backs," and they have been the Galápagos ever since.

Their other nickname, "the Enchanted Islands," sounds like a twentieth-century marketing slogan, but it isn't: apparently a group of Francisco Pizarro's men accidentally found their way there in 1546 and gave them that name because of the way they appeared and disappeared in the mists.

Buccaneers and Whalers

For years the islands were ignored, but in the 17th century the far-roving ships of pirates and whalers realized that they made a great place to stop and gather provisions. It was during this time that animals such as goats and pigs were released on the islands, so that future visitors would find a source of food there. Rats and mice also escaped off of the ships and onto the islands, where they remain a pest to this day.

It wasn't long, however, before these passing ships realized that the giant tortoises of Galápagos made for much better provisions. The tortoises were easy to catch and lived for a long time at sea, providing sailors with fresh meat whenever they wanted it. They didn't even eat or drink much while on board. During this time, thousands of Galápagos tortoises were captured and hauled off on pirate and whaling boats.

Seal hunters also visited the islands, driving the Galápagos fur sea lion population to the brink of extinction: fortunately, the pelt of the Galápagos sea lion is not as good, so those animals were not hunted nearly as much. To this day, Galápagos Fur Sea Lions are much more shy of humans than their Galápagos Sea Lion cousins.

Besides the introduction of unwanted species and the predation of the tortoises, the most lasting effect of these visitors was the establishment of Post Office Bay, where sailors from all nations would leave letters home and take those of other seamen with them if they were headed in that direction. The tradition continues to this day.

In 1684, English buccaneer William Ambrose Cowley was the first to make a navigational chart of the Islands, naming them after prominent British noblemen, including King Charles, King James, Admiral Narborough and the Duke of Albemarle.

These British names are still sometimes used, although not as common as the Spanish names. Other famous privateers and pirates to visit the islands included William Dampier and Woodes Rogers.

Several of the Spanish names have to do with Christopher Columbus and his 1492 voyage, as the official name of the Islands is "the Columbus Archipelago" (Archipiélago de Colón). Isabela refers to Queen Isabela, Pinta was one of his ships , etc.

Colonies and Penal Colonies

During the 19th century, Ecuador established colonies on the islands, in part to firmly establish their ownership of the islands—many nations, including France and the United States, had their eye on them.

The first great pioneer colonist was General José de Villamil, a leader of Ecuador's independence movement. He established a colony on Floreana in the 1830s consisting mostly of recaptured deserters from the army and convicts. They scratched out a meager existence as farmers, often selling whatever excess food they had to passing ships.

Another penal colony, named El Progeso, was the one led by Manuel Cobos (box, p.130). Located on San Cristóbal in the 1870s, the colony was a sort of forced-labor camp led by the tyrannical Cobos. Cobos would later be attacked and killed by his own workers, who he maintained in conditions of near-slavery. Isabela Island was home to yet another penal colony: unruly cons were sent to work on the "Wall of Tears" which can still be seen today. By the 1950s there were no longer any penal colonies on the Islands, but many a native islander can trace his or her roots to these convicts.

Norwegians and Germans

In the late 1920s, Galápagos was the destination of a most unlikely set of settlers: Norwegians. In 1907, a group of Norwegian sailors were forced to abandon their ship, the Alexandra, which had been carrying coal from Australia to Panama. They made it to Floreana, and from there to San Cristóbal and then to Guayaquil. The stories of the returned sailors lit a spark in the collective imagination of the people of Norway. Their tales of laden fruit trees, sunny climes, tasty tortoises so slow a toddler could catch one and even buried treasure converted the rocky, barren islands into an exotic tropical paradise. Eventually a few small groups of adventurous Norwegians would find their

The Angermeyer Family

Although the Angermeyer family history reads like something dreamed up by a novelist with a singularly wild imagination, the trials and triumphs of the foremost family of Galápagos were all very real. The most well known member of the family is Johanna Angermeyer, author of the acclaimed book My Father's Island: A Galápagos Quest, a combination of interviews with long-time residents of the islands, her own experiences in Ecuador, and her family's tempestuous history.

Johanna's father, Johannes Angermeyer, arrived in Galápagos in 1935. Five Angermeyer brothers left for South America in order to escape Hitler's Germany. Due to a shipwreck, only four of them made it to Galápagos, where they proceeded to live Robinson Crusoe-style among the fearless creatures of the Enchanted Islands.

Johanna's mother Emmasha had similarly tumultuous origins. American by birth, she lived in Ecuador with her first husband, a famous aviator, whose plane crashed in the Andes as he rushed to his wife's side following the birth of their first son. Emmasha later remarried to Johannes Angermeyer and relocated to Galápagos, where they had a daughter, Mary. Following the attack on Pearl Harbor in 1941, all American citizens living in Ecuador were forced to return to the United States, where Johanna was born. Her father died of tuberculosis shortly afterwards, far from his beloved islands.

Driven by a desire to learn more about the father she barely knew, Johanna developed a fascination with Galápagos at a young age, shortly after her family returned to Ecuador. What she learned about the islands and her own history eventually developed into several books about the islands, including several illustrated works for children. She still lives there today, writing in a small cabin surrounded by forest and animals.

The Angermeyers played a significant role in the Galápagos history and are, without a doubt, among Ecuador's most interesting residents. Angermeyer Point in Puerto Ayora is named for them, and the family also runs an environmentally sustainable cruise business in the islands. Whether you want to learn more about the islands or are just looking for some entertaining literature for the plane ride, it is well worth picking up one of Johanna's books before making your Galápagos trip.

way to the islands; the Ecuadorian government even granted them land and exclusive hunting and fishing rights. Most of them didn't last— the island reality was far too harsh. Still, a couple of hardy families did remain, and their descendants are there to this day.

Meanwhile, a handful of Germans decided to colonize the islands, the most noteworthy of which were the Wittmer and Angermeyer families, whose descendants are still there.

The Galápagos Affair
The Galápagos Islands came to world attention in 1934, when a bizarre string of deaths and disappearances took place among the European population of Floreana Island. Known as "the Galápagos Affair," the scandal was avidly followed around the world (see box, p.134).

The US Air Base
When World War II broke out, everyone realized the strategic importance of the Panama Canal. The USA decided that in order to win the war and protect its interests, the Canal must remain safe from Japanese or German occupation. To this end, they arranged a deal with Ecuador to put a military base in Galápagos. For several years, US airmen and sailors lived on Baltra, where they had not only an air base but also a barracks, store, bar and even a bowling alley. The US left in 1947, turning over the base to Ecuador. Some of the buildings are still there...as is the most famous ghost in Galápagos, "the Headless Gringa." (see box, p. 122)

Growth of Tourism
Galápagos was still considered a remote backwater well into the 1960s. The inhabitants of the towns made a living mostly by fishing or small-scale agriculture. Visitors were generally limited to scientists wishing to follow in Darwin's footsteps or those tourists who had their own yachts. In 1959, the National Park was established, imposing rules on visitors for the first time.

In the 1960s and 1970s tourism began to be an important industry. As airplanes could now reach Ecuador easily, Galápagos was no longer quite so remote. Ecuadorians were delighted (and perhaps a little surprised) to find that so many well-heeled foreigners would travel so far and pay whatever it cost to see Galápagos.

It wasn't long before hotels, restaurants, tour agencies and cruise ships started popping up, and by the late 1970s tourism was beginning to replace fishing as the main economic activity in the islands.

Special Laws for Galápagos
In the late 1990s, it became clear that greater protection for the islands was in order. Because of the tourism boom, thousands of poor Ecuadorians from the mainland had gone to the island to look for work. The people were creating a strain on the environment and the population of the towns was booming in an alarming fashion. Laws were passed to limit the people who could stay and kick out those who could not.

In addition, stricter laws were passed to help the island ecosystems. Certain fruits and vegetables were prohibited, and pets such as dogs and cats were put under stricter control. Efforts were made to eradicate introduced species and prevent new ones from arriving.

The Islanders Take Over
For decades, Galápagos was a backwater province, a place no decent Ecuadorian wanted to go. A few hundred hardy pioneers, half-cracked German settlers and irredeemable criminals in penal colonies scratched a meager living out of the volcanic rocks. They were subsistence farmers and fishermen, and thought nothing of eating the tortoises, birds and other animals that the islands are now famous for. The Ecuadorian government was far away and frankly couldn't have cared less about them.

TOURISM BOOMS
For years, tourism was limited to a few stray boats that visited, and there were really no controls. It wasn't until the 1950s that tourism began to be a serious industry in the islands, and not until the 1970s that it started to show signs of the boom that it is now.

Although tourism was embraced by some of the islanders, most notably the descendants of the salty German settlers of the early 20th century, most viewed it with a mixture of suspicion and resentment.

As tourism increased, Ecuadorian and foreign experts came to the islands and began telling the islanders what to do: "Don't eat the tortoises! Don't kill the sharks! Don't plant non-native plants!" For a rugged people that had been totally ignored by mainland Ecuador for decades, this new do-what-we-say attitude was offensive.

FISHING VS. TOURISM

Conflicts between the two major industries—fishing and tourism—continued to grow. In the islands, the two are often at odds with one another; the aggressive fishing of sharks (for their fins) and sea cucumbers has crippled the island ecosystem, which in turn means less wildlife for tourists to see. Fishermen have been known to blockade certain islands in order to have their demands for more liberal quotas met by the government.

NO MONEY FOR THE ISLANDERS

Historically, the biggest complaint of the islanders with tourism is that much of the money that comes into the islands does not stay there. Many visitors book their cruises and flights abroad, come to the islands, pay their park fee, and go right to their ship. Locals rarely see much money from these sorts of tourists. Only those who work on the ships or sell the occasional souvenir in town see any real profit from the elusive foreigner

The Galápagos Fishing War

There is constant tension in Galápagos between the two main industries in the islands: fishing and tourism. Those in the fishing industry are always pushing for ecologically questionable concessions from the government such as long-line fishing, long seasons for valuable species such as lobsters and sea cucumbers, and removal of protections on marine reserves.

Long-line fishing is particularly destructive—it involves baiting several hundred hooks on the same heavy line. Used to catch swordfish and tuna, it also results in a lot of "by-catch," or unintended catch, including sea turtles, sharks, rays, sea lions and even marine birds such as the albatross, all of which are protected in Galápagos. Ecologists are aghast that this fishing method is even being considered in such a fragile ecosystem.

Catch levels are way down in recent years, yet short-sighted fishermen continue to push for longer seasons and larger catch limits. What is worse, there is a lot of illegal fishing being done in Galápagos, both by foreign vessels fishing in Ecuadorian waters near the islands as well as local boats engaged in poaching out of season or of illegal species. In particular, sharks in Galápagos are being hunted to near extinction: they are caught for their fins, which bring a lucrative price in Asia. Sharks are caught by unscrupulous fishermen (sometimes using chopped-up sea lions as bait), their fins are cut off, and they are dumped back into the water. There is a ban on shark fishing, but Ecuador does not have the resources (or desire, apparently) to enforce it.

The tourism operators in the islands favor stringent restrictions, as unchecked fishing is severely detrimental to the ecosystem. For example, the sea cucumber, one of the most highly sought-after species in Galápagos, is a key link in the marine food chain.

Most Galápagos life ultimately depends on the sea: many birds feed on fish, and if the marine ecosystem collapses, there will be no more boobies, frigates or albatrosses for tourists to come and see. Therefore, tour operators are constantly pressuring the Ecuadorian government to enact and enforce strict rules for those who want to fish in Galápagos.

Most of the residents of the islands are either fishermen themselves or have family members who fish. This is true of many of the park rangers, who are charged with enforcing the rules: they often look the other way if they catch family or friends doing something illegal. The fishermen are very powerful in the islands: on more than one occasion, they have blockaded whole islands from tour vessels to protest a new ban or law, and once they even took over the Charles Darwin Research Station, held the scientists hostage, and threatened to kill Lonesome George.

Although the two sides seem beyond any sort of agreement, there are those who are working on compromises and new solutions; large tour operators Metropolitan Touring and Lindblad Expeditions support projects such as the "Teachers on Board" plan, in which schoolteachers from Galápagos spend time on cruise ships, learning about the islands from a tourism perspective. Metropolitan also has a project in which fishermen are paid to pick up trash off the islands. Perhaps in the future, fishing, wildlife and tourism will be able to coexist in these fragile islands.

NEW LAWS
In the late 1990s, several initiatives were passed to allow the islanders to take more control over the tourism industry. One of the first laws to be passed was one specifying that guides must be Galapagueños, and could no longer come from abroad or the Ecuadorian mainland. Even those non-native guides who were grandfathered in under the new law are being muscled out by aggressive unions. This law had the desired effect, as many locals became guides and started to earn very good money working for the tour companies.

Unfortunately, the overall quality of guides suffered, because the foreign and mainland guides in general are better educated and speak more languages than the locals. Also, once the law was passed, the pool of available guides decreased dramatically and ships were forced to grossly overpay unqualified guides in order to meet park regulations. In some cases, guides that were repeatedly accused of sexually harassing visitors continued to easily find work, simply because there was no one else to take their places.

OWNERSHIP AND NEW TAXES
More initiatives have passed to benefit the islanders. In the future, all ships must have all-Galápagos staff and even be at least 51% locally owned in order to operate.

A new $100 tax on all arriving tourists will be divided among the three towns in the islands: it should add up to millions of dollars. Within a few years, the entire tourism industry should be controlled locally.

ISLAND ATTITUDE
There is a new attitude among the islanders. They feel that for too long they were ignored or bossed around by the mainland, and now they are ready to seize control of the lucrative tourism industry for themselves. Ask any islander about it and they will rant and rave about the injustices of the past, when rich tourists came to the islands but all their money stayed in Quito and Guayaquil. Some of them are quite militant and hostile about the whole issue.

A GOOD THING?
One of the first casualties of this movement has been some of the tourist services themselves. One example is the combination diving-cruise tour, which had been popular in the islands for decades. Now, ships must declare themselves to be either a dive ship or a land tour ship, but not both. This new law forces SCUBA divers to stay on the islands, which will increase earnings for hotels, restaurants and dive shops at the expense of mainland-owned tour operators and ship owners. That's great for the locals, but bad for mainland businesses...and for tourists as well, who suddenly have fewer tour options.

THE GOOD NEWS
Those who view the changes optimistically say that this new control over tourism will bring with it education, and that the islanders, who love their home, will learn to take care of it better than any foreigner could. They say that with their newfound wealth, islanders will provide better facilities and services to visitors. The islands will never reach their full potential, they say, until the "bloodsuckers" from Quito and Guayaquil are out of the picture.

THE BAD NEWS
Meanwhile, pessimists point out the example of the guides: what was a benefit for the locals nevertheless meant a significant overall decrease in the quality of service for foreign visitors. If in the future, tour companies have to scramble to hire crews, cooks and other staff from a limited population, the result will be higher prices for visitors along with poor service. As for improving the island ecology, pessimists only need to point out the islanders' long history of apathy, ignorance and willful exploitation of nature to make their case that some things are better left in the hands of mainland experts or international organizations.

For better or worse, the islands will soon be in the hands of the islanders. Some see a rosy future, while others see a looming disaster: only time will tell who is right.

Towns in the Galápagos

PUERTO AYORA

The main town in Galápagos is Puerto Ayora, located on Santa Cruz island. It's a friendly, medium-sized town of some 20,000 inhabitants. The majority of land tours, scuba-diving tours and adventure tours originate and/or are based here.

Visitors intending to arrange cruise tours locally will stay here waiting for availability on boats to open up. Virtually every cruise tour makes a day stop here—usually near the half-way point of an eight-day trip or at the extremes of the four or five-day trip—so that visitors can visit the Charles Darwin Research Station and highlands and stock up on medicine, film, batteries and snacks if supplies were beginning to run low. Since Puerto Ayora caters to tourist activities, visitors can find almost any item unintentionally left behind.

There is a wide assortment of hotels, restaurants, bars, stores, tour agencies, dive shops, internet cafés and phone centers. There is also a post office, airline offices, a basic public hospital and a hyperbaric chamber.

Puerto Ayora Services

PUERTO AYORA SHOPPING

For the most part, if you're shopping in Puerto Ayora, you're looking either for supplies, such as sunscreen, or souvenirs. Things like medicine, food and sunscreen are available, but expensive, so stock up on those things before you go.

There are plenty of souvenir shops in Puerto Ayora, each of them selling coffee mugs, T-shirts, postcards and other touristy stuff, most of which seem to have some sort of Booby joke printed on them. Feel free to stock up on such things for friends and family back home. It's a big boost to the local economy.

Lately, there has been an increase in high-end shops specializing in jewelry, art and quality handicrafts from Ecuador and elsewhere. You can't miss the shops, which line Charles Darwin Avenue from the pier to the research station.

INTERNET IN PUERTO AYORA

There are literally dozens of internet cafés in Puerto Ayora and they're spread out so you're bound to find one handy just about anytime. Rates for internet use are about $2 per hour, including use of Skype if you have it. Internet cafés are also a good place to make cheap phone calls home.

One good internet café is Galápagos On-line, on Charles Darwin Avenue across from the naval base. It's very popular with gringos.

Galápagos is not known for crime, but if you're surfing the net, best to keep an eye on your stuff.

Things To See and Do

There are lots of things to see and do in Puerto Ayora. There are a handful of semi-regulated visitor sites in and around the town and it's possible to visit them without a naturalist guide.

There are some good beaches in town and nearby. The most convenient is the Station beach, not far from the Charles Darwin Research Station, but the ones at Garrapatero and Tortuga Bay are much nicer.

In the highlands, there are giant tortoises to view as well as lava tubes to explore. Hikers may want to visit Cerro Crocker, the highest point on Santa Cruz. Los Gemelos is a pair of sinkholes which are popular with birdwatchers.

If these sites aren't enough, it's possible to arrange day tours to nearby islands like Santa Fe or Floreana.

To read about all of these activities and more, visit the Visitor Sites chapter.

Chi Spa

Chi Spa is a small day spa located on the edge of town along the road that goes to the Charles Darwin Research Station. It offers a variety of treatments including massages, wraps, reflexology and more. It has a steam room and sauna as well. Packages start at $90. It's possible to make reservations through its website. Av. Charles Darwin. Tel: 593-09-513-9784/783-8830, E-mail: info@chispagalapagos.com, URL: www.chispagalapagos.com.

Puerto Ayora Tour Agencies and Dive Shops

There are many tour agencies in Puerto Ayora, ranging from competent, experienced professionals to sleazy con men on the street who would gladly sell their own mothers to a passing battleship if there was $5 in it for them.

To avoid the latter, stick to places that have a real office and NEVER deal with anyone who approaches you in the street. If you can, check the website of a place you're thinking of doing business with. If it looks serious and professional the place is probably okay. Stay away from the cheeseball hole-in-the-wall places near the old pier (close to the Proinsular supermarket).

Many of the hotels have travel desks to help their guests. If yours does, take advantage of it. These are a great way to set up little tours, buy tickets for the ferry, etc.

Shark Friends

A relatively new dive shop, Shark Friends goes to all of the usual Puerto Ayora dive spots: Daphne, Seymour, Gordon Rocks, etc. They offer a variety of dive courses from discovery SCUBA for beginners to Dive Master. A two-dive day will cost you around $140, three dives $180, including gear, guide and lunch. Some of their packages are a good deal. See their website for details.

They also do some basic local tours, such as biking, going to see the tortoises in the highlands, fishing, etc. Booking ahead is a good idea if you can, but walk-ins are welcome. Tel: 593-05-252-6854/08-504-4995/683-7342, E-mail: sharksfriendsgalapagos@hotmail.com, URL: www.sharksfriends.com.

Academy Bay Diving

Academy Bay Diving is a locally owned and run business. They offer single and multi day dive packages, PADI courses—Open Water to Dive Master, island tours, last minute cruises and a wealth of local information. The crew is fun and professional, and the equipment is of good quality and regularly serviced. Av. Charles Darwin. Tel: 593-05-252-4164, URL: www.academybaydiving.com. Updated: Aug 09, 2012.

Moonrise Travel

A reputable local travel agency in central Puerto Ayora (It's more or less across the street from the Banco del Pacífico near the fishermen's pier), Moonrise is a good place to organize day trips such as highland tours, snorkeling, etc. You can also get tickets here for the ferries to San Cristóbal and Isabela. If you contact them before you go, they will help arrange tours, hotels, etc. Their website is a little problematic, but the form for contacting them should work. Charles Darwin 160 and Charles Binford. Tel: 593-5-526402,/526403/526348/526589, URL: www.galapagosmoonrise.com.

Puerto Ayora Hotels

As the main point of entry for Galápagos, Puerto Ayora has the best selection of hotels. You'll find everything from the battered Pensión Gloria ($10 per night) to the $1,000 per night Prince of Wales Suite at the Royal Palm Hotel with plenty of options in between.

As in all of Galápagos, there has been a hotel boom recently, with most of the new construction taking place a couple of blocks off of the main drag, Charles Darwin Avenue. Some of the new hotels are quite nice and reasonably priced.

In Puerto Ayora, you'll find a couple of flat-out budget places, a glut of forgettable rooms in the $25 per night range, a few more for $40-60 or so, another glut of rooms in the $70-110 range, and a handful of excellent places for over $110 or so. Unless you're spending a wad of cash, you'll usually have to decide on some sort of trade-off. You may have to choose between being close to the main drag or having air conditioning, having a nice pool or having a nice view, etc. Look at the room options carefully!

Hotel rooms in Puerto Ayora tend to book up in the high season (June-September, December-January) but the town itself rarely gets so packed that nothing is available. You should book ahead to make sure you get your first choice of hotels and aren't settling for something sub-standard.

! = Recommended by Viva!

BUDGET

Pensión Gloria

(ROOMS: $5-10 per person) Pensión Gloria is the best option for the backpacker who has overstayed his welcome and overspent his budget. It is the least expensive—and least frilly—place to stay in the Galápagos, at $10 per person per day (you

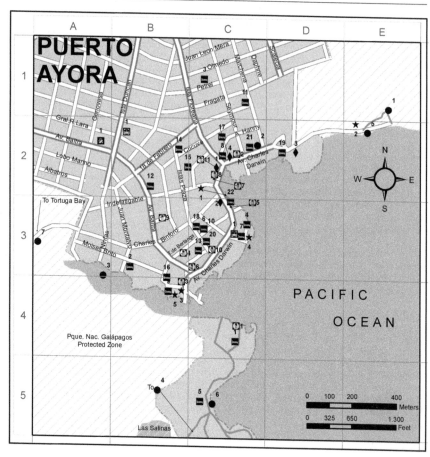

may get them as low as $5 per person if you stay for five or more days). There are a few (dark) rooms opening out to (an even darker) courtyard, each with fans and their own flair (the walls have painted Galápagos scenes). Bathrooms are shared, and kitchen facilities can be made available upon request. Av. Charles Darwin near Seymour. Updated: Aug 02, 2012.

Hotel Santa Cruz

(ROOMS: $7 per person) The Hotel Santa Cruz is popular with backpackers and low-budget Ecuadorians. It is a bit far from the boardwalk (in Puerto Ayora standards) and accommodations are basic. There are eight rooms—two singles, four doubles, one triple and one quadruple—with private bathrooms, tepid-water showers and portable fans. Some rooms have a TV, but no cable—local channels only. Av. Baltra and Indefatigable, near the market.Tel: 593-05-252-6573. Updated: May 12, 2013.

Hotel España !

(ROOMS: $15/person) Hotel España, the best budget option in Puerto Ayora, is clean, friendly and has been recently been renovated. The hotel is in a good location, plus the rooms are neat and tidy, and the mattresses have all been recently replaced. There is a new, attractive downstairs common area and even some hammocks for hanging out.

Most of the rooms have air conditioning (it costs a little more if you want to use it) and the showers are heated by gas heaters, not the lethal little "electric showers" most other hotels in the same price range have. The owner, Genoveva, is a friendly local lady who likes helping travelers find the right tours for them, and her daughter Esther is a SCUBA guide who can also answer any questions about the islands or about what you should see and do there. They help their guests with tours, ferry tickets,

● Activities
1 Charles Darwin Research Station E1
2 Chi Spa C2
3 Laguna Las Ninfas A4
4 Las Grietas B5
5 Playa de la Estación E2
6 Playa de los Alemanes C3
7 The Miguel Cifuentes Arias Community Center A3

◎ Eating
1 Angermeyer Point C4
2 Café del Mar C2
3 El Descanso del Guía B4
4 Galápagos Deli B3
5 Garrapata C3
6 Henán Café C3
7 Il Giardino C2
8 Isla Grill C2
9 Kioskos B3
10 The Rock C3
11 Tintorera C2

★ Services
1 Bank C2
2 Galápagos National Park Office E2
3 Information Center (Itur) B4
4 Police C3
5 Post Office B4

ⓩ Shopping
1 Market A2

▦ Sleeping
1 Angermeyer Waterfront Inn C4
2 Casa del Lago B3
3 Casa Natura C1
4 Estrella del Mar C3
5 Finch Bay C5
6 Gardner C3
7 Grand Hotel Lobo de Mar C3
8 Hosteling 10-28 C2
9 Hotel Castro B4
10 Hotel España C3
11 Hotel Fernandina C1
12 Hotel Santa Cruz B2
13 Lirio del Mar C3
14 Maidith B2
15 Mainao B2
16 Ninfa B4
17 Pension Gloria C2
18 Red Booby C3
19 Red Mangrove D2
20 Salinas C3
21 Silberstein C2
22 Sol y Mar C3

♦ Tour
1 Galapagos Sub-Aqua C2
2 Moonrise Travel Agency C3
3 Scuba Iguana D2
4 Shark Friends C2

▦ Transportation
1 Airline B2, C3

TOWNS

etc. The hotel tends to fill up, so you should either make reservations or call ahead before going to Puerto Ayora. Hotel España is priced comparably with the Hotel Gardner next door (although the hotels are not affiliated). The two hotels are probably the best value for budget lodging in town, so if one is full, your first stop should be the other

Hotel España

that's right next door. Tomas de Berlanga and Islas Plazas. Tel: 593-05-252-6108, E-mail: hotelesgalapagos@yahoo.es.
Updated: Feb 22, 2013.

Hotel Gardner
(ROOMS: $25 per person) The Hotel Gardner is one of Puerto Ayora's better budget options. The rooms are spacious and neat with proper ventialation. Some of the downstairs rooms are windowless, and can get quite dark. Ask for one of the sunnier upstairs rooms if they are available. Each room has a private bathroom, floor fans and TV, although only with local channels. There is a large room on the top floor with five beds in it, which is a pretty good option if you're traveling in a larger group or with a family.

There is an attached travel agency next door operated by the owners: it's a good place to book simple daytrips like tours of

Academy Bay. The Hotel Gardner is located next door to the Hotel España, which is similarly priced and also a very good value: the two hotels are not in any way affiliated. Islas Plazas between Bolivar Naveda and 12 de Febrero. Tel: 593-5-252-6979/8-800-3285, E-mail: hotelgardner@yahoo.com. Updated: Apr 07, 2013.

Hosteling 10-28

(ROOMS: $30 per person) Wedged in between a dive shop and a trinket store, Hosteling 10-28 is cramped but friendly, and efforts to improve the place seem to be ongoing, which is always a good sign. The tiny pool does not inspire much lounging about, but should suffice for a quick dip to cool off. There are only five rooms here, each suitable for 2-4 people. Rooms have cable TV, air conditioning, hot water and a small fridge. Tel: 593-2-255-0090/222-2156, URL: www.1028hostalgalapagos.com.

Hotel Lirio del Mar

(ROOMS: $15-45) A decent option for budget travelers, the Hotel Lirio del Mar is a three-story hotel with conspicuous orange walls and a second-floor terrace overlooking Academy Bay. Although its exterior is not lacking for character, the rooms are fairly basic and ordinary. Twenty-four single, double, triple and quadruple rooms have private hot baths and fans. There is also a small, dark lounge area near reception that has sofas and a TV. Islas Plaza between Tomas de Berlanga and Av. Charles Darwin. Tel: 593-5-252-6212. Updated: Nov 22, 2012.

MID-RANGE

Hotel Salinas

(ROOMS: $25-78) Hotel Salinas is one of the more spacious and professional low-mid-range hotels in Puerto Ayora. It has 22 plain yet comfortable rooms with private baths, which are distributed on three floors. As you climb the courtyard staircase, you encounter more frills and perks. First floor singles and doubles have tepid water and fans. Second floor doubles, triples and quadruples have hot water and fans. Third floor suites have hot water, air conditioning and cable. This results in a bewildering array of prices. It almost seems as if each room has a different cost! It's best to go, see what they have available, and negotiate a price.

The hotel also offers 24-hour coffee, laundry, and tour information services. The small central garden also provides a refreshing area for sipping cold drinks or chatting with new friends. Price includes taxes and breakfast is included. All meals in the small attached restaurant cost $4.48 except platos á la carte which cost $7.84 (not including tax). Islas Plaza between Av. Charles Darwin and Tomas de Berlanga. Tel: 593-5-252-6107, E-mail: reservashotelsalinas@hotmail.com. Updated: Jan 12, 2013.

Hotel Castro

(ROOMS: $50-70) Hotel Castro is a pleasant surprise. It's a clean and friendly place in a good location and reasonably priced. The interior is a bit gloomy and the 19 rooms are small and boxy, but overall the place is pretty good for the price, especially if it's hot out, as all rooms have air conditioning. If a/c is a must, this place might be your best bet in town if you're on a budget. Av. Los Colonos, near the old pier. Updated: Jan 12, 2013.

Hotel Estrella del Mar

(ROOMS: $47-83) The Hotel Estrella del Mar is the only mid-range hotel that can offer ocean views. Four of the hotel's 12 rooms face Academy Bay and receive fresh breezes off the water through their screened-in windows. All other rooms are ccomfortable, clean, and spacious, and have private hot showers and fan. A few select rooms have air conditioning and TV at the same prices, so request these rooms if you come between February and April and need solace from the unbearable heat. It is a friendly place near the water with a comfortable eating area (breakfast is available for a small price), self-service coffee bar, and lounge. 12 de Febrero, just off Academy Bay. Tel: 593-5-252-6427, E-mail: estrellademar@islasantacruz.com. Updated: May 12, 2013.

Casa del Lago

(ROOMS: $87-170) The Casa del Lago is part of an effort to offer tourists alternatives that emphasize social and cultural responsibility. Suites are rented on a daily, weekly or even monthly basis. Recycled glass fragments in window frames play with incoming light, hand-painted tiles add flair to showers and staircases and wild fabrics give the walls, ceilings and beds a spicy character.

The suites are all furnished with hot water, a private bathroom, cable and wireless internet. All suites have a private terrace with gardens. Breakfast is not included. Other meals in the caféteria range in price from

$6-10. The residence is adjacent to the Casa del Lago Café Cultural and looks out on the Laguna Las Ninfas. This is a comfortable and affordable option for travelers looking to venture outside the norm. The owner can also arrange custom-designed tours for student groups and other parties interested in educational tourism. Tours visit local hot-spots, farms and residences and generate proceeds that directly benefit Santa Cruz residents. Calle Moises Brito and Juan Montalvo, near the Ninfas Lake. Tel: 593-5-252-4116/9-971-4647, E-mail: info@galapagoscultural.com, casadellago@galapagoscultural.com, URL: www.galapagoscultural.com.
Updated: Apr 28, 2013.

Hotel Silberstein

(ROOMS: $113-165) The Hotel Silberstein is a modern, intimate and beautifully-landscaped hotel. It has 22 clean, romantic rooms, each containing a private hot bath, ceiling fan and air conditioning, and a view toward the lush courtyard/swimming pool area.

There are 11 matrimonial double rooms, eight double rooms with twin beds, and three triples. Comfort, style and attention to detail (not to mention price) are at a maximum at the Hotel Silberstein. A sandy space near the pool can serve as a playplace for youngsters. The garden surrounding the open-air bar provides a diverse, eye-catching landscape (as well as interesting data for plant and bird surveys conducted by the Charles Darwin Research Station). The hotel partners with the Galextur to offer four to eight-day tours with overnight accommodations in Puerto Ayora. It can also arrange cruise tours and any sort of day trips. Av. Charles Darwin and Seymour. Tel: 593-5-252-6277, E-mail: blectour@iuo.satnet.net.
Updated: Aug 02, 2012.

Galápagos Organizations

The Galápagos is a world-famous destination, and fortunately there are a number of organizations, based in Ecuador and throughout the world, that are dedicated to protecting and conserving it. The islands still suffer from problems regarding invasive species and illegal poaching and pollution, but several conservation organizations have made significant headway in solving these problems, largely thanks to the passionate support of donors, staff and volunteers.

The Charles Darwin Foundation, founded in 1959, is one of the oldest Galápagos protection organizations. Supported by UNESCO and the World Conservation Union, the Foundation works together with the Ecuadorian government to protect the islands' ecosystems. Most funding goes to the foundation's headquarters, the Charles Darwin Research Station (CDRS), which conducts scientific research and promotes environmental education, particularly to residents of the islands. It works closely with many other organizations that have similar conservation goals.

Agrocalidad is an Ecuadorian organization that manages farming practices on the Galápagos, running five inspection points throughout the islands where incoming agricultural produce is examined to make sure it is not an invasive plant species. It is also their duty to enforce quarantines of introduced flora and fauna, and they run educational seminars that stress the importance of their work.

CIMEI (Inter-institutional Committee for the Management and Control of Introduced Species) is another Ecuadorian organization that also focuses on managing invasive species on the islands, particularly domestic animals such as dogs and cats, which have presented a huge threat to the native wildlife that is unaccustomed to predators. Some of their work includes granting pet licenses to residents of the Galápagos and assisting the Charles Darwin Foundation in the eradication of introduced pests, such as rodents.

While invasive species of animals and plants can be problematic, so can invasive tourists if they do not respect the environment. Capturgal is an Ecuadorian agency that deals with this issue. They do a lot of work teaching tour operators about ecotourism, offering seals of approval to companies that meet their standards for safe and environmentally friendly cruises and trips.

Maidith Galápagos Apartments and Suites !

(ROOMS: $75-122) Don't let the name fool you, Maidith is a hotel, not a set of apartments or suites for long-term rental (although it seems they used to be). What's more, it's a very nice hotel and one of the best deals in Puerto Ayora.

Maidith is about as different from other Galápagos hotels as it is possible to be. That's a good thing. It's never blocky, boring, dull or forgettable. Instead, the hotel is a colorful maze of rooms and stairways, all different, all brightly but tastefully decorated with bits of tile and stone. It looks a bit like a candy house that someone made at Christmas come to life. Kids will love exploring the place. The rooms are all suites and each one is different and suitable for a different number of guests. The largest suite sleeps five.

There is a Jacuzzi and each of the rooms has all the expected comforts such as air conditioning, hot water, etc. There is a small kitchen available to some of the suites. Make sure you reserve the right room if you want it. Management is friendly and helpful. It's on a sleepy street a couple blocks off of the main drag; this is a boon for those who like it quiet. The website is Spanish-only but fairly easy to navigate if you want to see photos, make reservations, etc. Features: hot water, fridge, microwave, Jacuzzi, kitchen, TV cable, internet and restaurant. Tel: 593-8-456-8171/5-252-6311, E-mail: magreda@maidithgalapagos.com, URL: maidithgalapagos.com.

Hotel Ninfa

(ROOMS: $65) Remember that one spring break back in college, when you and a bunch of buddies went to Fort Lauderdale? And you had booked the cheapest hotel in town, because you figured, hey, I'll be too busy partying to care what the place looks like? And it had a pool, so how bad could it be? And you got there, and found a squarish, whitewashed place with flaking paint, tired-looking palm trees and cracked tiles that looked like it had weathered one hurricane too many? Well, that hotel has been shipped brick-by-worn-out-brick down to the Galápagos, where it has been rebuilt and renamed the Ninfa.

Right down to the sagging hammocks and broken pool table, it's all there. I'm not saying this is a bad place. I'm just saying you shouldn't buy the "high-class luxury hotel" line that you'll get from their official websites and literature. The Ninfa owns a small cruise ship and package tours are available. Calle Los Colonos S/N. Tel: 593-5-252-6127. Updated: Dec 11, 2012.

Hostal Mainao

(ROOMS: $119-197) The Hostal Mainao (don't be fooled by the name; it's no hostal but a hotel) is a pleasant, clean, multi-story hotel located a couple of blocks off the main street in Puerto Ayora. The staff is friendly, the location is convenient, and the included breakfast is quite good. The rooms are clean, airy and comfortable, and the maids do a good job keeping them clean. There are 19 rooms, for a maximum capacity of about 45 people. The rates reflect different seasons: prices will go down May-June and September-October. Check the hotel website for the latest information. The higher prices are for nicer suites. All of the rooms have air conditioning and fans to keep you cool.

Prices are a bit steep for a hotel with no ocean view or cable TV. Still, the Mainao is quite nice and you're bound to find it charming. If you're looking for something upper mid-range in terms of price it's worth checking out. About two blocks off of the main drag in Puerto Ayora, turn near the fishermen's dock. Ca. Matazarnos and Indefatigable, Pelican Bay Neighborhood. Tel: 593-9-415-1847/8-921-8349, Fax: 593-252-7029/252-4128, URL: www.hotelmainao.com. Updated: Jan 15, 2013.

Hotel Red Booby

(ROOMS: $100-110) The dolled-up Red Booby occupies a very specific place on the food chain of Puerto Ayora Hotels. It's nice and expensive enough to keep out the riff-raff, but doesn't really hit the four-star status that it obviously desires. The bedspreads and curtains are very nice, but that can't change the fact that the rooms are boxy, bare and a little grim.

Still, the pool is cool, as it occupies the whole top floor and has a great view. It's perfect if you want to spend a little more on a nicer hotel, but can't go all-out and stay at a place like the Finch Bay. It will appeal to this 'tweener crowd only, however: most visitors will either decide to pony up a few more bucks for a nicer place or sacrifice the nice pool and pretty bedspreads for the sake of cutting their hotel bill in half and staying somewhere like the Hotel Castro. P.S. In case you're confused, no, there is no such thing as a Red Booby—Red-**footed** Booby, yes;

TOWNS

Red Booby, no. This apparent lack of creativity seems odd until you consider the Red Booby's motto: "Enjoy the comfort and elegance of Red Booby." I sure hope they didn't pay some ad guy very much for that one. Av. Plazas and Charles Binford Islas. Tel: 593-5-252-6485, E-mail: info@hotelredbooby.com.ec, URL: www.hotel-redbooby.com.ec. Updated: Mar 20, 2013.

Grand Hotel Lobo del Mar

(ROOMS: $82-158) The Grand Hotel Lobo del Mar may be "grand" in terms of size due to its recent four-story addition, but it is nowhere near grand in terms of service, despite the variety of activities it coordinates. The hotel has a day-boat and a cruise-boat and it also has partnerships with a variety of day-tour operators. This means that if you booked the cruise outside of Galápagos, you may wind up having to stay in the already paid for Lobo del Mar, and it is a toss-up whether you will be placed in the swanky, newer, more expensive section of the hotel or the lifeless, older, more economical section.

Academy Bay, Puerto Ayora

If you are lucky, you will have one of the newer rooms, complete with lush comforts, TV and air conditioning. Less fortunate tourists will get a room in the older, darker section, which comes with a fan and private hot bath. Communicating objections to reception staff over the location (and subsequent worth) of your room will result in the standard apology, graceless smile, and no change. 12 de febrero just off Av. Charles Darwin toward the bay. Tel: 593-5-252-6188, URL: www.lobodemar.com.ec. Updated: Apr 15, 2013.

Casa Natura

(ROOMS: $100-145) One of the better options in the upper-middle price range in Puerto Ayora, Casa Natura is a clean, attractive, well-run place a few blocks off of the main street. The rooms are spacious, airy and clean, there's a pool and a small restaurant,

and the beds are comfortable. Like most of the nicer hotels, there is someone to help you book tours, buy tickets to the ferry, etc.

It's owned and operated by Via Natura, a growing Quito-based tour company with agencies in Peru and Chile. They also own the Monserrat yacht, a Galápagos cruiser. Booking combination packages with everything from Machu Picchu to Galápagos is possible. Via Natura is an eco-friendly organization and a member of the rainforest alliance and other eco-organizations. Petrel and Floreana. Tel: 593-2-246-9846/847, URL: www.vianatura.com, www.casanaturahotel.com.

Hotel Fernandina !

(ROOMS: $122-158) The Hotel Fernandina is a family-run place on the edge of town, but still not too far from where the action is. It's a great choice for the upper mid-range traveler who likes some luxuries. They have a swimming pool, jacuzzi, on-site restaurant and WiFi in the common areas. They have a travel desk and are happy to assist you in booking day trips and local tours. Try to get one of the upstairs rooms as they have a nicer view. Price includes taxes and buffet breakfast. Here's a bonus: the pool is available ($3) even if you're not staying there! Av. 12 Noviembre and Piqueros. Tel: 593-5-2526/499, URL: www.hotelfernandina.com.ec/eng.

HIGH-END

Hotel Sol y Mar

(ROOMS: $175-195) The Hotel Sol y Mar has 17 rooms, each with a private balcony and stunning sea view. The rooms are spacious, immaculate, and secure, and come with air conditioning and a bar. A small deck with picnic tables serves as a great resting or meeting area, with views of nearby Academy Bay. The on-site restaurant overlooks the bay. A family owned and operated establishment, Hotel Sol y Mar guarantees personalized, caring, and detail-oriented service. A mini buffet breakfast is included in the price. Av. Charles Darwin between Tomas de Berlanga and Charles Dinford (next to the Banco del Pacifico). Tel: 593-5-252-6281, Fax: 593-5-252-7015, E-mail: info@hotelsolymar.com.ec, URL: www.hotelsolymar.com.ec. Updated: Jan 20, 2013.

Red Mangrove Adventure Inn

(ROOMS: $192-550) The Red Mangrove Adventure Inn is one of Puerto Ayora's better hotels. Each room is clean, comfortable, and equipped with a private hot bath and ceiling fan. There is also a small pool, a meeting area with plush tables and chairs, a common room with television, and plenty of hammocks for lounging.

The Red Mangrove Adventure Inn is pricey, but it backs it up with good service and facilities. The inn coordinates a variety of tours, including camping, sea kayaking, fishing, mountain biking and horseback riding. As such, it offers excellent, custom-tailored alternatives to pre-arranged tours. The Red Mangrove has affiliated hotels on Isabela and Floreana and offers island-hopping packages. Av. Charles Darwin near the cemetery. Tel: 593-5-252-7011, Fax: 593-5-252-6564, E-mail: recepcion@redmangrove.com, URL: www.redmangrove.com. Updated: Aug 02, 2012.

Finch Bay Eco-Hotel !

One of the newer deluxe hotels in the islands, Finch Bay is owned and operated by the prestigious Metropolitan Touring, an Ecuadorian tour company that also owns three luxury Galápagos yachts. The Finch Bay hotel is a first class facility tucked away on Playa de los Alemanes, or "German Beach."

The hotel is rather expensive, but it's the only hotel in Puerto Ayora on a beach, the pool is very refreshing, and the rooms are classy. Naturally, everything you could ask for is available. They do tours of the island, kayaking, snorkeling, birdwatching, etc; there is a fancy restaurant and bar on the premises; they'll send someone to get you at the airport; you name it.

It goes without saying that the six suites and 21 regular rooms have air conditioning, hot showers, mints on the pillows, etc.

Many people who stay at the Finch Bay have booked cruises on the Santa Cruz, Isabela or Pinta, Metropolitan's three Galápagos cruise ships, so sometimes the place fills up. Better make reservations well ahead of time. How to get there: It's on Playa de Los Alemanes on Angermeyer Point. You'll have to take a water taxi from the pier (just tell them Finch Bay). Costs: Finch Bay runs more on packages and specials than per night. Check their website for the latest deals, but assume approximately $300/night/person, but that includes tours, guides, etc. Features: Jacuzzi, outdoor pool, restaurant, bar, gift shop, ice machine , laundry, phone, fax, safe box, and hair dryer. E-mail: info@metropolitan-touring.com, URL: www. metropolitan-touring.com.

Angermeyer Waterfront Inn

(ROOMS: $175-350) Marine iguanas and plunging blue-footed boobies are a natural part of the landscape at this tranquil seaside inn. It is known for great service and facilities. For being one of the original Galápagos hotels, it's very modern. You can even check out photos and other information about them on Facebook.

It has arguably the best location of any Puerto Ayora Hotel, right on a peninsula on Academy Bay. It is connected by land to Puerto Ayora, but due to the restrictions of the National Park it is not possible to walk there. Instead it can easily be reached by a 2 minute water-taxi ride right to their doorstep. Tel: 593-9-472-4955, E-mail: angermeyerwaterfrontinn@gmail.com, URL: www.angermeyer-waterfront-inn.com. Updated: Jun 01, 2013.

Puerto Ayora Restaurants

Along Avenida Charles Darwin in Puerto Ayora there are a variety of open-air cafés, restaurants and bars (or sites serving as all three). Seafood and Italian cuisine seem to dominate the food scene, but you can also find sandwiches, salads, amazing coffee and juices, and home-made ice cream. Even if you don't want to dine, stop in any street-side establishments, order a refreshing beverage, and watch the mesmerizing mix of people walk by.

For less expensive eats, head away from Av. Charles Darwin and find a local eatery, where you can ask for the fixed menu (usually a lot of fish or chicken and rice). This will fill you up for under $5. There are also some food stands at the municipal market.

Note that most restaurants will add 10% service onto your bill. Look for it there, because if they have already added it, there is no need to leave a tip unless service was outstanding. Not all restaurants do this, so look at your bill closely. Also, not all restaurants will accept credit cards. If you're paying with plastic, it's always a good idea to ask before ordering.

ASIAN

Red Sushi

(ENTREES: $6-17) Red Sushi, in the Red Mangrove Adventure Inn, is a bar/restaurant specializing in Japanese delights. The sashimi and maki rolls are perfectly delectable, and popping them in your mouth in the colorful, waterfront establishment makes the dining experience truly enjoyable. There is also a selection of Japanese soups and main dishes, as well as a full menu of exotic drinks served at the bar. The menu also has steaks, pastas and other dishes for those not interested in raw fish. Av. Charles Darwin, near the cemetery. Updated: Jan 12, 2013.

ECUADORIAN/SEAFOOD

Kioskos

(ENTREES: $3-8) Eat at the kioskos, a series of outdoor food stands, and you will get the tastiest, most reasonably priced, and fastest fresh food in town. Most locals eat here, so don't be surprised if you have to fight for a seat during the dinner hour. Almost all of the stalls have the same menu: beef, chicken, fish, and/or shrimp prepared according to your tastes or encocado style, covered in a delicious coconut sauce.

Most dishes come with rice, beans, and salad and cost around $5. Some stalls will also serve lobster, an especially tasty treat, for a pretty price. Ca. de los Kioskos, an extension of Charles Binford between Islas Plaza and Av. Baltra. Updated: Jan 12, 2013.

Restaurante El Descanso del Guia

(ENTREES: $5-8) The eclectic Restaurante El Descanso del Guia is a local staple. It is popular for breakfast. Try the bolon de verde, a giant ball of cooked plantain, it's about as 'typical' as it gets. Also good are the fruit salads and the secos de carne and pollo (chicken and beef soups) available for dine-in or to-go. A sign at the restaurant says "Rincon del Asado," so there may be some confusion about the name of the place. Av. Charles Darwin, next to the bus station. Updated: Jan 12, 2013.

Angermeyer Point

(ENTREES: $30-40) One of Puerto Ayora's finest restaurants was founded by the Angermeyers, one of the earliest colonist families. Set in the one-time cabin of Karl Angermeyer, it is decorated with photos and memorabilia of those early days of island life. On the deck facing the bay, you can enjoy an evening meal of fish or Galapagos beef, as succulent as that of Argentina. Meat portions are generous. The sides are delicious but disappointingly small. This is an unforgettable dining experience that is well worth the expense. Open evenings. Updated: June 01, 2013.

Il Giardino

(ENTREES: $5-13) One of the newest and best restaurants in Puerto Ayora, Il Giardino is a favorite of locals and visitors alike. The airy dining area is divided into several areas connected by a labyrinth of stairways and wooden walkways. Look around for a place you like (if the restaurant is empty enough for you to be choosy). The menu features fresh seafood, pasta and more, with enticing daily specials. There is also a fine selection of ice cream and desserts. The owners also have another restaurant in the highlands, but they only open it for groups. Inquire if interested. Closed Mondays. Reservations may be needed on a busy night. On Charles Darwin and Charles Binford, across from Banco Pacífico and near the fishermen's pier.

Isla Grill

The Isla Grill is one more place on the restaurant-heavy stretch of Charles Darwin Av. near the Banco del Pacífico and the fishermen's pier. As its name suggests, it specializes in grilled meat and seafood. The grill itself is right inside the restaurant near the entrance, presumably so that the smells of fresh meat and seafood sizzling will lure in customers off the street! In addition to grilled steaks and fish, they have burgers, pizzas and salads. The view is relatively lousy (you'll have a wonderful vantage point for observing the bank and traffic on Av. Charles Darwin), so if a romantic view is on your list, head over to Il Giardino instead. Av. Charles Darwin, across from the Banco del Pacífico.

Argemeyer Point

The Rock

A hip, airy dining area, full menu and cool bar are the attractions at the Rock, named for the US airmen's nickname for Baltra in the 1940s. The food is pretty good, and the service isn't too bad (by Galápagos standards). It's a good place to kick off a fun

TOWNS

evening with a drink or two. They sell T-shirts with their logo on them for those who really want to remember their trip here. For some reason, locals seem to avoid The Rock. One nice bonus: their menu is online at their website www.therockgalapagos.com. Corner of Charles Darwin and Islas Plaza. Tel: 593-5-252-4176, E-mail: info@therockgalapagos.com.

TOWNS

The US Military Base

Most visitors to the Galápagos are unaware of its brief stint as a U.S. military base. Concerned about a possible invasion of the vitally strategic Panama Canal from the Pacific during World War II, the United States decided that it would be desirable to have an Air Force base off the coast of Ecuador. In 1942 construction began for a base on barren, arid Baltra Island.

The plan was flawed from the start. For one thing, a written agreement for the construction of the establishment of the base between Ecuador and the U.S. was never produced, causing uneasiness since it meant that the U.S. could lose the privilege of using the island at any time. In addition to this, the harsh, lava-rock-strewn environment of the island made it difficult to construct runways, build barracks and dig latrines. Further problems were caused by the fact that it took a long time for any sort of supplies to reach the island, including fresh water, which had to be imported.

Called "The Rock" by the servicemen, the base at one time had barracks for the servicemen, airstrips, a casino, movie theater and even a small bowling alley. Ships kept the base well supplied with food and water.

Four difficult years later, with no enemy attacks in sight, U.S. forces decided that the most practical thing to do with their troublesome base would be to give it back to Ecuador. Today, Baltra is still an official Ecuadorian military base, and some of the original buildings are still in use. Until 1986, it was also the only airport in the Galápagos. If you fly into or out of Baltra, look around on the bus ride from the airport to the ferry and you'll see some of the remains of the famous U.S. base.

CAFÉS / BARS

Hernán Café

(ENTREES: $5-10) Hernán Café/Bar/Restaurante has a decent menu and a great location on a bustling corner not far from the new pier. The airy dining room and good food make it a favorite for locals and visitors alike. The menu has everything from sandwiches to pasta and is varied enough to be a good choice when your group can't agree on what to eat. Everyone will find something. They sell ice cream at one end of the restaurant and locals often hang out there. It's one of the only places in all of Galápagos where you can get a decent cappuccino, not a small consideration for serious java-heads. Service can be lethargic enough that you may suspect that someone has put a waiter's uniform on a giant tortoise, so skip it if you're in a hurry or the sort to get irritated by wait staff watching soccer when you want to order. Av. Baltra and Charles Darwin.

DELI

Galápagos Deli ♪

Tucked away around the corner from the hospital is one of Puerto Ayora's best finds, Galápagos Deli. There they sell hot sandwiches and homemade ice cream, the best in the islands. Their menu is limited, but it's a great place to go for a snack or dessert. On Tomas de Berlanga near the corner of Baltra.

INTERNATIONAL / VEGETERIAN

Casa del Lago Café Cultural

(ENTREES: $4-9) The Casa del Lago Café Cultural serves organic coffee grown on the islands and fantastic coffee drinks, perfectly complemented by homemade ice cream. It also serves tasty and inexpensive breakfasts and vegetarian dishes, including healthy soups, salads, middle-eastern food and bagels. Internet, musical instruments and board games are available for short-term use, and there are paintings and wooden crafts created by local elderly residents. Picture windows face the Las Ninfas Lagoon. Moises Brito and Juan Montalvo, near Las Ninfas. Tel: 593-9-971-4647, E-mail: info@galapagoscultural.com, casadellago@galapagoscultural.com, URL: www.galapagoscultural.com.

Garrapata

(ENTREES: $10-15) Garrapata is often considered (by tourists and locals alike) to be the best restaurant in town. It serves fresh seafood and creative meat dishes, as well as different pastas. The restaurant also features a friendly waitstaff, ample bar, and candle-lit outdoor seating. If the food alone does not sell you, a stroll past the romantic atmosphere and full tables will convince you to stop in and eat before hitting the bar down the way. Try the lobster. Av. Charles Darwin between 12 de Febrero and Tomas de Berlanga. Tel: 593-5-252-6264. Updated: Mar 20, 2012.

Café del Mar

(ENTREES: $8-10) The aroma of grilled meats and the sizzle of the fire greet you as you walk into this brightly lit, cavernous space with bamboo walls and large, wood slab tables. On one wall, a TV screen usually shows Galápagos videos. Café del Mar is a parillada, or grill, restaurant. Vegetarians may want to go elsewhere. There are some sandwiches and burgers for less than $5, and a heaping plate of meat will run you about $8-10. Try the grilled octopus. Prices are pretty competitive with the rest of the restaurants in Puerto Ayora.

Café del Mar has a full bar. The wines are a bit overpriced. Open evenings after 6:30 p.m. Av. Charles Darwin, across from the WWF (World Wildlife Fund) offices. Updated: Nov 19, 2012.

Tintorera

(ENTREES: $5-12) Tintorera is a popular restaurant with a fresh, eco-friendly spin. Produce is organic and locally grown; cheeses are made locally; jams are produced by the Orgnization of Artisan Women in Isabela; and reusable glass soda bottles, not plastic throw-aways, are used. Ice cream, cakes and bread products, including bagels, are homemade and mouthwatering. Breakfast is

the best meal here, not only because of the fresh baked goods, but also because you get a bottomless cup of tea or organic Galápagos coffee. Lunches, however, are not far behind: sandwiches on homemade bread, bagel sandwiches, veggie burgers, salads, soups and middle-eastern food provide delicious vegetarian options. Be sure to check out the executive lunch menu on the chalkboard if you're coming at lunchtime— it's a good deal. Av. Charles Darwin and Isla Floreana. Updated: Jan 12, 2013.

PUERTO BAQUERIZO MORENO San Cristobal

The capital and administrative center of the Galápagos, Puerto Baquerizo Moreno, has the second largest population in the archipelago after Puerto Ayora. Although the tourist infrastructure is less advanced here than in Puerto Ayora, visitors to Puerto Baquerizo Moreno are not without options. Hotels, stores, restaurants and travel agencies line the main street, and internet cafés, telephone centers and banks are common. There is also a small post office, police station and hospital. The Galápagos campus of the San Francisco University is also in Puerto Baquerizo Moreno, so university staff and students reside here.

Day trips to various onland, offshore and marine sites are available and can be arranged through travel agencies and dive centers located in town. Private vehicles (taxis) provide fairly inexpensive and reliable transportation and are often a good alternative to arranged tours when visiting highland sites. There are also infrequent public buses that run from Puerto Baquerizo Moreno to the village of El Progreso (8 km/5 mi to the east).

Some boats begin their tours here, and periodic closings of the Baltra airport for cleaning or maintenance can cause tourist activity to shift to San Cristóbal. As a result, visitor services and facilities are constantly improving in Puerto Baquerizo Moreno to provide alternatives for tourists and to meet tourist demand.

Services

Puerto Baquerizo Moreno is basically a smaller version of Puerto Ayora. There are shops, internet cafés, hotels and restaurants spread around along the main drag and nearby, none of which really stand out much.

TOWNS

TOWNS

SHOPPING

If you're in the market for T-shirts, playing cards, shotglasses and other tourist stuff, Puerto Baquerizo Moreno is the right place. They have all the same things as Puerto Ayora and it's a little cheaper. No fancy high-end stores yet, though.

INTERNET

Internet service is bad in town; apparently one lazy provider has quite a monopoly on the connection. There are internet cafés all over, but if one of them is down, they probably all are, a situation that is far too common. In general, the closer you are to the tourist pier, the more reliable the internet cafés are.

OTHER SERVICES

The post office is at the end of Charles Darwin Avenue near the sea lion beach. There are numerous places where you can drop off a bag of dirty laundry and they'll wash it for a couple bucks. The best place to make international phone calls is at the internet cafés: USA is $0.50 per minute, Europe slightly higher. There are a couple of ATM's near the tourist pier.

Things to See and Do

The Galápagos National Park Interpretation Center

Inaugurated in 1998, the Galápagos National Park Interpretation Center, located on the northeast side of Puerto Baquerizo Moreno, has a series of interactive exhibits providing information about the history and biodiversity of the Galápagos Islands. The self-guided walking tour lasts about one hour, is offered in English and in Spanish, and is appropriate for all ages. Updated: Nov 21, 2012.

Visitor Sites and Beaches

Puerto Baquerizo Moreno has several interesting visitor sites nearby. You should definitely check out the visitor's center and the trails behind it, which lead to a great beach (Cabo de Hornos) and a superior snorkeling lagoon (Cerro Tijeretas). In the town, Playa Mann (across from the university) is as nice a beach as you can find in a town anywhere.

Puerto Baquerizo Moreno is known for surfing, and there are several surf sites scattered around the island, all of them accessible from town. There are good dive sites nearby as well.

It's also possible to go to the highlands and hike or see tortoises. All of these activities and more are detailed in the Visitor Sites section.

El Refugio del Pirata

El Refugio del Pirata ("Pirate's Refuge") is a liquor store and pool hall. There are two battered tables and it costs $2 per hour to play. They sell cold beer for carry-out as well. Eyepatches and parrots optional. Av. Jose de Villamil, a half-block from Avenida Charles Darwin.

Puerto Baquerizo Moreno Tour Agencies and Dive Shops

Chalo Tours

Chalo Tours, conveniently located on the main drag across from the malecón, does a little bit of everything: SCUBA diving, snorkeling, day trips, surfing and more. They do dive courses and surfing classes as well. They rent all the necessary gear as well as other fun things like ocean kayaks and underwater cameras. Rates for excursions are reasonable for San Cristóbal—about the norm. Walk-ins welcome. Try the day trip to the highlands, with a downhill bike ride from El Junco Lake to the tortoise breeding center. Tel: 593-5-252-0953/430, Quito: 593-2-273-2416, E-mail: chalotours@hotmail.com.

Franklin Dive Center

Franklin Dive Center goes to all the usual dive sites near Puerto Baquerizo Moreno: Kicker Rock, Isla Lobos, etc. Rates are typical for San Cristóbal. They can rent all necessary gear and equipment.

One feature of this dive shop is that they'll let you use their underwater camera at no extra charge; just bring your own chip and a CD and they'll burn you a copy of your photos! They also do snorkeling trips. Teodoro Wolf and Ignacio Hernandez. Tel: 593-5-252-1543, E-mail: franklindivecenter@hotmail.com.

Wreck Bay Dive Center

Wreck Bay offers a lot of services for a dive shop: they can help you get to and from San Cristóbal and set up just about any day trip you're interested in, including tours of the highlands. They can arrange island-hopping trips, too. They do all the usual nearby dive sites, but for a large enough group they can go to sites which are further away, like Gardner Reef or Española. Walk-ins are welcome, or you can contact them before your trip and set something up. Charles Darwin and Teodoro Wolf. Tel: 593-5-252-1663/8-728-4164, E-mail: wreckbay_divingcenter@yahoo.com, URL: www.wreckbay.com.

Galápagos Fishing Adventures

Galápagos Fishing Adventures specializes, of course, in fishing. The owner has a couple of fishing boats, and different tours will have different costs. The fishing here is expensive ($1,300 for a day-long Marlin Fishing trip for up to three people) but they are by far the most experienced and professional fishing outfit in Galápagos. More economical tours are available as well. They are also a dive shop and tour operator and can do day tours of the highlands and beaches on San Cristóbal as well as dives and snorkeling. Av. Jose de Villamil y Malecón. Tel: 593-5-252-1537/9-404-0714, E-mail: Gustavo@galafishing.com.ec, URL: www.galafishing.com.ec.

Dive & Surf Club

Dive & Surf Club is pretty self-explanatory—it's a friendly dive shop that also has surfing stuff. San Cristóbal is well-known as a surfing destination, and Dive & Surf Club is your best bet of the places in town if you're going to hit the waves. They do courses (diving and surfing) and their dive shop visits all the usual San Cristóbal sites. They do snorkeling and day trips too. They also do some camping on the island. You might want to look them up if that appeals to you. Ca. H. Melville and I. Hernandez. E-mail: Wendyadira81@yahoo.es, URL: www.divesurfclub.com.

Come to Galápagos 🏃

A full service travel agency based out of San Cristóbal, Come to Galápagos is run by an American/Ecuadorian couple. They do everything from arranging your flights to finding hotels, booking tours and hiring your guides. They don't really do walk-in business: you should plan on contacting them long before your trip and setting something up. The fact that they are based in the islands is an enormous bonus, as they'll deal directly with your hotel or guide and any problems are resolved very quickly. They recently sponsored the first ever Galápagos Marathon, which was a big hit. They hope to make it an annual event. This travel agency is particularly involved with the community, so if you want a place that is making a positive difference, this is it. Tel: 593-5-252-1251/9-115-2102, E-mail: rickandbere@cometogalapagos.com, URL: http://cometogalapagos.com, http://galapagosfamilyvacations.com.

Puerto Baquerizo Lodging

Of all the three towns, Puerto Baquerizo Moreno is the one with the highest percentage of bland, square rooms for about $25 per night. There are a couple of cheaper options, however, as well as some nicer places for those with a little more to spend.

Many of the hotels in San Cristóbal are clustered along the waterfront, including, oddly enough, almost all of the high end AND extreme budget options. Get away from the water and all of the hotels start looking the same.

It seems like feast or famine for the Puerto Baquerizo Moreno. The hotels are usually mostly empty, as visitors tend to go to the centrally located Puerto Ayora or the more hip Isabela. They can fill up fast, however, if there is a conference of some sort going on– remember, Puerto Baquerizo Moreno is the capital of Galápagos.

It also may fill up during the annual Galápagos marathon. In other words, book early, even though you may find when you get there that the town is nearly devoid of tourists.
Updated: Sept 13, 2012.

BUDGET

Hotel Albatros

(ROOMS: $10 per person) The Albatros, along with its next-door-neighbor the Hotel San Francisco, represents the least expensive lodging option in Puerto Baquerizo Moreno. The rooms are all located on the third floor or higher, making this a bad choice for those who can't climb a couple flights of stairs. The rooms are basic, although most have TV (there are five or six local channels only) and a fan. If you want hot water, a couple rooms have it, but it will cost you more. The location is quite good, on the main drag across from the Malecón. It's really about what you'd expect for the price. Tax is included, but not breakfast. Av. Charles Darwin y 9 Octubre, across from the Malecón. Tel: 593-5-252-0264, E-mail: Marita0422@hotmail.com.

Hotel San Francisco

(ROOMS: $8-12/person) At the bottom end of the hotel spectrum is the Hotel San Francisco, a basic, no-frills place that happens to be the cheapest place in town. It's well-located, right on the main drag across from the malecón. Rooms are blocky and unattractive, but most of them have a TV with five or six local channels (no cable) and a fan (no air conditioning). There is no hot water. If your goal is to spend

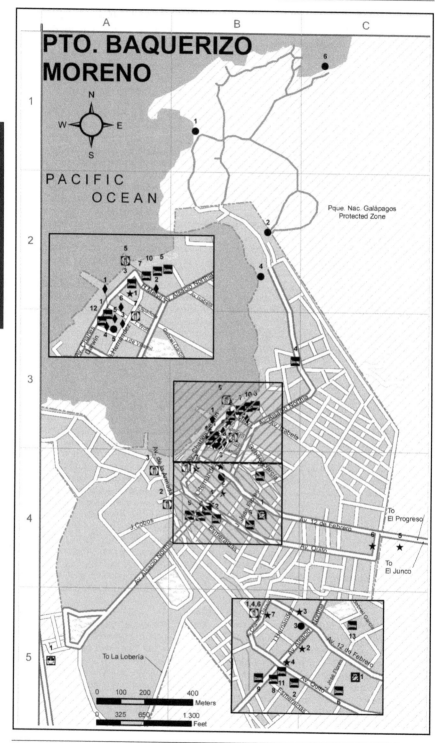

● **Activities**

1 Cabo de Horno B1
2 Centro de Interpretación B2
3 Cyber Dolphin B4*
4 Playa Man B2
5 Refugio del Pirata B3*
6 Tijeretas C1

🍴 **Eating**

1 Calipso B4*
2 Cormorant A4
3 La Playa A4
4 Miramar B4*
5 Muana Café B3*
6 Puerto Lobo B4*
7 Rosita B3*

★ **Services**

1 Bank B3*
2 Church B4*
3 Cruz Roja B4*
4 Hospital B4*
5 INGALA C4
6 Police C4
7 Post Office B4*

🛍 **Shopping**

1 Market B4*

🛏 **Sleeping**

1 Albatros B3*
2 Algarrobos B4*
3 Bellavista B3*
4 Casa de Nelly B3
5 Casa Opuntia B3*
6 Hotel Cactus B4*
7 Hotel Casablanca B3*
8 Hotel Paraíso Insular B4*
9 Mar Azul B4*
10 Miconia B3*
11 Residencial Doña Pilo B4*
12 San Francisco B3*
13 Wilmar B4*

◆ **Tour**

1 Chalo Tours B3*
2 Dive and Surf Club B3*
3 Franklin Dive Center B3*
4 Galapagos Fishing Adventures B3*
5 Sharksky Tours B3*
6 Wreck Bay Dive Center B3*

🚌 **Transportation**

1 Airport A5

* See inset maps

the least amount of money possible, this is your place (or the similar Albatros next door). If you can budget an extra $10 per night, you might consider an upgrade, if only for the sake of a hot shower. They do not have E-mail or a website, so if you wish to make reservations, you'll need to call. Av. Charles Darwin across from the Malecón. Tel: 593-5-252-0304. Updated: Sept 27, 2012.

Residencial Doña Pilo

(ROOMS: $15/person) A half-step up from the cheapest places in town, Residencial Doña Pilo is a small, family run place only a couple blocks off of the main drag. It's upstairs from the cheery Kicker Rock Cafetería. There are only four rooms, each of which has three or four beds each, so getting a single might prove problematic unless the place is mostly empty. The rooms have fans but no air conditioning, hot water (electric shower) and cable TV. There is a kitchen available. It's a pleasant enough little place, and probably worth the extra couple bucks that set it above the least expensive hotels in town. Av. Quito y Northia. Tel: 593-5-252-0409. Updated: Sept 27, 2012.

Residencial Wilmar

(ROOMS: $20/person) It doesn't look like much from outside, but the Residencial Wilmar isn't your worst choice in town. The place is clean, the owners are friendly,

and it's $5 cheaper than comparable places, probably because it's a couple of blocks from the main drag. The rooms are the typical San Cristóbal cells with a walled-off bathroom, a TV (no cable), small fridge and an air conditioning unit. Look at all the available rooms (there are only 6 in total). Some rooms have a bad view of the neighbor's ugly house, while other rooms have an even worse view of a cement brick wall. The best part is the covered rooftop terrace with a great view of the town and Shipwreck Bay. The friendly owners will help you arrange local tours and day trips if you ask. Features: small common area, air conditioning, TV, private baths, and access to a kitchen. Cost includes taxes but not breakfast. However, breakfast can be arranged if you're there with a large group. No credit cards accepted. Ca. Gabriel Garcia Moreno and Vicente Rocafuerte. Tel: 593-5-252-0135, Cel: 593-8-555-4518, E-mail: rafaelr@easynet.net.ec.

Hostal Los Algarrobos ♪

(ROOMS: $25 per person) One of the top choices in the great glut of hotels that cost around $25 per person per night, Hostal los Algarrobos is located a couple of blocks off of Avenida Charles Darwin but worth the walk. The rooms are your standard San Cristóbal style—squarish, cell-like and forgettable— but the Algarrobos has two things the others do not, reliable free internet on three downstairs computers and a spiffy game room on an upper floor. There is a little restaurant as well and the top floor features a good view of the town and bay.

Hostal los Algarrobos is best for small groups who can take advantage of the triples or quads (one of the quads has a balcony) and want a nice place to hang out. The service at Algarrobos is professional enough that tour agencies in Quito will send groups there: their confidence speaks volumes about the place. Cost does not include taxes. Includes TV, cable, air conditioning, hot water with electric shower and a game room. Supposedly includes breakfast (I'm skeptical if there are not many guests there). Tel: 593-5-252-1010/252-0034, Cel: 593-8-582-9467, E-mail: hostallosalgarrobos@gmail.com, paulavera1969@hotmail.com. Updated: Sept 27, 2012.

Hotel Mar Azul

(ROOMS: $20-70) An undistinguished little place a couple blocks off of the main drag, the Mar Azul used to include the two buildings that are now the Grand Hotel Paraiso Insular, but for whatever reason the management split them up. The Mar Azul got the short end of the stick, settling for one low structure full of the same blocky rooms as everywhere else in town. The selling points are air conditioning, electric showers and a relatively noise-free neighborhood. They'll serve breakfast if the hotel is full. Bugs in rooms are sometimes an issue.

It's best for people looking for a cheap sleep and who don't plan on spending much time in their rooms or hotels. It's far away enough from the airport that you'll want to take a taxi ($1-2). You can walk there in ten minutes from the tourist pier, but if you have heavy luggage you'll also want a taxi. Avenida Alsacio Northia and Esmeraldas. Tel: 593-5-252-0107/252-0139, E-mail: marazul@seamangalapagos.com, URL: www.hosteltrail.com/hotelmarazul. Updated: Sept 27, 2012.

MID-RANGE

Grand Hotel Paraiso Insular

(ROOMS: $20-95) Don't let the fancy name intimidate you. The Grand Hotel Paraiso Insular is but an above-average hotel with two locations almost across the street from one another on Avenida Alsacio Northia. Try to get into the newer building if you can (it's the one a little farther from town). The rooms in the newer structure have gas-heated hot water as opposed to the "electric showers" at the older building.

The rooms are your typical blocky San Cristóbal fare, mostly with cable TV and small refrigerators. Some have air conditioning, and some have a fan. Rooms with a/c cost about $20 more per night. Some of the rooms have a distant view of the ocean, but it's nothing to get too excited about. The hotel has many rooms, making it popular with groups and organized tours.

The Grand Hotel Paraiso Insular used to be affiliated with the "Mar Azul" hotel across the street, but no longer. The administration of the hotel is more or less professional. The girl in reception can help you book tours and trips if you can get her off the phone with her boyfriend. Unlike many of the other hotels in the low-medium price range, the Paraiso Insular can accept credit cards. Av. Alsacio Northia and Esmeraldas. Tel: 593-5-252-0091/252-0761/252-1573, E-mail: grandhotelparaisoinsular@hotmail.com, URL: www.grandhotelparaisoinsular.com. Updated: Sept 27, 2012.

Hostal Los Cactus

(ROOMS: $30-55) Los Cactus is a friendly little place located a few blocks off of the main drag in Puerto Baquerizo Moreno. The clean, comfortable rooms are a bit larger than the average in town, and there is one family room that sleeps four and has a little mini-kitchen. Owners are cheerful, speak some English, and seem to try a little harder than most places in town.

They can help you book tours, including fishing with a local guide, and they also have a restaurant in the San Cristóbal highlands which can be opened for larger groups. It's a good choice for couples or a family on a budget. The only drawback is the distance from the center of town, but it's only about four blocks. Rooms include Wifi, air conditioning, hot water, fridge, and TV (no cable). A 12% tax will be added to the bill. Service is not included. Breakfast is not included, but it can be for an additional $3. No credit cards accepted. Juan Jose Flores y Quito. Tel: 593-9-731-8278/5-252-0078, E-mail: Hostal_cactus@hotmail.com, URL: www. opuntiatravel.com.ec. Updated: Sept 27, 2012.

Hotel Casablanca

(ROOMS: $40-100) Casablanca is a pleasant, small (7 bedrooms) bed and breakfast conveniently located on the main street, across from the bay. The rooms are attractive, airy and eclectic. Each one is different and memorable. If you can afford it, the Cúpula suite is the way to go, as it features a terrace and ocean view. On the main street, not far from the pier. E-mail: jacquivaz@yahoo.com.
Updated: Feb 18, 2013.

Bellavista !

(Rooms: $45-65) Bellavista is a family run hotel with a prime location in Puerto Baquerizo Moreno, right next to the tourist pier on the main street. Bellavista's waterfront location provides great sunset opportunities at the memorable Wreck Bay. The hotel's nine rooms can accommodate up to 18 guests. Each room comes equipped with WiFi, cable TV, air conditioning, mini-bar, and 24-hour hot water. Charles Darwin Ave. and Hernan Melville. Tel: 593-5-252-1147/ 0352, E-mail: robertandradetorres@yahoo.com and agat74@yahoo.com.
Updated: Oct 19, 2012.

Hotel Miconia !

(ROOMS: $65-187) Hotel Miconia is one of the better visitor options in Puerto Baquerizo Moreno. The rooms are neat and airy, the staff friendly, and you'll find a Jacuzzi, small exercise room and bar there. On mainland Ecuador the prices would be scandalous for what you get, but they're pretty fair by Galápagos standards. The location is great, right smack in the center of what limited action Puerto Baquerizo Moreno has to offer. They'll even set up tours of the island if you wish. Av. Charles Darwin, more or less across from the pier . Tel: 593-5-252-0608, E-mail: hotelmiconia@yahoo.com, URL: www.miconia.com.
Updated: Feb 09, 2013.

Casa de Nelly

(ROOMS: $20-30/person)This friendly hotel has a B&B sort of feel to it. The rooms are your standard San Cristóbal cell-like affair, but an effort to keep them airy and attractive has been made, and there is a large marine mural on the wall downstairs adding a splash of color to the place. There are a variety of rooms available, all with air conditioning, TV and gas-heated water. The owner, Nelly, used to rent out suites and apartments on a monthly basis, but they're moving away from that. There are still little mini kitchens spread around, so if you want to use one, just ask for a room with one attached or nearby. Even though she's officially out of the apartment-renting business, this would be a good place to try if your stay is a little longer. Casa de Nelly is close to the university, and visiting professors often stay there. The best part is the rooftop deck with hammocks. This hotel is located close to the trails behind the interpretation center. If you plan to visit the beaches and snorkeling sites there frequently, you should check this place out. Av. Alsacio Northia (sector Playa del Oro). Tel: 593-5-252-0112/982, saltosnelly@hotmail.com.
Updated: Sept 27, 2012.

Casa de Nelly

HIGH-END

Casa Opuntia Hotel

(ROOMS: $89-163) San Cristóbal's newest luxury hotel occupies a privileged spot on the refurbished boardwalk within walking distance of the Playa del Oro beach. The beachfront rooms offer a spectacular view, and the pool, bar area and airy, air-conditioned rooms offer a welcome respite from the harsh Galápagos climate. The attached gourmet restaurant is worth a visit even if you're not staying there. The Casa Opuntia will appeal to travelers who want to spend a couple of extra days in Galápagos after a multi day luxury cruise, or for those who don't want a cruise but prefer to island hop in style. For the latter travelers, the Opuntia hotels group offers lodging at the Angermeyer Waterfront Inn in Puerto Ayora and the Iguana Crossing Hotel in Puerto Villamil. There are photos of the hotel on their website and on Facebook as well for those who want a peek before booking. There are only 10 rooms, so book in advance. Pasaje Cordova N23-26 and Wilson (Quito). On the waterfront (San Cristóbal). Tel: USA/Canada: 1-800-217-9414, Ecuador: 593-2-222-3720, Email: info@opuntiagalapagoshotels.com, URL: www.opuntiagalapagoshotels.com.

Grand Hotel Chatham

(ROOMS: $60-$216) The Grand Hotel Chatham is about as close to a luxury hotel as you'll find in Puerto Baquerizo Moreno. It has a pool, the rooms are pleasant enough and the prices can be a bit steep during high season. It's recently (2011) had a complete overhaul and renovation but it's already beginning to show a bit of wear. Room costs vary greatly, depending on the season and how fancy a room you want: the lowest will run you about $50/person in a double, which is pretty fair, actually. Services here are good and include wi-fi, on-site bar and restaurant, TV room, air conditioning and a small library. As with any halfway decent hotel here, they can help you plan day trips and small excursions. Service can be a bit sluggish, even by island standards. Book early, as this place fills up with tour groups. Avenida Armada Nacional and Alsacio Northia. Phone: (593) 5-2520 923. URL: www.grandhotelchatham.com. ec, Email: info@grandhotelchatham.com.

Casa Baronesa

(ROOMS: $1,00 for 2 people / $1,400 for 6 people) Casa Baronesa is a gorgeous, two-story and three-bedroom house which overlooks its own little piece of the beach right on the waterfront of Puerto Villamil. The creature comforts and service that are catered to your individual (or group) needs here are remarkable. Ranging anywhere from tours and activities around the island all the way to having a personal chef come over to cook you a delightful meal, Casa Baronesa truly serves as a platform for being pampered. The place also comes with packaged deals that include romantic meals for the honeymooners; or just come in a group and you can all share and cherish this wonderful little house to yourselves. On the waterfront, Tel: 1-800-217-9414 / 02-604-6800, Email: cs@ecuadoradventure.ec, URL: www.opuntia-galapagostours.com.
Updated: Aug 1, 2013 .

Restaurants Puerto Baquerizo

CAFÉS/BARS

Puerto Lobo

(ENTREES: $4-7) Living up to its name ("Sea Lion Port"), you'll probably have to step over or around several sea lions to enter this small, airy restaurant. Puerto Lobo serves mostly crepes, snacks and desserts—if you're looking for a steak, keep looking. The food, service and coffee are good, but a bit unreliable. It's open whenever someone is in there, and

it's often closed at strange times. If you're in the mood for a light lunch you might give it a shot, especially because it has such a nice view overlooking Shipwreck Bay. The evening shift likes to watch the Jesus channel on the lone TV there, so either bring your bible or avoid the place as you see fit. Crepes $4-7, breakfast $4.25, and desserts $2-5. Av. Charles Darwin at the end of the Malecón, downstairs from Miramar and around the corner from Calypso. Just follow the sea lions.
Updated: Sept 27, 2012.

Muana Café

(ENTREES: $3-5) Located right on a major intersection across from the pier and downstairs from the Casa Blanca Hotel, Muana Café gets a lot of business. The food and coffee are good, and so is the ice cream. They don't have an actual printed menu; look on the chalkboard behind the counter to see what's available. It features mostly snacks, sandwiches and desserts. Across from the tourist pier and under the Casa Blanca Hotel.
Updated: Sept 27, 2012.

Café del Mar

(ENTREES: $3-7) Café del Mar is easy to find: it's got the best location in Puerto Baquerizo Moreno, right on the seaward side of the main drag. It's a stand-alone, square-ish building, brightly painted – you can't miss it. It's a café and light restaurant: it has ceviches, burgers, sandwiches, pasta dishes, etc. Prices are reasonable, given the location. It also serves drinks and has live music at night, so it's as good a place as any to go out in sleepy San Cristóbal. No reservations needed. Charles Darwin, Malecón 593. Phone: (05) 252-0658.
Updated: June 10, 2013.

SEAFOOD

La Playa ♪

One of the best restaurants in Galápagos, La Playa is a casual, laid-back place with an ocean view. Nothing about the restaurant's plain exterior will cause you to suspect how good the food is. Specializing in seafood, La Playa is a local favorite and often fills up on weekends. There is a full menu, with non-seafood options for those who wish.The service is a bit surly, and the prices are quite steep by Puerto Baquerizo Moreno standards, but you'll forget all about that when the food comes. If you're very hungry, try a plate of chicharrón de pescado—little fried bits of fish served with a dipping sauce—as an appetizer. Av. Armada Nacional. Tel: 593-5-252-0044,
Updated: Nov 21, 2012.

Galápagos Coffee

Responsibility for bringing coffee to the Galápagos goes to Manuel Cobos, the self-titled "Emperor" of the Islands who endeavored to start a lucrative coffee farm on San Cristóbal in 1879. The rocky soil and lack of fresh water on many of the islands are not ideal for farming, so efforts were concentrated on San Cristóbal alone, home to the Galápagos' only fresh water lagoon. Cobos initially planted 250 acres of coffee trees on the Hacienda El Cafétel, a farm that was more like a prison camp, since he took advantage of free inmate labor. Cobos' business plan hit a wall in 1904 when his laborers revolted and killed him, and the plantation would be abandoned for over a century.

The Cafétel was resurrected in the 1990s when the Gonzales family, upon purchasing the land, discovered that Cobos' coffee plants had continued to thrive despite years of neglect. Today, a modernized version of the old plantation (manned by adequately compensated workers) is back in business, producing what many describe to be a rich, caramel-hinted brew. Their Galápagos Coffee can be ordered or found in specialty stores all over the world, but nothing beats sipping a cup while looking out over the lush greenery of San Cristóbal.

Ceviches del Colorado

(ENTREES $9-15) A cheery little outdoor cevicheria with plenty of shade, Ceviches del Colorado has a limited menu of mostly seafood. It's good seafood, however, and you won't regret taking a break here on a hot day. Portion sizes are large. Open daily 9-4. Avenida Armada Nacional and Ignacio Hernández.

INTERNATIONAL

Restaurante Miramar

(ENTREES: $8-19) Miramar has a winning menu of tempting international food, and obviously is taking a shot at being a very fancy restaurant in a town that currently does not have one. The food (and prices) are spot-on: the entrees are tasty and priced where you'd expect, at about the $8-19 range. The service and facilities don't quite make the cut, however. You think of a fancy restaurant, what do you think? Candles, wine, fancy tablecloths, hostess, free water, elegant waiter, little basket of bread...right? Here you'll get no bread, no tablecloth, no candles, no water, no hostess and a waiter in sneakers (wine was available, though, so maybe they're starting to get it). The point is that depending on your definition of what makes an upscale restaurant, you may or may not be hugely disappointed by Miramar.

The food is good and has some nontraditional options, such as Tequila shrimp, but the restaurant itself misses the cut by a mile. If you're all about the food, give it a shot. If style points matter, take a pass. I heard elsewhere in town that Miramar makes an effort to use locally grown produce and meat in an effort to help the island economy. If this is so, they don't advertise it at the restaurant itself. Av. Charles Darwin at the end of the Malecón, on the second floor above Puerto Lobo and around the corner from Calypso. Updated: Sep 27, 2012.

Calypso

(ENTREES: $5-17) Calypso is a happy little place that always seems packed with locals and visitors, which means the food must be really good, because its location is not great (a sort of half-basement next to a busy street) and prices are a bit high for Puerto Baquerizo Moreno. They have a good selection of burgers, pizzas, pastas and other main dishes. Come early or you might not get a seat. Patrons tend to linger, either because of the chilled-out atmosphere or because of the speed of Galápagos service. You can't miss Calypso: it's in the port authority building between Avenida Charles Darwin and the ocean at the end of the malecón. It's on the same block as Miramar and Puerto Lobo. Updated: Sep 27, 2012.

TRADITIONAL ECUADORIAN

Rosita

(ENTREES: $4-10) Restaurant Rosita is a friendly place, open and breezy, located a few blocks from the beach. It has a definite beach-place vibe to it, from the photos of fish on the walls to the ship's wheel hung near the bathrooms. The menu is varied enough to be interesting. The seafood and traditional Ecuadorian dishes are recommended here. They also have set menus at reasonable prices. It's as good a place as any in Puerto Baquerizo Moreno to unwind after a day of diving, exploring or snorkeling, even if it's just to have a cold beer served in a frosty glass! Corner of Hernandez and Villamil. Updated: Sep 27, 2012.

Cormoran

(ENTREES: $2-9) One of the classier budget eating options, Cormorán is located near the little creek that runs through town to empty into the ocean. It's an airy, family run place with a good variety of ceviches, sandwiches, seafood and even some vegetarian options. There is a massive TV there and the place fills up with locals when an important soccer game is on. Open for lunch and dinner. Cross the bridge at the end of the malecon and it's right there. Down the street a bit from La Playa restaurant. Updated: Sep 27, 2012.

PUERTO VILLAMIL

The charming town of Puerto Villamil on Isabela Island is probably the best kept secret in Galápagos. It's very small and underdeveloped—none of the streets in town are paved—but there's a lot to see and do, and it's well worth spending a couple of days here if you're doing the whole island-hopping thing.

First stop, the beach. Puerto Villamil is located right on one of the best beaches in all of Galápagos, a spectacular two-mile stretch of silky bone-colored sand and palm trees. Since there are fewer than 3,000 full-time residents in Puerto Villamil, the large beach never gets packed, even on the hottest days.

Locals seem divided about the tourism boom. Some have embraced it, while others can still be a little surly to outsiders. Service in hotels and restaurants is by far the worst in the islands, as hotel operators and waiters seem at best clueless and at worst apathetic. There are a few notable exceptions. See the hotel and restaurant descriptions for suggestions.

Puerto Villamil Services

Services in town are pretty basic. There's a post office, some laundry places, a couple of internet cafés, one dive shop, a small hospital and an assortment of hotels, tour agencies and restaurants of varying quality.

Although there is a co-op sort of bank, it is worth remembering that there is no ATM in Puerto Villamil, and if you run out of cash here, it's next to impossible to get more. According to locals, the bank did put an ATM in once in response to their complaints, but it was a fake one—simply a front with a screen that said "Out of order, please come back later!"

Eventually they even took that away.

Things to See and Do

Puerto Villamil is a paradise for those who like outdoor activities. It's possible to snorkel in several nearby places, including La Calera, Tintoreras and Concha de Perla. Just hiking around town will lead you past a couple of salt lagoons often filled with swimming and wading birds. Popular hikes include the Sierra Negra Volcano, the trail to the visitor center and a coastal walk to the Wall of Tears, built by convicts during the time that Isabela was home to a penal colony.

All of these visitor sites and more are covered in the Visitor Sites section.

Puerto Villamil Tour Agencies and Dive Shops

Isabela Dive Center

There's only one dive shop in Puerto Villamil, and that's the Isabela Dive Center, where divemaster/owner Pablo Constante will be happy to show you the best nearby dive sites. There are basically three places he goes to regularly: Roca Viuda, Cuatro Hermanos and Isla Tortuga (see descriptions of these under Diving Visitor Sites). Isabela Dive Center can do basic certification courses. They can also do snorkeling and other guided day trips. Dive prices vary depending on the number of divers and destination. You're better off in a small group. One example is Isla Tortuga. It'll cost you $120 per person with three or more, but $140 per person for two (and presumably much more expensive for only one diver if they'll go at all). They have all the gear you'll need, including masks, fins, weight, air tanks, etc. Escalesia and Antonio Gil. Tel: 593-9-466-6568/5-252-9418, E-Mail: info@isabeladivecenter.com.ec, URL: www.isabeladivecenter.com.ec.

Puerto Villamil Lodging

There are certain laws in Galápagos which make it very difficult for outsiders—that is, anyone not from the Islands—to own or operate any sort of business there. Nowhere are the effects of this law in greater evidence than on Isabela Island, which began to boom long after the law had taken effect.

The law has prohibited outsiders from coming in and setting up fancy hotels and restaurants, and instead has left such activities up to the people of Puerto Villamil, with mixed results. It seems everyone within a couple of blocks of the beach has built a hotel in their back yard. The rooms are mostly the same.

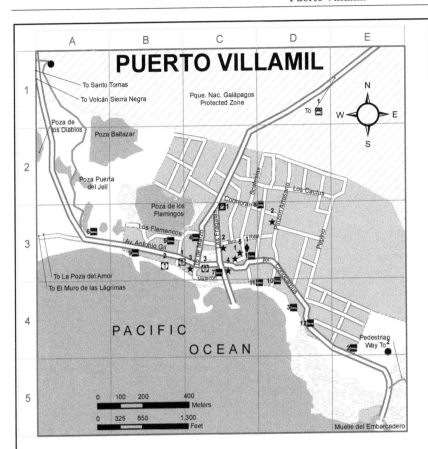

Activities
1 Centro de Crianza A1
2 Concha Perla E4

Eating
1 Aloha Betsy B3
2 Bar de Beto B3
3 Cesar's C3

Services
1 Bank C3
2 Church C3, D3
3 Medical Center C3
4 Police C3
5 Post Office C3

Shopping
1 Market C3

Sleeping
1 Brisas del Mar C3
2 Hospedaje Plaucio E4
3 Hostal La Casa de Marita D4
4 Hostal Villamil C3
5 Hotel La Laguna B3
6 Iguana Crossing A3
7 Pensión Albemarle C3
8 Pensión San Vicente D3
9 Pink Iguana B3
10 Red Mangrove Isabela Lodge D4
11 Sol Isabela D4
12 The Wooden House D4

Tour
1 Isabela Dive Center C3

Transportation
1 Airport D1

Twenty dollars will get you a square room with one to three beds and a walled-off bathroom in the corner. At least they're all new, so they're all still in pretty good shape.

Most of the hotel owners still don't "get it," and by "it" I mean the whole concept of hotel service. They don't answer their phones. You'll show up and no one is at the hotel. They'll say they'll pick you up at the pier and they don't. If there's a soccer game, they'll blow off all their guests to go play. I'm sure this carefree attitude is great for their blood pressure, but it's bad for yours. At least if you're expecting a complete lack of professionalism, you won't be shocked by it. Don't say I didn't tell you!

There are exceptions, of course. A couple of the hotels are indeed managed by responsible tourism professionals—these will usually be noted in the hotel description. There are no "neighborhoods" as such in tiny Puerto Villamil and all of the hotels are within a few blocks of one another.

BUDGET

Hospedaje Plaucio

(ROOMS: $10/person) Plaucio is an eccentric local artist who has built a couple of concrete rooms near his home, which is located on the main street leading from town to the new municipal dock. What the four simple rooms lack in amenities, they make up for in character, thanks to the friendly, one-of-a-kind Plaucio, who is happy to sit and chat about anything. He has decorated the rooms and grounds with paintings and knick-knacks, and the hospedaje is friendlier than it looks from the road.

There is a flat space out back where he'll let you pitch a tent (negotiate a price) if you have one with you. There's a small kitchen and a sink and clothesline for doing your own laundry. It's rustic and "different" and most people will either love it or hate it. The rooms have a fan and electric shower, but no air conditioning. Look for the sign on the road between the new dock and the town, or ask anyone—everyone knows Plaucio. Updated: July 24, 2013.

Hostal Villamil

(ROOMS: $15 per person) Hostal Villamil is a tiny hotel almost lost on a side street, but it's worth checking out if you're on a budget. It's located next to the larger George's Corner Inn. The seven rooms face out onto a tiny courtyard. Like most places in town, it's family run. It's clean, neat and bright and the location isn't too

bad. Some of the rooms have air conditioning. Rooms are all doubles and triples. 16 Marzo y los Flamencos. Tel: 593-5-252-9180/186/9-121-0686, E-mail: hostalvillamil@hotmail.es. Updated: Nov. 24, 2012.

Brisas del Mar

(ROOMS: $15-20/person) Brisas del Mar is a typical Isabela Hotel, insomuch as it's a concrete bunker in someone's backyard. That being said, it's not too bad. An effort has been made to make the rooms as attractive as possible, the management lady who lives there is friendly and the prices are reasonable for what you get. There are two parts to the hotel, an older part in front and a newer sort of tower in back. The newer rooms are nicer, have air conditioning and cost an extra $10. The older rooms are smaller and a little grim, and the façade of the hotel could use some work (I thought the hotel was not in service until I went around back). Some of the rooms can sleep up to five people. Try to get a discount if you're with a group. There is a large patio with hammocks, but you'll probably prefer to hang out at one of the bars on the beach. It's only a block or so from both the beach and the main park. Conocarpus and Escalecia, Barrio Central. Tel: 05-269-1511 / 08-697-4657. Updated: July 24, 2013.

Caleta Iguana (Casa Rosada)

(ROOMS: $15 per person) An endearing little hostal run by a cast of characters right out of a sitcom, Pink Iguana is not to be confused with the Iguana Crossing Hotel down the street. The two are as absolutely unalike as it is possible for two hotels to get. Pink Iguana is a laid-back place popular with backpackers, surfers and dudes. It's right on the beach and there are plenty of hammocks and benches strewn around for folks to make themselves at home.

There are some board games and puzzles inside for those so inclined. Prices are as low as you can get, and the place fills up fast. It is by far the least expensive place on the beach. The area to one side serves as the bar as well, and the happy hour is worth a visit even if you're not staying there.

The hostel gets its name from the hundreds of marine iguanas that live on the premises, climbing up its fluorescent pink walls to get some sun. Ask the owner to tell you the story of "Gringo Juan" if you can. The hostal is also known to locals as the "Pink

House" (la Casa Rosada). Tel: 593-5-252-9336, E-mail: info@caletaiguana.com. Updated: April 2, 2013.

George's Corner Inn/Rincón de George

(ROOMS: $20 per person) Yet another half-assed family affair with blocky rooms, George's Corner Inn is located across from the municipal buildings and central park. On my visit, the owner passed on answering my questions to run off and play soccer. I think that's all you need to know about the level of professionalism you can expect. There is no reception area for the place, either. However, there is a "boutique" located on the ground floor instead. The rooms aren't too bad and the bathrooms are relatively clean and nice, and if you run out of other options you might consider this one as your best bet. Just don't go by if there is a soccer game going on somewhere. Services include air conditioning, fridge and TV. 16 Marzo, across from the municipal buildings and the park. Tel: 593-5-252-9405. Updated: July 24, 2013.

San Vicente ♪

(ROOMS: $20-25/person) For a tourist class hotel on Isla Isabela, San Vicente does a pretty good job. Picnic tables and hammocks line the courtyard and a raised, open-air dining room serves both breakfast and dinner to guests. Single and double rooms come with air conditioning and private bathrooms. Singles go for $25 a night with breakfast included; doubles and triples are $20 per person. San Vicente also organizes daily horseback riding tours to the Sierra Negra Volcano as well as tours of the bay. Service here is very professional, a welcome break from the rest of Puerto Villamil. Cormorant and Escalecias. Tel: 593-5-252-9439, E-mail: ventas@hotelsanvicentegalapagos.com. URL: www.hotelsanvicentegalapagos.com, www.isabelagalapagos.com.ec.

MID-RANGE

Hotel La Laguna

(ROOMS: $60-168) One of the newer and spiffier places in town is La Laguna, which offers a view of one of the salt lagoons instead

The Electric Shower

The hotel advertises "hot water," but you're surprised to find only cold coming out of the bathroom sink. You look in the shower and see...something a little scary.

The use of the "ducha eléctrica" or "electric shower" is common in Galápagos, particularly on San Cristóbal and Isabela Islands. An electric shower is a bulbous attachment where the showerhead should be, which is connected via electric cables to the room's power grid. It looks like (and it is) a cross between a toaster and a showerhead. For those of us who have been taught that electricity and water don't mix, it looks lethal.

Hot shower or killing machine? You decide

How does it work? When you turn on the water, it comes through the shower head, automatically turning it on. There is a heating element inside, and the water warms up

as it runs over it and down into the shower. Older ones had to be switched on manually, and you had to be careful to turn them on and off while the water was already running or the heating element would burn itself out extremely quickly (none of the new ones are like that, so don't worry).

Because the water cools the heating element, using an electric shower is an exercise in finesse. If you want hot water, turn the pressure lower. If you want it cooler, turn the water up. You can basically choose between a cold shower with good pressure, a lukewarm shower with so-so pressure, or an impractical trickle of very hot water.

Is it as deadly as it looks? Not really. I've used them all over the world and I've only been zapped two or three times. It's not something I'm looking forward to repeating soon, but it's far from lethal. Some people report them shooting off sparks and even catching on fire from time to time.

Want to avoid them? All of the nicer hotels in Galápagos use gas heaters and you don't need to worry. If you're staying at the cheaper places, simply ask "Ducha eléctrica o calefón?" or "Electric shower or gas heater?"

of the ocean. The rooms are clean and neat, and offer just about everything a traveler could want, such as hot water, private bathrooms, air conditioning, cable TV, etc. It's operated by the same people who run the efficient Hotel San Vicente, so you can be sure of professional service. The best part is the airy terrace restaurant. La Laguna can help you arrange island tours and trips on Isabela and also help you get there and back from Puerto Ayora. All in all, a good choice in the mid-budget range. Services include WiFi, air conditioning, cable TV, tour desk, restaurant, bar, hot water, private baths, Jacuzzi and airport pick-up. Tel: 593-2-290-8725/5-252-9140/9-274-7880, E-mail: hotelsanvicentegalapagos@hotmail.com, URL: www.accommodationgalapagosisabela.com, www.sanvicentegalapagos.com.

La Casa de Marita !

(ROOMS: $45-180) Back in the day, the Casa de Marita was just about the only place you could stay in tiny Puerto Villamil. Marita and her family had a head start on other lodging options in town, and they have made good use of it. What was once a little guesthouse has evolved into a classy, well-run beachfront hotel. If you were there years ago, you may not recognize it. It's gone upscale, with nice rooms, a fancy restaurant and prices to match. It's well-located on the beach and the rooms are clean, airy and nice. The suites all face the ocean. It's best for middle or high-end travelers who want to spend a few days on Isabela and who want to save some money by avoiding the much more expensive Iguana Crossing and Red Mangrove Hotels. The staff there will help you book trips while on Isabela. Even if you're not staying there, the hotel restaurant is very good, with locally produced food. The hotel includes a restaurant, bar, laundry and room service, private bathrooms, hot water, air conditioning, minibars, hair dryers, telephones and WiFi. Tel: 593-5-252-9301, E-Mail: info@casamaritagalapagos.com, URL: www.galapagosisabela.com. Updated: July 24, 2013.

Hotel Albemarle

(ROOMS: $122-305) Location is everything, and Hotel Albemarle has the best location of any hotel on Isabela Island. It's right between the beach and the main park, where all the action is (or whatever action tiny Puerto Villamil has to offer, anyway). It has an impressive façade, and the interior is stately, if a little small and oddly structured. Check out the ocean view from the roof deck. Prices

for the rooms vary depending on whether they face the ocean or not. The ground floor restaurant has good food and service. There is a small swimming pool near the restaurant. Like most upscale hotels on Isabela, Albemarle can help set up tours and transportation. The Hotel Albemarle (and the restaurant) is one of the only places in town that will take credit cards, an important thing to remember if you forgot to bring cash with you. Services include hot water, air conditioning, private baths, restaurant, cable TV, phones in the rooms, safes, WiFi, travel info desk, pool and Jacuzzi. Tel: 593-5-252-9489, E-mail: info@hotelalbemarle.com, URL: www.hotelalbemarle.com. Updated: July 24, 2013.

Hotel Sol Isabela

(ROOMS: $70) A friendly, airy, whitewashed beach hotel with a good location, Sol Isabela is a good choice in the middle price range, especially as it's flanked by the much more expensive Red Mangrove and Casa de Marita. It's located a half-block from the old pier, so it has good access to town. Of the 11 rooms, eight somehow face the ocean and three do not. Make sure you know which you are getting. There are some hammocks hung around for excellent lounging opportunities. Sol Isabela does not have a restaurant, but it's right next to places that do. The website is a little wonky. Services include air conditioning, hot water, kitchen, fridge and bottled water. URL: www.hotelsolisabela.ec, Tel: 593-5-252-9183, E-mail: info@hotelsolisabela.ec. Updated: July 24, 2013.

The Wooden House (La Casa de Palo) !

(ROOMS: $70) The Wooden House is a small but nice-looking hotel on the outskirts of Puerto Villamil on the way to the new municipal dock. As of recently it is under new, more professional management who have made a lot of positive changes to the place. As you might guess from the name, it's made of volcanic stone and attractively painted and stained wood. It has a sort of rustic yet comfortable feel and there is a nice second floor lounge for hanging out.

There is a small but inviting pool. Try to get a room on the second floor, as they're brighter. It's on the main drag outside of town on the way to the municipal dock. Tel: Quito 593-2-250-3740, Isabela 593-5-252-9235/9-949-2624, E-mail: info@woodenhouse.com, info@scubagalapagos.com, URL: http://www.thewoodenhouse.com.ec/

HIGH-END

Red Mangrove Isabela Lodge

(ROOMS: $200) The original Red Mangrove Hotel is in Puerto Ayora, but in recent years they have opened "branches" on Isabela and Floreana and now offer island-hopping tours. The Red Mangrove Hotels are all professional and offer high-quality facilities and service...at a corresponding price, of course. The Isabela branch is no different. The rooms are spacious with two queen size beds in each one. The rooms supposedly all face the beach, although some may actually open out onto mangroves. The Red Mangrove can help you book tours. In fact, if you're staying here you're probably booked through Red Mangrove and staying with them throughout your Galápagos trip. The Red Mangrove also features one of the better restaurants on Isabela. Prices are not listed here. Depending on the package you get and how many Red Mangrove hotels you're staying at on the various islands, the cost will vary. It is possible to book this hotel directly without staying at other Red Mangrove Hotels or taking tours with them. Check prices, but it's around the $200 per night range. Walk-ins may be treated rudely. Av. Conocarpus on the beach. Tel: 593-5-301 7069, URL: www. redmangrove.com/lodging/isabela.html. Updated: July 24, 2013.

Iguana Crossing Hotel

(ROOMS: $200-400) Located at the southern edge of town where the National Park starts, the Iguana Crossing hotel has enviable beach access in addition to good views of the ocean and Sierra Negra Volcano. Modern, clean and cool, the rooms at Iguana Crossing benefit from central air conditioning, which is a big bonus in Puerto Villamil, which can get quite toasty. The Iguana Crossing Hotel is expensive by Ecuadorian standards, and will appeal to luxury travelers who want to spend a couple of days in Galápagos after a cruise, or to those who wish to go island hopping in style. The hotel can arrange for guides to take visitors on day trips to official sightseeing spots on Isabela Island or other western Galápagos Islands. For island hoppers, Iguana Crossing is affiliated with the upscale Casa Opuntia Hotel on San Cristóbal and the Angermeyer Waterfront Inn in Puerto Ayora. Package deals to visit all three are available through their website or via phone. Av. Antonio Gil, on the road to the tortoise breeding center. Tel: 593-05-252-9485 / 09-521-0279, E-mail: info@iguanacrossing.com.ec, URL: www.iguanacrossing.com.ec.

Puerto Villamil Restaurants

Puerto Villamil has a handful of look-alike restaurants, all serving seafood and simple plates. If you want something fancy, you'll have to head to one of the upscale hotels like the Iguana Crossing or Red Mangrove and eat there.

But why would you? You're in a remote fishing village, after all. Head down to one of the ramshackle places on the waterfront around the time the locals like to dine (they eat around 8 or 9 p.m.), have a seat and order up a plate of the fish of the day. There isn't really such a thing as "regional food" on Isabela, so there's nothing you must try, just order what looks good. Meals are surprisingly expensive (around $10-12 for an entree off the menu at one of the beach places), but if you go with the lunch or dinner of the day (just ask what they have) it will usually be much cheaper.

Cesar's

(ENTREES: $6-12) Cesar's is one of four or five look-alike restaurants on the main drag across from the park. It's popular with locals and gringos alike for the good, simple seafood dishes. They have a decent menu to choose from, including chicken, fish, shrimp, etc. Ask for whatever fish they caught that day if you're going for the seafood. Updated: Aug 15, 2012.

Aloha Betsy

(ENTREES: $6-22) Located just off the main park, Aloha Betsy features typical beach-side fare—plenty of seafood with rice and plantains. It's family run and has a laid-back atmosphere very typical of Puerto Villamil. The $4 set lunches are a good deal. They also have a good selection of juices. Located on Antonio Gil across from the Park Office. Updated: Aug 15, 2012.

Bar de Beto

Beto's beach bar is a far cry from the overly commercial Puerto Ayora. Here, the beach is the bar. Wooden tables set in the sand are warmed nightly by a log-fed bonfire. Cocktails are pricey, but no more so than in any other part of the Galápagos. Four dollars will buy you a caipirinha, cuba libre or gin and tonic. The décor and ambience is great, but with one caveat, the music is similar to a Starbucks' playlist. Norah Jones, Jack Johnson and Joan Osbourne played back to back. On La Playa Grande next to El Cormorán Cabins. Tel: 593-5-252-9015. Updated: Aug 15, 2012

Galápagos Cruises and Land-Based Tours

Cruise Tours

The most popular way to see the Galapagos islands is by cruise ship. These ships become the visitors' homes for the duration of their tour, and all activities (eating, sleeping, relaxing, partying, etc.) take place onboard. Due to the increasing popularity of the Galápagos, some 75 tourist vessels are now available for cruises, ranging from small but charming sailboats, to elegant, custom-designed motor yachts and luxurious, mid-sized cruise ships. Most, but not all, of them are listed here: this is due to some ships being in and out of service recently.

ITINERARIES

Because park rules limit the number of ships visiting each island, each cruise carries a fixed trip length and itinerary. Voyages vary in length from four to fifteen days, although currently most cruises are excursions lasting four to eight days, counting the days you arrive and depart at the airport.

Ship tours combine land and marine visits on the islands. Tourists usually visit two different land sites and one or two snorkeling sites on each full day of the tour. Usually, guests staying a full week get to spend some time in the highlands of Santa Cruz or the visitor center on San Cristóbal while the guides pick up new passengers and drop off those who are departing.

You can get a taste of the Galápagos in four days, but since each island has its own unique characteristics, you will see a broader variety of plants and animals with each additional day's visit. Besides, since the first and last days of the tour include a morning flight, a four-day tour yields only two full days and two half-days in the islands. Because of travel time required on each end of the trip, a longer trip is recommended.

In 2011, many ships switched to a 15-day cycle, divided into three crusies of six, six and five days. Basically, this change was made to reduce wear and tear on major visitor sites. That's great for the boobies, but not for the tourists, who can no longer see all the major islands in one week. Generally, the three tours are divided into Western Islands (Isabela and Fernandina), Eastern and Southern Islands (Española, San Cristobal and Floreana) and Central and Northern Islands (Santa Cruz, Genovesa and Santiago).

Each of these tours has its highlights, but unfortunately if you want to see all of Galápagos you'll need to spend two weeks on board!

La Pinta

Checking the ship's itinerary should definitely be an important part of your booking process. Itineraries change frequently and are partially controlled by the park service, so make sure you're looking at information that is up-to-date.

See this book's section on visitor sites to help you make up your mind. For instance, those interested in birds will want to prioritize ships that visit Española to see the Waved Albatross and Genovesa to see Red-Footed Boobys.

Those who want to snorkel with sea lions will want cruises that stop at the Devil's Crown (Floreana) or Isla Lobos (San Cristóbal). Between the visitor sites and the itineraries, you should be able to quickly pick a good cruise for what you want to see and do.

Updated: May 7, 2013

CRUISES

GUIDES

Each boat is required to have one or more naturalist guides who is in charge of providing daily island briefings, natural history information on flora and fauna of the islands, and suggestions for island conservation. Each guide is responsible for up to 16 passengers and no one is allowed to go onto the islands without a guide. There are over 200 certified naturalist guides in the Galápagos (not all work concurrently), who are qualified with a level I, II, or III according to their educational background.

Guides can have a profound effect on your Galápagos Experience

Generally speaking, level I guides have their high school diploma; level II guides have a bachelor's degree and some foreign language training; and level III guides have an advanced degree or specific training in the biological sciences and fluency in a foreign language. Lamentably, these are fairly arbitrary designations that do not take into account years of experience in Galápagos, naturalist behavior or group facilitation style.

Guides can make or break a tour, so it is prudent to ask for additional recommendations and/or qualifications that clarify the ranking of the guide assigned to your cruise. Unfortunately, since most guides are hired on a tour-to-tour basis (some have semi-permanent placements on boats), visitors have very little control over guide selection.

CREW

Galápagos cruisers are crewed almost exclusively by Ecuadorians, most of them from the Galápagos. There will be captains, mates, cooks, panga drivers and in some cases engineers and even doctors. Most of the time, the crews are very friendly and professional, but there are a few bad eggs. Some visitors have reported sexual harassment and petty theft. The higher the cruise class you choose, the less likely it is that you'll have a bad experience.

Most crew members only speak Spanish, but they're usually able to communicate with just about anyone. In general, ships have one crew member for every two or three passengers. Remember to tip them if they provide good service!

Galápagos Cruises: What's Included?

A Galápagos cruise is an expensive proposition, usually costing at least around $2,000-$3,000 for a full week. Unless your name is Bill Gates, that's a lot of scratch! Almost everything is included in the price...almost. Here's what's usually included and not. Check with individual cruises for details.

USUALLY INCLUDED:

Cabins
All food
Transportation while in the islands
Visitor sites
Admission prices
Occasional special cocktails
Services of guides
Fuel surcharges
Basic medicines, such as seasickness tablets
Guide

USUALLY NOT INCLUDED:

Galápagos park fees
Tips for guides and crew
Drinks other than water

SOMETIMES INCLUDED:

Airfare to and from Galápagos

Choosing a Galápagos Cruise

The things to consider when selecting a cruise are your expectations for price, boat quality, trip length and itineraries. In the Galápagos, the adage "you get what you pay for" is most definitely true.

Because new tourist boats occasionally arrive in the Galápagos, antiquated boats stop running tours, and Galápagos boats are periodically renovated or rebuilt, the class system is dynamic. Tourist boats can move up, down, or straddle the line between two categories in the class hierarchy according to specifications set in a particular period of time.

CRUISES

SHIP CATEGORIES

The tourist vessels in the Galápagos Islands are regularly inspected and categorized according to a set of fixed standards, including facilities, amenities, construction, maintenance and safety.

V!VA Travel Guides divides Galápagos ships into six categories: cruise ships, luxury ships, first class, mid-range, budget and diving ships. This is to help you decide which category of ship best suits you.

LARGE CRUISE SHIPS

There are a handful of large cruise ships in Galápagos, each carrying between 48 and 100 passengers. These ships are known for great stability and service, comfortable accommodations and superior food (lunch buffet? Woo-hoo!). Because they are larger than the others, they have ample public areas like bars and sun decks.

The cruise ships are fairly expensive, matching prices with first-class and luxury-class ships, but their facilities are comparable. They all have air conditioning, ocean-view cabins, gift shops and other luxurious facilities.

Cruise ships are best for those travelers who tend to get seasick, as there is considerably less motion as they cruise around the islands. They often have doctors on board, so they are a good choice for elderly or unwell travelers. They are also best for meeting people: obviously, if there are 90 passengers on your ship, you're bound to make some new friends!

Typical cruise ship rates run about $500-$900 per person per day, depending on season, what sort of room you want, etc. An eight-day cruise can cost $4000-$7000/person. Prices vary greatly among the big cruisers: La Pinta and the Eclipse are significantly more expensive than some of the others.

LUXURY YACHTS

Luxury yachts are the most expensive, since they have the most lavish accommodations, the most professional crews, the highest quality food, and the most in-demand naturalist guides. Yachts receiving this designation have air conditioning, hot water, ocean-view cabins with private facilities, and spacious social areas (dining room, living room, sun decks).

Eight-day luxury cruise tours generally cost between $4,000 and $7,000, or around $600 to $900 per day. Four- and five-day

tours aboard the luxury yachts are not as common, but they do exist.

The newest ships in Galápagos usually fall into this category. Many of the best luxury yachts are catamarans, which makes them more spacious and almost as stable as the cruise ships.

The luxury class is best for those travelers for whom money is not an object. If you want the best there is and are willing to pay, these are the ships for you. A great, memorable experience is practically guaranteed.

FIRST-CLASS

First class cruise yachts have spacious, comfortable and handsome accommodations, very experienced crews, gourmet food and some of the most knowledgeable naturalist guides. Yachts in this category also have air conditioning, hot water, ocean-view cabins with private facilities, and spacious social areas. Although first-class yachts have unique, distinctive features that contribute to an extra-pleasurable experience, they lack the extravagant perks that would catapult them into the luxury class. These boats can range in size, but most are well-designed, stable and fast.

Prices for eight-day tours aboard these yachts range from $2,900 to $4,300, or about $350 to $550 per day. Four- and five-day tours are more common on first-class cruise boats, and they range in price from around $1,600 to $2,200 for four days or $2,000 to $2,800 for five days (all prices per person). Again, these are cruise prices only and do not include airfare, national park fees or beverages.

First-class ships are best for those who want to splurge a little bit on a good experience but who don't want to break the bank. The crew and staff will be very professional and the guides very good.

MID-RANGE

Boats in the mid-range category tend to be slightly smaller, less private and less fancy. Yachts receiving a mid-range designation have air conditioning and hot water (although it may not be fully functional), double cabins with private facilities that may be below deck or with access to the outside, and moderately spacious social areas. These boats have good quality food and a professional crew. Occasionally ships in the mid-range category will save money by hiring guides with less experience or questionable language skills.

A good example of a mid-range ship might be a past-its-prime yacht with a professional crew that tries hard to keep it shipshape and make the passengers happy.

Prices range from $2,300 to $3,500 for an eight-day tour, or $300 to $450 daily. Four-day tours cost about $1,300 to $1,800. Five-day tours cost about $1,800 to $2,200 or so. Last-minute cruises on these yachts are common.

Mid-range ships are best for those with just enough money to climb out of the murky waters of the budget category. If you can spare an extra couple hundred bucks to take a mid-range cruise instead of a budget-level one, it will be money well spent.

BUDGET

Budget-class ships are the least expensive, and as such, offer the lowest level of service. Conditions can be cramped, uncomfortable and primitive. These yachts often do not have air conditioning or hot water (or any water at all); double, triple, or quad cabins with private or shared facilities; and small social areas. The food, crew, naturalist guide and itinerary are all decent but pale in comparison to the higher category yachts.

Wet landing: keep your camera dry!

These yachts offer budget travelers and last-minute shoppers (these boats often have availability) an opportunity to experience the wonder of Galápagos by ship, but unless you have a thriving spirit of adventure and zero claustrophobia, it is worth spending a few hundred extra dollars to travel comfortably.

Economy class boat tours cost between $1,800 and $2,500 for eight days, or $225 to $300 per day. Four-day tours cost around $900 to $1,300, and five-day tours are about

$1,150 to $1,500. Shorter itineraries are almost always offered in this class (and may just coincide with the maximum length of time you can tolerate the sub-par conditions!).

Horror stories on budget-class ships are not uncommon. Visitors who arrive to find that their ship has been overbooked and they have been placed on another one (with no say in the matter and no refund if the second ship is worse than the original), defective air conditioning that causes passengers to sleep on the deck, or snorkeling equipment that is unacceptable are some of the usual complaints. Breakdowns, bedbugs and cabins that reek of diesel are the norm on the less scrupulous budget ships.

If you do have a problem aboard a budget-class cruise, it is nearly guaranteed that the management will completely ignore any complaints or demands that you make.

The crew and captain of the ship will usually be fair, but the guide may not speak English or other languages besides Spanish. The bottom-of-the-barrel guides find work on budget ships: you may even find guides who have been blackballed from superior ships for things such as sexual harassment of guests, gross incompetence or drunkenness. Petty theft is common, so lock up your valuables as best you can.

The worst-case scenarios described above may not apply: hundreds of visitors annually have good experiences aboard these ships.

In recent years, complaints about the budget ships seem to be decreasing, possibly because some of the worst offenders have gone out of business (or sank, to tell the truth).

Budget-class ships are best for backpackers and those who wish to see the Galápagos for the lowest possible price.

DIVING SHIPS

Serious divers will want to consider a live-aboard cruise. There are a select few ships in the Galápagos which offer live-aboard diving trips. They're usually quite comfortable and have top-notch gear and guides.

Most of the dive ships correspond in price and service to first-class land tour yachts. All of them will have gear for rent and skilled divemasters with years of experience. Prices vary, but are comparable to first-class cruises.

CRUISES

The diving in Galápagos is unforgettable, and these live-aboards offer the chance to head out to the remote islands of Darwin and Wolf, where seeing Whale Sharks, Hammerheads, Manta Rays and other spectacular marine life is commonplace.

Note that these dive ships are not allowed to visit traditional landing sites, so guests will not get to see tortoises, land iguanas, etc.

Where to Book Your Galápagos Cruise

FROM ABROAD

Most visitors arrange their tours before arriving to the islands. Since the Galápagos are becoming ever-more popular and high-season tours sometimes fill up over a year in advance, arranging your tour early is often the only guarantee that you will get what you want. You can do this through a travel agency in your home country, but understand that while the process may be more efficient, you will pay more (commission cost, package fees, national taxes, etc.) and have fewer options (only those ships partnered with your home agency—usually the top-end ones).

You can also contact the boats directly, via the internet: pick a ship you're interested in by searching our V!VA Travel Guides database, and go through the official website for the tour company that owns or operates the ship.

ON THE MAINLAND

You can arrange tours (cruises and day tours) in Guayaquil or Quito, either through the ships' city offices or through any number of travel agencies. During the low season, you may find a well-priced tour with openings leaving in only a few days, but expect to have to wait a month or more for availability during the high season.

ON THE ISLANDS

During the low season, some visitors opt to organize their Galápagos tour from Puerto Ayora or Puerto Baquerizo Moreno. Tour agencies based in the islands will often offer last-minute deals on cruises, which can save you up to 50%.

If you have substantial travel time and a limited budget, you may save some money by flying to the islands, staying in an inexpensive hotel and trolling the tour agencies in town.

The best-case scenario: you fly to Puerto Ayora and immediately find a first-class ship leaving the next day with an opening, and you pay a fraction of what you would have had you booked ahead. Worst-case scenario: you spend the week looking for a ship with an opening and find nothing, so you do day trips and some SCUBA diving. Still not too bad! Finding boats in the high season (June-August and December) is exponentially more difficult.

Important Note: the worst ships in the islands often are not full, so a common "scam" on the part of the operators is to send a cheery fellow to the airport who catches people off the plane, saying he has a first-class or mid-range ship with a couple of sudden vacancies, and he'll sell the spots half-off or more. It's not exactly illegal, but if you take him up on his offer, you may find yourself on an unsafe or filthy ship.

Only book through reputable agencies with an actual office, or at the very least demand to see the ship before making up your mind. If he makes an excuse, he's probably playing you.

FINDING LAST-MINUTE DEALS

If you can book a last-minute tour, you can often save quite a bit of money, even hundreds of dollars.

If you have a few extra travel days in one of the big cities or the islands, go to a number of different agencies to inquire about last-minute tour availability and prices. You may happen upon a cancellation or a tour looking to fill spaces on departures leaving right away that may offer you a last-minute bargain (especially in the low season).

If you're really lucky, you may find a travel agent who works directly with boat owners and offers you the at-cost (no commission) tour price. Hanging around in Quito and working the last-minute tour agencies can cut as much as $500 off your trip (but there is no guarantee you will get a trip at all!).

Special Galápagos Cruises

Tour companies—in conjunction with private agencies—sometimes offer special tours for families, SCUBA divers, photographers, students, alumni groups and scientists, to name a few. Most of the time, these tours are coordinated by private organizations, which charter a boat

2>

2>

to meet their special needs, and thus are not available to individual tourists. This mostly applies to photographic, student or research expeditions.

Family tours are not uncommon in the Galápagos. A few boats—especially the bigger cruise ships—will have special family promotions in order to attract (and concentrate) younger visitors. Although the Galápagos vacation is more meaningful for visitors who can understand the evolutionary dynamics of island biogeography, students of all ages, young and old, can learn important lessons from their Galápagos tour. If you want to bring young children, it is worth your while to look for a family tour: other families will be present with playmates for your children, and your guides will have some experience with younger visitors.

If you have a group of sixteen passengers, it's possible to charter the ships. Contact the ships directly for details. Remember that the itinerary is set by the park and in most cases out of the hands of the ship operators.

Galápagos Islands Cruisers

The following is a fairly comprehensive list of the ships that currently offer cruise tours in the Galápagos Islands. They are organized according to class: cruise, luxury, first class, mid-range, budget and diving. Ships may change their categorization as they improve (or diminish) the quality of services provided.

Please visit the V!VA Travel Guides website-after your tour and be sure to rate your boat and add comments so our reviews can stay as accurate and up-to-date as possible!

Galápagos Cruise Ships

- Eclipse
- Silver Galapagos
- Galápagos Legend
- Isabela II
- National Geographic Islander
- National Geographic Endeavor
- La Pinta
- Santa Cruz
- Xpedition

Eclipse

If it's space you're looking for, the Eclipse is your ship. This luxury ship claims to be the most uncrowded vessel of its size in the Galápagos. The Eclipse has a capacity for 48 passengers, housed in four suites, eight staterooms, 13 doubles and two singles.

All rooms are indeed very large and have a private bathroom with hot shower and are fully air-conditioned. Dining Eclipse-style is alfresco, with the dining area located around the 20-foot (six-meter) pool.

Other amenities include a library/video room, an on-board shop and an observation deck. Tours of the islands are broken down into groups of no more than 12, divided between the naturalists on-board. The Eclipse offers a variety of tours from four to eight days. The Eclipse offers special family cruises in March, April, July, August and December where there are games and special activities for kids. URL: www.eclipse.com.ec.
Updated: May 14, 2013.

Galapagos Silver

Formerly named the Galápagos Explorer II, Galapagos Silver is a 100-passenger cruise ship with 50 ultra-elegant suites, each with television, DVD, mini-bar, and satellite communication, in addition to the standard private facilities, hot water and air conditioning. It is one of the fastest, most modern and most luxurious tourist vessels in the Galápagos, blending comfort, adventure and environmental preservation. Social areas—including sun decks, a bar and lounge, and a library—offer the amenities of a world class cruise liner. The Explorer II was purchased in 2012 by the prestigious international cruise company Silversea Expeditions, which immediately refurbished, refitted and renamed it. They also set about poaching the best guides from other cruise ships, showing that they're serious about providing a good experience for their guests. URL: http://www.silversea.com/expeditions/silver-galapagos/
Updated: May 3, 2013.

Galápagos Legend

The 90-passenger expedition ship, Galápagos Legend, is a well-regarded cruise ship known for good service, good food and well-maintained facilities. There is a kids' room, which should come in handy for families. Deluxe amenities—including numerous sun terraces, a small swimming pool, an outdoor bar area, mini-cinema, music lounge, and a well-stocked library—may make you want to stay onboard and forget about blue-footed boobies and hammerhead sharks. URL: www.kleintours.com/en/Galápagos-legend.html.
Updated: May 10, 2013.

Isabela II

The 40-guest Isabela II, with 20 spacious cabins with private bathrooms, hot water and air conditioning, offers an elegant yet relaxed atmosphere for experiencing the full adventure of the Galápagos. It has three public decks, stocked with a bar-salon, dining room, sun deck and jacuzzi. It also has a complete reference library, with a large selection of books on Ecuador and the Galápagos, nature and conservation videos, and nightly multimedia presentations and lectures. Tours are divided into northern, southern and central islands. URL: www.metropolitan-touring.com. Updated: Nov 2, 2012.

National Geographic Islander

The Islander is a small cruise ship with capacity for 48 guests. It has a very good reputation in the islands for service, facilities and quality guides. All rooms and common areas are air conditioned, elegant and tastefully decorated. The mahogany and brass fixtures give the Islander a real classic shippy vibe. It has internet, an on-board doctor and videographer. The food is excellent: it's international with just enough Ecuadorian dishes to give you a taste of local life. Snorkeling gear is available and well-maintained. It is run by the internationally known Lindblad Expeditions in partnership with National Geographic. URL: www.expeditions.com. Updated: April 17, 2013

National Geographic Endeavor

The Endeavor, a classy veteran of cruises all over the world, has settled nicely into the blue waters of Galapagos. Run by the reputable Lindblad Expeditions in conjunction with National Geographic, good service and facities are guaranteed. A spacious, massive cruiser, the Endeavor has room for 96 guests. The extras are nice: quality snorkeling gear, a full time photographer/videographer, kayaks and a glass-bottom boat. Guides are top-notch. Often sold as part of larger combination tours to Machu Picchu and other South American highlights. URL: http://www.expeditions.com/our-fleet/endeavour. Updated: May 8, 2013.

The Pinta

The Pinta is a roomy, recently renovated cruiser with space for 48 guests in comfortable, luxurious double cabins. Owned by Metropolitan Touring, which has decades of experience in Galápagos, the Pinta features outstanding service, dedicated crew and knowledgeable guides. Its large size makes it stable, so it's good for those who are prone to seasickness. The facilities are top-notch and include a TV room, bar/salon, briefing room, restaurant, deck and individual air conditioning for rooms. The Pinta also prides itself on being a good cruise for families and kids, in part because some of their cabins inter-connect, a rarity on Galápagos ships. Check the itineraries carefully to make sure the ship visits the places you want to see. URL: www.yachtlapinta.com. Updated: May 2, 2013

The Santa Cruz

The Santa Cruz, a 90-passenger cruise ship, is one of the only large vessels exclusively designed for exploring the Galápagos. The 47 cabins are well-maintained and relatively spacious, each equipped with private facilities, hot water and air conditioning. Comfort is a priority on the Santa Cruz, which has three decks filled with lounge chairs, a solarium, Jacuzzi, reading room, and well-stocked bar and lounge.

The Captain and officers of the Santa Cruz

The Santa Cruz has gained worldwide recognition for its excellent standards, including superb service, expert crew, the most knowledgeable multilingual naturalist guides and menus that feature the very best Ecuadorian and international cuisine. Quality snorkeling equipment is provided free of charge. URL: www.metropolitan-touring.com. Updated: May 4, 2013

Celebrity Xpedition

A large cruiser with capacity for 92 guests, the Xpedition is roomy, classy and elegant. It's what you'd expect from a cruise ship: spacious with nice social areas and comfortable rooms. The crew and guides are first-rate. It has a hot tub, sauna and other

CRUISES

amenities that simply won't fit on smaller vessels. Cabins are strategically placed to minimize rocking and seasickness. It offers room service, something you see on very few ships in the Galápagos. A good fit for those who want a larger ship with a touch of luxury. One bonus: access to the pangas from the ship is better than on most of the other large ships, so elderly or less-mobile passengers may prefer the Xpedition. Their website is useful but a little confusing. URL: http://galapagosxpedition.co.uk/ Updated: May 8, 2013

Luxury Class Galápagos Cruises

- Anahi
- Athala II
- Cormorant
- Evolution
- Grace
- Ocean Spray

Anahi
The Anahi is a classy catamaran with luxurious cabins and ample public areas. It has a Jacuzzi, bar area, sundeck, lounge, restaurant, etc. Staff to guest ratio is high, assuring a comfortable trip. The Anahi is one of the more affordable catamarans in its class, but does not skimp on comfort or service.

The Athala II

It's operated by Andando Tours, a reputable company owned by the Angermeyer family, pioneers in Galapagos. URL: http://www.visitgalapagos.travel/index.php/anahi-galapagos-cruise. Updated: May 10, 2013.

The Athala II
The Athala II is a spiffy new catamaran that has been drawing rave reviews from visitors. As a recently built catamaran, it is very spacious for a 16-passenger vessel and quite stable. The Athala is somehow roomy without losing the intimacy of a smaller boat: it's a great choice for someone who wants just the right amount of space vis-à-vis the

other passengers and crew. It features eight tastefully furnished double cabins, each with private bath, air conditioning, hot water and closet. The ship itself has a bar area, Jacuzzi, library, TV/DVD, and sunny observation deck in addition to the dining area. The food is outstanding and the staff and guides are very competent and professional. The Athala II tends to book up early, so make your plans in advance. URL: http://www.sanctuaryretreats.com/galapagos-cruises-athala-ii Updated: May 12, 2013

Cormorant
The Cormorant, sometimes referred to for reasons unknown as the Cormorant Evolution, is a classy catamaran which has been serving Galapagos since being built in 2011. Its prices are good for a ship in its class, so it tends to fill up. It has six spacious cabins and two luxurious suites, each with a private balcony. It's very well designed, with ample space in public and private areas. It's operated by the reputable Haugan Cruises, based in Quito. Not to be confused with the ill-fated Cormorant II, which sank in 2009. URL: http://www.haugancruises.com/cormorant-galapagos-cruise/index.html. Updated: May 9, 2013

M/V Evolution
The M/V Evolution, with a capacity for 32 passengers, has 15 total twin and double cabins and two suites, each beautifully furnished with private facilities, hot water, air conditioning and more. The Evolution caters to passengers seeking rest, relaxation and lavish accommodations, as well as families or charters. A few important extras—most notably an open-air dining area, small heated pool, multimedia room, and infirmary—set this cruise experience apart in terms of comfort. It also has ample deck space for sunbathing and a boutique for shopping. The design of the boat is reminiscent of the 1920s, but charming details and deluxe amenities provide modern-day comforts. URL: http://www.galapagosexpeditions.com/cruises/evolution-galapagos-ship.php Updated: May 13, 2013

Grace
If you like a bit of history with your ship, the Grace is for you. Originally built in 1928, the Grace has sailed for many owners under many names: she is currently named for one-time owner Princess Grace of Monaco. She even served some time in World War Two

and saw plenty of action, sinking an enemy submarine before being refitted as a hospital ship! Today, Grace is a stately yacht, known for service, good food and all of the amenities you'd expect, such as good snorkeling gear, kayaks, top-notch guides, etc. The large staterooms are quite posh if you can afford them. URL: http://www.galapagosexpeditions.com/cruises/grace-galapagos-ship.php. Updated: May 10. 2013

Ocean Spray

The Ocean Spray is one of the newest luxury catamarans in Galápagos, and as such offers top-of-the-line service and comfort. Ocean Spray makes the most of being a large catamaran: the spacious cabins each have a balcony, large windows and air conditioning. The common areas are also roomy and tastefully done. Details are always looked after: the snorkeling equipment is in good shape, there is a welcome cocktail, guests have access to airport VIP lounges, etc. The guides and crew are first-rate. Four to fifteen day itineraries include stops at visitor favorites like Punta Espinoza and Punta Suárez and memorable snorkeling spots like Vicente Roca Point. All of the major Galápagos species, including finches, giant tortoises, Flightless Cormorants and Galápagos Penguins can be seen at least once during the longer itinerary. URL: http://www.haugancruises.com/ocean-spray-galapagos-cruise/index.html Updated: May 15, 2013.

First Class Galápagos Cruises

- The Beagle
- Beluga
- Cachalote
- Coral I and Coral II
- Eric
- Flamingo I
- Galápagos Voyager
- Galaxy
- Letty
- Mary Anne
- Millenium
- Queen of Galápagos
- Sea Man II
- Tip Top II
- Tip Top III
- Tip Top IV

The Beagle

The Beagle is a 105-foot, two-masted, steel-hulled schooner/motorized sailboat with enough space to comfortably accommodate 13 passengers in its seven double cabins,

each with private bathroom, hot water and air conditioning. Snorkeling equipment is available. It's good for families or other groups and is available for charters. The crew prides itself on personal service and great food. Although it is motorized, it has a distinct sailboat vibe to it, even if it rarely sets sail. URL: http://www.thebeagle.com.ec/Beagle.htm. Updated: May 10. 2013

Beluga

The Beluga is a deluxe, 110-foot, steel-hulled motor yacht, which accommodates 16 passengers in eight double staterooms, each with private bathroom, hot water and air conditioning. It is very spacious, with lots of deck space, a sun deck, a dining room, a bar and a galley. It has twin dining rooms, each for eight passengers. It also has TV with DVD player and all the other modern amenities you'd expect. As a bonus, it's relatively fast, which will allow visitors more time visiting the islands and less time chugging from one island to another. The crew is well-trained and professional and takes very good care of their guests onboard and ashore. It's run by Enchanted Expeditions (they also operate the Cachalote), a member of Smart Voyager, the Latin American Travel Association and other certifying organizations for responsible travel. URL: http://www.enchantedexpeditions.com/english/galapagos/beluga.html. Updated: May 4, 2013

Cachalote

The ketch-rigged motor sailor Cachalote has capacity for 16 passengers in eight handsome double bunk cabins decorated in dark teakwood. Each cabin has two porthole windows, private bath, hot water and air conditioning. Other amenities include a large dining room, salon, bar and three ample wooden decks. The Cachalote was rebuilt and refurbished in 2002 to provide more space and to add modern touches to its Victorian style. Cabins are still a bit tight, but that's the norm for ships in this class. The attractive design of the Cachalote, its professional crew and excellent cuisine produces an ambience that enhances the character of the Enchanted Islands. Snorkeling equipment is available. URL: http://www.enchantedexpeditions.com/english/galapagos/cachalote.html.

Coral I and II

The Coral I and Coral II are both owned by Klein Tours: the Coral I is a larger (36 Passengers) version of the Coral II (20 passengers). Both ships are well-run and hire excellent crew and guides. The Coral I is a spacious motor yacht with standard (bunk-style), superior (twin double), and deluxe cabins, all of which have outside access, carpeted floors, handsome wooden furnishings, private bathroom, hot water and air conditioning.

The Coral II is also a three-deck ship which, like her twin yacht, provides privacy, personal attention and comfortable accommodations. Decorated in the same dark teakwood and sparkling bronze, the Coral II adds a touch of refinement to an open and spacious design, complete with ample social areas, large picture windows and an expansive observation deck. Both Coral ships pride themselves on their excellent food and service. URL: www.kleintours.com/en. Updated: Sept 18, 2012.

Eric

The Eric, in conjunction with her nearly-identical sisters, Letty and Flamingo I, was custom-designed for cruising the Galápagos archipelago. These three ships are reliable and consistent: they've been chugging around the Galapagos since 1991, leaving a trail of satisfied guests. Each of the three can accommodate 20 passengers in 10 double cabins on three decks—seven with two twin lower beds and three with one double bed—each equipped with private bathroom, hot water, air conditioning, intercom system and hair dryer. An ample dining space, a sun deck stocked with lounge chairs, and a conference area with television, DVD, stereo system, video collection and library add comfort, relaxation and modernity. Crew members provide dedicated and professional service, and naturalist guides—one per ten passengers—offer extensive and personalized information. Snorkeling equipment, sea kayaks, and beach towels are provided at no extra cost. URL: www.ecoventura.com. Updated: May 2, 2013

Flamingo I
See the Eric.

Galápagos Voyager
One huge perk of the Galápagos Voyager: all staterooms are on the upper and middle decks, which means no lower-deck rooms which are often noisy and/or smell like fuel. All rooms also have ocean view and modern conveniences like individual music

controls, in addition to private bathrooms (roomy showers!) and air conditioning. The social areas are also well-designed: there are two sun decks, a restaurant and lounge with TV/DVD. Their web site is rather quirky and not terribly informative. URL: http://www.galapagos-voyager.com/ Updated: April 29, 2013

Galaxy
The Galaxy is an attractive, single-hulled yacht well-suited for 16 passengers. It's classy, elegant and reasonably-priced for a ship in its class. The rooms are cozy but not cramped, and feature air conditioning and private baths. Social areas are ample and comfortable. The English-language part of the website is confusing and poorly-written, but clients generally have only positive things to say about the ship and her crew. The southeastern island itinerary is particularly good. URL: http://www.galapagosisland.net/cruises/galaxy-first-class/. Updated: May 7, 2013

Letty
See the Eric.

Mary Anne
The Mary Anne, a three-masted barquentine, is probably Galapagos' most easily recognizeable ship. If you want the experience of cruising the Galapagos on a genuine sailing ship, the Mary Anne is for you. It does have a motor, and usually chugs from one island to the next. It only rarely actually sets sail. Nevertheless, it does have a sort of "pirate shippy" vibe to it. Sailing vessels are notoriously cramped, so they compensate by having mostly individual cabins. It's run by the reputable Andando Tours, owned by the Angermeyer family, which has been doing tours in Galapagos as long as anyone. URL: http://www.visitgalapagos.travel/index.php/mary-anne-galapagos-cruise. Updated: May 8, 2013

Millenium
A classy and comfortable motor catamaran (making it one of the more stable cruises to ride on) with capacity for 16 passengers, the Millenium has six spacious double cabins with a private balcony view. Rooms are private with bathtub, hot water and air conditioning, and two suites also have a Jacuzzi included. Millenium also has ample social areas with views of the sea: a plush salon, communal dining room, well-stocked bar and four solaria.

Crew and staff work hard for guests, but guides have gotten mixed reviews. URL: http://www.millenniumyacht.com/ Updated: May 7, 2013

Queen of Galápagos

Queen of Galápagos is a modern, stately catamaran featuring lots of space in cabins and common areas. The rooms all have private bathroom, air conditioning and other modern amenities, including TV with DVD player. It's designed for 16 passengers in double occupancy. The Queen of Galápagos is one of the speedier ships in Galápagos: this is a good thing, as you'll spend more time snapping photos of iguanas and less time cruising from one island to another. As a catamaran, it's much more stable than the older yachts in the islands, good news for those who turn a little green while out at sea. Popular with families. URL: http://queenofgalapagos.com Updated: May 13, 2013

Sea Man II

The Sea Man II (you'll also see it listed as Seaman and Seaman Journey) is a roomy catamaran featuring nine large, beautiful and comfortable double cabins with outside views, private bathroom, cold/hot water, locker and closet, comfortable dining room, two bars and a lounge, library, full air conditioning with control in each cabin, TV, DVD, stereo, first aid, ice maker, water purifier, observation deck, and spacious sun deck with chairs for sleeping and relaxing. URL: http://www.galapagosisland.net/cruises/seaman-ii-luxury-cruise/index.html.

Tip Top II

The Tip Top II is a modern, steel-hulled motor yacht with a capacity for 16 passengers in eight double cabins—four below and four above deck—and one single cabin. Each double cabin has two twin beds, private facilities, hot water and air conditioning. It also has ample social spaces: a carpeted interior salon with fully-equipped bar, television, DVD player and full sound system, a plush dining room area, an extensive covered deck (perfect for relaxing or dancing the night away), open top-deck for star-gazing, and diving platform. Common areas are well-decorated and clean; food is well-prepared and varied; and navigational equipment is well-maintained and modern. SCUBA-diving facilities are available for two or more passengers. The Tip Top ships are operated by the locally famous Wittmer family: they give a lot back to the Galápagos community, so if that's important to you, give them a look. URL: www.rwittmer.com. Updated: Nov 1, 2012.

Tip Top III

The Tip Top III is the slightly more spacious equivalent of her sister ship, the Tip Top II. It also has capacity for 16 passengers, but in ten double cabins with two lower twin beds, private facilities, hot water and air conditioning. The Tip Top III is more modern, having been built in Guayaquil in 2001. Unusual for a small ship, different cabins have different prices: be sure to check when booking. URL: www.rwittmer.com. Updated: Nov 1, 2012.

The Humboldt Current

The incredible array of wildlife that the Galápagos is home to is undoubtedly enthralling. However, most people don't stop to think about what environmental factors make it possible for everything from sea lions and penguins to tortoises and iguanas to live in one place. The Humboldt current—unknown to most people, but hugely important to anyone who depends on the sea for their livelihood (or who lives in the sea, for that matter)—is a chief contributor to the diversity found in the Galápagos.

The Humboldt is a cold ocean current with a low salt level that flows along the west coast of South America, starting at the southern tip of Chile and going upwards past northern Peru to Ecuador. It is the dominant of five currents that converge around the Galápagos, creating a unique and varying oceanic climate. The chilly Humboldt is responsible for making the waters cold enough for sea lions, whales, penguins and other oceanic creatures that prefer a brisker environment. Aside from supporting the eclectic ecosystem of the Galápagos, the current is also the reason for the numerous of fish species off the coast of South America. When the current is occasionally disturbed by unseasonal storms, the effects can be devastating for marine life and fishermen alike.

Tip Top IV

The flagship of the Tip Top fleet, the Tip Top IV is one of the newer vessels in Galápagos, having been built in Guayaquil in 2006. It is an attractive, sleek vessel with airy common areas and spacious cabins. Naturally, the cabins and social areas are air conditioned and the ship features all other modern conveniences. Tip Top has decades of experience in Galápagos, and it moved all of its best captains, crew and guides to this ship when it launched, so you can be assured of great service and professionalism! Snorkeling gear costs extra, so pack it if you have it. URL: www.rwittmer.com.
Updated: May 10, 2013

Mid-Range Galápagos Cruises

- Aida María
- Angelito I
- Daphne
- Eden
- Estrella del Mar
- Fragata
- Galaven
- Monserrat
- San José
- Xavier III

Aida María

The 16-passenger Aida María was designed to combine style, comfort and efficiency. Eight double bunk cabins—each with outside access—are minimalist yet classy, and equipped with private bath, hot shower and air conditioning. Ample dining and social areas (most notably an expansive external sun deck) provide plenty of space for passengers to make themselves at home.

Although it has some of the problems common for ships in its class (some have complained of rooms smelling of diesel), the Aida María has a pretty good reputation. This has much to do with a hardworking crew who keep the Aida María shipshape. The price puts it right on the line between budget and mid-range. It's a good value and a smart upgrade from the cheapest ships. Contact them through their website for last-minute deals. URL: http://www.aidamariatravel.com/galapagos-cruises/aida-maria.html.
Updated: May 10, 2013.

Angelito I

The Angelito I is a comfortable, 16-passenger motor yacht with eight double bunk cabins, each with private bath, hot water, air conditioning and outside access. Four of the cabins are below decks.Frill-less yet efficient, the Angelito I has a professional crew, attentive service and excellent food. Social areas are roomy, but communal, so it provides the perfect atmosphere for groups or for making new acquaintances. Snorkeling equipment is provided free of charge. The Angelito is a very respectable, reliable and professional ship for its class. Angelito guides and chefs have gotten mixed reviews, but the crew is usually very good. Popular with German travelers, the website is also in German. URL: http://www.angelitogalapagos.com/
Updated: May 7, 2013

Daphne

The Daphne is a 16-passenger motor yacht with seven smallish but fully-equipped double-occupancy cabins and one fancy suite. Other amenities include a restaurant/bar, a small library, television and DVD, and solarium. Social areas and sun deck are surprisingly spacious given the Daphne's small size. Naturalists and crew are professional and experienced. It is one of very few Galápagos cruisers actually built in the islands.

The Daphne is certified by SmartVoyager, which recognizes contributions to the local community. May rock in rough seas. Squarely in the mid-range of ships, the Daphne is comfortable and unmemorable, which can be a very good thing, if you think about it. The web site is confusing, but should get you the information you need to know. URL: www.daphnecruises.com.
Updated: May 7, 2013.

The Daphne

CRUISES

Eden

The 16-passenger Eden is equipped with eight tight but comfortable double cabins, each with private bath, hot water and air conditioning. Her elegant interior and refined details—complemented by a library, television, DVD and full bar—provide a touch of class to enhance the cruise itinerary. An ample sun deck and accessible upper deck provide added comfort to an already luxurious trip. The Eden is relatively classy and well-appointed for a ship in its class. The dining area is particularly well-done. Snorkeling gear and wetsuits are available. URL: http://www.aidamariatravel.com/galapagos-cruises/eden-yacht.html
Updated: May 7, 2013

Estrella del Mar

The Estrella del Mar is a well-designed motor yacht with capacity for 16 passengers. Double cabins have private bathroom, hot water, air conditioning and views of the sea. Wood-paneled staterooms have twin beds instead of bunks, which means a little more elbow room. The Estrella del Mar also has a comfortable lounge and dining areas with plush booth seating. Ample sun decks are well-stocked with cushioned lounge chairs. Some of the indoor social areas are also air conditioned, a nice touch for when it gets hot. There is, of course, a TV with DVD player in one of the lounges. The Estrella del Mar has been in Galápagos for some 20 years, so it's getting a little weary, but the crew keeps it in good shape and most customer comments seem to be positive. URL: http://www.galasam.com/cruises-estrellademarI.php.
Updated: May 7, 2013

Fragata

The Fragata, a 16-passenger motor yacht with eight fully-equipped double cabins, is outfitted to provide comfortable cruising, fine dining and attentive service. Rebuilt in 2003, the Fragata combines modern style with spaciousness and comfort. It contracts experienced naturalist guides and maintains a professional crew, including talented chefs who take pride in the food. The Fragata sits on the line between mid-range and first-class: it's a good value, as the air contitioning usually works and the common areas are nice. Cabins have twin or bunk beds. URL: http://www.fragatayachtgalapagos.com/

Galaven

Galaven is a 20-passenger motor yacht featuring eleven cabins, each with private bath. The main deck cabins are a little tight, and two of them are right next to the engine room (=noisy), so avoid them if you can. Check their website for special deals and last-minute trips. Reviews of guides, service, food, etc. are almost always positive. One bonus: as a 20-passenger ship, it must have two guides, which means more quality time with your naturalist. It's pricing puts it squarely into the mid-range class. URL: http://www.galavengalapagos.com/index.html
Updated: May 8, 2013

Monserrat

The Monserrat is a 91-foot (28-m) motor yacht with capacity for 16 passengers in eight double cabins. The spacious cabins are equipped with double beds and upper berths or twin lower berths, private facilities, hot water and air conditioning. Social spaces include a comfortable lounge area with television and DVD, as well as a bar, communal dining room and sun deck. The upper deck cabins are greatly superior to the lower deck ones, so get into those if you can (it'll cost you an extra $300 but may well be worth it). The crew is attentive and professional. All in all, a solid choice in the mid-range category. URL: www.Galápagosislands.com/mid-range-cruises/monserrat/monserrat-yacht.html.
Updated: May 7, 2013

The Monserrat

San José

The San José is a large, stable, and comfortable motor yacht accommodating 16 passengers. The San José was built in Ecuador in 2003, so it's fairly modern and in good shape. The eight spacious double cabins on main and upper decks are equipped with two lower twin berths, outside access and windows on both sides of the stateroom, private facilities, hot water and climate control. Cabins are very large for a ship in its class. They're also located near the dining room (as opposed to near the engine) which makes them less noisy. Social areas are ample and comfortable. The indoor lounge has television, DVD, video collection and stereo system. The dining area has three communal tables and the covered observation deck is well-stocked with plush lounge chairs. Snorkeling equipment is available. A good bargain and a savvy choice for a ship in its class. URL: http://www.galapagosisland.net/cruises/san-jose-first-class/index.html. Updated: May 7, 2013

Xavier III/GAP IV
The Xavier III is a small ship, but it somehow seems to have a spacious deck and the cabins aren't too bad. How do they do it? Magic, maybe. It's built for 16 in eight double-occupancy cabins, each with private bath and either a porthole or window, so they all get at least a little natural light. The crew is solid (they even have formed a band and occasionally play for/with the guests) and the food is particularly good for a ship in its class. The Xavier occasionally has good last-minute deals, so ask about it if you're shopping for a good bargain and can go aboard on short notice. URL: http://www.galapagosisland.net/cruises/xavier-yacht/index.html Updated: May 7, 2013

Budget Galápagos Cruises
- Amigo I
- Darwin
- Encantada
- Floreana
- Golondrina I
- Guantanamera
- Merak
- New Flamingo
- Pelikano/GAP Adventure I
- Princess of Galápagos

Amigo I
The Amigo I is a battered, 16-passenger motor yacht with eight double cabins, each equipped with private bath and hot water. A small external sun deck provides a good place to catch some sun while cruising. The Amigo provides an adequate visitor experience for a reasonable price, offering seniors, students and groups special discounts. The Amigo has a kind of roly-poly Noah's Ark look to it

and is not great for those who get seasick in rough weather. Food is good, but portion size may leave something to be desired. Quality of guides/crew is patchy. Bugs have been reported by passengers, but most agree that the crew works hard to keep the ship clean. Air conditioning is inconsistent. All in all, the Amigo seems to get fewer complaints than the others in its class, which is probably a good thing, right? URL: http://www.galapagosisland.net/cruises/amigo-budget-class/index. Updated: June 7, 2013.

Darwin
The Darwin sits at the top of the list of budget-class ships with slightly better facilities (and corresponding slightly higher prices) than some of the others in its class. The 16-passenger motor yacht has eight spacious double cabins, each with private bath, hot water and air conditioning. It also has plenty of comfortable social areas: a plush dining room, living room area, bar and sun deck. Snorkeling equipment is also provided. The guides on board have gotten mixed reviews. The Darwin has the distinction of being one of the few ships actually built in Galápagos. A good place to look for last-minute deals if you want to save some money and avoid the bottom-of-the-barrel ships. URL: http://www.darwinyacht.com/ Updated: May 7, 2013

Encantada
The Encantada is a candy-apple red, 12-passenger, motorized sailing boat (it never sails, by the way, preferring to chug between islands with its motor). It has six double bunk cabins with private bath, a small conference room with television and DVD player, a sun deck, and an internal and an exterior dining room. Like other boats of its class, it is cramped and noisy, and the facilities on board are not always in working order (i.e. intermittent hot water). Some passengers have complained of roaches, bedbugs and cabins that reek of diesel. Decent food and cheerful crew make up for some of the afformentioned discomforts. Guides get mixed reviews (at best). Not advisable for those prone to seasickness. Generally popular with backpackers and those who wish to find the cheapest cruise they can, regardless of comfort. URL: http://www.encantadasailboat.com/. Updated: May 5, 2013

Floreana

The Floreana is a motor yacht that accommodates 16 passengers in eight double cabins containing private facilities and hot water. Amenities include comfortable bar and lounge areas equipped with television and DVD, sun deck, and indoor and outdoor dining areas. Quality snorkeling gear is available. It was formerly known as the San Juan. The Floreana, with dark wood paneling and tasteful social areas, is more attractive than most other ships in its class. It has a good reputation for helpful crews and good facilities. Guides have been described as "adequate," which is actually a ringing endorsement in this class of ship. It's a family operation: your captain may well be the owner. The Floreana is at the top-end of the price range for the budget class of ships, but it's probably money well invested to get you out of the dregs. URL: http://www.galapagosisland.net/cruises/floreana-tourist-yacht/index.html. Updated: May 8, 2013

Golondrina I

The Golondrina I is another option for visitors who do not require privacy or posh rooms. With capacity for 10 passengers in double bunk cabins with shared bathrooms, the Golondrina I provides only basic comforts and facilities. Still, it has a good reputation, based on the crew trying hard to make up for what the ship lacks in comforts. For a small yacht, it does have a sizable sun deck and a comfortable dining room. The cook specializes in Ecuadorian dishes and seafood. URL: http://www.galapagosisland.net/cruises/golondrina-tourist-yacht/index.html. Updated: May 7, 2013

Guantanamera

The Guantanamera has capacity for 16 passengers, distributed among two belowdeck matrimonial suites—with double lower and twin upper berths, two belowdeck double cabins, and four upper-deck double cabins. Each mid-sized, simple cabin is equipped with private bathroom, hot water, and oftentimes frigid air conditioning, which passengers must adapt to since they cannot control it from their staterooms. External deck space is fairly ample, with a few front-facing lounge chairs providing excellent sunbathing and dolphin-watching opportunities, and a covered conference area with tables and chairs. Unfortunately, this is the limit of the social space: the indoor lounge consists of two cushioned benches directly in front of the television/video and minimalist library facilities, while the dining/bar area includes three cramped—but plush—booths and a hallway doubling as a buffet area. Not for those with weak stomachs, the Guantanamera is somewhat top-heavy and tends to wobble in high seas. Crew members are friendly and competent. Guides get mixed reviews. URL:http://www.galapagosisland.net/cruises/guantanamera-tourist-yacht/index.html. Updated: May 7, 2013

Merak

The Merak is a small motor sailboat with limited lounging space and privacy. It has four double cabins, accommodating eight passengers, and two shared bathrooms. Social areas include a communal dining area and outdoor solarium. The Merak caters to small groups looking for the intimacy of their own sailboat at a reasonable price. Like others in its category, it is cramped, and air conditioning and hot water do not always work. There have been complaints about bugs, surly crews and clueless guides. The motor is loud and usually runs even on those extremely rare occasions when the Merak uses its sails. Although the Merak has snorkeling gear, it's not reliable, so bring your own. Brace yourself, keep your expectations low and if the trip turns into hell on Earth, remind yourself of the money you saved by booking here. URL: http://www.galapagoscruise.com.ec/merak-yacht. Updated: May 9, 2013.

New Flamingo

Look out! There are two cruise ships named Flamingo working in Galápagos, and there is quite a difference between them. The Flamingo owned by Ecoventura is a first-class luxury yacht, and not to be confused with the "New Flamingo," which is most definitely not. The 10-passenger New Flamingo offers your typical economy-class amenities: five tiny double bunk cabins, which are all below deck, a small bar and dining room, a sun deck that also serves as the upper deck (or roof) of the boat and almost no public space. Privacy is at a minimum. By the way, there's nothing "new" about it except the name: it's actually sort of old, saggy and worn-out. Passengers have reported power outages, no hot water, noisy generators, bugs and not-infrequent problems with the ship itself. (One passenger reports that a screw came loose on the rudder and the ship went in circles until the captain himself dove down to fix it!) By most reports, the crew tries hard to make up for these deficiencies. It's also priced accordingly, and is definitely among the least expensive ships to cruise the Galápagos. Caveat emptor. URL: http://www.galapagosisland.net/cruises/flamingo-economic-cruise/index.html. Updated: May 8, 2013

Pelikano

The 16-passenger Pelikano (a.k.a. GAP Adventure I) is one of the more comfortable of the lower-priced yachts, with eight double cabins, each with private bathroom and showers. Cabins are frill-less and small—although all have easy access to the eating area—and social space is limited to the dining room and upper deck, causing conditions to feel a bit cramped. If you are friendly, adventurous and on a strict budget, the Pelikano is one of your better options. Snorkeling equipment is provided. Reviews of service and guides are generally good. Price is at the high end of the budget range. URL: http://www.galapagosisland.net/cruises/pelikano-yacht/index.html. Updated: May 10, 2013

The Pelikano

Princess of Galápagos

The Princess of Galápagos (also known as the San Juan II) is fairly small for a 16-passenger ship, yet somehow they have managed to squeeze in eight double cabins with private bath, hot water and air conditioning. Try to get one of the upstairs rooms, as some passengers have complained that the lower ones smell of fuel. The Princess of Galápagos has two decks, a sun deck and a roof deck,

and the dining area is open-air towards the stern. Princess of Galápagos is sort of in the middle of the budget category: it's not the bottom-of-the-barrel, but it will most likely leave you underwhelmed. URL: www.princessofgalapagos.com.
Updated: Nov 2, 2012.

Galápagos Live-Aboard Dive Cruises

- Aggressor I and II
- Buddy Darwin and Buddy Wolf
- Deep Blue
- Humboldt Explorer
- Sky Dancer/Galápagos Sky

Aggressor I and II

Custom-built for Galápagos diving, the Aggressor I and II have been operating in the islands since the early 1990s, so there is a lot of experience on board in the form of captain, crew and divemasters. They're part of a world-wide diving fleet. Both ships prioritize diver safety and have taken steps to minimize their impact on the local ecosystem. Their week-long itinerary takes them to most of the best sites in Galápagos, including remote Darwin and Wolf.

They have all the gear a diver will need available for rent. The ships are nearly identical. Both have room for 16 passengers, well-appointed, wood-paneled social areas, well-designed diving deck and partially-covered sun deck which also serves as the bar. There are two different kinds of stateroom available: one is larger and therefore more expensive, but even the cheaper ones are fairly roomy. All staterooms have air conditioning and private bathroom. A reliable, professional dive operation. URL: www.aggressor.com. Updated: May 3, 2013

Wolf Buddy/Darwin Buddy

The Wolf Buddy and the Darwin Buddy are twin dive cruisers relatively new to the islands. They offer elegant cabins with air conditioning and DVD player, a roomy dive deck and cassy social areas. Prices are higher than some of the other dive cruisers (and go up during the May-December "Whale Shark Season"), but these cruisers are first-class and designed for those who want to dive and cruise in comfort. They rent all the gear any diver could need. URL: http://www.buddydive-galapagos.com. Updated: May 12, 2013

CRUISES

Deep Blue

The Deep Blue is a well-designed diving cruiser with airy dive deck, eight double cabins, nice social areas and library with TV/DVD player. The food is quite good (and plentiful). Service is professional and the divemasters know what they're doing. The Deep Blue hits all the usual Galápagos diving sites, including Darwin and Wolf. It's currently one of the least expensive diving live-aboards in the Galápagos, but the service hasn't seemed to suffer, and the itinerary is just the same as the other ships (plus, the Whale Sharks won't know how much you paid!). They can rent gear. The crew is good but may get a little pushy when it comes to the tip box. URL: www.deepbluegalapagosdiving.com. Updated: Oct 20, 2012.

Humboldt Explorer

A shiny, new dive cruiser, the Humboldt Explorer is a luxurious, 16 passenger yacht designed and built for diving in the Galápagos. All eight double cabins are roomy, with air conditioning, private bath, TV and ocean view. The social areas are well-done and the lounge is also air conditioned. There is a Jacuzzi and even a BBQ grill! The Humboldt Explorer goes to Darwin, Wolf and all of the other major dive sites. It has a satellite phone for making calls worldwide while on the trip (in case you want to gloat to your diver friends back home). Divemasters are professional and have all of their licenses up to date. It's a popular dive ship, and tends to book up, so look for space ahead of time if you're interested. URL: http://humboldtexplorer.com. Updated: Nov 16, 2012.

Sky Dancer/Galápagos Sky

The Galápagos Sky is a well-outfitted diving ship that hits all of the major Galápagos dive sites, including a trip to far-flung Darwin and Wolf Islands. The Sky features

The Skydancer

eight double cabins for a maximum of 16 passengers (each with private bath and all the amenities), an ample stern deck for ease of water entry and exit for divers, and spacious social areas including a bar, lounge and restaurant. The food is excellent.

But of course, divers don't care about food: They want hammerheads! The crew and divemasters onboard have been doing these dive trips for a very long time and they are excellent at what they do. Expect to be pampered after every dive with towels, bathrobes and juice handy. The captain and divemasters speak good English, but the crew does not. It's operated by the same people who run the first-class cruisers Eric, Letty and Flamingo, so service is a priority and customer satisfaction is important. All in all, a professionally-operated ship which will most likely leave divers very happy and satisfied. URL: www.ecoventura.com. Updated: Nov 20, 2012.

Galápagos Land-Based/ Island-Hopping Tours

Ships aren't for everyone, and many Galápagos visitors decide they'd rather spend their nights on solid ground. It used to be that land-based tours or "island hopping" was difficult to do, but that is no longer the case and increasing numbers of visitors are seeing the islands in this fashion.

WHO SHOULD DO ISLAND HOPPING?

Island-hopping tours are for those who want to spend their nights ashore or who want to see the Galápagos but cannot afford a cruise. It's not just for backpackers: well-heeled visitors can stay in fancy hotels in all three towns, although the activities will be about the same.

Divers also tend to do island hopping if they cannot afford a live-aboard cruise. It's easy to arrange dives in the three towns, and staying there gives them the flexibility to do some hikes or spend a day at the beach if they want.

ADVANTAGES OF ISLAND HOPPING

It's more flexible: If you're staying in a hotel on an island, you can pick and choose the day trips you want to take, and you can decide when to go to the other islands and how long to stay there. Cruise ships are great, but they must stick religiously to their itinerary, which is set by the park.

Island Life

Most humans get to know the Galápagos Islands only from the lens of a tour. But what is it really like for 21st-century Homo sapiens to live in this enchanted world?

To limit environmental damage, the number of cargo ships allowed into Galapagan waters is restricted. Much of the supplies they bring in head to tourist hotel and boat pantries. When the largest one arrives, residents of Puerto Ayora clasping their monthly shopping lists clear the freshly stocked supermarket shelves. During the rest of the month, locals pick up fresh produce and meats at the market and the Saturday morning Feria Libre, and fish at the Muelle Pescador.

Only Floreana and San Cristóbal Islands have permanent sources of fresh water, which provide drinking water. On the other islands, including Santa Cruz, desalinization plants prepare water taken from grietas, or fissures in the lava rock.

Getting ill or having a baby on the Islands present other adventures. The hospitals on Santa Cruz and San Cristóbal Islands are very basic and not equipped to handle acute emergencies. Those who can afford it go to the mainland for medical attention. Puerto Ayora does, however, have a hyperbaric chamber and various specialists in town that attend to tourists. Residents living on Isabela face even more rudimentary health care.

Galapagans have many environmental projects, like recycling (including batteries and oil), car ownership restrictions, good public transportation, the Cambio para la Vida campaign promoting bicycling, alternative energy projects and pet management. A special needs school, third-ager activities and other programs have been created.

Galapagans get their fair share of culture with frequent artist exhibits and concerts at civic centers. Identidad Galápagos is a cultural group promoting Galápagos' home-grown expressions. The El Colono newspaper comes out twice a month or so and keeps islanders up to date on current events.

CRUISES

It's less expensive: A cruise ship will cost you at least $150 per night...and that's if you get a good price on a crappy ship. Figure $200-$250 if you want living conditions that aren't sub-human.

In the towns, however, there are decent hotels in the $25/person/night range and it's possible to eat a meal for under $8 if you know where to look. Many of the best day trips from the towns are free!

There is a lot to see and do: It's easy to spend three or four days on each of the main islands of Santa Cruz, San Cristóbal and Isabela. All three have free visitors sites and good beaches within walking distance. There are dive shops in each town and all of them offer courses and excellent day dives.

Nightlife: On the cruises, unless you get lucky with a rowdy young group, everyone is usually beat after a long day hiking and swimming and they tend to pack it in early. If you're a night owl and want to dance and party, you'll want to be in

Puerto Ayora (the other two towns are pretty quiet at night).

HOW TO DO AN ISLAND-HOPPING TOUR

Before you go, you'll need to book your flights, hotels and the tours you want to take. Flights and hotels book up early, so make sure you plan far ahead, especially in high tourism seasons. Tours are easier to arrange later.

Figure out what you'll want to do and then set up an itinerary and budget. Remember that you can fly into or out of San Cristóbal or Puerto Ayora, so you may want to save yourself a ferry ride and fly out of a different airport.

Once you get into the islands, it's easy to find things to see and do.

SAMPLE TEN-DAY ISLAND-HOPPING ITINERARY AND BUDGET

Day 1: Fly into Puerto Ayora, arrive around 1:00 or so. Pass through migration, pay $100. Take the ferries and buses into town. Check into hotel, have lunch. Explore Puerto Ayora and see the Charles Darwin Research Station. After dinner, have some drinks out on the town.

Cost: Flight: $360 (round-trip)
$10 tourism control card
$100 Galapgos Park fee
$3 Ferries and buses
$20 meals
$25 hotel
$15 drinks
Charles Darwin Research Station: free!

Day 2: Morning: Tortuga Bay for swimming and relaxing on the beach. Return for lunch. Afternoon: boat tour of Academy Bay with snorkeling.

Cost: Tortuga Bay: Free!
Meals and hotel: $45
Academy Bay Tour: $35

Day 3: Morning: Snorkeling at Las Grietas, visit to German Beach along the way. Back to town for lunch. Afternoon: Highland tour to see tortoises, lava tunnels, etc.

Cost: Las Grietas/German beach: Free!
Meals and lodging: $45
Highland Tour: $40

Day 4: Morning: relax in Puerto Ayora, check e-mail, send postcards home and shop. Afternoon: catch the ferry to Isabela. Arrive Isabela 4:00. Check in, have dinner, explore town.

Cost: meals and lodging: $45
E-mail, postcards, gifts for friends at home: $30
Ferry: $30

Day 5: Sierra Negra hiking tour: climb Isabela's Volcano! Tour takes all day.

Cost: meals and lodging: $50
Tour: $60

Day 6: Isabela tour: includes wetlands, tortoise station, snorkeling in the bay, Wall of Tears, etc.

Cost: meals and lodging: $50
Tour: $60

Day 7: Morning ferry (6:00) back to Puerto Ayora. Lunch in Puerto Ayora. 2:00 Ferry to San Cristóbal. Arrive at Cristóbal around 4:00 p.m. or so. Explore town.

Cost: meals and lodging: $45
Isabela dock fee: $10
Ferrys: $60

Day 8: Snorkeling at Lobos and Kicker Rock with one of the dive shops. Day-long trip.

Cost: meals and lodging: $45
Snorkeling trip: $80

Day 9: Morning: explore the trails behind the interpertation center. Afternoon: highland tour to see tortoises and lagoon.

Cost: meals and lodging: $45
Trails: free!
Highland Tour: $40

Day 10: Morning: Visit La Lobería beach. Afternoon: fly back to Quito!

Cost: meals: $10
La Lobería: Free!
Flight back to Quito: Already paid for!

Total cost: about $1,500. The actual cost of an island-hopping trip will vary, of course. Some may spend more in town on gifts or meals, while others may stay in nicer hotels or take more expensive tours.

It's important to note that the sample itinerary hits many of the best island-hopping tours, but not all of them, not by a long shot! There are day-trips to other islands, dive tours, hikes, snorkeling, surfing, and much more.

Guided tours are available as well as tours to accommodate children, the elderly and the walking challenged. See the visitor sites section for help in planning your island-hopping trip.

)))))

Galápagos Islands Visitor Sites

Visitors to Galápagos will be amazed by the number and variety of visitor sites throughout the archipelago. There are over 50 visitor sites in Galápagos National Park territory, each offering its own unique history, landscape, vegetation and fauna. By seeing these sites, visitors can begin to understand the complex evolutionary processes that have shaped island biogeography. Most cruise tours generally visit two island sites and one or two additional snorkel sites per day.

The visitor sites in the islands are closely monitored by the Galápagos National Park. Even the itineraries of the ships are partially assigned by the Park Service. If you're planning your trip, it's a good idea to figure out which sites and islands you would like to see and then find a cruise ship that visits most or all of them.

Most of the sites are off-limits unless you're accompanied by a certified guide: there are some exceptions, usually in and around the towns. These exceptions are noted in the descriptions.

The descriptions also include which animals you may see. "Highly Probable" means that it is almost certain that you will see that sort of animal at that site. "Probable" means that you should see that sort of animal, but if you're unlucky you may not. "Possible" means that the animal in question has been seen there, but not every time. Bear in mind that other species may be seen at any given site that are not listed here: there are, after all, hundreds of species of animals and birds in the islands.

Trail Difficulty: all of the trails in the islands have been assigned a number from one to five. A one is very easy and short, while a five may be steep, rocky, muddy, treacherous or long. Note that these numbers are all relative to the islands only; in general the trails are not hard, and a fit 20 year old will barely break a sweat even on a "five." In other words, if the Punta Suárez trail is a five, then climbing Ecuador's Cotopaxi Volcano would be about a 793.

We have divided island and marine visitor sites into four regional categories: northern island sites, central island sites, southern island sites, and western island sites.

Northern Visitor Sites

Visiting the northern islands can be a special experience for tourists, because it involves a rite of passage across the equatorial line. Unfortunately, Marchena and Pinta are off-limits to tourists, but Genovesa is most certainly a Galápagos highlight. It is one of only two islands where you can see groups of Red-footed Boobies, and the surrounding bay is a great snorkeling site.

Although Santiago, Bartolomé (and nearby dive-site Cousin's Rock), Sombrero Chino and Rabida are closer to the central island of Santa Cruz than the three northern outliers, we consider them "northern islands," because they are located outside the central island conglomeration. These islands are geologically interesting and offer some of the best photographic opportunities in the Galápagos Islands.

GENOVESA CRUISE ONLY

Also known as Tower, Genovesa is north of the equator in the northeastern extreme of the archipelago. Because it's so remote, it's impossible to go there on a day-trip from Santa Cruz or San Cristóbal; you'll have to take a cruise. If you are interested in sea birds and exciting snorkeling opportunities, you may want to prioritize this island on your itinerary when selecting cruises.

Because it is isolated from the other islands, Genovesa became home to colonies of birds, but relatively few land animals. For example, no Giant Tortoise species ever developed on Genovesa.

Due to Genovesa's relative isolation and lack of fresh water, it has remained uncontaminated by invasive species, and naturalist guides will likely ask guests to take extra care not to track anything into the delicate Genovesa ecosystem.

Genovesa is fairly flat and round, with a large, almost landlocked cove on the south side called Darwin Bay. During the dingy ride from your boat to one of the visitor sites, Prince Philip's Steps, you will have a good view of Red-billed Tropicbirds, Great Frigatebirds, Swallow-tailed Gulls, Nazca Boobies and Red-footed Boobies flying, fishing and potentially nesting in cracks in the seaward side of the cliff.

Because of the steep underwater terrain of Genovesa, snorkeling conditions can vary. If you like to dive and can hold your breath for extended periods of time, you may see interesting bottom-dwellers, tropical fish found only in the northern archipelago, or even a hammerhead shark.

Darwin Bay
Darwin never visited Genovesa (Tower) Island in the northern part of the Galápagos archipelago, but he would have loved the bay named after him. The landing site is a spacious sandy beach with trails wending through mangroves and lava rock formations.

Darwin Bay, Genovesa

The birds are a marvel to see. Frigates with their dazzling chest sacs, Blue-footed and Red-footed Boobies, Swallow-tailed Gulls and more populate the sheltered bay. Genovesa is nicknamed "Bird Island" for good reason!

The easy trail winds in and out of nesting colonies of different bird species, allowing close-up photos of seldom-seen Galápagos species such as the Red-footed Booby or the Lava Gull. At one end of the trail, look for deep tidal pools, which occasionally trap a sea turtle or ray.

Trail Difficulty: 2/5
It's an easy trail that goes over some lava in places.

Wildlife:
Highly Probable to See:
* Red-footed Boobies
* Blue-footed Boobies
* Swallow-tailed Gulls
* Nazca Boobies
* Frigate Birds
* Yellow-crowned Night Herons

Probable to See:
* Genovesa Mockingbirds
* Large-billed Cactus Finches
* Lava Gulls

Possible to See:
* Red-billed Tropicbirds
* Whimbrels
* Wandering Tattlers

* Ruddy Turnstones
* Yellow Warblers
* Galápagos Doves ·
Updated: Aug 15, 2012.

El Barranco/Prince Phillips' Steps
El Barranco (a.k.a. Prince Philip's Steps) is a memorable site located on the flat area above the cliffs in Darwin Bay. After a challenging scramble up a rocky crevasse, the rest of the trail is very easy.

The first part of the trail goes through some scrubby trees and brush where you're likely to see some boobies (of all three varieties if you're lucky), Frigatebirds and Galápagos Doves. The trail then continues to a long stretch of rocky dune, on the ocean side of which it's possible to see the Short-eared Owl. Although the Short-eared Owl is fairly common in Galápagos, it's only seen at a handful of visitor sites, so make the most of the opportunity! They're hard to spot, so be patient and stay close to the guide. If you have binoculars or a major zoom lens for your camera, this is the place for it.

Trail Difficulty: 3/5
The first part is the hardest—if you can get up the crevasse onto the flat area on top, it's easy.

Wildlife:

Highly Probable to See:
* Galápagos Sea Lions (when arriving)
* Nazca Boobies
* Red-footed Boobies
* Frigatebirds
* Galápagos Doves
* Marine Iguanas

Probable to See:
* Mockingbirds
* Finches
* Galápagos Fur Sea Lions (from the panga)
* Short-eared Owls
* Galápagos Petrels
* Blue-footed Boobies

Possible to See:
* Red-billed Tropicbirds
Updated: Aug 2012.

MARCHENA DIVE ONLY

Also known as Bindloe, Marchena is a large, (130 km²/80.78 mi²) active shield volcano located due west of Genovesa. Although it is the seventh-largest island, it has a fairly desolate terrain and absolutely no visitor sites. There are some good scuba sites nearby, so you may get to see the island up close if you are on a dive tour.

Marchena played a bit part in the sordid history known as "the Galápagos Affair," (box, p. 134) for it was here that Rudolf Lorenz, suspect in the disappearance of the "Baroness" and her lover, met his end along with Norwegian fisherman Trygve Nuggerud. Apparently they washed up on Marchena and died of dehydration.
Updated: June 12, 2013.

PINTA

Also known as Abington, Pinta is an elongated shield located northwest of Marchena that used to serve as Lonesome George's abode. Visitation to the island is limited to researchers, who must get a permit before landing there. Updated: June 12, 2013.

SANTIAGO  Day trips

Also known as San Salvador or James, Santiago is the fourth largest island at 585 square kilometers (363.5 mi). This island is especially interesting for people interested in geology, volcanology or succession. Visitor sites include Buccaneer Cove, Puerto Egas and Sullivan Bay.

Buccaneer Cove
Buccaneer Cove, as the name suggests, is a small, sheltered bay once popular with whalers and pirates, who could re-stock fresh water and tortoises there while they repaired their ships. As a visitor site, it's a large cliff where you can see many birds, including

blue-footed boobys and Brown Noddies. In general, ships don't land at Buccaneer cove: the visit consists of a panga ride and some snorkeling, which is quite good when the water is clear.

Wildlife:
Highly Probable to See:
* Marine Iguanas
* Brown Noddies
* Frigate Birds
* Blue-footed Boobies
* Sea Turtles

Probable to See:
* Wandering Tattler
* Surgeonfish
* Mullet
* Nazca Booby
* Swallow-tailed gull
* King Angelfish

Possible to See:
* Sharks while snorkeling
Updated: May 30, 2013

Puerto Egas
Puerto Egas is a favorite visitor site, as it's a good place to see animals and birds and the hike itself is very easy. It's named for a man named Egas who had a salt mine there in the early 1960s; parts of the mine are still there, although they're not on the trail. Ask your guide to tell you the story of the crazy mine guard who remained there for some years after the mine folded.

Visitors disembark on a sandy beach and then head for the circular trail. Part of the trail heads into the interior of the island, and the scrubby brush is a good place to look for Darwin's Finches and other birds, including the pesky introduced Smooth-billed Ani. Near the landing site, look for sea lion pups.

The trail loops around once it hits the coast. The coastal walk features many tidal pools, which are a good place to look for marine life and shore birds like herons. You may even see a Yellow Warbler or two skipping along the seashore, nipping up bugs. Another highlight along the seaside trail is "Darwin's Toilet," which is a small, rocky pool fed by invisible underground channels: as the waves crash, the "toilet" fills and drains.

Near Darwin's Toilet, look for the rare Galápagos Fur Sea Lion. Your guide will point

VISITOR SITES

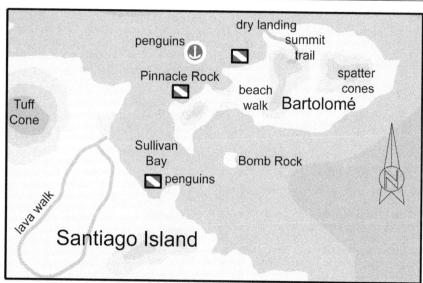

dry landing

penguins

summit
trail

Pinnacle Rock

spatter
cones

beach
walk   **Bartolomé**

Tuff
Cone

Sullivan
Bay

Bomb Rock

penguins

lava walk

Santiago Island

Sullivan Bay

them out: they look just like regular sea lions, but their coat is a bit thicker and their snout more blunt.

Ship crews are always happy to visit this site because there is a soccer field there and they can go play: join in if you're fit enough.

Trail Difficulty: 2/5
There are some rocks and slippery places along the seaside part of the trail.

Wildlife:
Highly Probable to See:
  * Marine Iguanas
  * Galápagos Fur Sea Lions
  * Sally Lightfoot Crabs
  * Galápagos Sea Lions
  * Darwin's Finches

Probable to See:
  * Whimbrels
  * Yellow Warblers
  * Galápagos Flycatchers
  * Ruddy Turnstones
  * Hermit Crabs
  * Striated Herons
  * Great Blue Herons

Possible to See:
  * American Oystercatchers
  * Sanderlings
  * Smooth-billed Anis
  * Galápagos Snakes
  * Herons

  * Galápagos Hawks
  * Vermilion Flycatchers
  * Storm Petrels
  * Brown Noddies
Updated: Aug 2, 2012.

Sullivan Bay
The eastern side of Santiago Island was volcanically active relatively recently (about 100 years ago) and Sullivan Bay is a great place to see lava, sometimes edged with black volcanic glass (obsidian). There is a small colony of Galápagos Penguins at the landing site, but visitors hoping to see a lot of wildlife will be disappointed. On the sun-baked lava, insects and lava lizards may hop around, but there's little else.

Still, the geology of the area is very interesting. You can see the path of lava flow as well as the various igneous rock structures formed from varying rates of flow, temperature of formation, and pressure. Here you can see examples of three lava types—pahoehoe (braided), aa (jagged and painful), and schrict (ropy). You can also find hornitos, little ovens, formed when bubbles escape from hot lava to form mini-volcanoes. Your guide may even point out holes where trees were vaporized by the hot lava!

The regeneration of the island is ongoing. Pioneer plants such as Brachycereus cactus and Mollugo carpetweed can be seen as well as colonizer animals like insects, lizards and snakes. The bay is also a good snorkeling site—fortunate visitors will get to take a dip after taking the lava hike.

Trail Difficulty: 3/5
Lava can be treacherous, and the hike can get quite hot in the sun.

Wildlife:
Highly Probable to See:
* Galápagos Penguins
* Sally Lightfoot Crabs
* Sea Lions
* Lava Lizards

Probable to See:
* Blue-footed Boobies
* American Oystercatchers
* Galápagos Hawks

Possible to See:
* Galápagos Snakes
* Sea Turtles (snorkeling)
Updated: Oct 28, 2012.

BARTOLOMÉ Day trips

Bartolomé, a small islet (1.2 km²/0.75 mi²) just off Sullivan Bay on Santiago, is probably the most recognizable point in Galápagos—literally. On one side of Bartolomé is the famous Pinnacle Rock, a rocky formation pointing skyward. Legend has it that Pinnacle Rock was bombed into shape in the 1940s by American servicemen testing their ordinance. There's a hike to the top of a hill where you'll have a great view of Pinnacle Rock and there is a small beach with excellent snorkeling.

Pinnacle Rock

La Escalera/The Stairs
"La Escalera" is a long, winding wooden staircase which leads up to the peak of the island, where visitors are rewarded with a magnificent view. Along the way, visitors hike through an arid, rocky landscape of reddish volcanic rocks that has caused many people to speculate if the surface of Mars looks similar.

Naturalist guides will point out the hardy pioneer plants that are slowly making the arid island livable for other species.

Other than the geology, there isn't much to see. Once away from the landing spot, there is little in the way of wildlife—look for Lava Lizards and brightly colored grasshoppers. The magnificent view at the top of Bartolomé is worth the climb, however. Don't forget your camera! There are usually Marine Iguanas, Sally Lightfoot Crabs and sea lions near the landing site.

Trail Difficulty: 3/5
The stairs make the going easy, but there are a LOT of them and the sun-drenched island is often very hot.

Wildlife:
Highly Probable to See:
* Marine Iguanas
* Sally Lightfoot Crabs
* Sea Lions
* Lava Lizards
* Grasshoppers

Probable to See:
* Blue-footed Boobies
* Frigatebirds
* Brown Pelicans

Possible to See:
* Galápagos Penguin (swimming near the landing site)
* Various Herons
Updated: Aug 15, 2012.

The Beach
Bartolomé Island is home to a beautiful white sand beach with a gentle surf. The beach is at the base of the famous Pinnacle Rock, the unmistakable rock formation allegedly blasted into shape by American forces during World War II.

Bartolomé is very narrow at this point, and there is a short, easy trail which leads to a scenic beach on the other side. The beach is nice, but you shouldn't miss the opportunity to snorkel while here. Beginners can putter around in the sheltered cove of the beach, but

VISITOR SITES

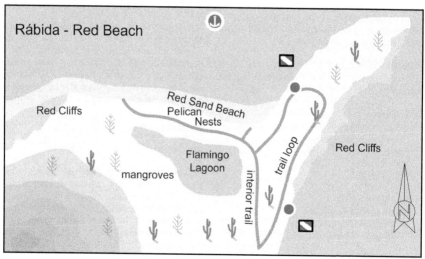

Rábida - Red Beach

Red Cliffs

Red Sand Beach
Pelican Nests

Red Cliffs

Flamingo Lagoon

mangroves

interior trail

trail loop

N

Rábida

if you head out and around Pinnacle Rock, you'll be rewarded with some truly awesome underwater life. Look for penguins, octopuses (they're tough to see but they're there), sea lions, sharks, rays and much more.

Swimming penguin, Bartolomé

Even the underwater rubble from the bombing is now grown over with algae and seaweed and makes for memorable seascapes. If you're on one of the larger ships, they may have a glass-bottom boat for those who do not wish to snorkel.

Trail Difficulty: 1/5
It's an easy trail from one beach to the other. Snorkeling Difficulty: Easy (near the beach) to Intermediate (deep water near Pinnacle Rock). Currents are not a danger here.

Wildlife:
Highly Probable to See:
 * Penguins
 * Sea Lions
 * Reef Fish

Probable to See:
 * Sea Turtles

Possible to See:
 * Sharks
 * Rays
 * Octopuses
 * Blue-footed Boobies (Fishing)
Updated: Aug 15, 2012.

RÁBIDA

Also known as Jervis, Rábida is a small island (5 km²/3.1 mi²) south of Santiago whose colorful splendor makes it a photographer's dream. Visitors will be struck by the sharp contrasts between the turquoise waters, maroon sandy beach, beige rock substrate, white trees and lush green highlands spread out before them. Note that there is only one visitor site on Rábida.

There is a wet landing onto the long, red beach where sea lions lounge, pelicans nest and the occasional manta ray jumps up out of the water in the distance. A short walk away from the beach takes you to a brackish lagoon, where you can sometimes see flamingoes wading in the water, all this despite the fact that sea lion fecal contamination has killed off most of the lagoon's crustaceans - the flamingoes' food source.

A 0.75 kilometer (0.46 mi) a circular trail begins at the lagoon, winding through a bunch of fauna - especially cacti (look for the one that's shaped like Mickey Mouse). The walk offers amazing views of the sea as well as the island's 367 meter (1,204 ft) volcanic peak.

VISITOR SITES

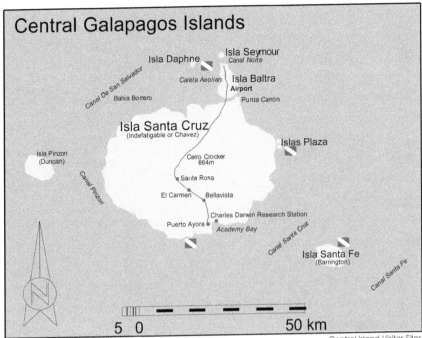

Central Galapagos Islands

Central Island Visitor Sites

You can also snorkel from the beach or take a dingy ride along the cove to look for green sea turtles, marine iguanas, and fur sea lions. The deep-water snorkeling off of Rabida's walls is fantastic.

Trail Difficulty: 1/5

Wildlife:
Highly Probable to See:
* Sea Lions
* Pelicans
* Hermit crabs

Possible to See:
* Flamingoes
* Fur Sea Lions
* Galapagos Hawks
Updated: Jan 3, 2013.

SOMBRERO CHINO

Sombrero Chino, or Chinese Hat, is a small islet which gets its name from its appearance—a yellowish, nearly perfect cone like hat worn in parts of Asia. Located off the southeastern tip of Santiago, Chinese Hat is a fairly recent volcanic cone with a few small but intact lava tunnels. The 400-meter trail starts on a small, white-sand beach, where you can often see American Oystercatchers

and sea lions. The trail continues along the cove, passing marine iguanas, Sally Lightfoot Crabs, and Lava Lizards. The trail is a good place to observe different lava formations—ask your guide for details.

If you visit during the cold season (May/June-November/December), the island may have some small tide pools lined with green algae, which attract more marine iguanas. From the beach you can swim in tranquil blue waters along the cove, playing with sea lions and spotting tropical fish.

Sombrero Chino is considered a fragile visitor site, and only certain cruise ships (those which don't carry many passengers) are allowed to visit; if you want to include Sombrero Chino in your itinerary, be sure to sign up with one of the cruise ships that goes there.

Trail Difficulty: 2/5
The trail gets rough in places, so bring good walking shoes.

Wildlife:
Highly Probable to See:
* Sea Lions
* Marine Iguanas
* Sally Lightfoot Crabs
* Pelicans

Probable to See:
* Lava Lizards

Possible to See:
* Galápagos Hawks
* Penguins (snorkeling)
* Rays (snorkeling)
* White-tipped Reef Sharks (snorkeling)
Updated: Jan 3, 2013.

Central Island Visitor Sites

The central islands of Santa Cruz and Baltra serve as the hub of tourist traffic, since the main town of Puerto Ayora and the airport are located here. The majority of organized tours and independent travelers begin and end their adventures here.

The surrounding islands of Daphne Major and Minor, North Seymour, South Plaza (and the nearby dive site of Gordon Rocks), and Santa Fe are thus the most visited by tourists due to their close proximity to Puerto Ayora. But they also offer some of the best opportunities for seeing sea birds and large marine creatures, like hammerhead sharks.

SANTA CRUZ

Tourist-friendly Santa Cruz (Indefatigable) Island is not only the home of Puerto Ayora, it's also the most centrally located island, meaning more visitor sites, dives and tours are available. Because the main airport is on nearby Baltra, most visitors to the Galápagos Islands will wind up in Puerto Ayora at some point, and the town has the best hotels, restaurants and nightlife in the islands. It's also home to the Charles Darwin Research Station, former home of Lonesome George and a must-see for any visitor to Galápagos.

Santa Cruz is more than just Puerto Ayora, however. There are 22 land and marine visitor sites on and around the island. The lush green highlands are home to tortoises and birds, the beaches are among the best in the islands, and even Puerto Ayora's Academy Bay is worth checking out.

There are several dive sites near Puerto Ayora, and plenty of dive shops in town to take you there. The best known site is probably Gordon Rocks, where different sharks, including hammerheads, are often seen.

Santa Cruz is a great place to see Giant Tortoises. There are some at the Charles Darwin Research Station, but it's better to go to the highlands to see them in their natural habitat, munching on vegetation, wallowing in mud and lumbering around. El Chato reserve is a good place to start: in addition to the tortoises, there is a freshwater lagoon that attracts ducks and other birds, and some lava tunnels that can be explored. Also in the highlands, Los Gemelos ("the twins") refers to two sinkhole craters formed by collapsing underground lava tunnels. They're a great place to see birds (keep an eye open for the brilliant red Vermillion Flycatcher) and native plants.

There are also some beaches in and around Puerto Ayora, including Tortuga Bay, Station Beach, German Beach and Garrapatero.

Some of the visitor sites on Santa Cruz are only for cruise ships, while others are open to the public. Of all the sites listed here, Las Bachas and Cerro Dragón are only for cruise ships and off-limits to day trippers from Puerto Ayora; the rest of the sites are either public or visited from Puerto Ayora as part of a tour.

The Charles Darwin Research Station

In 1959, the same year the National Park was established, the Charles Darwin Foundation—an international non-governmental organization—was formed. Its basic objectives were to promote scientific studies and environmental education in partnership with the Galápagos National Park, through the management of an on-site investigative facility, the Charles Darwin Research Station (CDRS). Since its foundation, the Charles Darwin Foundation and its Research Station have gathered baseline scientific data for a variety of conservation initiatives.

An important nexus of these conservation efforts has been the mitigation of the harmful effects of introduced species and the regeneration of native populations, a process that visitors to the CDRS can watch with their own eyes. Until his death in 2012, the station was home to Lonesome George, the last of the Pinta Island Giant Tortoise subspecies.

At the station you will also see the solution to the turtle population problem: a tortoise captive breeding center that has been successful in restoring healthy populations to the wild.
Updated: Jan 3, 2013.

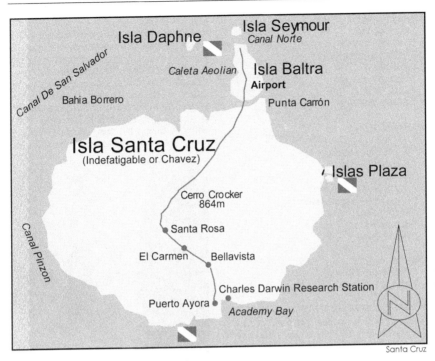

Santa Cruz

Other attractions at the CDRS include close-up views of several of the 11 subspecies of tortoise, land iguanas, and Darwin's Finches, paths through coastal and arid-zone vegetation, including salt bush, mangroves, prickly pear, and other cacti, an elaborate presentation and video of the station's conservation efforts in the Van Straelen Exhibition Center, and the customary souvenir kiosk, whose profits go to support the station (since it is 100% privately funded, receiving zero support from the Ecuadorian government).

You can't miss the Research Station: it's right outside of town.
Updated: May 6, 2013

Playa de la Estación/Station Beach

Station Beach is a small, rocky beach located off of the road that leads to the Charles Darwin Research Station. It's the closest beach to town and the easiest one to reach, so sometimes it fills up. The small patch of white sand is bordered on either side by some jagged lava rocks, where you might see some shore birds like pelicans or gulls, and marine iguanas are common. It isn't the best beach, but it is close to town. It's free and there are no restrictions.

It's possible to snorkel here, and you may see some bright reef fish near the rocks on either side.

Don't bring any valuables to the beach, and if you do, keep a close eye on them.

Trail Difficulty: 1/5
Open hours: 6 a.m. to 6 p.m.
Updated Aug 20, 2012.

Playa Ratonera

From Playa de la Estación, a path leads south to Playa Ratonera. This white-sand beach is a perfect place to watch the sun set over Academy Bay. Despite the rocky outcrops, this is a favorite place for Puerto Ayora's surfers. Often sea lions swim by to wave to anyone hanging out. When the sea goes out, tidal pools form in the lava-rock basins in which sea slugs, eels, octopus and a myriad of fishes may be studied. Shore birds are also frequent visitors. At the north end are mangrove stands. Beach morning glory, salt-bush and sea purslane embroider the sand.

Trail Difficulty: 2/5
It's about 5 minutes past Playa de la Estación. Beware walking on the rocks when tidal pooling, as they can be slick. Open Hours: 6 a.m.-6 p.m.

Highly Probable to See:
  * Lava Lizards
  * Marine Iguanas
  * Sally Lightfoot Crab
  * Finches
  * Great Frigatebird
  * Lava Gull
  * Brown Pelicans

Probable to See:
  * Sea lions
  * Great Blue Heron
  * Striated Heron
  * Ruddy Turnstone
  * Semipalmated Plover
  * American Oystercatcher
  * Wandering Tattler
  * Whimbrel
  * Sea urchins

Possible to See:
  * Blue-footed Booby
  * Moray Eel

Playa de los Alemanes

Playa de los Alemanes (German Beach) is an easy visit from Puerto Ayora and one of the better easily-accessible beaches. Simply take a water taxi (should cost about $1) to the pier on Angermeyer Point (just tell the water taxi guy that you want to go to Playa de los Alemanes) and you'll get there in about a minute or so.

From there, it's an easy walk of five minutes; you'll pass some saline pools on the way, so keep your eyes open for some wading and swimming birds.

The beach itself is a crescent of white sand framed by a boardwalk behind and mangroves on either side. It's sheltered, so the water is great for swimming and snorkeling (although you shouldn't expect to see anything spectacular, like sharks). German Beach is great for kids.

There are no public changing or restroom facilities located here. Nearby is the ultra-fancy Finch Bay Hotel—they'll probably let you sit in the shade at the bar and order a cool drink if you like, but the pool is only for guests.

As always, keep an eye on your valuables. German Beach is free and you do not need to be accompanied by a naturalist guide to visit. If you keep walking past the Finch Bay Hotel, you'll find the path to Las Grietas.

Las Grietas

A postcard-perfect swimming hole located in a lava crevasse on Angermeyer Point, Las Grietas is a great place to cool off on a hot Galápagos afternoon. The crystal clear blue water is as smooth as glass, and it's a great place for beginner snorkelers. It's very popular with day-trippers from Puerto Ayora but there isn't a lot of room to put your stuff. In fact, petty theft is common there when there are a lot of people, so you should only bring what you really need.

Las Grietas

The trail to Las Grietas goes through a rocky, dry forest of tall cacti; you'll want good walking shoes and a bottle of water.

Walking there will take you about 15-20 minutes from the Finch Bay Hotel. You'll pass a couple of salt lagoons, but don't expect to see a lot of wildlife on this trail.

Las Grietas is free, and you do not need to be accompanied by a naturalist guide. Hours: 6 a.m.-6 p.m.

Trail Difficulty: 3/5
It's rocky, involves some climbing, and the last part down to the water can be treacherous.

Wildlife:
Possible to See:
  * Finches
  * Lava Lizards
  * Pintail Ducks
  * Wading Birds

Updated: Aug 10, 2012.

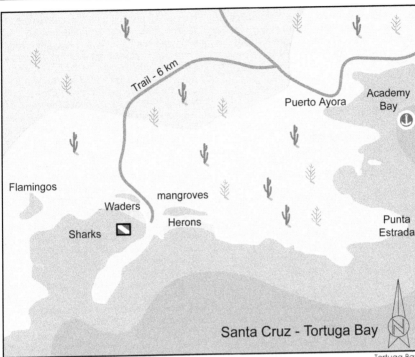

Santa Cruz - Tortuga Bay

Tortuga Bay

Laguna Las Ninfas

Laguna las Ninfas is a crystal blue lagoon located only a block away from a busy street in Puerto Ayora. For many years, it was run-down, full of garbage and a favorite place for surly Puerto Ayora teenagers to hang out and grumble about how much their lives sucked.

I'm happy to say that has all changed. The garbage is out of the lagoon and there is a lovely boardwalk most of the way around it with interesting signs describing the local plant and animal life. Even the teenagers are gone, perhaps because the lagoon is no longer a depressing place. You can swim in the lagoon now, although some locals say that runoff from farms upriver makes doing so questionable.

Las Ninfas is a brackish lagoon: in other words, it's where sea water meets a creek bearing freshwater. As such, it is home to some fish, animal and plant species you may not see elsewhere.

Seeing Las Ninfas won't take more than an hour and I highly recommend it if you're spending a couple days in Puerto Ayora. It's off the main drag near the Casa del Lago Hotel. Any local will give you directions to find it.

Trail Difficulty: 1/5
It's the easiest trail in Galápagos.

Possible to See:
* Finches
* Brown Pelicans
* Fish
* Rays
Updated: May 6, 2013.

The Miguel Cifuentes Arias Community Center

Located a short walk from the main road and at the head of the trail that goes to Tortuga Bay, the Miguel Cifuentes Arias Community Center is a small complex of buildings housing some classrooms (would-be islanders must take a short class there before receiving their residency) and a tiny museum dealing with the marine reserve. There are some informational displays as well as a couple of aquariums with lobsters and eels in them.

It's named for Miguel Cifuentes Arias, former head of the Charles Darwin Research Station, director of the Galápagos National Park and Mayor of Puerto Ayora.

It's worth a quick stop on your way to or from Tortuga Bay. Seeing the marine reserve room shouldn't take you more than 15 minutes. Also, there are bathrooms here, the closest ones available to the beach at Tortuga Bay. Updated: Aug 10, 2012.

Tortuga Bay

Tortuga Bay is a pristine, gorgeous white sand beach located within walking distance from Puerto Ayora. It's part of the park system, but it's free and you don't need a naturalist guide to go there. It's popular with locals and often you'll see families there on weekends.

The trail to get there leaves town not far from the Ninfas Lagoon. Just head further outside of town until you see signs for the Miguel Cifuentes Arias Community Center—the trail is right behind it. There are restrooms at the community center, but none at the beach, so plan ahead.

You'll have to pass through a sort of checkpoint where you'll sign in and out; this will also be your last chance to buy water, snacks, etc., as there is nothing at the bay. There are no trash cans there either, so plan on bringing back any empty bottles, chip bags, etc.

The trail itself is easy and paved. The sign says it's a 45-minute walk, but I was able to do it in 30 by myself, walking briskly. There's no need to hurry, though, because you'll most likely see some interesting bird life as you go, including mockingbirds, finches, flycatchers and Smooth-billed Anis. I also saw a feral cat on the trail once: they're shy so keep your eyes peeled. It's the only feral cat I've ever actually seen, although they're quite numerous on Santa Cruz.

The trail goes through some thick scrubland, and before long you'll have some respect for whoever made it—it must have been some hard work over the rough rocks and through the thorny trees! About halfway along the trail there is a little gazebo-looking structure where you can sit down and have a rest.

The trail emerges at Playa Brava, a wide and lovely beach that stretches for over a kilometer. You can surf there—several places in Puerto Ayora will rent you any gear you need. The mounds behind the beach are off-limits. That is where sea turtles nest. On a clear day, Carmaaño Islet (the Lobería) at the mouth of Academy Bay, Santa Fe Island and Floreana can be seen on the horizon.

The west end of Playa Brava, pools form at low tide. These are popular snorkeling spots for local school kids. The beach seemingly ends at a rocky point. A trail goes around this spit of land, full of marine iguanas—some of the largest you'll see so close to civilization. (Stay on the path, because this is also their nesting grounds). Offshore, you'll see sea turtles hanging out. The path loops around to the other side of the peninsula to Playa Mansa. Along this stretch, Blue-footed Boobies dance.

Playa Mansa is a perfect piece of paradise. The turquoise waters are perfectly tranquil. At times, even sea lions, Eagle Rays and mating sea turtles come to enjoy this warm cove. Between dips, rest on the makeshift benches beneath the trees. Occasionally there is a guy there who rents out kayaks, but there are no other vendors of any sort.

At the far end of Playa Mansa, past the mangroves, are some salt flats and marshes where a variety of waterfowl and shore birds, including flamingos, are seen.

Some petty theft has been reported at Tortuga Bay. Be sure to take care of your valuables.

Trail Difficulty: 2/5

It's paved, but long, and it can get quite hot. There are a few ups and downs. Bring bottled water for sure. Trail length: 2,500 meters (8,202 ft).

Open Hours: 6 a.m.-6 p.m.

Highly Probable to See:
* Finches
* Galápagos Flycatchers
* Galapagos Mockingbird
* Lava Lizards
* Marine Iguanas
* A wide variety of shorebirds

Probable to See:
* Noddy Terns
* Brown Pelicans
* Blue-footed Boobies
* Lava Gulls

Possible to See:
* Feral Cats
* Galápagos Dove
* Spotted Eagle Rays
* Sea turtles
Updated: January 12, 2013.

Playa de los Perros

The "Beach of the Dogs" is a quick, 10-minute boat ride from Puerto Ayora. It's a pleasant enough white sand beach, with a nearby pool where you can see White-tipped Reef Sharks if you're lucky. Playa de los Perros is often included with tours of Academy Bay.

Trail Difficulty: 2/5
There is a short walk from the landing site to the actual beach.

Wildlife:
Highly Probable to See:
 * Marine Iguanas
 * Blue-footed Boobies
 * Sally Lightfoot Crabs
 * Frigatebirds

Probable to See:
 * Brown Noddies
 * Finches
 * Sea Lions
 * Brown Pelicans
 * Swallow-tailed Gulls

Possible to See:
 * White-tipped Reef Sharks
Updated: Aug 10, 2012.

Lava Tunnels

Lava Tunnels are natural volcanic rock formations left behind when a stream of lava flows out of a volcano. The outer magma cools while the inner magma continues to flow, resulting in an underground stone tube of sorts. There are lava tunnels all over Galápagos, in all shapes and sizes.

There are several lava tunnels in the highlands near Puerto Ayora. They're often located near the farms where the Giant Tortoises hang out, so tours to see the tortoises will usually stop at a lava tunnel as well. The ones usually visited by tourists either have lights installed or are short enough that visibility is not a problem. The lava tunnels are interesting, but not so much so that you'd really want to go out of your way to see one unless you're a geology buff. Best to catch one on a tortoise or highland tour. The tunnels are popular with barn owls, so keep your eyes open near the entrance. Updated: Aug 10, 2012.

Cerro Crocker

Cerro Crocker (Crocker Hill) is the highest point on Santa Cruz Island, which isn't saying much (860 m/2,821.5 ft). It's fairly easy to hike, and you'll be rewarded at the top

with a good view of Puerto Ayora. The terrain is leafy and green (and muddy when it rains, so bring good shoes). Part of the trail goes through agricultural areas, and part is the Galápagos National Park.

A guide is legally not needed, but you'll definitely want one so that you don't get lost. Also, the trail winds its way through several vegetation zones, including some rare endemic plants and introduced species. Without a guide to tell you what they are, you might just assume that they are just some plants and walk right past them!

The Cerro Crocker hike is your best chance to see the elusive Galápagos Rail, a bluish purple-black bird that hangs out mostly on the ground.

Trail Difficulty: 3/5
Long and occasionally muddy.

Wildlife:
Highly Probable to See:
 * Finches
 * Galápagos Flycatchers
 * Mockingbirds

Possible to See:
 * Galápagos Rails
 * Galápagos Petrels
 * Vermilion Flycatchers
Updated: Aug 10, 2012.

El Chato Reserve

Located in the green, hilly highlands of Santa Cruz Island, the El Chato Reserve is one of the best places in the islands to see the Giant Tortoises in their natural habitat. The reserve is free and open to the public, but a guide is highly recommended, as in recent years some visitors have gotten lost, and one died before he could be found.

The tortoises are easy to spot, lumbering around eating grass and leaves and wallowing in the small pools that are common in

Tortoise watching in the highlands

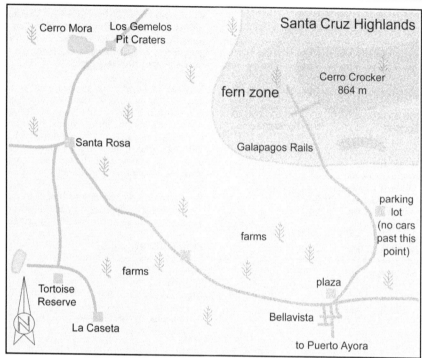

Cerro Mora   Los Gemelos   Santa Cruz Highlands
                Pit Craters

                                  Cerro Crocker
fern zone   864 m

Santa Rosa

                Galapagos Rails

                                        parking
                                        lot
                                        (no cars
                        farms   past this
                                         point)

        farms
                                plaza
Tortoise
Reserve
                            Bellavista
    La Caseta

                        to Puerto Ayora

Los Gemelos, Santa Cruz Highlands

the reserve. You may also spot some highland birds, like Cattle Egrets, mockingbirds,
finches or flycatchers.

There is a trail through the reserve, leaving
from the little town of Santa Rosa. From the
"caseta" or little house where it begins, figure
on about a three or three and a half hour hike
round trip. It's possible to hire horses and
guides in Santa Rosa. There are also several
lava tunnels in the reserve, a couple of which
are open to the public. There is also a small
lagoon covered in red algae.

In addition to the El Chato reserve, there are
a couple of private farms in the highlands
where visitors can see the tortoises. That's
another reason to go with a guide, as they'll
tend to know where the tortoises are at any
given moment.

Trail Difficulty: 5/5
It's long and tends to get muddy. Watch
your step!

Wildlife:
Highly Probable to See:
  * Galápagos Tortoises
  * Finches

  * Mockingbirds
  * Cattle Egrets

Probable to See:
  * Galápagos Flycatchers
  * Yellow Warblers

Possible to See:
  * Galápagos Rails
  * Short-eared Owls
  * Paint-billed Crakes
  * Barn Owls
  * Vermilion Flycatchers
  * Herons
  * Pintail Ducks
  * Whimbrels
  * Gallinules
Updated: Aug 20, 2012.

Los Gemelos

Located in the Santa Cruz highlands, Los Gemelos ("The Twins") refers to two large sinkholes
which were formed by collapsing underground
lava tunnels. As paths to and around the sinkholes have improved, they have become more
popular with visitors, who are kindly asked to
stay far from the edges of the sinkholes and not
to throw anything (i.e. rocks) into the craters
themselves.

VISITOR SITES

The big attraction here is the Scalesia forest. Scalesia is a sort of tree endemic to Galápagos. Many endemic and native species call Los Gemelos home.

Los Gemelos is the best place in Galápagos to see the dazzling, elusive Vermillion Flycatcher. Darwin's Finches are also commonly sighted there. Los Gemelos is often combined with trips to other highland locations to see Giant Tortoises.

Trail Difficulty: 3/5
You have to be careful not to get too close to the edge of the sinkholes, as it's not safe. The trail can get muddy, and parts of it involve a scamper up some rocks.

Highly Probable to See:
* Mockingbirds
* Darwin's Finches
* Galápagos Doves

Probable to See:
* Vermilion Flycatchers
* Carpenter Finches
* Yellow Warblers
* Warbler Finches

Possible to See:
* Short-eared Owls
* Galápagos Rails
* Dark-billed Cuckoos
Updated: Aug 20, 2012.

Las Bachas Beach
Las Bachas is a beautiful white-sand beach on the northern coast of Santa Cruz Island. There isn't much to do there except lounge on the sand, go for a stroll or do some easy snorkeling in the gentle surf. Rough, right?

There are a couple of salt lagoons behind the sandy berm—lucky visitors will spot a flamingo or two. You can also look for a rusted pontoon, a relic of the Second World War. In fact, "bachas" is a poor pronunciation of "barges," two of which were wrecked offshore at that time.

Sea Turtles lay their eggs at the edge of the vegetation—be sure to obey the signs to stay away.

It's possible to snorkel in the gentle surf; you're unlikely to see much, given the sandy bottom and cloudiness of the water, but if you stay near the rocks you should see some fish, or a shark or turtle if you're lucky.

Trail Difficulty: 1/5
Lovely white sand beach - it doesn't get any easier.

Wildlife:
Highly Probable to See:
* Sally Lightfoot Crabs

Probable to See:
* Flamingoes
* Black-necked Stilts
* Whimbrels
* Hermit Crabs
* Blue Herons
* Brown Pelicans
* Blue-footed Boobies (fishing)
* Sanderlings
* Wandering Tattlers
* Semipalmated Plovers

Possible to See:
* Sea Turtles
* Yellow Warblers
Updated: Nov 10, 2012.

Cerro Dragón/Dragon Hill
The aptly named Cerro Dragón ("Dragon Hill") is a memorable visitor site and one of the best places in the islands to see land iguanas. The site is on the other side of the island from Puerto Ayora and consists of a trail in a sort of lasso shape: a trail leads inland to the hill, up and around the hill, and then back out the same trail to the beach.

Along the trail, it is possible to see land iguanas and several species of birds. It's lucky that there are land iguanas on Santa Cruz at all. As the most inhabited island, it is also the one most plagued by introduced species such as goats, cats and dogs, all of which wreak havoc on land iguana populations. Goats eat up all the available vegetation, cats eat baby iguanas and eggs, and a pack of dogs can gobble a fully grown iguana.

These introduced pests were devastating the Santa Cruz iguana population, to the point that researchers and Park Service officials relocated some of the iguanas to a nearby islet (with no dogs, cats or goats) so that if the Santa Cruz population were wiped out, they would be able to repopulate it.

Fortunately, intensive efforts to remove the offending introduced species have been successful, and the resident "dragons" are no longer seriously threatened. Efforts to control introduced plants and animals on this part of Santa Cruz are ongoing, and Cerro Dragón is one of few places on the islands where tourists and scientists may cross paths.

The path is one of the longer ones in Galápagos. From the top of the small hill is a nice view, and the trail itself goes through Palo Santo trees and cacti forests.

There is a saltwater lagoon where lucky visitors may see Pintail Ducks or Flamingos.

Trail Difficulty: 3/5
A relatively long hike that includes some rocky scrambles. Infirm hikers may want to check with the guides before attempting it. It can get a little muddy during the rainy season.

Wildlife:
Highly Probable to See:
  * Land Iguanas
  * Marine Iguanas
  * Flamingoes
  * Sally Lightfoot Crabs

Probable to See:
  * Galápagos Pintail Ducks
  * Galápagos Mockingbirds
  * Darwin's Finches
  * Galápagos Flycatchers

Possible to See:
  * Lava Herons
  * Black-necked Stilts
  * Wandering Tattlers
  * Whimbrels
Updated: Sep 10, 2012.

Garrapatero Beach

Located outside of Puerto Ayora, Garrapatero Beach is a favorite among locals and visitors alike. It's a gorgeous white sand beach perfect for swimming, lounging or even a bit of snorkeling. There are mangroves around it and even the little trail to the beach is interesting.

Getting there is a bit of a trick; you'll have to take a taxi and the ride is about 40 minutes or so. The taxi will not wait for you, but will come back for you if you tell him when. There are usually no taxis waiting there.

Once you reach the parking lot, there is a 15 minute walk to the beach along an easy trail. You can also get here by bike—it's about a two hour ride from Puerto Ayora.

There are no souvenir stands, restaurants, drink vendors or anything else at the beach— that's the whole charm of it, but be sure to bring everything you need. There are no trash cans either, so bring a bag for your garbage and be sure to take it out with you.

Beware of the manzanillo trees: they're poisonous. They're labeled, so just don't eat the little apples or sleep under the tree.

Although it's part of the park system, it's public access, so anyone can go there from Puerto Ayora with no need of any naturalist guides. There is sometimes a park ranger patrolling the area to make sure all regulations are complied with. Keep an eye on any valuables as petty theft is not unheard of.

Trail Difficulty (from parking lot): **1/5**

Wildlife:
Highly Probable to See:
  * Sally Lightfoot Crabs
  * Marine Iguanas

Probable to See:
  * Mockingbirds
  * Finches

Possible to See: (in a little lagoon nearby)
  * Galápagos Pintail Ducks
  * Flamingoes
  * Oystercatchers
  * Stilts
  * Herons

Dive Sites Near Puerto Ayora

Puerto Ayora is by far the best of the three towns for divers. There are several dive shops to choose from, all of which go to the same sites. Perhaps because of its central location, the variety of sites is very good: you could stay a week in Puerto Ayora and not dive the same site twice

North Seymour

There are five different immersion sites on North Seymour, a small island not far from Puerto Ayora, making it good for all levels of diving skill. Currents can be strong. Highlights include a garden eel colony and a chance of sharks including Galapagos Sharks and Hammerheads.

Distance by boat from Puerto Ayora: 1 ½ hours.

VISITOR SITES

Floreana Island

There are nine sites off of Floreana, which is good because if the water is rough at one site, the divemasters will usually just go to another one. There are sea lions at some of the sites and it's possible to watch them frolic underwater. It's also one of the only places in the Islands with significant coral formations.

Distance from Puerto Ayora: 1 hour, 45 mins.

Bartolomé Island/Cousins Rock

Bartolomé Island is usually combined with nearby Cousins Rock when organizing dives. Both dives are wall dives, best for intermediate to advanced divers.

Highlights include the chance to see frogfish, sea horses and sharks.

Distance from Puerto Ayora: 2 hours.

Academy Bay Tour, or a Dude with a Boat

If you're staying in Puerto Ayora for a while, a day tour of Academy Bay is a great way to spend the time. The city is located right on the bay, and it's tempting to overlook it because it's so close, but the bay has a lot to offer.

There are several "tour boats" which will be happy to sell you a spot on a bay tour; these range from genuine, safety-inspected motorboats with qualified, official guides to smelling-of-fish converted water taxis featuring a driver/guide who is perhaps best described as "a local Dude with a boat."

Surprisingly, when all is said and done there is little difference, and what the "Dude with a boat" may lack in wimpy things like safety inspections, life jackets and radios, he may make up for in local color and personality. As long as you don't need a lot of in-depth information—the Dude will not know the geological history of every island, or the name of Charles Darwin's dog, or any of that other stuff that they teach in guide school—you won't know the difference. Anyone can operate a motor and point out a Blue-Footed Booby. Besides, you'll be in sight of Puerto Ayora the whole time. Radios are for pansies.

There are little travel agencies literally everywhere—you can't swing a dead cat in Puerto Ayora without hitting a "tour operator." To book a bay tour, just walk into the nearest agency and set it up. They go every day, and should cost you about $15-25 depending on where you want to go and your negotiating skills. They generally go from about 1 or 2 in the afternoon to 5 or 6 p.m.

Bay tours generally include some or all of the following: you may go snorkeling at La Lobería, which is a small island in the bay with a sea lion colony, snorkeling along the rocky coast (where you might see a shark), a visit to a half-sunken fishing ship, and a walk along a short trail where you can maybe see some sharks in a narrow "canal." Some tours go to Playa de los Perros. Your guide (or Dude) will point out sea turtles, rays, fish and birds as they present themselves.

Bring a camera, a windbreaker, some walking shoes (tevas are fine) and perhaps a bottle of water.

You'll also want to bring your own snorkeling gear; you should be able to get it from the "tour operator" before you go. They will tell you that the Dude has all the snorkeling gear you need, and they will be lying. The Dude will have a few leaky masks that look like they were left on the islands by Charles Darwin himself because they were too crappy and beat-up to take back to England. He will have no fins. There will be snorkels, but what do you think the Dude does in his spare time? Wash snorkels with an appropriate solution of water, salt, Listerine and bleach? Not on your life! God only knows where the Dude's snorkels have been since the last time they were properly washed.

Tour Dude in his Boat

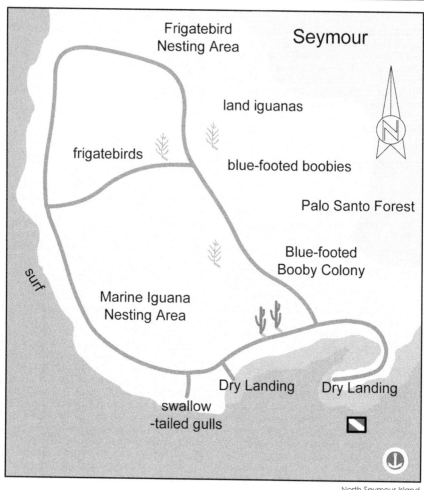

North Seymour Island

Academy Bay

Often overlooked, Academy Bay—the wide bay that serves as home for Puerto Ayora—is a superlative dive site in itself. There are five sites scattered around the bay, none of which is more than 20 minutes away from town by boat. It's good for beginners, and when people are staying for a few days, dive shops like to warm up here before heading to more difficult and remote sites. Good for rays, sea lions and perhaps a Galapagos Shark.

Distance from Puerto Ayora: n/a.

Santa Fe Island

The waters off of perennial favorite Santa Fe are calm and clear but still full of marine life, making it a must-do for divers of all levels. There are four different sites here, and your

divemaster will pick the one most likely to have lots of marine life. Look for rays, eels, turtles and sharks.

Distance from Puerto Ayora: One hour.

There is great SCUBA diving near Puerto Ayora!

Gordon Rocks

Another must-do, Gordon Rocks is a submerged tuff cone that consistently draws rave reviews from diving magazines and websites. Two of the four dive sites there are good for beginners, but the other two can be very challenging. It's a wall dive, and the wall goes very deep. Schools of Hammerhead Sharks are frequently seen, but other large marine life like rays and other shark species are common. Gordon Rocks is sometimes done in conjunction with North Seymour or Mosquera.

Distance from Puerto Ayora: One hour.

Mosquera

A good site for beginners, Mosquera Islet is home to a huge Garden Eel colony. The dive follows the reef which connects Mosquera to Baltra Island. There are other types of eel there, too, as well as sea turtles, a variety of rays including Manta Rays and a chance to see sharks. The currents can get strong sometimes.

Distance from Puerto Ayora: 1.5 hours

Daphne

There are three dive sites spread out in this smallest of islands including Daphne Major, Daphne Minor and El Bajo. One of the sites is perfect for mixed groups, as beginners will find it possible to do and experts will find lots of marine life to see.

Dive shops often take "Discovery Divers" (uncertified divers doing one or two dives only under the close supervision of a divemaster) to Daphne. The other sites can get a little rough, so beginning level divers should consult with the divemaster to make sure they're going to the right one!

Distance from Puerto Ayora: One hour.

NORTH SEYMOUR ISLAND

North Seymour is a small, flat island located near Baltra and Santa Cruz; it's possible to visit from Puerto Ayora as a day trip. It's a popular visitor site, as it is home to several species of birds as well as land and marine iguanas and sea lions.

The trail is about two and a half kilometers (1.6 mi) long and is rocky and treacherous in places. Following the trail along the beach, you should see Blue-Footed Boobies and pelicans fishing, Swallow-Tail Gulls and frigatebirds

flying, and marine iguanas resting on the rocky shore. If you take a rest on the rocks and patiently look out at the sea, you will probably see a sea lion or two surfing the waves.

Regardless of the time of year you visit, you are likely to observe some kind of courtship, mating, nesting or chick nesting on North Seymour. And since both boobies and frigatebirds often make their nests close to the trail, you may get a very good close-up shot. It's also not uncommon to catch frigates and boobies doing their courtship rituals. Further along the trail, you will see flocks of male frigate birds nesting—attracting females with their inflated red sack—and the occasional land iguana.

The land iguanas are found inland, where they feast on low-hanging cacti. Your guide will help you spot the bright yellow lizards among the plants and rocks off the trail. The iguanas here have an interesting history—they were brought here from Baltra in the 1930s and they thrived. Later, the Baltra population of land iguanas went extinct, but was repopulated by bringing some iguanas back from North Seymour!

The waters off of North Seymour Island provide some of the best diving and snorkeling opportunities in the islands. From the surface, you are bound to see White-tipped Reef Sharks, Triggerfish, Surgeonfish, and other colorful fish.

If you are diving in the Canal, you are likely see a host of Galápagos garden eels, moray eels, and the occasional diamond, golden, or manta ray.

Trail Difficulty: 4/5
The trail gets rocky and treacherous in places, and can get very hot on a sunny day.

Highly Probable to See:
* Blue-footed Boobies
* Frigatebirds
* Sea Lions
* Marine Iguanas
* Land Iguanas

Probable to See:
* Swallow-tailed Gulls
* Brown Pelicans

Possible to See:
* Red-billed Tropicbirds
* Galapagos Snake

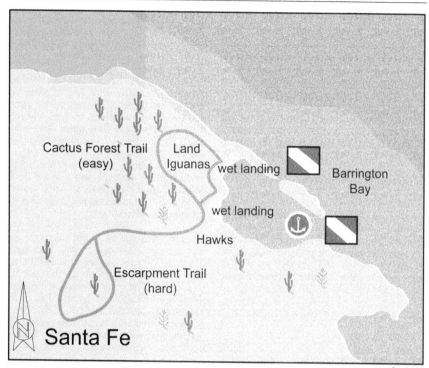

Cactus Forest Trail
(easy)

Land
Iguanas   wet landing

Barrington
Bay

wet landing

Hawks

Escarpment Trail
(hard)

Santa Fe

Santa Fe

BALTRA — AIR PORT.

Most visitors to the Galápagos archipelago arrive by plane to Baltra, also known as South Seymour. Baltra once served as a US military base. There are no visitor sites or accommodations on Baltra and the only facilities available relate to air traffic and transportation. From the airport you can catch a bus to the canal, where you catch the ferry to Santa Cruz, and to the port, where visitors with pre-arranged tours meet their boat. There is, however, a ghost on Baltra: see the box on "La Gringa sin Cabeza" on p. 122 for a first-hand account!

SANTA FE

Located about 20 kilometers (12.4 mi) southeast of Santa Cruz, the small island of Santa Fe (Barrington) is a popular destination for day trips and cruises. The trail consists of two loops separated by a walk of a couple hundred meters. The first loop, a 300-meter (984 ft) circuit, takes you to one of the tallest stands of opuntia cacti in the archipelago, some reaching heights of over 10 meters (32.8 ft). Look for the elusive Santa Fe subspecies of land iguana. You also might

see a park project of fire ant control. The other loop goes through a Palo Santo Forest, where you can also look for land iguanas.

Santa Fe is home to one of the two remaining species of endemic Galápagos Rice Rats, although it's very unlikely that you'll see one. There was once a species of Giant Tortoise on the island, but it has unfortunately gone extinct.Santa Fe is a popular day trip from Puerto Ayora because of the excellent snorkeling in the cove.

Note that only cruise ships are allowed to land on the island itself; if you're a day tripper, you'll come, snorkel and return without seeing the iguanas. It's also a popular SCUBA diving site.

Trail Difficulty: 2/5
It occasionally gets steep.

Wildlife:
Highly Probable to See:
  * Marine Iguanas
  * Sea Lions
  * Finches
  * Mockingbirds
  * Galápagos Hawks

La Gringa Sin Cabeza

Once in early 1989, while I was Captain of Port Seymour on Baltra Island, a navy guardsman banged noisily and incessantly on my door in the still darkness of the early morning. It was unusual that anyone would bother me so early, as they knew I would not be pleased, not to mention the fact that there was little that could happen in such a remote place that could not be straightened out later. I opened the door to find a grave-faced man informing me that the Headless Gringa had claimed another victim.

All of my subordinates knew exactly what I thought about that old ghost story, and they were alarmed at my insolence in doubting that a spirit had lingered for decades on that small, deserted island. As for myself, I always marveled at the fact that my adult soldiers—more than ten of them on the Naval base—all slept in the same dormitory simply to avoid being the prey of a satanic ghost that only attacked men who were alone.

During World War II, the US built a large base on Baltra, with beds for 5,000 men, two runways, a dock with generous reserves of water and fuel, some munitions bunkers, a hydroplane platform, and even a casino with bowling alley and a small movie theater.

The legend goes that one day a cuckolded American Marine threw his cheating girl-friend down the steep steps that led down the cliff from the command center to the pier. During this fall she lost her head, which had gotten spectacularly torn off as she tumbled. No one knew of this crime for years, because the Marine left no traces and stuck with the story that she had gone swimming and never come back, possibly on account of the love triangle in which she had become involved.

Nevertheless, her spirit lingered, even when the Americans left the base after World War II, their mission of protecting the vital Panama Canal no longer necessary. The base was turned over to the Ecuadorian government, which set up its own base there. Some of the installations were taken down, and the island returned to being the desert it had always been.

But the unhappy spirit remained, getting revenge for her tragic destiny by charming lonely men, sometimes appearing as a beautiful apparition, a sort of siren with an irresistible song, leading them to places where they would not be seen before un-leashing all of her bitterness and showing her true, headless form. She became known to the soldiers on the base as "la Gringa sin Cabeza" or the Headless Gringa.

Among her known victims was a young man posted to the Air Force base, a good-looking, smooth-talking fellow who was well-built and fearless. He was kind of cocky, especially when he was drinking. He was a big drinker, but then again so was pretty much everyone on the base. After all, what else was there to do to kill the time on that lonely outpost? They say it was his swagger that attracted the Headless Gringa.

He went missing, and after a day-long search, he was found on the eastern end of the island, near the lighthouse, where the view is magnificent and the sea is lit up in electrifying shades of blue. We weren't surprised to find our Don Juan foaming at the mouth, bound hand and foot and begging the "Gringa" to leave him alone.

The story he told of how he had been taken there was not unlike the ones we had heard before, except that this time he mentioned the scent of a strange and fancy perfume that the Gringa used. At first, it smelled like the Palo Santo trees found all over the island, before becoming the nauseating odor of a decomposing corpse later in their intimate encounter. We thought this dementia would be temporary, but he never really snapped out of it and had to be sent back to the continent a few days later by the Air Force.

There was an installation in the central part of the island which belonged to a group called DIREL 10, a mixed force of Army, Marine and Air Force soldiers who lived in the famous "Stone House," the impressive social club built by the Americans.

The Stone House had been an officers' club and bar during the war, and its thick stone walls, red roof, magnificent windows and 60 foot (18.3 m) wooden bar had all been restored to their original glory. They say that in its day the club had seen visitors including Marilyn Monroe, the President of the United

States and many others. They also say that when they restored the bar, they found at least three inches (7.62 cm) of chewing gum stuck beneath it all along its length.

Some 10 or 12 soldiers lived there, and they all slept together in a single room, except for their dog, "Rambo," who they always made stay outside "to protect them" no matter how miserable he looked or how much he whined. At the entrance to Stone House is a great cross made of thick, twisted Palo Santo branches. From the cross hangs a sign that reads "God is my savior, nothing will happen to me."

At night they always heard the seductive songs, which turned into piercing wails when they went unheeded. There was a small pickup truck at the house, and the horn would beep and the lights would flash, to the beat of the pathetic howling of the dog. But the soldiers never split up after dark, nor would they walk alone at night, because they knew what became of those who disrespected or were cheeky with the Headless Gringa.

The morning the guardsman woke me up, the Gringa had bewitched a sailor named Mendieta. He had been drinking and wanted to find more alcohol, so he had stolen the only truck in the port. Everyone knew I kept the keys to it in my desk. He apparently wanted to take the ghost somewhere, although there was nothing to do, nowhere to go and no store where he could get more alcohol. There wasn't even any light—the base was shrouded in darkness because we religiously shut off the generator at 10 o'clock at night until six o'clock the next morning.

The sailor sped around the base, found his way onto the only road on the island and proceeded to crash into the only radio pole on the base, in the process destroying the VOR communication system used by incoming airplanes and leaving us "incomunicado" for a long time. By some miracle Mendieta was alive, although with several fractures. According to those who found him, there was a penetrating, ominous odor of rot and Palo Santo at the crash site.

Our little truck was not so lucky. It was completely destroyed and there was nothing we could do about it, because even the Ecuadorian Navy had forgotten we lived there, and so it would be for some time.

I don't know if my luck was good or bad. Despite the fact that I refused to sleep with the others and was isolated in an officer's house some 500 meters (1,640 ft) away (where I felt acutely the "isolation of command"), I never saw the Gringa. I never even caught a whiff of her perfume.

What I would have given for a visit from the Gringa.

Captain Christian Cuvi Rinsche
September 29, 2010

MOSQUERA

Only about 600 meters long by 160 meters wide (1,968.5 ft by 525 ft) at its widest point, Mosquera is a small, rocky islet located between Baltra and North Seymour. It was once an underwater reef when a geologic force known as an uplift pushed it up above the water, forming an island. Because of this, Mosquera is very flat, not at all conical like other small islands in Galápagos.

There is a good beach on Mosquera, as well as a trail leading past a huge sea lion colony and a nesting area for Lava Gulls. It's possible to snorkel off of the beach, and there's a good chance swimmers will be joined by one of the numerous sea lions who make the island their home.

Mosquera is a popular dive site with operators from Puerto Ayora.

Trail Difficulty: 1/5
There is no real trail, just the chance to explore at leisure.

Wildlife:
Highly Probable to See:
  * Sea Lions
  * Lava Gulls
  * Blue-footed Boobies
  * Sally Lightfoot Crabs
  * Marine Iguanas

Probable to See:
  * Brown Pelicans
  * Herons
Updated: Sept 13, 2012.

VISITOR SITES

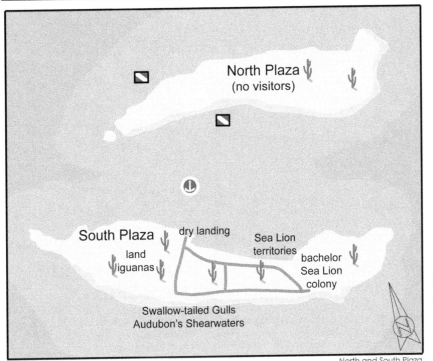

North and South Plaza

SOUTH PLAZA

South Plaza is a small island off the east coast of Santa Cruz. The small size of the island combined with interesting geology, flora and fauna make it a definitive highlight for cruise travelers or for day trippers from Puerto Ayora.

There is a dry landing onto a shore covered with white rocks, polished to a brilliant sheen by the oily sea lions as they travel up and down the shore. A one-kilometer (0.62 mi) trail circuit leads you through an opuntia cactus forest frequented by land iguanas, Yellow Warblers and finches. There is also a land/marine iguana hybrid that has been hanging out at the beginning of the trail since 2003, but it is only rarely seen. South Plaza is one of the best places to see land iguanas in Galapagos. The trail continues along a 25-meter (82 ft) high cliff, which provides excellent vistas of neighboring Santa Cruz as well as sights of numerous sea birds.

You may also see a conspicuous line of mullets swimming offshore and, if you are lucky, a shark or two lurking in the rocks below or a manta ray jumping in the distance.

Further east along the trail, you will encounter a sea lion bachelor colony, where males defeated in the battle for territory kick back for a bit before returning to challenge once again. The final part of the trail passes through a sea lion nursery, where you may see newborn pups (if arriving in October-December) or playful juveniles (February-April).

Trail Difficulty: 2/5

Wildlife:
Highly Probable to See:
 * Sea Lions
 * Nazca Boobies
 * Blue-footed Boobies
 * Sally Lightfoot Crabs
 * Marine Iguanas
 * Finches
 * Yellow Warblers

Probable to See:
 * Land Iguanas
 * Swallow-tailed Gulls
 * Frigatebirds

Possible to See:
 * Red-billed Tropicbirds

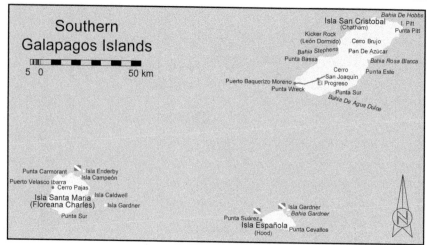

Southern Island Visitor Sites

VISITOR SITES

DAPHNE MAJOR AND MINOR

If you have the opportunity to visit Daphne Major, the island home where Rosemary and Peter Grant conducted their study on Darwin's Finches that inspired the novel, *The Beak of the Finch*, consider yourself among select company: the island is only accessible to one scientific group per month in order to mitigate erosion.

It is clear from the beginning of the visit—a landing which requires stepping from the moving dinghy onto a vertical cliff face and scrambling up the rocks to the head of the steep, rocky trail—that a trip to Daphne is a special experience.

The short trail leads up the side of the volcanic island to a 120-meter (393.7 ft) high summit, passing Nazca Boobies, Swallow-tailed Gulls, and finches along the way. At the top of the cone are two small craters, where hundreds of Blue-Footed Boobies and Frigatebirds settle to find their mates (a veritable bird motel!).

Daphne Minor is fairly eroded and not accessible to tourists, although the surrounding waters are a very popular dive site. The underwater geology of Daphne proves very interesting to those inclined to dive, with recesses and steep cliffs, and a high possibility of seeing sharks as well —White-Tipped, Galápagos, and occasionally even Hammerheads—along with sea turtles and rays here and there.
Updated: June 04, 2013.

Southern Island Visitor Sites

The three southern islands of San Cristóbal, Española, and Floreana provide some of the most exciting, unique and unforgettable visitor sites in Galápagos.

San Cristóbal and its main port town, Puerto Baquerizo Moreno, have the best surfing spots in the archipelago. There is good diving and snorkeling nearby, as well as some good beaches.

Española is famous as the only place in the world where the Waved Albatross nests. You can see their awkward waddling take-off during the months of the year when they are there.

Finally, the island of Floreana boasts one of the best snorkel spots in the islands, Devil's Crown, as well as some of the most interesting human history. Updated: Jun 04, 2013.

SAN CRISTÓBAL

San Cristóbal (Chatham) is the fifth-largest (558 km²/346.7 mi²) and easternmost of the islands. Rapid development of tourist and educational facilities, as well as the existence of an airport, has caused island visitation to grow in recent years, with a corresponding boom in tourism services.

San Cristóbal boasts the largest large freshwater lagoon in the archipelago, as well as beautiful beaches, amazing snorkeling and

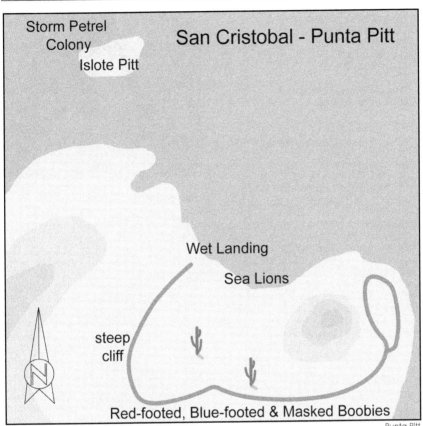

Punta Pitt

scuba-diving opportunities, and some of the best surfing spots in Galápagos.

The island also provides an interesting socio-environmental element missing from other islands—visitors interested in the human component of the Galápagos Islands can see colonial architecture, visit organic coffee plantations and other agricultural centers, and even check out local politics in the provincial capital, Puerto Baquerizo Moreno.

Some of the sites are only for cruise ships: these include Punta Pitt and Cerro Brujo. The rest can be visited from Puerto Baquerizo Moreno.

Punta Pitt

Located on the far eastern shore of San Cristóbal Island, Punta Pitt is a popular site for visitors, mostly because it's the only Galápagos visitor site where you can see all three types of Booby as well as both types of Frigatebirds.

After landing on an olivine beach, the trail runs up a dry creek bed between a couple of hills before leveling out. The trail then loops through a nesting area for the aforementioned birds. The scenery is beautiful: the scrambe up the creek bed to get to the top is well worth it.

Most visits to Punta Pitt include a boat ride past a small rocky islet not far from the landing site. Many species of birds make their homes there, including the elusive Red-Billed Tropic Bird.

Trail Difficulty: 4/5
One of the harder visitor site trails, it's long and treacherous in places. Bring good shoes and extra water.

Wildlife:
Highly Probable to See:
  * Galápagos Sea Lions
  * Blue-footed Boobies
  * Red-footed Boobies
  * Nazca Boobies

* Magnificent Frigatebirds
* Great Frigatebirds

Probable to See:
 * Lava Lizards
 * Mockingbirds
 * Red-Billed Tropic Bird
Updated: May 3, 2013

Cerro Brujo

Cerro Brujo, or "Warlock Hill," is named after the Vermilion Flycatcher, which is called Pájaro Brujo or "Warlock Bird" in Spanish. The hill used to be home to a handful of these colorful birds, although it's very rare to see one there now.

Instead, visitors will have to settle for the marvelous sandy beach and sea lion colony there. There is no trail as such, only a small one that connects the first beach, where pangas land, with the second one, where visitors can swim and snorkel. The beach is gorgeous and wide and great for a stroll. At low tide, rocks and tidal pools are exposed in the area between the two beaches; this is a great place to look for wading birds like Oystercatchers or Herons.

The visit to Cerro Brujo usually includes a short panga ride along the coast, where visitors can marvel at some interesting rock formations and even go through an eroded tunnel!

It's possible to snorkel here, although the sandy bottom and waves make it unlikely you'll see much other than a few fish or a stingray or two if you're lucky. Head towards the rocks and go a little deeper if you want to see anything.

Stay clear of the sand dunes behind the beach to preserve the vegetation.

Trail Difficulty: 1/5
The rocks and dunes between the two beaches can be slightly tricky, especially if you have to go around a sleeping sea lion.
Wildlife:
Highly Probable to See:
 * Galápagos Sea Lions

Probable to See:
 * Brown Pelicans
 * Marine Iguanas

Possible to See:
 * Whimbrels
 * Herons
 * Oystercatchers

Panga Ride, Cerro Brujo

Interpretation Center

The "Interpretation Center" on San Cristóbal is a small complex of buildings located at the far end of town, not far from Playa Mann and the university. It's a museum of sorts, with displays on the natural and human history of Galápagos—the human history part is by far the more interesting, although both are well done. It has fascinating displays on everything from the famous "Galápagos Affair" to the hardy Norwegians who settled Galápagos in the 1920s. The center is a must for anyone who wants to know more about the history of the islands.

There is also a conference room and small open-air theater, both of which seem to be rarely used. Behind the interpretation center is the trail that leads to the Cabo de Horno/Punta Carola beach and Tijeretas Hill and snorkeling lagoon. The trail itself is paved and well-marked—it's impossible to get lost. Updated: Aug 15, 2012.

Cerro Tijeretas

Cerro Tijeretas gets its name from the Frigate Birds, commonly called "fragatas" but also called "tijeretas" ("cerro" means hill). Chances are you'll see some frigate birds flying around.

Cerro Tijeretas is located on the trail behind the interpretation center on San Cristóbal. There are stairs to climb the hill, and once you're up there you'll see Shipwreck Bay as well as the ocean; the view is well worth the short walk to the top. If you're going to see all the points of interest on the trail—an old artillery piece, the Cabo de Hornos beach, a statue of Charles Darwin—go to Cerro Tijeretas first, because the whole trail is visible from the top and it will help orient you. Updated: Aug 15, 2012.

VISITOR SITES

At the base of the hill is a small, nearly enclosed lagoon that is perfect for snorkeling, particularly for beginners. There are no waves or currents, just underwater rocks where fish and other marine life like to hang out. The trail leads down to a small platform on the water where sea lions may be lounging.

There isn't much space on the little platform, so if a lot of people are there you may have to wait your turn to get into or out of the water (to avoid this, go in the morning). Don't leave valuables behind while snorkeling.

Cerro Tijeretas is part of the National Park, but you don't need a guide to go there. The trail from the interpretation center is very easy to follow.

Trail Difficulty: 2/5
There are some steps to get to the top of the hill, but nothing treacherous.

Wildlife:
Highly Probable to See:
 * Lava Lizards
 * Sea Lions
 * Frigatebirds
Updated: Aug 17, 2012.

Galapaguera de Cerro Colorado/ Red Hill Tortoise Breeding Center

The Cerro Colorado ("Red Hill") Giant Tortoise breeding center is a great place to see San Cristóbal Giant Tortoises in the wild (semi-wild, anyway). There is a small breeding center with a handful of tiny tortoises (ask to see "Genesis," the first one to hatch in the center a few years ago) and

Cerro Tijeretas

behind the building is a trail through the dense brush. Along the trail you can expect to see several fully grown tortoises eating, napping, wallowing in the mud, etc. It's one of the best places in all of Galápagos to see them: they're penned in at the Charles Darwin Research Station and the breeding center on Isabela, but here you can go right up to them for a good photo (no touching!).

This breeding center is very important because the San Cristóbal Giant Tortoises are in grave danger due to introduced animals including goats and cats; it is hoped that the consistent release of tortoises into the wild will stabilize the population until the pests can be eradicated.

Keep your eyes open for birds; they love the scrubby trees. You may see finches, mockingbirds and other small land birds flitting around.

You can go to the breeding center from Puerto Baquerizo Moreno—it's about a 40 minute drive. It's often included on day tours of the area which also include Playa Chino and the Cerro Colorado Lookout. Cruise ships often take their passengers there, especially if they're picking up new passengers at the San Cristóbal airport.

How to get there: You'll have to arrange transportation from Puerto Baquerizo Moreno: negotiate with a taxi driver.

Trail Difficulty: 2/5
It's rocky and dense in places.

Wildlife:
Highly Probable to See:
 * Giant Tortoises
 * Mockingbirds
 * Finches

Possible to See:
 * Yellow Warblers
 * Galápagos Flycatchers

Galapaguera Natural (Natural Giant Tortoise Breeding Center)

On the northern end of San Cristóbal Island is a natural protected zone for the San Cristóbal Giant Tortoises. A trail runs from the beach into the interior for about five kilometers (3 mi); visitors turn around and take the same path back out.

VISITOR SITES

The trail is tough and most cruise ships do not include it on their itineraries (if your itinerary says "Galapaguera" it's probably referring to the one at Cerro Colorado, which is much easier to visit). The only way to do this trail is to contract a guide in Puerto Baquerizo Moreno, and the only way to reach the trail is by boat.

Trail Difficulty: 5/5
The trail itself isn't too bad, but it's long, it gets really hot there and there is no breeze. Bring water and sunscreen, but try to avoid scented sunscreen as it may attract the aggressive wasps that are common along the trail.

Wildlife:
Highly Probable to See:
* Giant Tortoises
* Mockingbirds
* Finches
* Lava Lizards

Possible to See:
* Feral Goats
Updated: Aug 12, 2012.

La Lobería
La Lobería is a beach and small island located not too far along the coast from Puerto Baquerizo Moreno. It's not technically part of the Galápagos National Park, although the park rangers do help monitor it because of its ecological importance.

It's a nice beach and home to a very large pack of sea lions. It is not necessary to have a guide; there is a trail to get there from near the airport which takes about a half hour on foot. Some cruise ships stop there. It's possible to camp here overnight but you need previous permission from the National Park.

La Lobería beach is known as a good place to surf: check with the surf shops in Puerto Baquerizo Moreno if you're interested.

Trail Difficulty: 2/5

Wildlife:
Highly Probable to See:
* Sea Lions
* Lava Lizards
* Marine Iguanas
* Finches

Probable to See:
* Blue-footed Boobies
* Yellow Warblers

Possible to See:
* Giant Tortoises (along the trail)
Updated: Aug 17, 2012.

Laguna El Junco/El Junco Lake
One of the few bodies of fresh water in Galápagos, El Junco Lake is located in the green highlands of San Cristóbal. Don't go there expecting to water ski or fish for salmon—in the USA they'd call it a "pond" instead of a lake. Still, it's the largest body of fresh water in the islands, and it's a great place to see birds that you won't see anywhere else. Many cruise ships go there, and it's possible to visit on your own from San Cristóbal, without a guide, by taking a taxi ($10 round trip from town, including waiting an hour for you to walk), or tours can be booked in Puerto Baquerizo Moreno.

The lake is a dormant volcanic caldera at 650 meters (2000 feet) above sea level and the only year-round lake in all of the islands. On a clear day, the 360 degree views are unparalleled. Visible on a hill in front of the lake are three wind turbines that produce around half of the electricity for the island in an innovative project financed by the E8, a consortium of some of the largest electricity companies in the world, and the United Nations.

Frigate birds frequent the lake to clean the salt from their wings and Pintailed ducks are frequently spotted feeding in the lake. Miconia, an endemic plant that traps mist from the air, covers most of the mountain but has been threatened by introduced blackberry. The National Park and the Jatun Sacha Foundation are reforesting with miconia, and volunteers can participate (see volunteer section p. 48).

Trail Difficulty (from the road): 4/5

The walk from the parking lot is steep and takes about an hour to go up and back, and another half an hour to hike around the lake (highly recommended if you have a clear day). Parts of the trail can be muddy and very slippery, but about half of the trail up is a wooden boardwalk.

Wildlife:
Highly Probable to See:
* Frigatebirds

Probable to See:
* Pintail Ducks

Possible to See:
* Herons
* Egrets
* Common Moorhens
* Pied-billed Grebes

Playa Ochoa

Located about 30 minutes by boat from Puerto Baquerizo Moreno, Playa Ochoa is a great public beach with a large sea lion population. It's one of the places that Charles Darwin visited on his famous 1835 trip to the islands. It's good for snorkeling, as the surf and currents are not too rough. Cruise ships often stop here, and it's possible to visit from Puerto Baquerizo Moreno. A little ways inland is a brackish lagoon where Flamingoes are occasionally seen. Camping is allowed with a permit from the park.

Puerto Chino

Puerto Chino is a remote beach on the southern edge of San Cristóbal Island, located not too far from the Cerro Colorado Tortoise Breeding Center. The trail from the road goes about 1,500 meters (4,921 ft) to the beach. The beach is great for relaxing and surfing. The beach itself is smallish and surrounded by mangroves. Watch out for the poisonous Manzanillo trees. Most cruise ships don't visit Puerto Chino, and the only visitors are likely those who have booked a day surfing with a Puerto Baquerizo Moreno surf tour company.

Puerto Grande

Puerto Grande is a public beach on the coast of San Cristóbal Island not too far from Kicker Rock. It's accessible by boat from Puerto Baquerizo Moreno. It's popular with day-tripping families from town who have their own boat; cruise ships don't usually go there and it's unlikely to be included on any tour. It's a nice beach, and the swimming and snorkeling there are pretty good.

According to some locals, there is pirate treasure buried at Puerto Grande, although no one has ever found any. Most likely, the "treasure" is one of the best beaches in Galápagos!

Probable to See:
Brown Pelican

Possible to See:
Red-billed Tropicbird
Lava Heron
Swallow-tailed Gulls

Punta Carola

Located on the trails behind the visitor's center, Punta Carola is about a 45 minute walk from Puerto Baquerizo Moreno. Bring good walking shoes as the trail is rough. It's a small, sandy beach, home to sea lions and shore birds.

It's possible to snorkel there, but it can get a little rough; it's far better to walk 15 minutes over to the lagoon at Cerro Tijeretas. There's more space here, however, so if you're looking for a place to put down a towel and relax for a while, this is a better bet.
Updated: Jan 18, 2013.

Playa Mann

The best of the beaches right in Puerto Baquerizo Moreno, Playa Mann is only a short walk from downtown. It's right across the street from the university. It's a gorgeous white-sand beach, and you can swim and snorkel to your heart's content. It's free and there is no need of a guide.
Updated: Jan 18, 2013.

King Cobos' El Progreso

The settlement of El Progreso had its beginnings as Manuel Cobos' notorious plantation and sugar-refining operation, founded in 1869. Cobos used prisoners as his labor. As punishment, he sentenced them to hundreds of lashes or marooned them on waterless islands (a sure death). Mr. Cobos controlled all aspects of the economy—including minting the only money used on San Cristóbal, and owning the only boat that operated between the mainland and the island. He reportedly said, "I am King of San Cristóbal. I can kill. I will defend myself with my money."

In 1904, after a prisoner died from a 500-lash treatment, the others could take it no longer. They plotted to kill Cobos just before the ship was to come in. They took over the boat, loading up as many of the men, women and children as possible. When the ship arrived near the Ecuador-Colombia border, all were arrested. Government officials went to the San Cristóbal to check out the prisoners' accusations—and found them to be even more horrific. (One prisoner who had been marooned on another island was miraculously found still alive—four years after his "sentence"!). The ruins of the plantation and Cobos' grave are historical monuments.

San Cristóbal Dive Sites

San Cristóbal is known mostly for surfing, but there are a few dive shops in town and they go to some pretty cool sites.

León Dormido/Kicker Rock

The distinctive, boot-shaped Kicker Rock is a favorite Puerto Baquerizo dive site. It's for beginner-intermediate level divers. There are actually two rocks there, and the dive takes you down between them to the bottom, about 80 feet (25 meters). Along the way, you'll see numerous fish and possibly Hammerhead Sharks. It's possible to snorkel on the surface here, so snorkelers and divers can take the same trip.

Isla Lobos

A fun dive for beginners, Isla Lobos is located just up the coast from Puerto Baquerizo Moreno. There is a long, narrow island separated from the coast by a short distance. Between the island and the coast is a little lagoon of sorts, full of sea lions and marine iguanas. It's only about 30 feet (10 meters) deep, and there is little current. Most dive shops combine Lobos with Punta Pitt or Kicker Rock. Also great for snorkeling.

Distance from Puerto Baquerizo Moreno: 20 minutes

Five Fingers

Located just outside of Shipwreck bay, Five Fingers is a great place for colorful reef fish. It's a wall dive off of a very small island and there are some coral formations, but the walls go too deep to go to the bottom of them except in a couple of places. Be careful with the sharpness of them.

Distance from Puerto Baquerizo Moreno: 20 Minutes

Caragua

The Caragua is a 100-year-old wreck located just outside Shipwreck Bay. It has formed an artificial reef and is home to many fish, seahorses, coral, sea lions and more.

There is a moderate current, but the wreck isn't too deep, only being in about 15 meters (50 feet). It's just about the only wreck worth diving in the Galápagos.

Distance from Puerto Baquerizo Moreno: 15 minutes

Buried Treasure?

It's mandatory—anywhere there were once pirates, there must be buried treasure, right? The pirate literature classic Treasure Island does not lie! And just as there were once pirates in Galápagos, so legends of buried treasure persist.

On San Cristóbal Island, the natives of Puerto Baquerizo Moreno believe that pirates buried some treasure near Tijeretas Hill, behind the Visitor's Center (no, silly, the visitor's center was NOT there when the alleged pirates buried their alleged treasure). Some have even gone looking for it. But an old San Cristóbal legend suggests they might be looking in the wrong place.

The legend goes like this. Back in the 1930s, San Cristóbal was a tiny settlement, mostly supported by fishing and some basic agriculture. Of course, there were no motors back then, so fishermen had to sail and row to where they needed to go. Now, everyone knew that the fishing was good near Kicker Rock just off the north side of the islands. The fishermen would go there, camp overnight on the beach at Puerto Grande, and fish the next day.

One day, the old-timers tell, they were fishing off of Kicker Rock when a strange yacht no one had ever seen before came into view. It cruised towards the beach and stayed there for a while, but when the fishermen got back there, it was gone. The tents and belongings of the fishermen had been scattered and thrown aside, and there was a large, deep hole in the dunes where their tents had been. The smashed remains of wooden crates were everywhere. No one ever found out what was in the crates, and no one ever saw the strange yacht again.

Did the yacht have a treasure map? The old-timers don't know. The mysterious visitors certainly found what they were looking for. A tall tale? You be the judge, but would fishermen ever fib?

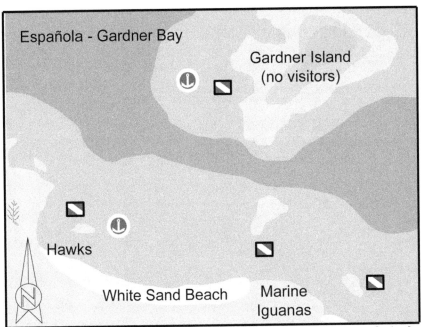

Española - Gardner Bay

Gardner Island
(no visitors)

Hawks

White Sand Beach   Marine
Iguanas

Gardner Bay

ESPAÑOLA

The southeasternmost of the Galápagos Islands, Española is also the oldest in geological terms. Like the others, it was created as the earth's crust moved over a geological "hot spot," spawning volcanoes which eventually created solid land.

Española (known to the British as "Hood") moved away from the hot spot long ago and is no longer volcanically active.

Española's main claim to fame is that it is the only nesting site of the Waved Albatross, a large, stately bird endemic to Galápagos. It's also where you'll find a subspecies of the Marine Iguana: the Española "Christmas Iguana" so named because the larger ones turn a distinctive red and green color during mating season.

There are two visitor sites on Española: Punta Suárez (Suárez Point) and Gardner Bay. Punta Suárez is one of the most memorable sites in all of Galápagos—it's the only place to see the brightly colored iguanas and the Waved Albatross. Gardner Bay is a gorgeous white sand beach known for friendly sea lions and good swimming and snorkeling.
Updated: Jan 18, 2013.

Gardner Bay/Tortuga Rock

Gardner Bay is one of the best beaches in Galápagos—a stunning stretch of white sand rocked by gentle waves, which dozing sea lions will grudgingly share with you. There's not much to see in the way of wildlife and no trail to follow: just a great beach to spend a couple of lazy hours. Observe the signs, which will keep you out of a sea turtle nesting area. If you go to the far end of the beach (where the black rocks are) you have a good chance of spotting a Marine Iguana or two.

It's possible to snorkel in the fairly calm waters of the bay, but don't expect to see much. Sea lions may get close enough for a good look, and rays are common in the area. Stingrays lurk on the sandy bottom; look for them starting just a few feet from shore. Manta and Spotted Eagle Rays occasionally pass through. You'll see some fish as well or a sea turtle or White-tipped Reef Shark if you're lucky; look for fish near rocks.

Just offshore, however, is Turtle Rock, the remains of a volcanic crater that, when viewed from the right angle, looks like a turtle surfacing. The snorkeling around Turtle Rock is excellent. On the calm (no current) side of Turtle Rock, look carefully in the sand for camouflaged Stone Scorpionfish lurking on the sandy bottom. Although there is a current, Turtle Rock

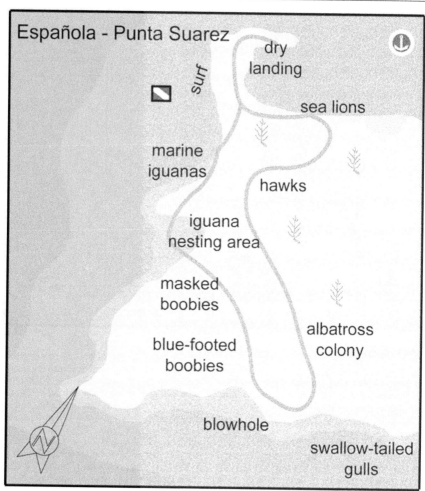

Punta Suárez

is a good place for intermediate snorkelers because one side of it is always sheltered from wind and waves. A good swimmer can make it from shore to Turtle Rock and vice-versa.

Trail Difficulty: 1/5
Sandy beach!

Wildlife:
Highly Probable to See:
* Sea Lions
* Hood Mockingbirds
* Stingrays
* Reef Fish

Probable to See:
* Darwin's Finches
* Hood Lava Lizards

Possible to See:
* Manta Rays
* Spotted Eagle Rays
* Green Sea Turtles
* White-tipped Reef Sharks
* Marine Iguanas
* Stone Scorpionfishs
Updated: Jan 27, 2013.

Punta Suárez

One of the best visitor sites in the islands, Punta Suárez is the only place where visitors can see the famous Waved Albatross. It's also a great place to see Boobies, Tropicbirds and other birds. Look for the red-and-green "Christmas Iguanas." There are a couple of sandy beach areas and a monument which is also a popular perch for the Galápagos

The Galápagos Affair

In 1929, Dr. Friedrich Karl Ritter, an eccentric Berlin doctor, arrived on Floreana Island with his mistress/patient Dore Strauch. Dr. Ritter had a medical degree, but he believed that the power of the mind could cure many diseases: today, we would call him a "holistic" doctor. They had each left their respective spouses to set up a sort of Eden in the far-off Galápagos Islands, and their scandalous affair made them into popular subjects for the European press.

ARRIVAL OF THE WITTMERS

Before long, they started getting curious visitors who came all the way from Europe. Most didn't last long, but in September of 1932, Heinrich and Margret Wittmer arrived with Heinrich's 12-year-old son from a previous marriage, Harry. They set up a homestead not far from Ritter and Strauch. The Wittmers and the Ritters didn't have much in common besides being German, and the two groups basically kept to themselves, which seems to be how they liked it.

THE BARONESS ARRIVES

Their peace and tranquility was about to be severely disrupted, however, with the November, 1932 arrival of "The Baroness." Looking like the star of a bad S&M movie—she regularly wore black boots and riding pants and kept a whip and a pistol handy—she went under the name of Eloise Baroness Wagner de Bosquet and claimed to be Austrian nobility. She moved into an abandoned Norwegian settlement in Post Office Bay with her retinue of three men: Germans Rudolf Lorenz and Robert Phillipson and Ecuadorian Felipe Valdivieso.

The German men were apparently both love slaves, and the Ecuadorian was there to do all the work. It was the Baroness' plan to construct a magnificent luxury hotel, to be called the Hacienda Paradiso.

TROUBLE IN PARADISE

Not long after her arrival, the three groups of settlers began to have problems. The Wittmers and Dr. Ritter and Ms. Strauch suspected that the Baroness was stealing items and mail from them and lodged several official complaints. The governor of Galápagos was eventually forced to come to Floreana to check out the reports, but he apparently fell under the spell of the Baroness and even invited her to his home.

By March of 1934, the situation of all three groups had taken a turn for the worse. The area was suffering from a severe drought, heightening the tension and requiring more work from everyone. Dr. Ritter was becoming more and more abusive to Dore Strauch, forbidding her from doing non-essential work (such as planting flowers). According to the Wittmers, Strauch showed no signs of wanting to leave the doctor in spite of his increasing violence and cruelty.

The Baroness and Phillipson

A MYSTERIOUS DISAPPEARANCE

Meanwhile, at the Baroness' camp, Rudolf Lorenz had apparently fallen out of favor, and Phillipson was beating and starving him. Lorenz would often show up at the Wittmer home for food, and would stay until the Baroness and Phillipson came for him.

One day, the Baroness and Phillipson vanished. According to Margret Wittmer, they told her that they were going to Tahiti on a ship that was waiting for them in the harbor. There is no evidence, however, that there ever was such a ship and a search of their home indicated that they had taken almost none of their possessions with them, including items that they would have wanted even on a very short voyage. They also never turned up in Tahiti.

Many locals and historians believe the two were murdered either by Lorenz or Ritter and the others went along with the Tahiti story.

Hawk. The trail is a loop; your guide may lead you to the left along the beach and into the interior, or to the right along the rocky coast. Either way, you'll get to see the whole trail.

Punta Suárez

Heading counter-clockwise along the coastal trail, you pass colonies of Blue-footed Boobies and Nazca Boobies nesting on the cliffs, most likely spot a finch or two, and probably see a few sea birds—the Red-billed Tropicbird or Swallow-tailed Gull—flying offshore.

You'll immediately learn to avoid the Lava Lizards darting under your feet and Mockingbirds begging for water.

THE DEATHS OF RUDOLF LORENZ AND DR. RITTER

Not long after, Lorenz left the islands, bound for Guayaquil. His ship also vanished, and the bodies of Lorenz and the ship's captain were later found, mummified and dessicated, on Marchena Island, where they had died of dehydration and starvation.

In December of 1934, Dr. Ritter died after eating some chicken that had gone bad. As he died, he cursed Dore Strauch, leading many to believe that she had poisoned him.

THE ENDURING MYSTERY OF THE GALÁPAGOS AFFAIR

Although there have been many inquiries, no one has ever gotten to the bottom of the disappearance of the Countess and the deaths of Lorenz and Ritter, and "The Galápagos Affair" remains one of Latin America's most enduring mysteries to this day.

Next, walk down to the beach where waves crash up on the rocks in a breathtaking display and where hordes of marine iguanas monitor the eggs they have laid between the months of January and March. If you arrive when the eggs begin to hatch, chances are you will see a Galápagos Hawk hovering around this area, waiting to prey upon the new hatchlings.

Just beyond lies a flat section of the trail, an "airport" where, from late March until late December, Waved Albatrosses can take flight, land, await the return of their mates from the mainland, or proceed with their elaborate courting rituals.

Further along the trail is a blowhole, a slit in the rocky coastline through which waves force water to spout about 20 meters (66 ft) in the air. Here you can sit on the cliff and watch the spectacle, relax and reapply sunscreen (you have probably already been walking for an hour!), and watch sea birds flying overhead.

The rocky trail back to the beach cuts inland through the dry vegetation of the island, where more albatrosses may be hiding. This part of the trail is the hardest, as the rocks can be treacherous and it gets very hot during certain times of the year.

Trail Difficulty: 5/5
One of the toughest trails in Galápagos, the Punta Suárez trail includes a scamper up from the coast to the cliff and goes over some large, rounded boulders where it's possible to turn your ankle. Reasonably fit people will have no problem; older or unwell travelers may want a good walking stick.

Wildlife:
Highly Probable to See:
 * Hood Lava Lizards
 * Blue-footed Boobies
 * Waved Albatross (except January-March)
 * Masked/Nazca Boobies
 * Marine Iguanas
 * Swallow-tailed Gulls
 * Hood Mockingbirds
 * Sally Lightfoot Crabs

Probable to See:
 * Darwin's Finches
 * Galápagos Flycatchers
 * Sea Turtles (swimming off shore)
 * Dolphins
 * Galápagos Hawks

* Brown Pelicans
* Frigatebirds

Possible to See:
* Galápagos Snakes
* Red-billed Tropicbirds
* Audubon's Shearwaters
* American Oystercatchers
Updated: Jan 27, 2013.

FLOREANA

Floreana (Charles) is one of the more historic islands in Galápagos, although there is little left there today to remind visitors of the past. Charles Darwin visited the island in 1835; at the time there was a penal colony there, with between 200 and 300 prisoners.

Floreana had many Giant Tortoises at the time, and they were taken as food by the prisoners and by passing ships, eventually becoming extinct.

Patrick Watkins

In 1807, Irishman Patrick Watkins decided he had seen enough of the sea. His ship was anchored at Post Office Bay, and he took the opportunity to desert, marooning himself in the process. For years he lived on the island, eating what goats and tortoises he could catch and occasionally raising vegetables and fruit to sell to passing ships...or, preferably, trade them for booze.

After a few years, he tired of the harsh life on Galápagos and decided to get back to civilization. He stole a small boat and some weapons...and then the story gets a little hazy. In some versions of the tale, he kidnapped three sailors; in other versions it was five slaves. According to the tales, he arrived in Guayaquil...alone. The Ecuadorian authorities, believing he had killed and eaten the others, threw him in jail.

Other versions of the story claim that he made it to the coast by himself, met a woman and convinced her to return to the islands with him. It was at that point that he was jailed, for trying to steal a boat.

No one knows for sure the ending of the tale of Patrick Watkins, first resident of the Galápagos Islands...fill in your own!

Perhaps because of the abundant tortoises, Floreana was popular with pirates and whalers who could take on food and water easily there. One remnant of this time is Post Office Bay, where whalers would leave letters for home (and pick up any if they were headed back). There is still a place to leave postcards and letters, and other visitors will deliver them for you!

Floreana was also the site of the infamous 1934 "Galápagos Affair" that left five people dead or missing in a few short months. The Wittmer family, which was involved in the affair, still lives on Floreana.

Floreana is also known as Santa María or Charles. The island was named for Juan José Flores, the first President of Ecuador. He never visited Galápagos.

Because of the long human history on Floreana, it is also one of the worst off in terms of introduced species. The island has always suffered from more than its share of introduced vermin, including mice, wasps, fire ants and more. The island also has a problem with introduced plants, such as the blackberry. In many places on Floreana, it is possible to see efforts to remove them, as Floreana has been targeted by the Charles Darwin Research Station for urgent removal of these dangerous species.

There are several places to visit on Floreana. The first is the tiny town of Puerto Velasco Ibarra, the smallest settlement in Galápagos, with fewer than 200 inhabitants. There is now a small hotel there, so it's possible to spend the night.

Post Office Bay includes a look at the famous post office site and some lava tunnels. The Baroness Lookout is a great site with a nice view. Punta Cormorant is a nice ocean walk and a good place to see flamingos. The Devil's Crown is one of the best snorkeling sites in the islands. Offshore, Champion Islet is a superlative snorkeling spot.

PUERTO VELASCO IBARRA

The tiny town of Puerto Velasco Ibarra has no more than 200 inhabitants, but does have a small hotel, restaurant and store operated by the Wittmer family, descendants of hardy German settlers who arrived in the 1930s, just in time to take part in the sordid "Galápagos Affair."

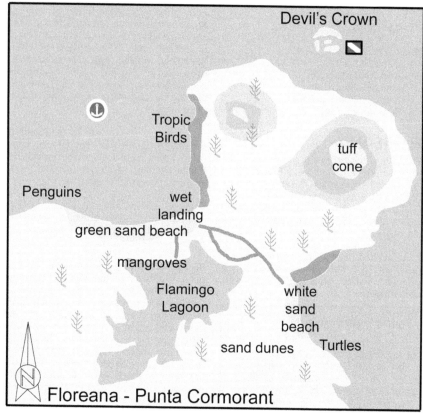

Devil's Crown

Tropic
Birds

tuff
cone

Penguins

wet
landing
green sand beach

mangroves

Flamingo
Lagoon

white
sand
beach

sand dunes   Turtles

Floreana - Punta Cormorant

Punta Cormorant

Most visits to the town take visitors up the hill to a lush area once owned by the Wittmer family; there is a small spring there, and you'll probably spot some birds.

Cerro Alieri/Alieri Hill

Cerro Alieri is outside of Puerto Velasco Ibarra, the tiny town of Floreana Island. To get there, it's a 15-minute ride in a truck followed by a two-hour hike (round-trip). The hike up to the top of Alieri hill is primarily notable for vegetation: most of the plant species are either native or endemic and the hike will be of great interest to botanists.

One of the plants is the endemic Scalesia tree, which was once abundant on Floreana. Now there are only a few trees scattered around; their decline is due to pressure from goats and early settlers, who cut down the trees to make their homes. For Galápagos, Cerro Alieri gets a lot of rainfall. The trail may be muddy, so pack accordingly.

La Lobería/Sea Lions Area

About one kilometer (0.62 mi) away from Puerto Velasco Ibarra is a small beach which is home to a colony of sea lions, as well as some marine iguanas. It's possible to walk there from the town for some recreational snorkeling. If you're lucky, the sea lions will come out to join you! Extremely fortunate snorkelers may spot a ray or a shark. It's also a popular spot for sea kayaking. You don't need a guide. Updated: Feb 01, 2013.

Asilo de la Paz/Asylum of Peace

The Asilo de la Paz hike on Floreana Island is primarily of historical interest for guests. It goes past a cave allegedly once used by maroonee Patrick Watkins and also visits a freshwater spring which served as a source of water for early settlers.

The hike, which can be done from the small town of Puerto Velasco Ibarra (or you can contract for a ride to take you most of the

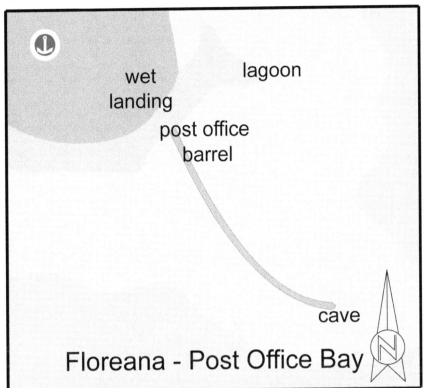

wet
landing

lagoon

post office
barrel

cave

Floreana - Post Office Bay

Post Office Bay

way), goes through the heart of Floreana's agricultural region. Early settlers planted trees including tamarind, plums and particularly citrus trees (according to legend, it was Watkins himself who introduced citrus trees to the Island).

The cave allegedly used by Watkins was later home to the famous Dr. Ritter and his girlfriend Dore Strauch. After Ritter died, the Wittmer family lived there for a time. Near Asilo de la Paz, there is a place where the Park Service has built a corral of sorts for Giant Tortoises. As the Floreana Island subspecies of Giant Tortoise is extinct, the corral houses specimens from other islands.

Look out for the introduced Polistes Versicolor Wasp—it's aggressive and common all over Floreana. You don't want to mess with them!

Trail Difficulty: 2/5.
It's an eight kilometer (5 mi) hike from town, but you can hire a driver to take you all but the last 1/4 mile or so.

Punta Cormorant

"Cormorant Point" is poorly-named, as there are no cormorants to be seen here. The other wildlife more than makes up for it, however. After a wet landing on a beach, visitors hike along a small trail over to the other side of the island. Along the way, there is a brackish lagoon where flamingoes feed and nest—there are a couple of good outlook points.

Watch the vegetation—you may see some wasp traps set out by the Park Service, as Punta Cormorant is a targeted area for getting rid of these introduced pests. The park advises visitors not to wear bright colors or use fragrant lotions or sunscreens, as these will attract the wasps, which sting.

On the other side of the island is a wide beach with a gentle surf, great for a leisurely barefoot stroll. Keep an eye on the water and you may see rays, turtles or sharks. Obey the signs to stay out of the area where sea turtles lay their eggs. Between the two beaches and the shallow lagoon, Punta Cormorant is one of the best places in the

islands to see wading birds such as Whimbrels, Herons, Stilts, Pintail Ducks, etc.
The beach where the zodiacs land is special; it gets its distinctive greenish color
from olivine minerals only found in certain
parts of Galápagos.

Trail Difficulty: 2/5
Getting up to the lookouts over the lagoon
can be a bit of a scramble. Otherwise, the
trail is short, quick and easy.

Wildlife:
Highly Probable to See:
* Hermit Crabs
* Flamingoes
* Sally Lightfoot Crabs
* Sea Lions

Probable to See:
* Stingrays (in the surf)
* Sally Lightfoot Crabs
* Yellow Warblers
* Galápagos Flycatchers
* Darwin's Finches
* Marine Iguanas
* Floreana Lava Lizards

Possible to See:
* Brown Pelicans
* White-tipped Reef Sharks (in the surf)
* Golden Cownose Rays (in the surf)
* Spotted Eagle Rays (in the surf)
* Pintail Ducks (in the lagoon)
* Wilson's Phalaropes
* Black-necked Stilts
* Great Blue Herons
* Whimbrels
* Ruddy Turnstones
* Wandering Tattlers
Updated: Jul 21, 2013.

Post Office Bay

Post Office Bay is a popular stop with visitors,
who get to soak in a little bit of the human
history of the islands, which can be refreshing
after days of natural history and animals.

Centuries ago, whaling ships would spend
years at sea hunting and rendering whales
for their valuable fat. Needless to say, the
sailors would miss home, and they would
send letters to loved ones. The best way to
do this was to drop the letters at places frequented by other whalers in the hopes that
some other ship heading for your home port
would take the letters with them. Apparently
the system worked, because Post Office Bay
was used by sailors for almost a century.

The traditional simple wooden barrel is more
elaborate and decorated now, but still serves
the same function. Just write a postcard or letter with an address and drop it in. No stamps
needed! In theory, the next person who lives
close to you will take it home and hand-deliver
it. It's a great way to make new friends! Visitors are encouraged to sift through the pile of
outgoing mail and take a letter or two home.
Remember, traditionally letters and post cards
are hand-delivered, so only take something
close to home. Taking a letter and then putting
a stamp on it and mailing it is against the rules!

Post Office Bay also includes the ruins of
a canning factory and a soccer field (your
ship's crew will probably come and play, and
visitors are usually encouraged to join in,
but watch out—they're good!). There's also
a lava tube: a cave-like tunnel formed ages
ago. There's a pool in the tube, good for a
nice swim in the dark.

Trail Difficulty: 1/5
Mostly flat. Wet landing on a sandy beach. A
ladder descends to the lava tube.

Wildlife:
Highly Probable to See:
* Sea Lions
* Sally Lightfoot Crabs
* Hermit Crabs
* Floreana Lava Lizards

Champion Islet

A small island off the coast of Floreana,
Champion is one of the top snorkeling spots
in the islands (the island itself is off-limits to
visitors). Occasionally, dolphins are sighted
as the boats approach the shore.
The snorkeling is truly phenomenal. Lucky
visitors will get to see White-tipped Reef
Sharks, Galápagos Penguins, sea turtles,
eels, and more in addition to the usual selection of dazzling reef fish.

Champion Island is special because it is
one of two places where the nearly-extinct
Charles (Floreana) Mockingbird is still
found. The other is Gardner Island, also
off the coast of Floreana. When Charles
Darwin visited the islands in 1835 Floreana
Mockingbirds were common, but hunting
and introduced species on Floreana caused
them to become extinct on the main island,
and the only survivors are now on Champion
and Gardner. Conservationists want to reintroduce them to Floreana, but conditions

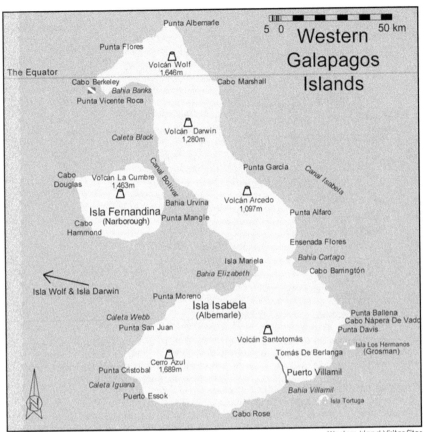

Western Island Visitor Sites

there are not yet right for the birds, which would not survive for the same reasons they died off there in the first place.

Walking on Champion is not allowed, but most operators will take visitors on panga rides around it, and lucky visitors may get to spot a Charles Mockingbird or other bird species such as Swallow-tailed Gulls, Nazca Boobies or Brown Noddies.

Champion Islet is also a popular SCUBA diving site, easily reached by Puerto Ayora Dive shops.

Wildlife:
Highly Probable to See:
 * Sea Lions
 * Reef Fish
 * Nazca Boobies

Probable to See:
 * Charles Mockingbirds

 * Swallow-tailed Gulls
 * Brown Noddies

Possible to See:
 * White-tipped Reef Sharks
 * Sea Turtles
Updated: Dec 02, 2012.

Western Island Visitor Sites

The western islands of Isabela and Fernandina are the least frequented by tourists due to their distance from the main islands. However, if you are lucky enough to visit them, you will have the rare opportunity to witness volcanology in action, to see the unusual Flightless Cormorant, and maybe even to cross paths with pods of whales and dolphins!

The islands of Darwin and Wolf are even more remote, so scuba-diving tours here

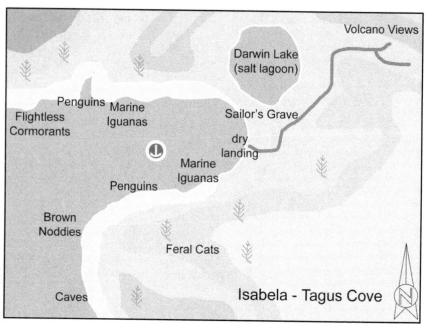

Tagus Cove

offer an extra-special occasion to experience some of the most abundant and diverse marine life in the world.

You also have the best possibility of encountering the big attractions, like whales, Hammerhead Sharks and Whale Sharks.

ISABELA

Isabela (Albemarle) is by far the largest island, and there are several great visitor sites there. Most cruise ships will go up along the western coast of the island to see some of the sites there and also visit Fernandina Island. There are essentially two sorts of visitor sites on Isabela: the ones that you can only get to if you're on a cruise, and ones that are do-able from the town of Puerto Villamil. Most of the cruise ship ones are on the western side of the island.

Cruise-only sites include Tagus Cove, Urbina Bay, Punta Vicente Roca and Punta Moreno. Sites very close to the town include Concha de Perla Lagoon, Tintoreras, the Centro de Crianza, Humedales and the Wall of Tears. The sites of Sierra Negra Volcano, Sucre's Cave and the Sulfur Mines are further away from town, but tours from Puerto Villamil can be arranged. Occasionally cruise ships

will visit Puerto Villamil and see some of the nearby sites, but if you're staying in town, you're not allowed to visit cruise-only sites like Tagus Cove or Urbina Bay.

Tagus Cove (cruise only)

A visitor favorite, Tagus Cove combines a panga ride around the cove with a hike along a stony trail to see lava formations and salty Lake Darwin. The cove is a good anchorage historically used by pirates and whalers who would carve or paint the names of their ships into a small cave near the beginning of the trail. Seeing this centuries-old graffiti is a highlight of the hike (nowadays the Park Service would kick any graffiti-carvers out of the islands!).

The hike is a fairly easy one, less than two kilometers (1.2 mi), and it leads past lava formations up the side of a volcano. Several small land birds can be seen, such as finches.

The trail winds through arid-zone vegetation before climbing for a great view. Volcanic formations can be seen, including spatter cones and tuff cones.

The panga ride is a lot of fun: lucky visitors will get to see Galápagos Penguins, Flightless Cormorants and other marine birds.

Did a unique trek? Got way off the beaten path? Tell other travelers at vivatravelguides.com

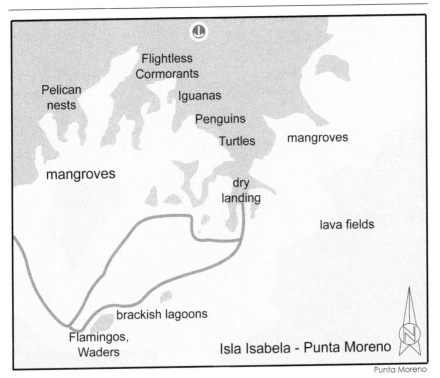

Isla Isabela - Punta Moreno

Punta Moreno

Highly Probable to See:
* Galápagos Penguin
* Flightless Cormorant
* Brown Noddy
* Blue-footed Booby

Probable to See:
* Brown Pelican
* Noddy Tern

Possible to See:
* Galápagos Hawk
* Whales
* Dolphins

Updated: Sep 22, 2012.

Punta Moreno — Cruise only

Located on the western shore of Isabela Island, Punta Moreno is a popular site where a lot of wildlife can be seen. The trip usually begins (or ends) with a panga ride along the rocky shore: keep your eyes peeled for Galápagos Penguins sunning themselves on the rocks. If you look in the water, there is a chance that you'll see sea turtles, rays or other marine creatures.

Once on shore, the trail winds its way through lava formations, mangroves and crystal-clear tidal pools. It's in these little pools where the action is—check them all out to see what was trapped there the last time the tide was high. There will certainly be all sorts of colorful fish, crustaceans and echinoderms, but there may be something spectacular such as a turtle, ray or shark. Updated: Jan 12, 2013

On a clear day, this visitor site offers a great view of some of Isabela's volcanoes.

Trail Difficulty: 3/5
The lava rocks can be treacherous, and watch your step around the tidal pools. Tip: This hike can get really hot: If you suspect it might, bring extra water and lots of sunscreen.

Wildlife:
Highly Probable to See:
* Brown Pelicans

Probable to See:
* Galápagos Penguins
* Herons
* Flightless Cormorants
* American Oystercatchers

Possible to See:
* Rays
* White-tipped Reef Sharks

VISITOR SITES

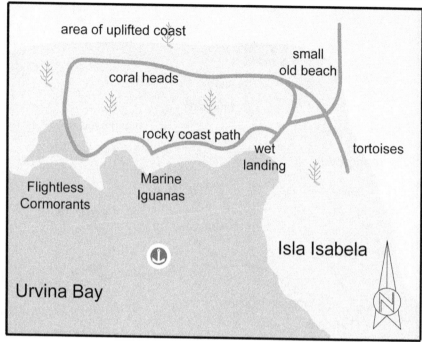

area of uplifted coast

coral heads

small
old beach

rocky coast path

wet
landing

tortoises

Flightless
Cormorants

Marine
Iguanas

Isla Isabela

Urvina Bay

Urbina Bay

* Green Sea Turtles
  * Pintail Ducks
  *Flamingoes
* Gallinules

Punta Vicente Roca Cruise only

Punta Vicente Roca (Vicente Rock Point) is a popular marine visitor site: there is no trail on land here. Typically, cruise ships will send passengers on a panga ride along the rocky shore, where they can often see Galápagos Fur Sea Lions, Galápagos Sea Lions and Galápagos Penguins. Lucky visitors might see a Flightless Cormorant too.

The highlight of the panga ride is a visit to a large, yawning cave; look for some birds nesting on the cave walls.

After the panga ride, visitors can snorkel in the area. It's a good place to see some sea turtles and sea lions, and maybe sharks or the famous Pacific Sunfish in the cave area or out a little deeper.

Wildlife:
Highly Probable to See:
* Galápagos Fur Sea Lions
* Galápagos Sea Lions
* Galápagos Penguins
* Galápagos Iguanas

Probable to See:
* Green Sea Turtles

Possible to See:
* Flightless Cormorants

Urbina Bay   Cruise only

One of the more fascinating Galápagos visitor sites, Urbina Bay (sometimes spelled Urvina Bay) was caused by a geological phenomenon in 1954. An area that was previously underwater suddenly was thrust up into the air 5 meters (16 ft.), creating land where there had previously been none. Local fishermen discovered it because of the odor of rotting marine life that had been too slow to escape!

The hike therefore winds through coral formations and recent pioneer plants, giving geologists and botanists an illuminating look at how new lands are colonized by plants and animals in Galápagos.

Located at the base of the Alcedo Volcano, the trail is over 3,000 meters (9,843 ft) long and can be taxing for weaker hikers, especially on hot days. It's one of the few places to see grasshoppers. Look for land iguanas feeding on manzanilla apples: deadly poison for humans, but a tasty snack for an iguana!

It's possible to snorkel at Urbina Bay and many ships allow their passengers to do so; it's not the best snorkeling in the Galápagos as the water is often cloudy, but a lucky snorkeler might see a green sea turtle or a stingray.

Tips:
Bring water
Look out for turtle nesting sites
Don't touch the fragile coral formations in the uplifted area.
The landing can be rough: protect your camera gear and other stuff.

Trail Difficulty: 4/5

Wildlife:
Highly Probable to See:
 * Marine Iguanas
 * Ground Finches
 * Sally Lightfoot Crabs
 * Yellow Warblers
 * Lava Lizards

Probable to See:
 * Land Iguanas
 * Brown Pelicans
 * Flightless Cormorants
 * Giant Tortoises
 * Galápagos Penguins

Possible to See:
 * Galápagos Hawks
Updated: Sep 22, 2012.

Las Tintoreras
Las Tintoreras is a memorable visitor site for those who get to go there. It's a small trail along a rocky island in the harbor off of Puerto Villamil. The trail goes past several channels and tidal pools, which for some reason are home to White-tipped Reef Sharks, sometimes as many as dozens of them. "Tintoreras" is, in fact, the local name for the White-tipped Reef Shark. The sharks usually hang out in a shallow, narrow channel, allowing visitors to get quite close and take good photos.

The trail itself is rocky but not too long or difficult. In addition to the sharks, it's common to see other marine life such as rays in the tidal pools, and sea lions and marine iguanas are abundant.

Once you're done, you can snorkel around the rocks nearby (you cannot snorkel in the little channel, and even though the sharks are harmless you probably wouldn't want to, especially if you've ever seen *Jaws*).

There is also another crevasse nearby where you can go if you're with a guide. Chances are good that you'll see more sharks while snorkeling around the rocks or in the other crevasse.

Some cruise ships will visit Las Tintoreras, but not all of them are permitted to snorkel there. Check and see if swimming alongside dozens of sharks appeals to you. If you're staying in Puerto Villamil, it should be pretty easy to find a guided group headed there; it usually costs about $25 or so, and is well worth it. Updated: Sep 22, 2012.

Centro de Crianza "Arnaldo Tupiza"
The Centro de Crianza (or "Rearing Center") is a sort of nursery for Giant Tortoises located within walking distance from Puerto Villamil. There are several pens housing grown tortoises, mainly from the different volcanoes on Isabela Island, as well as dozens of young tortoises in protected cages. Look for the ones from Cerro Paloma—the adults there were the only six left of their species in 1994, although now there are some little ones at the center.

An easy paved path leads through the penned-in area and ends up at an information center (and gift shop, naturally).

Unlike the Charles Darwin Research Station, the pens here are not open and you can't go in with the tortoises to have your photo taken. The walk is shadier though.

Although you can take a taxi to the Centro de Crianza, it's much more fun to walk. The trail leads outside of Puerto Villamil near the Iguana Crossing Hotel and winds through mangroves, swamps and salty lagoons where you can see ducks, flamingoes, herons and other wading and swimming birds. The trail takes about 40 minutes to walk, but it's in good shape and pretty easy. You do not need a guide to walk on the trail or visit the Centro de Crianza.

You can book a half-day tour in Puerto Villamil which will include the trail, the Center and the Wall of Tears for about $20, but this is all as long as there are enough people who want to do it.

It isn't a bad idea, as a guide will help spot wildlife and tell you about the plants and animals that you're sure to see on the trail as well as the history of the wall. The center is a popular stop with cruise ships that visit Puerto Villamil.

VISITOR SITES

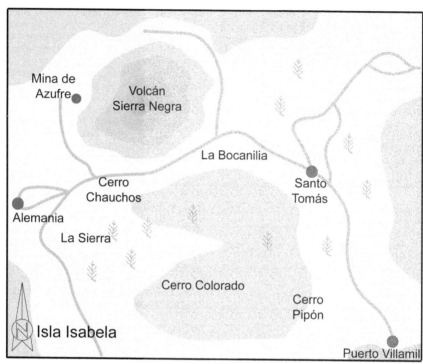

Isla Isabela - Sierra Negra Volcano

Trail Difficulty:
1/5 (center)
2/5 (lagoons and mangroves: it can get a little hot so bring water).

Wildlife (including the trail AND the center):
Highly Probable to See:
* Giant Tortoises
* Lava Lizards
* Marine Iguanas
* Finches

Probable to See:
* Flamingoes
* Pintail Ducks
* Gallinules

Possible to See:
* Common Moorhens
* Herons
Updated: Sep 22, 2012.

Sierra Negra Volcano

Sierra Negra Volcano is the closest one to Puerto Villamil and it makes for a popular hike. It's a day-long affair and you'll definitely want to have a guide because it's possible to lose the trail, especially if

it gets rainy or foggy, which it often does. Usually trips will take a van or truck to a dropping-off place near the base of the mountain.

Sierra Negra is the oldest of Isabela's volcanoes, and was active as recently as 2005. The hike passes through several different vegetation and geological zones. Generally, guided tours will reach the summit of Sierra Negra and also visit nearby Volcán Chico.

It's possible to rent horses for the same trip; they usually cost about $10 more. Typically, you'll pay roughly $35 for a tour of Sierra Negra on foot and $45 if you want a horse. Sierra Negra last erupted in 2005, so if you rent a horse, make sure to ask for the fastest one they have.

Trail Difficulty: 4/5
You should be in decent shape to attempt it.

Concha de Perla

Concha de Perla is a gorgeous lagoon located not far from the new municipal dock of Puerto Villamil. There is a trail through a dense mangrove to get there, but they've made a

Shark-watching at Las Tintoreras

sort of boardwalk so it's an easy five-minute walk from the main dirt road.

The lagoon is perfect for swimming and snorkeling, as it's protected from the ocean surf and currents. Lucky swimmers will get to see plenty of fish and probably a couple sea lions or rays.

Note that the pier at the end of the trail is very small: there isn't much room to hang out or leave your stuff, so if you go there at a popular time—say, on a sunny weekend afternoon—the little pier will be full of locals lounging around and taking up all the space. You'll be able to squeeze past them into the water, but don't plan on laying out a towel or anything. Also, there have been some reports of petty theft, so don't bring anything valuable with you. It's perfectly acceptable to go there in your swimsuit with your towel and snorkeling gear only. You won't need your wallet.

Concha de Perla is free and open to the public during daylight hours.

Trail Difficulty: 1/5

The trail leads off the main road, about a 15 or 20-minute walk from town. If you're at the new municipal pier, it's only five minutes away. Look for the wooden sign. You can take a bicycle as far as the entrance to the boardwalk.

Wildlife:
Highly Probable to See:
 * Sea Lions
 * Brown Pelicans
 * Fish

Possible to See:
 * Rays
Updated: Sep 22, 2012.

Sulfur Mines

Deep in the interior of Isabela Island are some old sulfur mines that it's possible to visit. You'll need to take a tour from Puerto Villamil to get there, because there is some National Park paperwork that must be provided for permission and getting there is hard. Most tours go by horseback after an approximately 45-minute drive from Puerto Villamil. As a result of all this, very few visitors ever get there.

It's possible to camp here, but again, you'll need a guide and permission. The mines themselves are cool, with interesting sulfur formations. Nearby are several steaming fumaroles. The trail leads through a forest of introduced Guava trees: the Park Service is trying to remove them, but it's not an easy task. Updated: Sep 22, 2012.

Humedales/wetlands

The Humedales, or "wetlands," are a can't-miss for those staying a couple days in Puerto Villamil. The humedales consist of a good trail through mangroves, pools, beaches and rocky shores. It's well worth a visit, as many different types of birds nest there.

The trail also ends up at Isabela's old cemetery, which is interesting because some of the earliest colonists are buried there. You'll also find the Wall of Tears not to far from here.

Along the trail you'll find Orchilla Hill, which is an easy climb. From the top there is a nice view of town and Isabela's volcanoes. Also look for "La Playita," a small, secluded beach. The park has released some Giant Tortoises into the wild near here, so keep an eye open for them too!

There is a picnic area popular with locals, but don't plop down just anywhere, out of respect for the nesting birds.

Trail Difficulty: 2/5

Wildlife:
Highly Probable to See:
 * Flamingoes
 * Marine Iguanas
 * Finches

VISITOR SITES

Probable to See:
* Pintail Ducks
* Brown Pelicans
* American Oystercatchers

Possible to See:
* Giant Tortoises
* Galápagos Penguins

Updated:Aug 18, 2012.

Wall of Tears

The Wall of Tears serves as a bleak reminder of Galápagos' darker history. Located on Isabela Island, the wall was constructed by convicts from a penal colony that inhabited the island between 1946 and 1959. Building the wall was a form of punishment, as moving huge blocks of lava in the searing heat was torturously difficult. Many of the convicts, denied proper nourishment and medical care, were worked to death building the wall.

Photo by: Eric Schmuttenmaer

The Wall of Tears is not a protected visitor site—anyone can go. Just follow the trail outside of town or ask any local how to find it. It's about seven kilometers (4.3 mi) outside of town, and you can reach it by bike, which are easy to rent in town. Bring water.

The Wall of Tears is generally included in any tour of Puerto Villamil, but cruise ships stopping in town rarely go there, so don't expect to be taken there if you're on a boat.

Sucre's Cave

Located in the farmlands outside of Puerto Villamil on Isabela Island, Sucre's Cave is actually a visitor site protected by the National Park. More than just a cave, the hike, about a half kilometer (0.31 mi) in length, is mostly designed to show the ongoing restoration efforts of the humid rain forests in Isabela's agricultural zone.

Along this path, scientists and rangers have been working hard to eradicate introduced species and reintroduce native and endemic

ones. Visitors will get to see the plant nursery used to repopulate the area as well as a small home for rangers and volunteers. There is, of course, a cave as well; it's a relatively small lava tunnel but fun and interesting to explore. It's possible to volunteer to work at this site; see rangers or Park Service for details. **Tips:** Bring a flashlight to explore the cave.

Isabela Dive Sites

The SCUBA diving in Isabela is much more limited than in Puerto Ayora or Puerto Baquerizo Moreno. There is only one dive shop in Puerto Villamil—Isabela Dive Center—so you're pretty much stuck with it, at least for now. It basically only go to three dive sites: Tortuga Island, Cuatro Hermanos and Roca Viuda, although if you're staying there for a few days and want to dive more, it's possible the dive center could find some more places to go. Isabela has excellent snorkeling, so it's a good place to go if some members of your group dive and some prefer to snorkel.

Tortuga Island

A moderate to strong current, but the underwater landscape is spectacular and the chance of seeing impressive marine life is good. Look for Hammerheads, Galápagos Sharks and large rays in addition to dazzling fish like Moorish Idols and Parrotfish. Distance from Puerto Villamil: 30 minutes.

Cuatro Hermanos

Cuatro Hermanos is a spectacular site, where you're likely to see seahorses, including the Giant Pacific Seahorse. There is an underwater cavern here, too, and there's a good chance of seeing sharks and rays there. Enormous Manta Rays are also often seen as well as lobsters, octopus and, of course, plenty of colorful fish. Distance from Puerto Villamil: 45 minutes.

Roca Viuda

The charmingly-named "Widow Rock" is one of the most challenging dives in Galápagos and only for advanced divers: it's on a wall and the currents are quite strong, occasionally carrying divers away from the site! Sometimes it's worse than others. Those who do it are rewarded with a truly astounding collection of reef fish: thousands of them literally everywhere. Not so many sharks and large rays, but the pretty fish make up for it.

Distance from Puerto Villamil: 25 minutes.

VISITOR SITES

FERNANDINA

Fernandina (Narborough), the westernmost (and youngest, geologically speaking) of the main islands is situated directly above a geologic hot spot and as such, has the highest volcanic activity of any of the islands. Many eruptions have been recorded since 1813, with the most recent one having occurred in early 2009.

There is one visitor site, Punta Espinosa, where Flightless Cormorants, pelicans, penguins, sea lions, and an abundance of marine iguanas reside.

The marine ecosystem around Fernandina, where the cold Cromwell current has its greatest impact on water temperature and nutrient upwelling, hosts organisms not found in other sectors of the archipelago.

In fact, Bryde's Whales, Pilot Whales, and Bottlenose Dolphins feed here, so keep your eyes open when you are cruising! This area is resource-rich and has been declared a Whale Sanctuary.
Updated: Jan 4, 2013.

Punta Espinosa

Fernandina's only visitor site, Punta Espinosa is a great place to see some Galápagos wildlife that you don't often see. Most noteworthy is the endemic Flightless Cormorant, which is only found in the western islands. After a dry-ish landing on a rocky shore, visitors will have the opportunity to peek into some tidal pools, which often are home to interesting marine life. You may even spot a ray or sea turtle in the lagoon.

After the landing, you'll head to the main trail, passing a large colony of marine iguanas as you do. Stop for some photos, and then head along the trail past a sea lion nursery to see the cormorants. If you're lucky, you'll be able to get a good look at them as they swim and flap their vestigal wings to dry them off. The other end of the trail leads to some interesting lava formations, an abandoned ship's engine and some more lagoons. Along the rocky shore near Punta Espinosa, visitors will occasionally see the rare Galápagos Penguin. If you're lucky, your cruise ship will send pangas or zodiacs along the shore, where your keen-eyed naturalist guide will help you spot the penguins—they're difficult to see against the black lava background.

VISITOR SITES

Galápagos Sailing Adventures

For centuries, navigating around the Enchanted Islands was difficult. Sailors tell of winds falling calm for days on end. Captain David Porter of the USS Essex recounted in 1812 that a British ship escaped in a gust of wind while his ship lay becalmed. The most nightmarish experience was when the schooner Tartar, captained by Benjamin Merrill of New York, was caught between Isabela and Fernandina Islands just when a volcano blew its top:

"14 February. On Monday the fourteenth, at two o'clock a.m., while the sable mantle of night was yet spread over the mighty Pacific, shrouding the neighboring islands from our view, and while the stillness of death reigned everywhere around us, our ears were suddenly assailed by a sound that could only be equaled by ten thousand thunders bursting upon the air at once; while at the same instant, the whole atmosphere was lighted up with a horrid glare that might have appalled the stoutest heart! I soon ascertained that one of the volcanoes on Narborough Island had suddenly broke through with accumulated vengeance.

At 3 a.m. I ascertained the temperature of the water, by Fahrenheits thermometer, to be 61, while that of the air was 71. At eleven a.m., the air was 113 and the water 100, the eruption still continuing with unabated fury. The Tartar's anchorage was about ten miles to the northward of the mountain, and the heat was so great that the melted pitch was running from the vessels seams, and the tar dropping from the rigging.

Our situation was every hour becoming more critical and alarming. Not a breath of air was stirring to fill a sail, had we attempted to escape; so that we were compelled to remain idle and unwilling spectators of a pyrotechnic exhibition which evinced no indications of even temporary suspension."

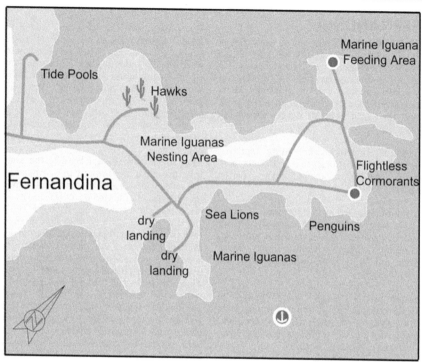

Fernandina - Punta Espinosa

Trail Difficulty: 2/5
It crosses some treacherous lava in some places, but otherwise it's pretty flat and easy.

Wildlife:
Highly Probable to See:
  * Flightless Cormorants
  * Marine Iguanas
  * Lava Lizards
  * Sally Lightfoot Crabs
  * Sea Lions
Probable to See:
  * Green Sea Turtles
  * Hermit Crabs

Possible to See:
  * Galápagos Hawks
  * Galápagos Snakes
  * Galápagos Penguins
Updated: Nov 30, 2012.

Certain species of tropical Indo-Pacific fish and coral can only be found here, but the main attraction for divers is the high possibility of seeing big stuff, and lots of it, like whales, Hammerhead Sharks, and Whale Sharks.
Updated: Jun 04, 2013.

DARWIN AND WOLF

Darwin (Culpepper) and Wolf (Wenman) are two tiny, outlying islands in the northwest archipelago that harbor an incredibly diverse and abundant marine life. As such, the islands are only visited on live-aboard scuba diving tours.

Galápagos Wildlife Guide

As spectacular as the waters, islands and beaches of Galápagos are, there is no doubt about what visitors have come to see: the animals. Because the archipelago was undiscovered until very recently (geologically speaking), the endemic species of Galápagos never learned to fear humans, as animals and birds did in every other corner of the globe. In other words, the animals on the islands see the lumbering hairless monkeys that smell like sunscreen, but do not identify them as something predatory or dangerous. For this reason, you can get very close to them before they spook and run away.

Some animals are more skittish than others: migratory birds, including many of the shore birds, will not let you get too close, because they've encountered mankind in other parts of the world. Other animals, like marine iguanas, barely seem to notice you at all. Many careless travelers have accidentally stepped on them—they blend right in with the black lava rocks. The sea lions will let you get fairly close, as will most of the sea and land birds, but watch out. Get too close, and a sea lion or booby will give you a good nip!

Galápagos is home to several species of reptiles, including the giant tortoise, marine iguana and land iguana. However, there are very few native mammals in the archipelago, the most noteworthy of which is the Galápagos Sea Lion.

The birds of the Galápagos are easily divided into categories. Land birds are generally seen inland where they feed and nest. Some endemic Galápagos land birds include the Galápagos Hawk and different species of Darwin's Finches. Shore birds may nest farther inland, but they are most commonly seen along the shoreline and in tidal pools and mangroves where they feed. Sea birds nest on land but feed exclusively on fish, squid and other marine life.

The marine life in Galápagos is impressive, which makes the snorkeling and diving in the islands world-class. There are many different fish, sharks and rays that are easy to spot and identify.

Unfortunately, not all of the wildlife in Galápagos belongs there. Introduced species remain a major ecological problem, although scientists and park rangers are dedicated to removing them.

Please note that there are many other species not included here—the islands are home to thousands of different kinds of animals, birds and fish, and there is only room in this guidebook to include the most common and interesting ones. Local Spanish names are given in parentheses where appropriate.

Sea Birds
Bird life is everywhere in Galápagos , and the marine species are particularly fun to watch and identify. Because of the cold-water currents that cruise through the archipelago, there is an unusual abundance of marine life, which in turn supports large colonies of different avian species.

The Galápagos bird species are specially adapted to working together. Take the three species of booby, for example. The Blue-footed Booby fishes close to shore—thrilling visitors by putting on a fantastic show of plummeting after fish. The Nazca Booby fishes at an intermediate range from shore and most visitors will never get to see them in action. The Red-footed Booby fishes far out to sea, often flying many miles simply to find a good fishing spot. In this way, the three booby species do not compete with one another for food resources.

Some species of sea birds are endemic to the Galápagos Islands. The three most noteworthy are the Flightless Cormorant, the Waved Albatross and the Galápagos Penguin.

There are many other sea birds in the islands. Shearwaters and petrels can be seen skimming the waves, if you look for them. There are plovers and terns, and other species of gull that are not endemic to the islands. A knowledgeable guide should be able to point out most of these species to you as you spot them.

Blue-footed Booby
The Blue-footed Booby (piquero patas azules) is most easily identified, as its name suggests, by its bright blue feet. It has brown upper plumage and white lower plumage, with wings that are a slightly darker brown than the rest of

WILDLIFE

the body. Juveniles are completely brown and receive their coloration after about one year.

Males are slightly smaller than females and perform an elaborate, rather entertaining mating dance to attract a partner. He begins by lifting up his enormous clown feet, one-by-one, and then stops in a distinctive pose, beak raised skyward, announcing his studliness with a loud whistle, sticking out his tail and opening his wings. This is accompanied by a love-offering of sticks and twigs. Females join in the mating dance, following the same movements, but respond with a guttural honk. Besides their distinguishing sounds, the females also have larger eye pupils.

Blue-Footed Booby

Breeding can take place at any time of the year when the food supply is abundant, and also varies from island to island. Up to three eggs are laid in a "guano ring," or circle of booby dung. When food is scarce, the oldest sibling will push younger sibling(s) out of the guano ring in an act of "cainism." This form of natural selection is effective, because chicks outside of the ring are refused care and ultimately perish. It is nature at its most cruel, but the stronger chick survives.

The young take two to six years to mature, at which time they will return to their island birthplace to mate. Meanwhile, they travel among the islands feeding on fish, which are caught in a graceful plunge dive. Watching the boobies fish—either from the air or underwater—is a major highlight in Galápagos.

Blue-footed Boobys are common throughout the archipelago and can be seen on several isalnds.

Red-footed Booby
The Red-footed Booby (piquero de patas rojas) can be easily identified by its distinctive red feet, blue-gray bill, pinkish facial skin and brown outer plumage. A certain percentage of them are mostly white instead of brown, but they're the same species. It is the smallest of the three booby species in Galápagos and nests in treetops and ledges, instead of on the ground.

Courtship among Red-footed Boobies is similar to the blue-footed variety, but it is performed in the trees. Unlike the Blue-footed Booby, the Red-footed Booby lays a single egg on a platform of twigs and guano. The egg is then incubated by both parents for 45 days. The chick is dependent on its parents for food for about a year. The Red-footed Booby feeds exclusively on fish, which are caught far away from land.

Red-footed Boobys are common throughout the islands, but best seen on Genovesa.

Nazca Booby
The Nazca Booby (Piquero Nazca) is alabaster white with a black tail and black ends to the primary feathers on the wing. Some black skin at the base of the bill serves as a distinctive Zorro-mask. The Nazca Booby is the largest of the three booby species in Galápagos.

Galápagos Nazca Boobies were once thought to be the same as Masked Boobies, but are now considered different enough to be their own species. Nazca and Masked Boobies look almost identical, and many in the islands (including some guides) may still refer to them as Masked Boobies.

As with other boobies, the Nazca Booby feeds entirely on fish and follows the same courtship ritual, although it's a bit less elaborate. Males and females look alike, so the best way to distinguish them is by their sounds: the males whistle and the females quack.

Nazca Boobies are commonly seen at Punta Suarez (Española), Punta Pitt (San Cristóbal), Daphne Major and Genovesa.

Frigatebird
There are two species of Frigatebird in Galápagos, Great Frigatebirds and Magnificent Frigatebirds. They're hard to tell apart: both are large black birds with a long beak, hooked on the end. Male Frigatebirds of both species are most recognizable by their

WILDLIFE

dazzling red skin flaps, which they can in-flate to volleyball-sized balloons to attract females. Immature Frigatebirds have a white head and neck and a pale beak.

Males construct nests out of twigs in low trees or shrubs and wait in the nests with their pouches inflated until a female arrives to mate. Frigatebirds spend much of their time offshore, but return to land to mate, nest, and rear their young.

Since Frigatebirds do not secrete enough oils to waterproof their feathers, they can-not swim, even though they are sea birds. As such, they steal fish from other birds (especially the Blue-footed Boobies, who are excellent fishermen) or force them to regurgitate the food. Oftentimes, Frig-atebirds will raise their young near Blue-footed Booby colonies so that they have a food source nearby and readily available. Because of this behavior, Frigatebirds are considered kleptoparasites or pirates.

In Galápagos, both varieties are most com-monly seen on Genovesa and North Seymour.

Great Frigatebird
The Great Frigatebird (fragata común) is a bit smaller than the Magnificent Frigatebird and has a green sheen to its black feathers. It also has the same courtship and klepto-parasitistic behaviors (although Great Frig-atebirds are a little less aggressive in their stealing of food than their Magnificent cous-ins). Great Frigatebirds are found all over the world, including the Pacific, Indian and South Atlantic Oceans.

Magnificent Frigatebird
The Magnificent Frigatebird (fragata real) is the larger of the two species of Frigate-birds found in Galápagos. Male Magnificent Frigatebirds can also be distinguished from Great Frigatebirds by the purple sheen cast on their jet-black feathers and blue circles around their eyes. Females are slightly larger than males and also entirely black, except for a white breast and shoulders.

Waved Albatross
The Waved Albatross (albatros) is the larg-est bird that breeds in Galápagos, with a wingspan of almost 2.5 meters (8.2 ft). It has brown upper parts and wings with gray, waved bars (hence its name), a white neck, a cream-colored nape and a handsome yellow beak. Males are a bit larger and have thicker

eyebrows than females. It looks a little like a duck on steroids.

There are about 12,000 monogamous pairs of Waved Albatrosses that fly back and forth from the Ecuadorian coast and northern Peru to their only breeding ground in the world, Española Island.

The males return first to Galápagos in late March or early April and wait for the arrival of their mates, at which time they begin an elaborate courting ritual: pairs dance with each other in an awkward waddle, move their necks up and down in rhythm, clack and encircle their bills, and raise their bills skyward with an abrupt guttural release, reminiscent of a cow's moo. Albatrosses perform this unforgettable courtship display before, during and after they lay their eggs, so you can witness it from mid-April to as late as November. Waved Albatrosses mate for life and can live 45-50 years.

Albatrosses are expert flyers, but they re-quire a significant amount of space and en-ergy to get airborne. Often, you can see them jump off nearby cliffs and catch offshore winds as a method for getting aloft.

Flightless Cormorant
The Flightless Cormorant (cormorán) is unmistakably recognized by its stubby vestigial appendages that were once wings. Although they cannot fly, they are excel-lent swimmers and feed on small fish, eels and octopuses. Adults have black upper feathers and brown under feathers, but they—like the juveniles—look completely black when wet. They also have short black legs; large, black webbed feet; brilliant turquoise eyes and a hooked, black bill. Although the cormorant is a common bird around the world, flightless ones are only found on Galápagos.

Flightless cormorant

WILDLIFE

Like many other sea birds, Flightless Cormorants have an elaborate courtship display: pairs begin with an aquatic dance, followed by an unusual "snake necking" embrace, where necks are intertwined in a snake-like spiral. The mating ritual continues with some swimming back and forth, a continuation of the dance on land and a final presentation of a seaweed nest to the female by the male.

Most females lay their eggs between May and October. The eggs are then incubated for about a month before hatching, and the chick is reared for about nine months by both parents. If, however, food supplies run low, the female may leave the male to care for the chick while she looks for another, more apt, mate.

Flightless Cormorants can be seen in Punta Espinosa (Fernandina) and the western visitor sites of Isabela.

Galápagos Penguin
The endemic Galápagos Penguin (pinguino) is the only species of penguin found north of the equatorial line (a good trivia question!). At only 35 cm tall, the Galápagos Penguin is also one of the world's smallest penguins. Adults have black outer feathers, white under feathers, an irregular black band across the breast and a distinctive white stripe passing from the eye to the throat.

There are only about 1,000 monogamous pairs of Galápagos Penguins, which can breed at any time of year when resources are plentiful and water temperatures are cool. They lay one or two eggs in shady holes or caves nestled along the shoreline. Pairs take turns incubating the egg, for a period of about 40 days. Chicks can fend for themselves after two months, but often stay in swimming groups with the adults.

Galápagos Penguins can best be seen at Punta Espinosa (Fernandina), at various west coast Isabela visitor sites and Bartolomé.

Brown Pelican
The Brown Pelican (pelícano) is an unmistakable bird with a large, heavy body and an enormous, deep bill. Mating adult pelicans have a striking white head and maroon neck; when they do not have their breeding plumage, their necks are gray.

Brown Pelicans breed individually or in small colonies, making their nests in mangroves on virtually all of the islands in the archipelago. The female lays three large eggs, usually during the colder months of May to July, which are then incubated by both parents for about one month (if they are not eaten by the Galápagos Hawk).

They feed mainly on large fish, which they catch by plunging into the ocean (a graceless but effective dive), filling their pouches with sea water and filtering the food out by draining the pouch.

Brown Pelicans are common throughout the islands. A good place to see them is at the fishermen's pier in Puerto Ayora as they try to mooch a free meal.

Red-billed Tropicbird
The Red-billed Tropicbird (ave tropical) is a spectacular, solitary bird with white feathers, black barring on the back and a bright red bill. Its most distinguishing characteristic, however, is its long white tail, which can reach up to a half-meter in length.

During the breeding season, which varies in the archipelago, the Red-billed Tropicbird performs a courtship flight characterized by a shrill, "knee-knee-knee" call. The female lays a single egg in a fissure of a cliff, which is then incubated by both parents for about six weeks.

Red-billed Tropicbirds are best seen off the cliffs of South Plaza, Española, Daphne Major and Genovesa.

Swallow-tailed Gull
The endemic Swallow-tailed Gull (gaviota de cola bifurcada) is the only nocturnal gull in the world. Adults have a distinctive black head with a red ring around the eyes; a black bill with a gray tip; a white, forked tail; and red, webbed feet. They often have white spots on their back, which resemble guano and help them to camouflage with their rocky cliff habitat. Immature gulls are white with dark brown spots on their backs and a black band on their tails.

Swallow-tailed Gulls nest in small colonies on islands concentrated in the eastern archipelago, breeding throughout the year. Their courtship ritual involves mutual preening, head-tossing and regurgitation of food by the male. The young have a recognizably harsh call, consisting of an initial scream that displays their red gape and tongue, an unnerving rattle, and a final clicking noise, which some experts think may also be used for echo-location during night feeding.

The most common places to encounter Swallow-tailed Gulls are Genovesa and South Plaza.

Swallow-tailed Gull

Brown Noddy

The Brown Noddy (gaviotín de cabeza gris) is a common seabird found all over the world. A member of the tern family, they get their name from the nodding motions they make. It's a medium-sized seabird (larger than a finch, smaller than a booby) easily recognized by its brown plumage and the grayish "cap" on top of its head. They can occasionally be seen while feeding: they fly low and nip up small fish and other marine creatures that swim too close to the surface.

Otherwise, the best place to see them is in their nests. In Galápagos they are often seen in seaside caves and crevasses nesting on precarious ledges. Mated pairs will return to the same nesting spot year after year.

Fun fact: a group of noddies is correctly referred to as a "niddle," an "affirmation" or a "sleepiness" of noddies.

Lava Gull

A largish member of the gull family, the Lava Gull (gaviota de lava) lives only in Galápagos. There are estimated to be only about 400 mated pairs of this extremely rare bird. Although the population is stable, it is considered threatened because of numerous dangers, including loss of habitat and introduced animals.

The Lava Gull is easily identified by its nearly-uniform gray color, black tail feathers and black-and-white eyes. It can quite easily blend into the lava formations where it makes its home (hence the name). It is a relative of the Laughing Gull native to North America (it also has a similar, distinctive laugh-like call).

As special and rare as the Lava Gull is, its behavior is much like that of other gulls. It feeds on small fish, crustaceans, lizards, carrion and whatever it can find washed up on shore. They'll follow boats waiting for cast-offs and scavenge in ports and towns.

The best places to see one are in the towns, where it's easier for them to scavenge. They can also often be seen on Genovesa/Tower Island and North Seymour Island. Occasionally they'll perch on a cruise ship, hoping some soft-hearted tourist will toss them a tasty morsel!

Shore Birds

One of the best places in all of Galápagos to see birds is right along the shoreline. Many of the most interesting species in Galápagos are wading shore birds who feast on small fish, crabs, snails, small marine iguanas and other creatures that live in the mangroves and tidal pools of the islands.

Since most of the visitor sites in Galápagos involve a transfer from the cruise boat to the island, usually by means of a zodiac or panga, visitors to the islands have a good chance of seeing one or more shore birds.

American Oystercatcher

The American Oystercatcher (ostrero americano) is a distinctive shore bird found up and down the eastern coast of North America, the Gulf of Mexico and the western coast of South America. They are a common sight in Galápagos, where they can be seen on the coast poking around tidal pools and along rocky shores. Some ornithologists consider the Galápagos American Oystercatcher to be an endemic subspecies, known as Haematopus palliatus galapagensis.

The American Oystercatcher is easily identified by its red-rimmed eyes, black head, white body, grayish-black wings and white legs. Its most distinctive feature, however, is certainly its long, thick, bright orange beak, which looks, from afar, like a large plastic drinking straw.

WILDLIFE

As you might imagine, the preferred food of the American Oystercatcher is shellfish. Using its sturdy beak, an American Oystercatcher can pry apart an oyster, clam or mussel. It then snips the muscle that holds the shells together and eats the oyster at its leisure. Their long beak allows them to poke into small nooks in tidal pools that are too deep for other predators. American Oystercatchers are shy and will dart or fly away if closely approached.

American Oystercatchers can be seen on any island where there are tidal pools along the shore.

Greater Flamingo

The Greater Flamingo (flamenco) receives its characteristic pink color from the pigments consumed in its diet of crustaceans and shrimp larvae. Legs are gray or flesh-colored; feet are webbed for swimming; primary feathers are black; and bills are pink with a black tip. Young flamingos are pale white until about three months, when they begin to feed on their own and become a richer pink color.

This species of flamingo is thought to have arrived from the Bahamas during a one-time intense tropical storm. Since they did not have the flying capacity to return, they made their homes in the brackish lagoons of the archipelago.

Around July and August, the male flamingoes perform their courting ritual: they join in fixed lines, moving and swaying together in a sensual, flamenco-like dance. Monogamous pairs will lay their eggs in cone-shaped mud nests nearly 25 cm high, which have a 28-day incubation period before hatching in September and October. Chicks are born with a straight bill, but it starts to curve after about three weeks. They live about 20-30 years.

There are currently about 500-600 flamingoes on the various islands. They are most commonly found at Punta Cormorant (Floreana), Puerto Villamil (Isabela) and Las Bachas Beach (Santa Cruz).

Yellow-crowned Night Heron

The distinctive Yellow-crowned Night Heron (garza nocturna) can be easily identified by its yellow crown and a white stripe under its eye. They are gangly birds, with heads that seem a little too large for their bodies. During the day, they can often be seen poking

around rocky shorelines. They are more active at night and sometimes even come into the towns to feed near streetlights.

Yellow-Crowned Night Heron

Yellow-crowned Night Herons can be found all over North America and in northern South America. Those in Galápagos are considered by some scientists to be a sub-species.

The Yellow-crowned Night Heron mostly feeds on crabs, which it snatches off the rocks and downs in one big gulp. They're also known to eat shellfish, snails, fish and small reptiles. They nest in branches and mangroves that hang over water.

They can be seen on just about every island, but they're most common on Genovesa.

Lava Heron

Scientists are currently debating whether or not the Lava and Striated Herons are, in fact, separate species. While we all wait for them to make up their minds, your guides will probably refer to them as two different types of heron, and we'll list them separately here for now.

The Lava Heron (garza de lava) is very similar in appearance to the Striated Heron: they're the same size and shape, and have roughly the same coloration. You can tell them apart easily, however—the Striated Heron has a black crown and dappled wings,

WILDLIFE

whereas the Lava Heron is a uniform gray color. Some experts believe that the heron has adapted to blend in easily with the lava rocks of Galápagos. During mating season, male Lava Herons develop brightly colored feet and their beaks turns a glossy black. The Lava Heron is also called the Galápagos Heron because it is endemic to the islands.

The Lava Heron perches on rocks or branches in mangroves, tidal pools and along any shore where small crabs and fish can be found. It waits, still as a stone, before suddenly lunging forward to snatch up its prey. They are very efficient hunters and fishers—some Lava Herons have been observed catching up to three small crabs per minute.

Lava Herons are less shy than their cousins, the Striated and Great Blue Herons; if you move slowly, you can get quite close to them before they spook and fly off.

Lava Herons can be seen on any of the islands.

Striated Heron
The Striated Heron (garza estriada) is a fairly common sight in Galápagos tidal pools, mangroves, ponds and rocky shores. Similar in size to a Lava Heron, the Striated Heron is also rocky gray in color.

Striated Herons are common around the world, from Japan to South America, Africa and Russia. They usually perch on a branch or rock near the water's edge, head back, waiting for small fish or crustaceans to swim by. They then lunge forward, trapping their prey in their sharp beaks and quickly gobbling it up. The Striated Heron is a clever bird, occasionally dropping a leaf into the water and snapping up fish that come to look at it.

Striated Herons can be seen on most islands.

Great Blue Heron
Yes, the Great Blue Herons that you may have seen in the USA and Canada are the same as the ones in Galápagos. The Great Blue Heron (garza morena) is a large, majestic bird that is relatively common in the United States and Canada, as well as Mexico and the West Indies. They can be found in South America as well. Great Blue Herons living in Canada and the northern United States migrate south to spend the winter. They can be seen year-round in Galápagos.

Great Blue Heron

The Great Blue Heron is a shore bird, and can often be seen wading in tidal pools looking for small fish. They have also been known to eat reptiles, turtles and even rodents. Great Blue Herons nest in colonies, occasionally with or near other heron species. They tend to fish alone, however, stalking their prey both during the day and at night. Males can be identified by the small patch of feathers sticking out of the back of their heads.

Snowy Egret
The Snowy Egret (garceta blanca) is a long-legged white bird a little larger than a Lava or Striated Heron. It's native, but not endemic, to the islands. Their plumage is entirely white, with a dark beak and legs and a yellowish face. They're fairly common in North and South America, if you know where to look for them. They look an awful lot like the Cattle Egrets very common in the Galápagos highlands. The two species can be differentiated by the color of their beaks—Snowy Egrets have grayish bills while those of the Cattle Egrets are yellow. That, and Snowy Egrets consider hanging out with cows "uncool."

They're not easily seen in the islands, although you might get lucky in the highlands of those islands that have highlands. One good place to see them is the brackish pool in the town of Puerto Baquerizo Moreno (San Cristóbal) where the little creek empties out into the ocean.

WILDLIFE

Ruddy Turnstone

The Ruddy Turnstone (vuelve piedras) is a stocky, smallish shore bird found all over the world, including every island in Galápagos. Built roughly like a pigeon but a little bigger, the Ruddy Turnstone has a white breast with a blackish-brown "collar" that extends back to the mottled brown wings, speckled with black and white. It has reddish-orange feet and legs. Its medium-sized beak is black and pointed. In mating season, the Ruddy Turnstone changes colors: the black and white of the breast and collar sharpen, and the brown wing feathers become brighter. The legs and feet turn from orange to dazzling red.

Ruddy Turnstones have a hugely varied diet, including small fish, crustaceans, carrion, insects, garbage, other birds' eggs and even occasionally coconuts. They prefer rocky shores and tidal pools where they dart quickly about, searching for morsels. They get their name from their tendency to flip over stones with their beaks to see if there isn't something delicious hiding underneath. They nest in a shallow, scraped-out hole in the ground. Shy by Galápagos standards, it is difficult to get within 20 feet (7m) of them before they scurry away or fly off. They're common on shorelines throughout the islands.

Land Birds

There are relatively few land birds in Galápagos, and most of them are endemic. In general, their coloring runs in grays, browns and blacks, with the dazzling Vermilion Flycatcher being the most obvious exception.

Like most Galápagos birds, they can be surprisingly tame and even friendly to humans. Darwin's Finches—the famous little birds that helped to inspire their namesake's evolutionary theories—are known to land on your dinner table (or in your hand, if there are crumbs in it). Mockingbirds like to land nearby and hop over for a closer look, perhaps even perching on your feet to ask for a drink of water.

Other Galápagos land bird species are less outgoing: the Galápagos Hawk prefers to soar and to majestically sit on the treetops rather than associate with lowly humans, the Short-eared Owl is usually busy looking for a meal, and the Galápagos Dove will dart away if approached. On the far end of the spectrum, the Galápagos Rail is shy and only very rarely seen.

Even though they're considered land birds, some of these Galápagos species are only one step or so removed from the sea. The hawk eats marine iguanas, the Yellow Warbler sometimes eats bugs at the waterline, the Short-eared Owl eats small sea birds, etc. This is one more reminder of how interconnected the island ecosystems can be.

Yellow Warbler

The Yellow Warbler (canario maria) is frequently spotted in Galápagos flitting across the trail or snapping up bugs near the water's edge. The Yellow Warbler is the only small, dazzling, yellow-colored bird with black stripes on its wings in the islands—you can't mistake it for anything else. Male Yellow Warblers have distinctive reddish stripes on their breasts and a reddish "cap" on top of their heads. Females are a little drabber and have duller stripes, or may lack them altogether. Their song sounds a little like "sweet, sweet, sweet."

Yellow Warblers are not endemic to Galápagos. They're found all over the western hemisphere, from Alaska to Peru.

Yellow Warbler on Santiago

In other parts of the world, the tiny warblers prefer the edges of boggy wetlands and fields with trees. In Galápagos, you'd expect to see them feeding on the ground or in a low tree. Nevertheless, they have found that there are more insects along the shoreline than in the dry interior of the islands. They also occasionally feed on seeds or fruit. They're found throughout the islands: look for them at the Puerto Egas visitor site.

WILDLIFE

Darwin's Finches

The 14 species of Darwin's Finches (pinzón) that are found in the Galápagos are perhaps the most famous and sought-after land birds on the islands. This is probably due to the ecological significance of differences in the species' beak morphology and its link to feeding behavior.

All of the finches are sparrow-sized with mottled gray, brown, black or greenish feathers and short, rounded wings. Because all 13 species have similar superficial characteristics, it is difficult, and at times nearly impossible (even for naturalist guides), to distinguish them. The only clues they provide are the shape of their beak, the type of food they eat and the type of habitat they occupy.

Although they all originated from a single ancestor, individual species have formed as niche specialists: some eat seeds, some eat leaves, some eat cacti and some eat insects. One species found on Wolf drinks the blood of Nazca or Red-footed Boobies, a habit that has led to its being dubbed a "vampire finch." Three other finch species—the small, medium and sharp-billed ground finches—have the distinction of eating the ticks and mites off of reptiles. There are even two species—the woodpecker and mangrove finches—that use twigs or spines as primitive tools to extract hidden insect larvae or grubs from holes in tree branches.

courts the female by building an elaborate dome-shaped nest made of twigs, grass, bark, feathers and other materials, which he locates in his firmly established and highly protected territory. The male will continually attend to the female at the nest, while she lays and incubates her eggs (two to five, on average), and during the first weeks of the fledglings' lives.

Finches are found on all major islands, with each species distributed throughout the archipelago (and within the islands) according to its desired habitat. They are also common in towns, where they'll sit around at outdoor restaurants hoping for a handout. Darwin would approve of them adapting to this new food source!

Galápagos Mockingbird

There are four similar-looking species of endemic mockingbirds in very different home ranges throughout the Galápagos archipelago: The Charles Mockingbird (Nesomimus trifasciatus, cucuve de Floreana) is found near Floreana on the islands of Champion and Gardner. The Hood Mockingbird (Nesomimus macdonaldi, cucuve de Española) is found on Española. The Chatham Mockingbird (Nesomimus melanotis, cucuve de San Cristóbal) is found on San Cristóbal. The Galápagos Mockingbird (Nesomimus parvulus, cucuve de Galápagos), lives on most of the remaining major islands.

Galapagos Mockingbird

Darwin Finch

The mating season of finches generally begins after the first major rainfall of the rainy season (around February). The male

All four species of mockingbird are thrush-sized, long-tailed, gray and brown streaked land birds. The mockingbirds, especially the Hood variety, will greet you inquisitively with a loud, piercing call, loosely translated as "give me any liquid beverage—even your spit will do." Resist the temptation to quench their thirst: years of successfully begging tourists have caused an increasing reliance on them for water.

WILDLIFE

The mockingbirds have an extremely interesting social structure. During the breeding season, they form cooperative groups comprised of a breeding female, her mate and the offspring of her previous broods, all of whom participate in the raising of the next brood and maintenance of the territory.

During the rest of the year, large communal territories are formed with as few as nine and as many as 40 individuals, each contributing to territory defense. It is a hoot (no pun intended) to watch these birds defending their territories; individuals will face off across the imaginary frontier in linear fronts, each enemy pair squawking, flicking their tails, and rushing at each other.

Mockingbirds are omnivorous, but they occasionally exhibit aggressive, predatory behavior. They will eat just about anything: seeds, insects, baby turtles, young finches and sea lion placenta.

Galápagos Hawk

The Galápagos Hawk (gavilán de Galápagos) is an impressive, large, dark brown bird of prey. Adults have a dark banded tail, yellow hooked bill and strong yellow talons. The female has the same general features but has a larger, more imposing stature. Juveniles are a lighter brown and heavily mottled.

Nests—large, disorganized conglomerations of twigs—are usually constructed in trees or on a rocky outcrop. Following an unusual mating system termed "cooperative polyandry," each female will mate with up to four males, who take turns incubating the two or three eggs in the nest and raising the young. Young birds are expelled from the territory after about four months and begin to breed two years later.

A fearsome predator and scavenger with no natural enemies, the Galápagos Hawk delights in a smorgasbord of foods, especially baby iguanas, lizards, small birds, dead goats or sea lions and sea lion placenta. It can often be seen flying or perching impatiently near an iguana nesting area during April and May, when baby iguanas begin to emerge from their eggs. The hawks are best viewed at Punta Suarez and Gardner Bay (Española), South Plaza, Santa Fé, and Punta Espinosa (Fernandina).

Short-eared Owl

The Short-eared Owl (lechuza de orejas cortas) is the most commonly seen owl in Galápagos. It is dark brown in color with light mottled markings, a dark facial disc, yellow eyes, and a dark bill. You are most likely to see the diurnal hunter in the early morning or evening, when it is out looking for its next meal of small birds, rats or mice. It makes its nests on open ground, where it lays three to four eggs. This species is found on every major island except Wolf. The best place to see them is on Genovesa.

The Vampire Finch

Many people shudder at the mention of a vampire bat, but attaching such a monstrous name to a pretty, delicate animal like a finch seems ridiculous—like imagining a vampire kitten. However, vampire finches are very real and, in many ways, just as brutal as the bats that share their name.

An endangered species, the vampire finch can be found only on Darwin and Wolf Islands in Galápagos (although you can see the closely related sharp-beaked ground finch on Genovesa, Santiago, Pinta and Fernandina). They are one of the 14 species of Galápagos finches that adapted a specialized beak to suit food sources particular to the island they inhabit—in this case, a small, narrow bill that is used to puncture the flesh of larger birds in order to drink their blood.

Although Vampire Finches eat seeds and insects for the most part, occasionally these food sources are scarce on the tiny island, so the innovative birds resort to drinking the blood of their larger cousins. The Blue-footed Booby is their usual victim. The finch typically executes its assault by landing on the tail of the bird, pecking at the base of the wing feathers until the skin breaks, and then sipping the oozing blood. Other finches will patiently queue up behind the booby to take their turns at the gruesome fountain. Oddly enough, the boobies don't offer up a whole lot of resistance; scientists believe this is because they think the finches are picking parasites off their flesh.

As cringe-inducing as the feeding methods of the Vampire Finch are, you can't help but admire what are inarguably some very tenacious and inventive survival skills.

WILDLIFE

Galápagos Barn Owl

The Galápagos Islands are home to a thriving population of barn owls (lechuza de campanario). They're easy to spot with their distinctive owl faces and mottled brown and white coloring. Galápagos Barn Owls are not considered an introduced species and are actually a subspecies of the Common Barn Owl. Although probably as common as the Galápagos Short-eared Owl, they're much harder to spot because of their nocturnal habits.

Like their mainland cousins, they like to nest in airy structures, including buildings and lava tubes. They feed mostly on rodents and smaller birds. Seeing one is rare, as most visitor sites are closed at night. Your only real chance is to spot one on the outskirts of one of the towns at night or in a lava tunnel during the day.

Galápagos Dove

The endemic Galápagos Dove is one of the more spectacular land birds, with a chestnut-brown back, reddish-brown head and belly, bright red legs, and a conspicuous pale blue ring around the eyes. They nest year-round, but peak breeding season usually starts in February. Courtship behavior includes exaggerated flying patterns, a bowing ceremony, and the males' deep, soft cooing call. The female will lay two eggs in nests built under rocks or nests vacated by mockingbirds.

The curved shape of the Galápagos Dove's bill is indicative of its chosen food: seeds picked from the ground, mainly dropped by the opuntia cactus. They will also eat caterpillars and insect larvae. The Galápagos Dove can be seen in the drier areas of most islands; a slightly larger subspecies is found on Darwin and Wolf. Puerto Egas (Santiago) and Prince Philip's Steps (Genovesa) are good places to look for them.

Galápagos Martin

A rarely seen member of the swallow family, the endemic Galápagos Martin (golondrina de Galápagos) is mostly blue-black to brown. It feeds in the air, gracefully swooping about to catch airborne insects. It may be related to South America's Southern Martin. They nest in holes in cliffs.

They're occasionally seen near Bachas beach. If you hike to the rim of one of the volcanoes on Isabela, you may see them feeding in the caldera. Look for them near cliffs.

Galápagos Flycatcher

The Galápagos Flycatcher (papamoscas de Galápagos) is occasionally mistaken for a finch, because it occupies comparable habitats and has similar coloring, if all you get is a quick look. Upon closer examination, you'll see that the Galápagos Flycatcher is a little larger than the average finch and also more brightly colored, with a yellow-greenish underbelly and brown and white wing feathers. Like the finches, they're not very shy and you can often get a good look at one perched on a nearby branch.

The Galápagos Flycatcher is common throughout the islands. They can be seen just about any time you're inland, flitting close to the trail.

Vermilion Flycatcher

One of the more dazzling birds in Galápagos (or anywhere, for that matter), the Vermilion Flycatcher is found in mainland Ecuador and is occasionally seen in Galápagos. The brilliant red males are more commonly spotted, with their bright red breast and black wings and "mask" across the eyes. Female Vermilion Flycatchers are a more drab grayish color with light pink breasts and can be confused with finches from afar.

Like all flycatchers, they feed on insects such as flies, bees and grasshoppers, which they can deftly snatch out of the air. In Spanish, they are called "pájaro brujo" or "warlock bird." Cerro Brujo, a popular beach visitor site on San Cristóbal Island, is named for this bird, although they're rarely seen there anymore. The best place to see the Vermilion Flycatcher is at highland ranches, where visitors often go to see the Giant Tortoises in their natural habitat. They can also be seen at the Gemelos site of Santa Cruz, a pair of verdant sinkholes.

Galápagos Rail

Seldom seen by visitors, the elusive Galápagos Rail (pachay) is a medium-sized bird which prefers wooded and grassy highlands. It is black with a grayish breast and white spots on its back. Visitors who get close enough will notice its red eyes.

The Galápagos Rail is nearly flightless, preferring to dart quickly through grasslands and forests, digging in fallen leaves for invertebrates such as worms, amphibians and insects.

It is considered a threatened species, as introduced animals such as cats, dogs, goats

WILDLIFE

and pigs devastate its habitat and eat the birds and their eggs. Increased efforts to eradicate these introduced species seem to be having a positive effect on Galápagos Rail populations. They can be seen in the highlands, usually in the morning.

Smooth-billed Ani

A large member of the Cuckoo family, the Smooth-billed Ani (Garrapatero) is a largish, black bird with a big, black beak (yes, the beak is smooth). It has a relatively long tail and tends to congregate in groups. A Smooth-billed Ani might be mistaken for a crow at a glance.

Common throughout South and Central America, it's an introduced species in Galápagos—rangers and visitors started seeing them around 1960. It has been speculated that they were deliberately brought there by ranchers, as the birds will peck ticks and other insects out of the tough hides of cattle.

They're considered a pest because, in addition to insects, Anis eat small birds and eggs. Endemic birds such as Darwin finches are in danger because of them and they can also eat lizards and snakes. The species has proven difficult to control, in part because of their high reproduction rate—a mated pair can turn out three clutches of eggs annually, which can hatch as many as 10 chicks each time.

The Smooth-billed Ani is more interesting than your average bird. Several females can lay eggs in the same nest. In Suriname, they believe that eating them (apparently they taste terrible) is a good cure for asthma. A group of Smooth-billed Anis is known as a "couch," a "silliness" or an "orphanage."

Inland Water Birds of Galápagos

Although the different islands that make up Galápagos are generally very dry and arid, there are a few ponds and streams, mostly in the highlands of the larger islands. These ponds and streams are home to a handful of species of water birds like ducks and grebes that visitors won't ever see out to sea or on the beach. The most famous is probably the endemic Galápagos Pintail Duck, which can be seen in the highlands of Santa Cruz, Isabela or San Cristóbal.

Common Moorhen

Also called the Common Waterhen and Common Gallinule, the Common Moorhen (gallareta común) is a familiar sight in many areas of the world. A member of the Rail family, it is a medium-sized bird somewhere between a pigeon and a chicken in size. It has black feathers with a few white ones in the tail and wings. It is most easily distinguished by its bright red "face" around the eyes and over the bill. It also has skinny, bright yellow legs.

The Common Moorhen eats small insects and plants, and can often be seen puttering around ponds and lagoons. El Junco Lake on San Cristóbal Island is a good place to spot one.

Pied-billed Grebe

The Pied-billed Grebe (zambullidor de pico grueso) is a water bird resembling a small grayish-brown duck. The easiest way to recognize them is the black stripe on their bills (which are pointier than that of a duck). It looks like someone put a black rubber band on its bill to keep it closed.

The Pied-billed Grebe can often be seen puttering around freshwater highland ponds or brackish inland lagoons. They're pretty quiet and shy, preferring to quickly swim away if approached. They eat frogs, bugs and small fish. They can also eat their own feathers to aid in digestion.

Galápagos Pintail Duck

The Galápagos Pintail Duck (patillo de Bahamas) is a medium-sized duck with brown and white feathers. It is easily identified by its white cheeks and colorful red and blue bill. It is a subspecies of the Bahama or White-Cheeked Pintail and is endemic to the Islands.

Ducks are rare in Galápagos, but there are enough highland ponds and coastal lagoons for the Pintail to thrive. Like other endemic species, it has adapted well to Galápagos life, feeding and breeding opportunistically as conditions permit. Look for them in any inland lake or lagoon—the brackish pools on Isabela Island are a good place to find them.

Whimbrel

Brown, medium-sized birds commonly sighted along the seashore, Whimbrels (zarapito) are most easily identified by their long, narrow, curved beaks. They're common in Galápagos and in much of the world. Whimbrels migrate, preferring to nest in colder northern climes.

Whimbrels eat small fish, insects and crustaceans. They are commonly seen in or near tidal pools, poking around for a good meal.

WILDLIFE

Galápagos Reptiles

Reptiles dominate the animal scene in Galápagos, due to their ability to cross long distances (i.e., from the mainland to the archipelago) without food or water. Giant tortoises and large land iguanas play the ecological role of the larger mammals on the mainland. There are 23 species of Galápagos reptiles, 21 of which are endemic to the archipelago. In 2009, the Galápagos Pink Iguana was identified as a separate species, which split off from other iguana species about 5-6 million years ago.

Galápagos Giant Tortoise

The Galápagos Giant Tortoise (tortuga gigante) is the namesake of the archipelago. The word "galápagos" refers to an old Spanish saddle very similar in shape to the shell of one of the two major types of tortoises: saddleback and dome-shaped. The saddleback tortoises have long necks, are smaller in stature, and live in low areas with little vegetation. Dome-shaped tortoises live in the highlands of the larger islands. Males have longer tails and are bigger than the females. Within these two categories fall 14 subspecies (three of which are extinct) of Galápagos Giant Tortoise, each having evolved differently due to habitat isolation.

The Galápagos Giant Tortoise is most well-known for its immense size. It can grow to over 1.5 meters (4.92 ft) in length and up to 250 kilograms (551.2 lb) in weight. Growth ring approximations on their shells indicate a life span of at least 150 years. The rate of growth is controlled by the availability of food, their food of choice extending to over 50 species of plants, including poison apple, guava, cactus pads and more.

Giant tortoises at the breeding station on Isabela

Female tortoises reach sexual maturity at between 25 and 30 years of age, at which time they will mate and then migrate to the lowlands, locate a suitable earthy area, dig a shallow pit and deposit between two and 16 ping-pong ball-sized eggs. They will cover the eggs with mud and urine and leave the eggs incubating for 120 to 140 days. The distance traveled by female tortoises to lay their eggs is the greatest distance any tortoise will travel in its lifetime; males only move 4-5 kilometers (2.5-3.1 mi) per year and can often stay for days in their mud holes without moving.

The most famous Galápagos Giant Tortoise was Lonesome George, the last of the Pinta Island subspecies and an important symbol of the plight of the tortoises due to human activity until his death in 2012. Because tortoise populations have been drastically reduced from predation by introduced species, the Charles Darwin Research Station has spearheaded a very successful captive breeding and reintroduction program.

The easiest places to see Galápagos Giant Tortoises are at the Charles Darwin Research Station or at the breeding centers on Isabela or San Cristóbal and in the wild in the Santa Cruz highlands.

Galápagos Lava Lizard

There are seven endemic species of Lava Lizard (lagartija de lava) in Galápagos. They are easily recognizable by their small size (up to 30 cm in length) and interesting coloring. Males and females of all species are wildly different. Males are up to three times heavier than females, have more patterned skin, and have a clearly visible black or yellow throat. Females, on the other hand, are smaller and have a bright red or orange throat.

All Lava Lizards also perform a characteristic "push-up" behavior to show territorial aggression or courtship tendencies. Interestingly enough, this display is a vivid example of character divergence among species. This is because each of the islands' populations (even ones harboring the same species) have a slightly different display pattern.

Lava Lizards feed primarily on small insects, but they are omnivores and can occasionally eat plant material or even blood if a nearby bird or iguana is bleeding. Activity is closely dependent on daily

WILDLIFE

temperature fluctuations, so you will probably see most lava lizards during the cool morning and mid-afternoon hours.

Lava Lizards can be seen darting around underfoot on every major island.

Green Sea Turtle

The only marine turtle to breed in Galápagos is the Green Sea Turtle (tortuga marina verde), which has a hard, dark green to black shell and can weigh up to 150 kilograms (330.7 lb). Unlike the giant tortoise, the female is larger than the male.

Peak mating season is from November to January, when both males and females will choose various partners with which to mate. You can often see a mating couple bobbing offshore or swimming near the surface of the water.

The female then goes ashore to prepare her nest, a large "body pit" with a smaller flask-shaped pit inside where the eggs are laid. She may come ashore as many as eight times at two week intervals, each time depositing 70 to 80 eggs. The small hatchlings emerge after a three-month incubation period, only to be confronted immediately with the reality of their delectability—only about one percent will survive predation by crabs, birds, sharks, or introduced cats, dogs or rats.

Snorkelers will see Green Sea Turtles all over the archipelago. You can also look for them while taking panga rides in calm, shallow waters.

Galápagos Land Iguana

There are two endemic species of land iguana (iguana terrestre) in the Galápagos archipelago, not counting the Pink Iguanas of Isabela: the more common Land Iguana and the island-specific Santa Fé Land Iguana. Both species look very similar, with pale to dark yellow coloring, but the Santa Fé Land Iguana is paler, has a more pronounced crest, and is covered with a distinctive pattern resembling military camouflage.

There are also rare examples of land and marine iguanas hybridizing, the result of which is a land-loving iguana with dark skin, light-colored bands, a small spinal crest and webbed feet.

During the period of reproduction (the end of the year), males take on a brilliant red color to attract the females and become extremely territorial. After a somewhat violent copulation, the females will then lay six to eight eggs in underground nests, usually between January and March. The eggs are incubated for about 45 to 50 days, after which time young iguanas face the formidable challenge of surviving natural and introduced predators (especially the Galápagos Hawk). It is estimated that 70 percent of young land iguanas survive. The average life span is 45 years.

Land iguanas have a fairly limited home range of about 100 meters (328.1 ft), which means that they feed in a small area, mostly on pads and fruit from the opuntia cactus, and thus can be affected by localized climatic changes. The best places to see them are at Cerro Dragon (Santa Cruz) and on North Seymour. Sometimes they are seen wandering around near the Baltra airport.

Diego, the Second Most Famous Galápagos Tortoise

Poor Diego. His neighbor, Lonesome George, used to get all the attention, when Diego's story is just as remarkable.

Diego is a tortoise of the Española variety, and he's believed to be about 100 years old. Back in the 1930s, he was taken from home by a passing yacht and eventually made his way to the San Diego Zoo. He stayed there, a favorite of visitors, until he was sent home to Galápagos in 1977.

It turns out that Diego was just in time. He was reunited with the final 14 surviving members of his subspecies—12 females and two males—found on Española and taken away for safekeeping. Ever since, he's been busy breeding, and the results are very positive. In recent years, well over 1,000 young Española tortoises have been returned to the island, a good number of which are Diego's offspring.

Unlike Lonesome George, Diego never had his own pen, his face on T-shirts, or any other special treatment. He is in a nondescript enclosure at the Charles Darwin Research Station with other Española tortoises. Ask station staff or your guide to point out the second-most famous Galápagos Tortoise!

WILDLIFE

Galápagos Pink Iguana

First discovered in 1986, the Pink Iguana was thought for a long time to be a subspecies of the Galápagos Land Iguana. In early 2009, however, researchers at a university in Rome released a study declaring the Pink Iguana to be a different species. There is only a very small population of Pink Iguanas in Galápagos, and they are all found on the slopes of Wolf Volcano, on the northern end of Isabela Island. They are considered critically endangered due to their small population, and efforts are under way to protect them. Currently, there are no visitor sites on Wolf Volcano, so visitors to Galapágos will not get to see them.

Galápagos Marine Iguana

Ask any biologist what they think is the most remarkable of the Galápagos reptiles and chances are he or she will tell you that it's the Marine Iguana (iguana marina). After all, it's the only sea-faring lizard in the world!

Adult Marine Iguanas are mostly black or dark gray, but some have a colorful red and green lichen-like covering on their backs, the result of their algal diet. They also have an elongated tail to help them swim, a flat head, a pronounced crest running the length of their backs, and large, webbed feet.

Galápagos Marine Iguana

Marine Iguanas live on land, but they feed on red and green algae in the cool ocean waters. Smaller iguanas keep to the intertidal zone, but others venture to depths of up to 10 meters (32.8 ft) and stay submerged for up to 10 minutes looking for food. After a swim, they will return to land to bask in the sun or huddle with others for warmth (they are cold-blooded) and perform an unforgettable sneeze-like snort in order to release an excess of salt from their nostrils.

Marine iguanas have the same general reproductive cycle as land iguanas, laying their eggs in the beginning of the year. Their mating behavior, however, is a bit different. Marine iguanas are polyganous, meaning female iguanas accept a number of male partners, often as many as 15. Females lay three eggs in their underground nests instead of one, which take up to three months to incubate.

Young Marine Iguanas face the same predatory threats when they hatch, but they have the added challenge of thwarting marine predators. If they survive through the formative period, they are expected to live for 40 years.

V!VA QUOTE

It is a hideous-looking creature, of a dirty black color, stupid and sluggish in its movements.

Charles Darwin, referring to the Marine Iguana

Galápagos Snake

The unassuming Galápagos Snake (culebra de Galápagos) is shy and difficult to see. They're found on all of the islands except for the northern ones including Genovesa, Pinta and Marchena. There are four basic species and three subspecies. Most of them are subclassified according to the different islands where they're found.

The majority are cream-colored with stripes, while others are darker. They resemble the garter snakes common in North America.

Galápagos snake, Fernandina

WILDLIFE

While technically venomous, their poison is not very dangerous to people and they're not aggressive in the least. Their teeth are designed in such a way that they cannot inject the poison when they bite. Instead, they use it in digestion once they already have caught and killed their prey. They're constrictors who crush their prey, typically small birds, lizards and insects. They, in turn, are hunted by the Galápagos Hawk and introduced species such as cats and rats. Look for them on Española and Fernandina Islands, although you might get lucky just about anywhere.

Mammals List

There are not many mammal species that are native or endemic to Galápagos, as getting there from the mainland is very hard. Reptiles, for example, are much more likely to live on some floating vegetation for the days or weeks necessary to make it to the islands than a mammal. Still, the islands are home to a handful of endemic and native mammal species, as well as some undesirable introduced species.

The endemic mammal most often encountered by visitors is without question the Galápagos Sea Lion. These friendly critters are found on every island and often seem to enjoy interacting with tourists, particularly when snorkeling. Their cousins, the Galápagos Fur Sea Lions, are much more reclusive and only can be seen at a handful of visitor sites. They can be tough to tell from the regular sea lions, but naturalist guides can spot the differences easily.

There were once several subspecies of the Galápagos Rice Rat, but pressure from the far more aggressive introduced Black and Norway rats have driven most of them to extinction and there are now only three subspecies left. Every effort is being taken to preserve them, but it's a difficult battle against the introduced rats, cats and dogs. Active only at night, Rice Rats are very rarely seen by visitors.

The Galápagos Bat, or Galápagos Red Bat, is the only endemic bat in the islands. There are Hoary Bats as well, but they're common elsewhere in the world. Both species nest in vegetation and mangroves and are active at night. The best place to see one is in one of the towns around dusk.

Galápagos is also home to several species of whales and dolphins. These are rarely seen from shore but occasionally from a ship. The strait of water between Isabela and Fernandina is a good place to see them. The most commonly seen ones are Bryde's Whales and Bottlenose Dolphins. Galápagos cruise ships will usually make an effort to see the whales if there are some in the vicinity.

There are, of course, several other mammal species in Galápagos, none of them helpful for the ecosystem. Early whalers and settlers brought domesticated animals to Galápagos, including pigs, dogs, cats, goats and donkeys. Unintentionally, they brought rats and mice as well. These introduced animals have become a true nuisance, destroying whole ecosystems and pushing Galápagos species to extinction. Aggressive extermination measures have greatly reduced the impact of these species, but the problem is not yet over.

Galápagos Sea Lion

The endemic Galápagos Sea Lion (lobo marino) is found all throughout the islands and is absolutely fearless of humans. You will definitely have the chance to watch some of the 50,000 inquisitive juvenile sea lions, playful adult sea lions, protective mother sea lions and competitive male sea lions found in the archipelago. Male sea lions can be aggressive and are potentially dangerous so be alert while in their presence.

Males, or bulls, can be distinguished from the females, or cows, by their thick necks, bumped foreheads, and immense size (full-grown males can weigh up to 250 kg). They jealously guard and protect their territory, a finite area covering land and water space, a harem of approximately 20 cows and any number of pups. When bulls lose land battles to other, more aggressive dominant males, they conglomerate in specific island sites, or bachelor pads, to heal and rest until the next challenge.

The mating season varies from island to island, but it generally occurs from June to November. Females give birth to four or five pups over their lifetimes, one every two years. Copulation usually takes place in the water four weeks after a birth, but due to "delayed implantation," the egg is not implanted into the womb for another two months. Gestation takes another nine months, thus finalizing the annual birth cycle.

Nine out of 10 sea lion pups are females. The males and females stay together in "kindergartens," swimming and playing in the shallow water. After five months, the pups can start fishing for themselves, although they still depend on their mothers. After three years, cows have reached sexual maturity and begin to reproduce. After five years, the slow-blooming males reach their adulthood. Most sea lions live for 15 years or so.

Sea lions feed mostly on sardines (the cause of their bad breath) and other small fish, for which they may travel 10 to 15 kilometers (6.2-9.3 mi) out from the coast over the span of days to hunt. It is in deep water that sea lions encounter and must defend themselves from their only natural predators, sharks.

A playful Galápagos sea lion

Galápagos Fur Sea Lion

Also known as the Galápagos Fur Seal (foca peletera), this local critter is much more difficult to spot than its cousin, the Galápagos Sea Lion. The two species can be tough to tell apart—they're about the same size and color and tend to hang out in similar places. Naturalist guides can tell the difference at a glance, however; the fur sea lion has a thicker coat, is slightly smaller, has a more rounded nose, and prefers rocky shorelines to sandy beaches.

The well-insulated Fur Sea Lion has a double coat of thick skin. That's why you won't see them sunning themselves on the beach. They prefer shady grottoes where they can keep cool. It is believed that much like the Galápagos Penguin, the Fur Sea Lions were brought from southern South America by strong currents and have been adapting to the warmer climate ever since. Fur Sea Lion pups are especially vulnerable to temperature and climate changes and El Niño years have been known to nearly wipe out an entire generation.

They feed at night on fish and squid, trying to steer clear of predatory sharks as they do so. They were once hunted (almost to extinction) for their skins but are now protected and their population levels are considered safe.

Good places to see them are at Puerto Egas (Santiago) and Punta Vicente Roca (Isabela).

Marine Life

The Galápagos Islands are an amazing place for exploring underwater habitats. Due to the collision of warm and cool ocean currents, there is an astounding diversity and abundance of Galápagos fish species. That does not mean, however, that mastering marine creature identification is impossible.

The following pages are an introductory guide to the most common shore animals, cartilaginous fish (sharks and rays) and bony fish that can be seen when snorkeling. Marine life is more diverse than land life, and there are hundreds more fish, mollusks, crustaceans, echinoderms and other watery critters than are listed here.

Sally Lightfoot Crabs

Sally Lightfoot Crabs (zayapa) are named for their ability to flitter across rock faces like the semi-mythological dancer. Adults have a dramatic red-orange color, with a blue underside. Since red is the first color to disappear underwater, this coloration serves to camouflage the crabs. Juveniles, which are heavily predated, also rely on camouflage—they are black so that they can disappear against the lava background that serves as their habitat.

They are found on rocky shores throughout the islands, but common sightings are in Las Bachas (Santa Cruz), Puerto Egas (Santiago) and Sombrero Chino.

SHARKS IN THE GALÁPAGOS ISLANDS

The White-tipped Reef Shark (tiburón aleta blanca) is a common sight in snorkel spots throughout the archipelago. It is easy to identify by its pointed nose, silvery-gray color, and the white tips on its tail and first dorsal fin. Most White-tipped Reef Sharks are about the same size as an adult human, 1.5 to two meters (6.56 ft) in length. They tend to rest around rocky inlays or in caves, often swimming very close to snorkelers. Don't worry about these sharks reenacting a scene from *Jaws*—they feed at night on small fish and are very docile.

They are commonly seen by snorkelers at North Seymour, Gardner Bay and Turtle Island (Española), and Devil's Crown

(Floreana). The place most famous for them is Tintoreras Islet near Puerto Villamil (Isabela), where visitors can see hundreds at a time if they're lucky. You can sometimes see them from the beach at Punta Cormorant (Floreana) and Bartolomé.

The Black-tipped Reef Shark (tiburón aleta negra) is less common than the White-Tipped Reef Shark, but it can still be seen by snorkelers. It is easily recognizable by its pointed nose, silvery-gray color, and the black (instead of white) tips on its fins. It is the same size as the White-Tipped Reef Shark, but it is more blatantly unassuming, usually swimming away at the sight of humans. These are sometimes seen at Devil's Crown (Floreana). Juveniles are common in Black Turtle Cove (Santa Cruz).

The endemic Galápagos Shark (tiburón de Galápagos) is a stout, silvery-gray to brown shark. Despite its smaller size (up to two meters/6.56 ft), it is, arguably, the most threatening of the Galápagos sharks both in appearance and behavior. It is an active carnivore, and known to eat other sharks.

It is rarely seen in the typical snorkel spots, but you might get lucky at Devil's Crown (Floreana) and at Leon Dormido (San Cristóbal).

The Hammerhead Shark (tiburón martillo) is instantly recognizable by its flattened head, peripheral eyes and nostrils and large (growing up to 4 m long) physique. Galápagos is famous for its abundance of Hammerheads—divers often see them in large schools of up to 30 or 40 individuals or even more.

The Sea Lions of San Cristóbal

Puerto Baquerizo Moreno, San Cristóbal Island, has finally come to an agreement with its oldest residents: a thriving sea lion colony. The city is located on picturesque Shipwreck Bay, one of the best natural harbors in Galápagos. The bay is deep but sheltered, the surf is gentle and it's a great place for fishing—all of which the sea lions figured out long before humans arrived.

Sea lion on the playground in Puerto Baquerizo Moreno

The playful sea lions can be something of a nuisance. They eat stinky fish and then climb onto anchored boats for a nap, letting nature take its course. Before you know it, your boat is full of fish-stinky sea lion excrement. They do the same thing on the beach. If you come too close, they may nip. Many a native of San Cristóbal has muttered under his or her breath about the sea lion colony, one of the largest in the islands.

Not that it's any picnic for the sea lions, mind you. Boats have sharp propellers, which can injure them or scare away the fish. At night, light and noise pollution affect sea lion habits. Fuel gets into the harbor, fouling it and killing the fish. Sea lions can get caught up in fish lines and nets. Presumably, the sea lions grumble under their breath too about their two-legged neighbors.

But these reluctant neighbors are entering a new era. The residents of San Cristóbal have decided to make the sea lions the semi-official mascot of the town, with a new campaign: "Sea Lions: the Face of San Cristóbal." It turns out the ornery critters are popular with tourists, and just maybe they're not so bad after all.

This new partnership is bringing benefits for feet and flippers alike. The sea lions are now monitored for health problems on a weekly basis, and they've gotten a nifty, large square platform anchored in the bay where they can go take a nap. The campaign, which includes education for San Cristóbal's youth, is drawing positive reviews from ecological groups. Everybody wins!

You are less likely to see them while you are snorkeling, but your best chance is at Genovesa. If you are extremely lucky, you may see juveniles in Black Turtle Cove (Santa Cruz) or Post Office Bay (Floreana).

The Whale Shark (tiburón ballena) is a massive (but harmless) shark found mostly around the western islands of Darwin and Wolf. Since divers tend to be the only ones to visit these outlying islands, they are the most likely to see one of these gentle monsters. It has a huge mouth (often lined with cleaner fish) that can swallow vast quantities of plankton.

RAYS IN THE GALÁPAGOS ISLANDS

The Manta Ray (mantaraya), with its large lobes, long mouth, thin tail and massive three-meter wingspan, is an amazingly beautiful, graceful and unassuming creature. Watching it swim or jump out of the water to remove annoying parasites or remora is a truly unforgettable experience. They feed on plankton near the surface of the water, making visual sightings from the ship or dinghy a fairly common occurrence.

They are often seen in open water between the central islands, most often from the cliff at South Plaza or from the beach at Rábida.

Golden Rays (raya dorada) are usually between a half-meter to a meter across the wings. They are aptly named for their golden-colored tops, but they can also be recognized by their blunt heads and long, whip-like tail. They are often seen in the major snorkel sites swimming alone, but they also swim in large schools in quiet lagoons. The best place to see schools of Golden Rays is at Black Turtle Cove (Santa Cruz).

Spotted Eagle Rays (raya águila) are also commonly sighted schooling in small lagoons like Black Turtle Cove (Santa Cruz).

How to Get Rid of Goats

Twenty years ago, goats were a serious problem on every major Galapagos Island. These animals had been left on the islands long ago by passing ships: the theory was that if you let a couple goats loose on every island, when you came back a couple years later, there would be plenty there to hunt for food. In fact, this theory worked...far too well.

For decades, park rangers and conservationists tried to eradicate them, to no avail. Rangers would carry guns and shoot any goat they saw, but the crafty creatures soon learned to avoid humans. Hunts were organized, and although thousands of goats were slaughtered, they never seemed to get them all, and the goat populations merely rebounded in a question of months.

Today, goats are gone from Pinta, Santiago, northern Isabela and some smaller islands, and the park service is confident of removing them from the rest of the islands at some point in the future. How did the park service begin to win the battle against the feral goats? By consulting international experts, mostly from Australia, New Zealand and Hawaii, the Galapagos conservationists were able to come up with a plan. Here are some of the strategies:

The Judas Goat: Goats are gregarious and like to travel in herds. This is a weakness their hunters can exploit. Sterilized goats with radio collars were released into the wild. These goats found the closest herd and joined it. Then, it's simply a question of following the radio signal and hunting.

Mata Hari Goats: "Mata Hari" goats are sterilized females who have been chemically caused to be in estrus. They are good for luring male goats out of hiding.

Helicopters: Helicopter hunting, especially in combination with the Judas Goats, has proven a devastating weapon against the goats. The Galapagos Islands are rocky, barren and harsh, but they're also small. Hunters in the air can cover a whole small island in a question of hours, and sharpshooting rangers can pick off goats at will.

Specially trained hunting dogs: hunting from the ground is still done, with specially trained hunting dogs. These dogs are trained in Galapagos with techniques from New Zealand. The dogs are trained to find the goats, round them up and keep them in one place until the hunters arrive. The dogs are also trained to ignore any other animals.

Such success comes with a cost: the final bill for Santiago Island alone was $6.1 million. Much of it came from park fees and donations from visitors.

WILDLIFE

They have pointed heads, long tails with a spiny point, and a wingspan ranging from one to two meters (3.28-6.56 ft), but their most distinguishing feature is the array of white spots that covers their black tops. They are also occasionally seen by snorkelers at Turtle Island (Española) or off Floreana.

Stingrays (raya sartén) are common residents of shallow beach areas and deeper sandy bottoms throughout Galápagos. They are gray with a flat body and long, narrow tail, which has the nasty stinger at its base. The size and shape of stingrays can vary, from the smaller, angular "diamond stingray" to the larger (up to two meter wingspan), circular "marbled" stingray.

You can spot stingrays lurking on the sea floor of some shallower snorkel sites or hiding out in the surf at Punta Cormorant and/or Post Office Bay (Floreana).

Fish in the Galápagos Islands

Galápagos is world-renowned as one of the best places in the world for diving and snorkeling. If you choose to dive, snorkel, or take a tour in a glass-bottom boat, chances are very good that you will see a number of beautiful, exotic fish and marine animals. Here are just a few of the dazzling fish you might see.

The Flag Cabrilla

The Flag Cabrilla is a favorite of divers and snorkelers in Galápagos, as it is very common, prefers shallow water and is not terribly timid. North American divers and snorkelers may think it looks like a bass. It has a greenish/olive to reddish to gray body and is easily identified by its numerous white spots and milky blotches. It also has a distinctive black spot on the upper side of the base of its tail. They prefer rocks and reefs and don't tend to move much—you'll usually see them lurking on ledges and in crevasses as you pass. Approach slowly and you should get a good look.

Zebra Moray Eel

Moray Eels are common in Galápagos. The elusive Zebra Moray Eel is smaller and shyer than its Moray cousins. It is blackish brown with distinctive white-green to white-blue stripes.
It also has a blunter nose than its Moray relatives. It prefers rocky walls and areas with boulders and rocks. It is shy and will hide from snorkelers and divers. It eats crabs and mollusks.

White-tail Damselfish

The White-tail Damselfish is a familiar sight to many Galápagos snorkelers and divers. This fish, much more spectacular when it is a juvenile, is found in most dive and snorkel spots in the islands, where they favor rocky formations in relatively shallow water. They are brownish gray to black. Adults and juveniles are identified by a white stripe at the base of their tail—in some adults, the stripe may disappear. They generally have a bright orange "eyebrow" that makes identifying them easy, and there is often a bright yellow stripe on their pectoral fins. They ignore divers, only retreating into holes and shelter if too closely approached.

Bat Fish

Just when you thought you knew everything there is to know about Galápagos, something like this pops up in your guidebook. Looking as though it had dragged itself out of a Hieronymus Bosch painting, the red-lipped bat fish is characterized by its scarlet mouth, compressed, horizontal body, and the wing-like fins it uses to walk along the ocean floor.

It is chiefly found in the waters around the Galápagos Islands, as well as around Cocos Island, off the coast of Costa Rica. True to its name, it prefers deep, dark waters, and can be found at an ocean depth of over 30 meters (100 ft). The bat fish is carnivorous and hunts for small fish and crustaceans using a small, worm-like extension from its head as a lure. Charles Darwin must have missed this little guy when he visited the islands, or there undoubtedly would have been plenty written in his journal about one of Galápagos' most bizarre residents.

King Angelfish

The only member of the Angelfish family to be found in Galápagos, the King Angelfish is a favorite of many snorkelers and divers. This very beautiful fish is common in most snorkeling and diving areas. They prefer rocky areas to sandy bottoms.

They are oval-shaped and have a dark blue body with a distinctive white stripe behind the gill. The top and back fins are yellow to orange. They are generally seen alone or in pairs—they occasionally school. Sudden movements will frighten them. It is best to approach slowly to get a good look.

Stone Scorpionfish

The Stone Scorpionfish is a master of deception, disguising itself as a rock, clump of vegetation or piece of coral. Loose flaps of skin and scale help it blend into the bottom, where it will wait motionless for prey to swim past. It can also change colors from gray to purple to red in order to better hide. The spines along its dorsal fin contain a painful poison—don't step on one! However, they are not aggressive and remain motionless if approached. They are fairly common, but often difficult to spot. Its Spanish name is brujo, or "warlock."

Bravo Clinid

This small, colorful bottom dweller can change colors rapidly to disguise itself into its environment. A member of the blenny family, the Bravo Clinid is endemic to Galápagos and common throughout the islands. It usually remains motionless when approached by a snorkeler or diver, allowing close inspection. They prefer rocks and crevasses to sandy bottoms.

Sergeant-Major

A member of the Damselfish family, Sergeant-Majors are commonly seen at most Galápagos snorkeling and diving sites (and around the world, in fact). They are small (up to 20.32 cm/8 in) oval-shaped fish, yellow-green with distinctive blue-black stripes. These stripes give it its name. They resemble the stripes on a sergeant-major's uniform. They are not terribly shy and can usually be easily approached by slow-moving swimmers.

Parrot Fish

A common sight for snorkelers and divers, the parrot fish is very colorful and not extremely shy, which makes it a favorite. Common at most of the dive sites throughout Galápagos, the Parrot Fish is a large member of the Wrasse family. It has a long body, large scales, and a distinctive parrot-like beak with which it crunches coral in order to eat the organisms inside. You can often hear their munching before you see them. Most are bluish-green with hints of yellow and orange.

Introduced Species in Galápagos

Ask any Galápagos guide or park ranger, and they'll tell you that the most serious problem currently facing the islands is the threat posed by introduced species. The animals that live in Galápagos have been there by themselves for centuries, allowing them to adapt to very specific island conditions. Some scientists estimate that if it were not for humans, one new species would arrive to Galápagos "naturally" once every hundred years.

But the presence of humans changed all that. Since the islands were first discovered in the 16th century, dozens of new species have been brought to the islands. Some of them were brought accidentally, like the Tree Frog (Scinax quinquefasciatus) or the Ship Rat (Rattus rattus), but many, such as goats and pigs, were brought intentionally. In centuries past, sailing ships such as pirates and whalers would often release goats, pigs and other animals on islands so that they could be hunted for food on return visits. Also, early settlers brought cats, dogs, donkeys and other domestic animals with them, which would often escape into the wild.

The damage wrought by these animals is tremendous. Introducing new animals into a closed ecosystem often greatly disrupts it. Take for example the endemic Galápagos Flightless Cormorant. It arrived ages ago to the islands and began evolving. Most cormorants around the world can fly and make their nests in trees or on cliffs. The Galápagos variety does not fly and makes only a rudimentary nest of twigs on the ground. These adaptations were possible because the Galápagos Cormorants have only one natural predator: the Galápagos Hawk, which can occasionally snatch a juvenile cormorant if the parent is inattentive. But when cats, dogs and rats were suddenly introduced, the cormorant, nesting on the ground and incapable of flying away, suddenly became vulnerable. Although the cormorant populations on the islands are not in any immediate danger, there is no doubt that their numbers are reduced from where they were before man arrived.

Almost every introduced species has caused great damage in the islands. Goats, one of the worst offenders, can pick an area clean of vegetation, leaving slower tortoises and iguanas to starve. Aggressive, introduced rats have muscled out the timid Galápagos Rice Rat. Cats eat bird eggs, small iguanas, snakes, lava lizards, turtle eggs and birds. Even introduced birds such as the Smooth-billed Ani carry diseases which infect local species.

Many invertebrates have arrived in Galápagos as well, including fire ants, wasps and the

WILDLIFE

Cottony Cushioned Scale (Icerya purchasi). The scale insect was doing so much damage to the mangroves that the ladybug was intentionally introduced simply to combat it.

PLANTS

Many visitors assume that the introduced animal species are the most harmful to the islands, but this is not the case. Introduced plants have been taking over the islands at an alarming rate, elbowing out native plants in the process. Most of the plants were brought for a reason, such as edible blackberries or the Red Quinine tree, which produces an anti-malarial medicine. These plants are extremely difficult to control or eradicate. It is easier to remove goats or even rats from an island than an invasive plant species.

HOW TO HELP

The various institutions that are in charge of the ecology of Galápagos, such as the national park and the Charles Darwin Foundation, are working aggressively to remove these invasive species and undo the damage they have caused. There have been some success stories. Feral donkeys, for example, have been eliminated entirely from the islands. Project Isabela, a ten-year, multimillion-dollar initiative, removed an estimated 130,000 goats from Santiago and northern Isabela. Next up: cats, rats and certain plant species, including the Red Quinine.

As important as eradication, of course, is controlling the arrival of new species to the islands. Airplane cargo holds are fumigated, fresh food is not allowed, and carry-on baggage can be inspected. The Galápagos Islands are probably about the only place in the post-9/11 world where airport personnel are more concerned with people carrying pears and apples on board than bombs! So do your part: be sure to follow the clearly posted restrictions when you visit Galápagos, so that it can be preserved forever just as it is.

Darwin in the Galápagos

Over the years, many famous people have visited the Galápagos, including actors, artists and politicians from all over the world. Without a doubt, however, the most famous Galápagos tourist of all time was British naturalist Charles Darwin, who visited while on a round-the-world trip with the HMS Beagle in 1835.

Evolution and Scandal

Most people know Darwin for the firestorm of scandal that marked his later life. In 1859, Darwin published On the Origin of Species, a book which shook the world to its foundations. Today, evolution is accepted as scientific fact by most people. Animals, plants and insects adapt to their environment in order to compete. As the environment changes, so do the animals. In 1859, however, most people had never heard of evolution, and believed that all animals existed in exactly the form that they were originally assigned by God.

The most controversial aspect of Darwin's book was the notion that mankind was not excepted. In many ways, man is an animal like any other, and can therefore be assumed to have evolved from lower life forms. The notion that our ancestors were some sort of ape scandalized the world and ignited a debate which continues to this day. Darwin only spent about six weeks in the Galapagos Islands in late 1835, but his time there was very important to his later work.

Role of the Finches in Darwin's Work

Darwin illustrated his theory of evolution with the finches of Galápagos. There are fourteen different species of finch on the islands, and they differ significantly. Some are large, some small, some have heavy beaks and some have small ones, some are brown, some are black, etc. Assuming that the finches all descended from one common ancestor who somehow came to the Galápagos eons ago, the differences can only be explained by assuming that they have changed over time, resulting in several different varieties.

Ironically, the finches did not interest Darwin on his visit. He collected only a few specimens and did not label them very well. He was initially more interested in the mockingbirds, which also differ from one island to another.

Charles Darwin in Galápagos Today

Darwin continues to be associated with the islands, where he is celebrated. Any number of hotels, ships, and businesses are named for him. There are even more than a handful of islanders named "Darwin!"

Quito

 2,850 m 2,239,191 02

Travelers worldwide are drawn to Quito for its spectacular mountain setting, its colonial historical center, near-by adventure travel opportunities, international cuisine, and the gentle, generous quiteño culture. The city is known for being home to some of the best Spanish schools in South America; there is a great backpacker community; and, the area offers plenty of activities to help you escape the typical tourist crowds. Don't miss out on socializing with the locals, quiteños tend to be relaxed, friendly and eager to make friends.

Planning a trip from Quito to other parts of Ecuador, or to neighboring South American countries, is also fairly easy. Most Quito hotels, travel agencies and tour operators can be found in the neighborhood of La Mariscal and are within a five block radius of each other. Transportation by land and air is also plentiful and generally inexpensive, depending on the time of year.

This rapidly growing capital city has a past that stretches back to before the Incas made Quito the second capital of their empire. It appears that only the mountains that cradle the city remain unchanged. The historic Old Town features colonial architecture which the Spanish constructed over the charred remains of the Inca city. Just north of Old Town, towering concrete and glass structures show off the modern structures of the business and tourist center of the city.

History of Quito
PRE-INCA CIVILIZATION
Despite its high altitude and scarcity of easily cultivable land, the area around Quito has been the scene of human settlement for nearly 10,000 years, dating back to the Quitu (who gave the city its name), Cara, Shyri and Puruhá indigenous groups. Due to its central location, Quito flourished as a permanent commercial trading center, or tianguez, for the peoples residing in the Amazon basin, the sierra and on the coast. The merchants traded products like salt, cotton and shells from the coast for cinnamon, medicinal herbs and precious metals from the Amazon region. Traders from the sierra sold potatoes, corn and other agricultural products native to the area.

INCA RULE
Those early inhabitants of Quito fiercely resisted the Inca invasion of the late 15th century; however, after more than a decade of fighting, Quito fell to Inca rule under Túpac Yupanqui and became an important part of his empire. Túpac Yupanqui's son, Huayna Capac, was born near Quito, making him the first Inca ruler to be born outside the confines of Cusco. A generation later, Atahualpa, one of Huayna Capac's sons, used Quito as his capital during his war against his brother. No architectural evidence of the pre-Columbian city remains, however, because it was destroyed by the Inca general Rumiñahui to keep it out of the hands of the Spanish conquistadors.

SPANISH RULE
Colonial officials rebuilt Quito in the style of a Spanish city, featuring a grid of narrow streets dotted with public squares, still largely intact today as the city's Centro Histórico. While it remained a compact city, colonial Quito was the capital of an administrative district larger than present-day Ecuador. The city also made an enormous contribution to the arts of the Spanish empire. Originally used as a means of inculcating the indigenous inhabitants of the region into Christianity, religious painting and sculpture flourished in the city. The so-called "Quito School" of the 17th and 18th centuries was marked by the use of dramatic, often quite gruesome, images to depict Biblical stories. Many of these works can still be viewed in Quito's art museums and colonial churches. Over time, Quito's native-born population chafed under the rule of the Spanish crown. This frustration resulted in the quiteños' declaration for independence in 1809. Quito's - and Ecuador's - independence from Spain was sealed on the slopes of Volcán Pichincha, high above the city, when José Antonio de Sucre's army defeated the Spanish garrison on May 24, 1822. Today, the site of the battle is commemorated by the military museum La Cima de la Libertad.

1869 - PRESENT
In 1869, President Gabriel García Moreno altered the constitution to make Catholicism the official state religion of Ecuador and required all voters and political candidates to be Catholic. The liberal opposition despised him for this, especially the self-exiled writer

QUITO

Juan Montalvo. Shortly after he began his third term, Moreno was attacked on the steps of the Palacio de Gobierno and hacked to death by a machete-wielding assassin in 1875. When Montalvo heard of Moreno's death, he proclaimed, "My pen has killed him!"

The conservatives continued their reign in the country, especially under the dictator General Ignacio de Veintimilla. Conservative rule ended in 1897 with the election of Eloy Alfaro. He was a revolutionary and fought against García Moreno's government during his youth. During his two terms as president, from 1897 to 1901 and 1906 to 1911, Alfaro separated church and state, severed ties with the Vatican, instituted divorce, and kicked out foreign clergy. He also helped complete the Quito-Guayaquil railway. In between terms, Alfaro's adversary General Leónidas Plaza became president. Plaza caused civil unrest amongst conservative Catholics and liberals and Alfaro's second term saw nearly half of the budget go towards the military for security reasons and fear of an uprising.

Civil war broke out when Alfaro's successor, Emilio Estrada, died shortly after his inauguration in 1911. Plaza's forces proceeded to defeat and kill Alfaro and his supporters, dragging them through the streets of Quito and finally burning their corpses at the Parque El Ejido.

Leonidas Plaza's son, Galo Plaza Lasso, became president in 1948. He had strong ties to both Liberal and Conservative parties, and strongly advocated democracy and freedom of speech, which caused him to become the first Ecuadorian president to serve a full term since 1924. The banana boom in the 1940s helped fund Quito's undertaking of new schools, an airport, hospitals and universities. It was also during this time, following the Second World War, that Quito expanded dramatically.

The wealthy abandoned the Centro Histórico for new neighborhoods farther north. Meanwhile, the difficulty of earning a living through agriculture and the availability of jobs in the city lured many people from the countryside to settle in the Quito's poorer neighborhoods, a migration which continues to this day. It was later, in the 1970s, that saw the oil boom transform Quito into the second most important financial center in the country.By 1991, the population of the city hit one million; and as the population began approaching two million in the new millennium, Quito implemented the Metrobus (Ecovia) which currently facilitates the commute across the city from north to south. In 2005 the renovation of La Mariscal - which was formerly considered a zona roja (red-light district) - saw the creation of new bars, cafes, hostels and restaurants.

2013 welcomed the new, larger airport for the city located on its outskirts to the east – an idea which took nearly 50 years to come to fruition.

Quito's Sectors

Divided into different neighborhoods (sectores), most tourists spend their time in the Mariscal, the area north of Parque el Ejido and south of Avenida Orellana. The Mariscal has the highest concentration of travel agencies, hostels, international restaurants and inexpensive bars, but there are a couple of other neighborhoods that are worth seeing— be sure to branch out. The Centro Histórico, for example, hosts a diverse and rich colonial history with some beautiful plazas, churches, museums and pedestrian walkways. Guápulo has a distinctly bohemian feel, and La Floresta and Northern Quito are considerably modern. Quito was originally contained within the limits of what is now called the Centro Histórico, but today it is about 35 kilometers (21 mi) long from north to south and on average 5 kilometers (about 3 mi) wide east to west.

When To Go to Quito

Quito has two seasons: spring with rain (September–April), and spring with sun (May–August). The city's location, about 40 kilometers (about 25 mi) south of the equator and at an altitude of 2,800 meters (9,180 ft) above sea level, makes for some startling temperature changes in a 24-hour period. The city gets downright cool when the sun is down (from 6:30 p.m.- 6 a.m. every day of the year) and when it rains. When the sun is out, however, you will find yourself in need of shorts and shade. Consequently, wearing layers is fundamental to being comfortable in Quito. Pants, a light T-shirt or tank top layered with a long-sleeve shirt and jacket or sweater should be fine throughout most of the year. Travelers coming from colder climates will be amused at the winter garb of most quiteños from September-April, which

QUITO

often includes jackets, scarves, gloves and hats. Winter is a strong word, but during these months, afternoon storms are common and tend to drop the temperature to around 10°C (50°F). During sunny days, the temperatures can rise up to 30°C (85 °F).

In addition to climate, things in Quito tend to heat up socially and culturally during *fiestas* (festivals) and cool down during *feriados* (holidays). The latter is ideal for visitors who wish to see Quito in a softer, quieter light - for it's during this time that the capital empties out as quiteños head to the coast to either party or rest. Carnaval (second week of February) and Semana Santa (Holy Week, end of March) specifically provide said windows of time.

Fiestas on the other hand are much more abundant and have the city bustling with parties, concerts and fireworks. Fiestas de Quito is perhaps the most iconic time of the year as quiteños celebrate - from the end of November to the 6th of December - the foundation of their capital.

From bullfights to opera and theater shows commemorating Quito's history and culture, quiteños party hard during this time, riding Chiva's (open party buses) or attending block parties and concerts hosted by the city.

Christmas and New Years might pale in comparison to the above, but these days still hold their own energy as the city goes into a shopping tizzy right before Christmas day, calming down for a week right after, and then jumping into the New Year with copious amounts of food, liquor, fireworks, and the traditional burning of the Año Viejo (a human mannequin with your choice of a politician or celebrity's mask, done to symbolize the letting go of the previous year).
Updated: Feb 28, 2013.

Getting To and Away from Quito

Quito is one of two main transportation hubs within the country, the other being Guayaquil. From the capital, you can pretty much get to anywhere inside of Ecuador, either by bus or plane.

In addition to being the center of the domestic transport network, Quito is also well connected to international locations by both air and long-distance buses.

BY AIR
All international and domestic flights arrive and depart from Quito's Mariscal Sucre International Airport (Code: UIO) which is 18 kilometers (11 mi.) east of the city, near the small town of Tababela.

TRANSPORTATION BETWEEN

THE AIRPORT AND QUITO:
The company Aeroservicios S.A. (www.aeroservicios.com.ec) runs WiFi equipped buses 24/7, leaving every 15 minutes at rush hour (7-10a.m., 4-7p.m.), or every 30 minutes during normal hours. Buses depart from the old airport to the new one at a rate of $8 per passenger, taking about one hour to an hour-and-a-half in getting there. Tickets can be bought online or before boarding.

Alternatively, public transit will provide buses departing from the Rio Coca terminal to the new airport every 15 minutes for $2. The catch is that you'll have to patiently wait through 5 brief stops before finally getting there. Estimated transport time between the two points will be at least an hour-and-a-half to two-hours until traffic conditions improve - specifically once the bypasses are constructed (the main Collas-Tababela highway that is being built from the city to the airport is not expected to be completed until April of 2014)

The third option is to take a Taxi, which will cost an estimated $25 to get to the airport from most places in Quito (and vice-versa).

From Quito it is possible to fly directly (nonstop) to the following destinations:

INTERNATIONAL FLIGHTS
In Latin America:
- Bogota or Medellín (Colombia)
- Caracas (Venezuela)
- Lima (Peru)
- Santiago (Chile)
- Saõ Paulo or Manaus (Brazil)
- San Jose (Costa Rica)
- Panama City (Panama)

In the United States:
- Miami
- Houston
- Atlanta

In Europe:
- Madrid (Spain)
- Amsterdam (Holland)

QUITO

DOMESTIC FLIGHTS
Served by three airlines: TAME (www.tame.com.ec), LAN (www.lan.com), and Aerogal (www.aerogal.com.ec). AeroGal and LAN are somewhat more expensive than their competitors, but generally receive high marks from travelers. The following are popular cities that have direct flights to and from Quito:

- Bahía
- Coca
- Cuenca
- Esmeraldas
- Guayaquil
- Galapagos
- Lago Agrio
- Loja
- Macas
- Machala
- Manta
- Portoviejo
- Tulcán

These national flights cost about $60-100 each way, except to the Galapagos where a round trip ticket will cost around $400. There are no departure taxes for flights within Ecuador except for trips into and out of the Galapagos.

BY BUS
Instead of one, centrally-located bus station, Quito has two terminals located at the north and south ends of Quito. These newer stations are intended to make travel more efficient and cost-effective, as well as reduce the number of long-distance buses passing through the city.

In the far north is Carcelén (Av. Eloy Alfaro and Av. Galo Plaza Lasso), with buses that go typically go north from Quito. At the southern tip is the brand new Quitumbe station (Av. Cóndor Ñan and Av. Mariscal Sucre), this terminal is most useful for buses heading south from Quito.

Some bus companies have locations in the Mariscal part of town, making the purchase of tickets in advance significantly easier thanks to its proximity. In many instances it is possible to simply turn up at the appropriate bus terminal and buy a ticket to your chosen destination.

However, those wanting to travel over public holidays are best advised to book tickets in advance (up to several days in advance to secure a seat).

Buses From The Quitumbe Terminal
This modern, new bus terminal is located at the Southern end of Quito. From here you can get to the Amazon, coast or any of the surrounding Mountain regions such as Baños and Cuenca. You can get here via the Trolebus or Ecovia ($0.25, 1 hour) or taxi from La Mariscal ($15, 30 minutes), for more info see Getting Around Quito). Av. Cóndor Ñan and Av. Mariscal Sucre

Buses From The Carcelén Terminal
The northern bus terminal in Carcelén is smaller and more grimy than the southern terminal. Buses here head north from Quito, the main reason to come here is to get to Otavalo or Mitad del Mundo. To get to this bus terminal via public transit you'll need to take the Metrobus and transfer at Estación Ofelia, which will take approximately one hour. From here you will have to take the "feeder buses" to get there. To get to the terminal via taxi will cost approximately $8 from La Mariscal, more during busier periods. The journey will take just 20 minutes or so with no traffic, longer during rush hour periods.

At this bus terminal you will find baggage storage, food stalls and telephone and Internet. There are 16 booths from which to buy a ticket. All have their destinations listed on the wall above each individual booth. Sometimes you can pick up a bus outside the terminal that is already leaving and just get on there, paying the driver instead of the company representative at the booth. Av. Eloy Alfaro and Av. Galo Plaza Lasso.

Bus companies and destinations from Carcelén:

Unión de Nor-Occidente
Leaves to Los Bancos, Puerto Quito, Santo Domingo, Mindo, Perovicente from booth 3 every 30 minutes from 5:00 a.m. to 10:00 p.m.

San Cristobal
Leaves to Tulcán from booth 6 every hour from 2:00 a.m. to 12:00 a.m.

Expreso Tulcán
Leaves to Tulcán from booth 7 every hour from 1:00 a.m. to 12:00 a.m.

San Gabriel
Leaves to San Gabriel from booth 10 every 30 minutes from 5:30 a.m. to 8:00 p.m.

Espejo
Leaves to Masquerida, Mira, San Isidro, El Angél, Otavalo, Ibarra and Tabacundo from booth 11 every hour from 4:30 a.m. to 7 p.m.

Flota Imbabura
Leaves to Atuntaqui, Otavalo, Ibarra, and Tulcán frequently from booth 12.

Taca Andina
Leaves to Ibarra and Santo Domingo every 20 minutes from 5 a.m. to 10 p.m. from booth 13.

Buses From The Mariscal

Buses that leave from the Mariscal are usually the most convenient for travelers or expats who want to get out of Quito for a while. This part of town is fairly central and easy to access, unlike the major bus terminals.

There are eight bus providers in the Mariscal, and they capitalize on their good location by charging a little more for their tickets than if you'd travelled from Quitumbe or one of the northern bus terminals. In a lot of cases, it is possible to get air conditioned buses that are non-stop from the Mariscal to your chosen destination.

The following is a list of long-distance bus companies, their destinations and contact information.

The price for these companies varies between $8-15, one-way.

Transportes Occidentales
Buses from this company go from Quito to: Santo Domingo, Quininde, Esmeraldas, Tonsupa, Atacames, Sua, Muisne, San Lorenzo, Guayaquil, Salinas, Machala, Pasaje, Santa Rosa, Huaquillas, Lago Agrio, Riobamba. 18 de Septiembre and Versalles. Tel: 02-250-2735

Reina del Camino
This company's buses go from Quito to: Canoa, Junín, Manta, Tosagua, Pedernales, San Vicente, Chone, Puerto Lopez, Bahía de Caraquez, Portoviejo. 18 de Septiembre and Manuel Larrea. Tel: 02-321-6633

Flota Imbabura
Flota Imbabura's buses head from Quito to Guayaquil, Cuenca, Manta, Ibarra and Tulcán. Portoviejo and Manuel Larrea. Tel: 02-256-5620

Transportes Aray
Transportes Aray has buses that head from Quito to: Manta, Santo Domingo, Chone, Ambato, Santo Domingo, Pedernales, San Vicente, Portoviejo, Bahía de Caraquez, Manta, Esmeraldas, Lago Agrio, Pichincha, Quevedo, Quininde, Jipijapa, Jama, Rocafuerte, Tosagua, Puerto Lopez. Portoviejo and Manuel Larrea, Tel: 02-275-0424.

Panamericana International
Buses from Quito to Guayaquil, Manta, Huaquillas, Tulcán, Machala, Cuenca, Loja, Milagro, Santa Rosa, Atacames, Esmeraldas. This company also has buses that go to Colombia and Peru.

La Mariscal Station: Av Colón, E7-31, between Reina Victoria and Diego de Almagro. Tel: 02-255-7133/7134. Tickets: ext.131, Secretary: ext.132. Fax: 02-251-5414 .Quitumbe Terminal: Av. Condor Ñan and Av. Guayanay. No. 45 Y 46. Tel: 02-382-4751

TransEsmeraldas
Buses head from Quito to: Muisne, Atacames, El Coca, Machala, Esmeraldas, Lago Agrio, Huaquillas, Santo Domingo, Guayaquil, Portoviejo, Salinas.

La Mariscal Station: Santa María y 9 de octubre. Tel: 02-250-5099. Quitumbe Terminal: Av. Condor Ñan and Av. Guayanay. Tel: 02-382-4791

BY TRAIN
Resurrected in late 2008, Ecuador's railroad system is back in full force and – starting June 2013 – provides affluent travelers with trips from Quito all the way to Guayaquil over the course of four to five days. Since 1975, the railroad system in Ecuador gradually decreased in popularity due to the growth of highway transportation and dwindling interest and investment on behalf of the government, inevitably leading to its demise and neglect. Back in April of 2008 however, attention to the old railroad system grew within government as it came to be regarded as a cultural and historical hallmark of the country, and as a result, they saw it fit to rehabilitate its lanes and trains. From Quito, it's possible to take day trips to Machachi, Boliche & Latacunga for about $10-30, round-trip. Estación de Trenes Chimbacalle, Sincholagua and Maldonado. Tel: 1-800-873637. www.trenecuador.com
Updated: Apr 12, 2013.

Getting Around Quito
GETTING AROUND QUITO BY BUS

The blue buses of Quito crisscross the city in every conceivable direction and, like other forms of public transportation, cost $0.25 cents (non-transferable). Easiest to navigate are the **Trolebus**, **Ecovia** and **Metrobus**, each of which run from north to south (and vice versa) across Quito on a dedicated pair of lanes that are sandwiched between the major avenues: 10 de Agosto, 6 de Diciembre, and La Prensa. Each trip costs $0.25 like the blue buses, regardless of the length of the journey. These three tend to be much more crowded than the blue buses due to their popularity.

Blue Bus

To figure out where a particular blue bus is headed, you'll have to quickly read the long, multi-colored destination list that's posted on the front window (as the bus is barreling toward you). If the bus is the one you want, simply wave it down and jump aboard. If you're not able to read the sign in time, or catch the tout's (the driver's partner who shouts out destinations and collects money) attention, don't worry - another bus will come along shortly.

Some buses have cashiers (behind a wooden desk to the left of the door) or touts who will take your 25 cents as you get on. Should you need a little more time to gather your payment, all operators will accept the fare as you leave or come to collect them during the trip. Make sure you have small change when you take the bus. Most operators are unable or unwilling to give change for currency larger than $5.

To get off the bus, stand up, walk to the front and indicate to the tout that you want to disembark. The bus should pause long enough for you to step off quickly to the curb.

Bus routes are so numerous and so varied that not all of them can be detailed here. but it's safe to say: if there's a part of the city you'd like to get to, then there's probably a bus that will take you there. Ask a local (most quiteños are very helpful) what bus you need to take to get to where you want to go. Intercity buses typically stop operating shortly after 8.

Trolebus

The Trole system runs down 6 de Agosto from the southern Terminal Quitumbe station to the northern Estación La "Y" (Tel: 593-2-243-4975). Along its trajectory, and worth noting, are three stops: Colón (outskirts of La Mariscal neighborhood), Plaza del Teatro and Plaza Santo Domingo (in the Old Town).

Troles have dedicated lanes and green, glass booths as their stops. Like theMetrobus andEcovia, the ride to any point along the Trole route costs $0.25 cents in exact change. If need be, you can get change for small bills or coins at the attendant's kiosk at any stop. Troles are handicap accessible, but the doors usually open and close quickly, so be prepared. Also, watch your valuables carefully, particularly if the popular Trole buses are jammed with people. If any one Trole seems too full, just wait for the next one.

Serving the city everyday is the Trole that runs from the northern terminal La "Y" to the southern station El Creo. The schedule for getting from these two places, and vice-versa is:

Monday-Friday:
5 a.m.-Midnight (every 8-15 minutes)

Weekends & Holidays:
6 a.m -10 p.m. (every 10-15 minutes)

Note: After midnight on any day of week, all the buses still continue to run once every thirty minutes; however, they do so with limited service, stopping only at every other (second or third) stop along the line. Starting at 2a.m., they run once every hour. On weekends the same applies after 10 p.m, but only running once every hour.

At three of the following main stations, the Trole splits off into a number of supplemental bus routes.

- At **Marán Valverde** you can continue on along   Camal Metropolitano, Cdla. Ejército, Guamaní and San Martin de Porras.

- **El Recreo** serves Solanda, Chillogallo, Lucha de los Pobres,   Oriente Quiteño (ending at Vilcabamba) and Ferroviaria.

- **La "Y"** connects to Cotocollao, Rumiñahui, Carapungo,   Kennedy, Comité del Publo (ending in Jiménez) and Los Laureles (to Rio Coca and Eloy Alfaro).

If need be, many Trole stations have route maps posted to help you find your destination. If you're still unsure, ask at one of the main stations for directions and a *"mapa de rutas y paradas del Trole"* (map of Trole routes and stops).

Ecovía

The Ecovía consists of a series of very popular, articulated buses that operate along Av. 6 de Diciembre. The Ecovía is one part of Quito's North-South public transportation triumvirate, and runs between Rio Coca to the north, and La Marin to the south.

Like the Trolebús and Metrobus, the Ecovías have dedicated lanes, covered stops and always cost 25 cents (no matter your destination). Conductors usually call out the next point along the line, but each Ecovía *parada* (or stop) is also indicated by a large, brown marker and pictographic signs. To use the Ecovía, walk into any of the stops along 6 de Deciembre. Each stop is a glass, rectangular booth. You will need to insert correct change into a machine to pass through the turnstile. If you don't have 25 cents, the booth attendants can convert coins and small bills for you. (Just don't ask them to change anything larger than $5).

Be sure to get on quickly, as the doors don't stay open for long. If you are confronted with an Ecovía that appears extremely full (which happens often), wait for the next one. Once you're on, make sure you grab one or two of the many handholds, since Ecovías stop abruptly. Food and uncovered drinks are not allowed on the Ecovias. Keep an eye and hand on your valuables at all times; if you're using a backpack or large bag, shift it to your front when you get on. Pickpockets have been known to target Ecovía passengers, particularly on crowded buses.

Ecovias pass by very regularly during their operating hours of 5 a.m. to 11 p.m., Monday through Friday, and 6 a.m. to 9:30 p.m. weekends and holidays. Outside of those hours (midnight-dawn), the Ecovía runs hourly Monday-Friday, and half-hourly Friday-Saturday.

Metrobus

Of all three lines (Trole and Ecovia being the other two), Quito's Metrobus line is the one that reaches farthest north. Barreling down America & La Prensa, the metrobus makes several stops within walking distance of several areas such as: Mañosca St., La Gasca, Iñaquito Alto, Urb. Granda Centeno, Quito Tennis, El Bosque, Pinar Bajo, Pinar Alto, and La Concepción. Terminus station to the south is Estacion Varela, and to the north is Estacion La Ofelia. The cost is $0.25.

In addition to taking you farther north, the Metrobus is actually your first step in getting from Quito all the way to Mitad del Mundo via public transit. Transfer at the final stop up north in Estación La Ofelia, making sure to check (by asking) which buses are leaving to Mitad del Mundo from there.

The Trole, Ecovia and Metrobus offices are located at Av. Vicente Maldonado y Miguel Carrión sector El Recreo in Quito. To reach the main line, call: 593-2-266-5023; fax: 593-2 266-5019; email:info@trolebus.gov. ec; or visit www.trolebus.gov.ec.

GETTING AROUND QUITO BY TAXI

If you are looking for a relatively inexpensive, safe and convenient way to travel, tapping into Quito's extensive taxi network is a good way to get around the city.

During the day, taxi drivers are required to use a taximetro (or meter) when they drive you around. When you climb in, the initial rate should be 35 cents. Always ask for the taximetro, which is typically located just in front of the emergency brake, between the driver and front passenger seats. You should always be able to easily see the meter and should check the amount as you arrive at your destination (before the taxista turns it off).

Some drivers have been known to tell passengers that their meter is broken or that they don't have one, particularly around large hubs such as Terminal Terrestre. Taxis are plentiful enough that, if your driver won't use his meter (or has a meter that seems to be going extraordinarily fast), tell him to stop, get out and hail a more honest cabbie. Most daytime trips around the city cost between $1.50 and $3. Given the distance, trips to the airport cost a lot more. The price of taxis to the airport are calculated by a fixed price chart (not a taximetro) which is based on the neighborhood you are departing to/ from. For the most part, a trip to the airport will cost around $25-30 from most places in Quito (and vice versa).

At night, within the city itself, rates increase by $1 (since few other public transportation services are available) and taxi drivers do not use their meters. Make sure to negotiate a price before you get into a cab. If the price is too steep, ask for a more reasonable rate or hail a different taxi. Drivers charge per ride, not per person. Make sure when you're taking a taxi that you have roughly the correct fare in small change. Most cab drivers won't have much money on hand and will not be able to handle large bills. Tips are also accepted but usually not expected

GETTING AROUND QUITO BY CAR
Renting a car can be a good way to get out of Quito and explore the surrounding, spectacular countryside. Whether it be for a short trip or a longer vacation, car rental is a good option for those who are prepared to brave the interesting traffic "rules" that Ecuador has. When renting a car, be sure to consider that in some cases, roads may not be in top condition, and a vehicle with 4-wheel drive might be the best option.

In order to rent a car, you must be at least 25 years of age. Drivers must hold a valid driver's license and own an international credit card. As a general rule, those renting cars can expect to pay anything from $50 to $120 per day.

Avis (tel. 02/2440-270; www.avis.com.ec), Budget (tel. 02/3300-979; www.budget-ec.com), Hertz (tel. 1800/227-767 toll-free within Ecuador, or 02/2254-257; www.hertz.com.ec) are the main car rental agencies, with offices at both Quito and Guayaquil airports.

GETTING AROUND QUITO BY BICYCLE
BiciQ is Quito's new public bicycle system, which aims to promote everyday cycling for both Quito residents and visitors to the city. Twenty five bicycle stations are located around the city, with a total of 425 bikes for use, allowing for easy mobility throughout Quito. In order to have access to the public bikes, you need to subscribe to the service, which costs $25 for the year; visitors can arrange monthly payments instead. Once registered—either online, at one of the BiciQ stations, or at the BiciQ administrative office—you will receive a BiciQ card that you will need to present at each station in order to borrow a bike.

BiciQ users have 45 minutes of free use between stations to return their bike, at which point they can trade it for another. Other rules do apply, including the city confines in which the bike can be used. You must be at least 18 years old to sign up; those who are 17 or 16 years old can register if a parent signs for them. BiciQ operates daily between 7 a.m. and 7 p.m. The main administrative office is located on Calle Venezuela, between Chile and Espejo streets in the Centro Histórico (Tel: 02-395-2300, E-mail: biciq@quito.gob.ec, URL: www.biciq.gob.ec). Updated: Apr 19, 2013.

Quito Lodging
Quito has accommodation options for travelers of any economic stature and for travelers with specific interests.

For the budget traveler: Keep an eye out for some basic amenities when looking for accommodations, especially when looking for cheaper places to stay. Cool evenings are year-round and heat in hotels is pretty rare, so hot water and thick blankets are a necessity. Many hotels have rooms with beautiful views of the Pichincha Volcano or city skylines at no extra charge, so it never hurts to ask.

If you're looking higher-end, there are large, luxurious hotels with solid reputations that are much pricier per night, but are often in safe enough locations and have great in-hotel restaurants. For anyone who wants to be in a central location with easy access to the New Town, the Old Town and tons of restaurants, then in or around the Mariscal is the place to stay, as there are hotels fitting into all price ranges in this bustling area.

For a complete list of hotels in Quito, visit: www.vivatravelguides.com/south-america/ecuador/quito/quito-hotels.

Quito Restaurants
Quito is a modern city with a wide variety of restaurants and places to eat, from Argentine steak houses to fancy Spanish restaurants to local holes-in-the-wall.

The Mariscal district is home to a variety of restaurants and wandering a few blocks in any direction will take you past several options. For a complete list of restaurants in Quito, visit www.vivatravelguides.com/south-america/ecuador/quito/quito-restaurants.

Holidays and Fiestas

The most popular "holiday and fiesta" is by far the Fiestas de Quito, a celebration of Quito's Independence Day, which technically falls on December 6, but really ends up taking the entire week leading before. Quiteños celebrate by drag racing colorfully painted, open-air buses called chivas, complete with beverage service and live music. They also hold beauty pageants for the "Queen of Quito," along with dozens of live concerts, bullfights and massive competitions of Cuarenta, Ecuador's national card game.

Other festivals unique to Quito take place mainly during August, leading up to El Día del Patrimonio, the day the Centro Histórico was named a World Heritage Cultural Site. These celebrations consist of outdoor concerts, theater and other cultural events. Throughout the year there are smaller, neighborhood celebrations, with parades (desfiles), costumes, street food, fireworks and the like, such as the Fiesta de Guápulo on September 7th, and Carnival in Centro Histórico's La Ronda, the three weeks leading up to the actual Carnival date in February.

Studying Spanish

Quito is a major hub for travelers who want to study Spanish. Most Spanish schools offer homestays, excursions and even other types of classes like cooking classes and salsa lessons. You will usually have a choice between group or private instruction, and many schools recommend or require a minimum hours per week. Rates range from around $5-10 per hour, but rates often reflect quality. If even the lower end of the scale is out of your budget, many schools will hire you as an English teacher and either give you a discount on your Spanish lessons or let you take classes for free. Classes are rarely less than one week and run as long as several months in length.

Yanapuma Spanish School

Yanapuma Spanish school is a unique, nonprofit school whose proceeds benefit Yanapuma Foundation and its sustainable development projects in Ecuadorian communities. It combines in-class learning with a wide variety of optional activities, including culturally and socially oriented weekday and weekend excursions, community-based Spanish study, and volunteering in poor neighborhoods of Quito. The school is located at the edge of the Mariscal (New Town), with many restaurants, bars, and other tourist amenities a short walk away. It offers free WiFi (with your laptop) or limited use of its computers, a language lab, and a TV and DVD player for watching Spanish movies and videos. All materials are included in the class price. Veintimilla E8-125 and 6 de Diciembre, Tel: 02-254-6709, E-mail: spanish@yanapuma.org, URL: www.yanapumaspanish.org

Academia de Español Guayasamín

(Weekly Cost: $150, four hours for one week to seven hours in eight weeks) Academia de Español Guayasamín offers affordable hourly group classes. Teachers are native Spanish speakers and all have at least seven years of experience. All materials are included in the price, along with salsa classes, city excursions, volunteer opportunities, and assistance with securing accommodation in a hotel or homestay. Class schedules are flexible. Programs are also offered on the coast and in the Amazon Jungle. Calama E8-54 and 6 de Diciembre, Tel: 02-254-4210, E-mail: info@guayasaminschool.com, URL: www.guayasaminschool.com.
Updated: Jan 08, 2013.

Academia Latinoamericana de Español

($165-290 per week, includes host family) At Academia Latinoamericana de Español, you will find yourself quickly learning Spanish amid friendly Ecuadorians and the mix of Spanish and indigenous history that defines Quito. Regardless of your proficiency level, you will find a program that suits your needs, goals and learning style here. The maximum number of students per class is four, and you will learn using the four language skills: listening, grammar, oral and written comprehension. The school arranges homestays with native, middle-class families within a 10-minute bus ride of school, providing a cultural complement to your language learning. Additionally, you can combine your Spanish study with volunteer programs and excursions in and around Quito. Noruega N10-31 and 6 de Diciembre, Tel: 02-225-0946/226-7904/7905, Fax: 02-226-7906, E-mail: info@latinoschools.com, URL: www.latinoschools.com.
Updated: Jan 08, 2013.

Amazonas Language School

(Weekly Cost: $450-630, Hours per Week: 20-35) Amazonas Language School features private or group Spanish classes for 20 to 35

QUITO

hours per week. Since the school is paired up with a travel agency, students have the advantage of learning about the country and language as they travel. Founded in 1989, the school is well-established and all teachers have degrees in language and literature, along with a minimum of six years of teaching experience. There are various options for study around Ecuador, including classes in Quito, the Galápagos Islands and the Amazon jungle. English, French and German language classes are also offered. Prices include homestay in a private bedroom with three meals a day and laundry service, airport transfer upon arrival, cultural activities once a week, study materials, salsa classes once a week, luggage storage and more. Those who commit to at least 100 hours of study also get access to the Hilton Health Club for two weeks, which has a pool, sauna, gym and Jacuzzi. Jorge Washington E4-59 and Av. Amazonas., Edificio Rocafuerte, Washington Tower, 3rd. floor, Tel: 02-254-8223/250-4654, Cel: 09-8328-0302/8321-1923, E-mail: info@eduamazonas.com / Messenger: languages.travel@hotmail.com, URL: www.eduamazonas.com / www.ecuadorandgalapagosislands.com / Facebook: www.facebook.com/amazonaseducation.
Updated: Feb 21, 2013.

Andean Global Studies

(Weekly cost: $200) Andean Global Studies is a Spanish school based in Quito and offers foreign students a wide variety of programs, such as: spanish immersion, medical Spanish, and volunteering. The school facilities are deigned with comfort in mind, providing Wi-Fi and computer access for their sutdents. The school has multiple classrooms, cafeteria and a recreational room with audiovisual material. It's also conviniently located in the heart of the city, surrounded by banks, parks, shopping malls and restaurants. If you would like to travel and study throughout Ecuador, AGS is a pretty good option given they have programs in Manta, Cuenca, and Montañita. El Mercurio 346 y La Razón, Tel: (593 2) 225 4928, E-mail: info@andeanglobalstudies.org, URL: www.andeanglobalstudies.org.
Updated: May 18, 2012.

Cristóbal Colón Spanish Language School

Private classes at Cristóbal Colón are reasonably priced and no registration fee is necessary, just pay as you go. Its library offers a selection of materials for your classes and

you have the option of changing teachers each week to practice a variety of accents and teaching styles. There are several ways you can get discounts at this language school, including working in the office, staying at the hostel next door, or printing out a brochure from their website. Extra services offered include excursions, English teacher placements around Quito, host family accommodation and more. Salsa classes, cooking classes, Internet facilities, and city excursions with your teachers are all included in the price. Av. Colón 2-56 and Versalles, Tel: 02-250-6508/222-2964, E-mail: info@colonspanishschool.com, URL: www.colonspanishschool.com.
Updated: Jan 08, 2013.

Simón Bolívar Spanish School

Located just three blocks from the center of the Mariscal area, Simón Bolívar Spanish School offers a wide range of extra services such as free Internet, airport pick-up, city tours, two salsa classes per week, cooking classes, and classes on culture, economy and other Ecuadorian subjects. Its flexible class schedules are also a plus. Simón Bolívar also has branches in Cuenca, just south of Puerto López on the coast, and in the Amazon rainforest. Homestays can be also be arranged on a weekly basis, with all meals included. Mariscal Foch E9-20 and 6 de Diciembre, Tel: 02-254-4558/223-4708, Fax: 02-254-4558, E-mail: info@simon-bolivar.com, URL: www.simon-bolivar.com.
Updated: Jan 08, 2013

Tour Operators in Quito

If you're looking to take a tour from Quito, whether it is a week in the Galapagos or a day in Old Town, La Mariscal is the place to book. Travel and tourism agencies have popped up around La Mariscal (specifically near Plaza Foch, the area's central meeting point) making it easy to book once you arrive and have figured out exactly what you would like to do while in and around Ecuador's capital.

While it can't hurt to book ahead, as tours are popular from Quito and often fill up, there are definitely risky but rewarding benefits in trying to catch last minute deals, specifically filling spots on Galapagos cruises.

Many tour agencies offer a range of options, from half-day trips to week-long excursions; be sure to shop around as something will surely meet your needs. La Mariscal tends to be the best place to scout around.

Colombus Travel !

Norwegian owned and based in Quito, Columbus Travel has access to a wide range of boats and cruises, providing an excellent booking service for Galapagos tours. As a result of selling more Galapagos cruises than any other company, they're able to negotiate some excellent discounts and prices which they make widely available to all travelers. They also know a lot about dive tours, hotels, island-hopping and can set up a wide variety of itineraries catered to their clients' tastes.

The service they provide is honest and reliable, and they're a good place to start if you find yourself having trouble on deciding what to do and where to go.In addition to offering tours of the Galapagos, Columbus also provides tours of Quito, Guayaquil, Otavalo, Papallacta, Mindo, Baños and Cuenca. Mariscal Foch 265 and 6 de Diciembre Avenue, Sonelsa Building 2nd and 3rd floors, Quito, Ecuador, Tel: 02-602-0851, URL: www.columbusecuador.com. Updated: Jan 08, 2013.

Biking Dutchman Cycling Trips

Since 1991, Biking Dutchman has been offering great cycling trips all throughout Ecuador, helping travelers enjoy the beautiful surrounding landscape. Whether you're a beginner or expert, Biking Dutchman has a variety of cycling adventures to suit your level of experience, comfort and interests. Trip lengths range from convenient and fun day trips to exciting week-long expeditions across the Andes and the Amazon. Foch 714 and Juan Leon Mera, Tel: 593-2-256-8323 / 593-2-254-2806, Fax: 593-2-256-7008, E-mail: biking.dutchman@gmail.com, URL: www.bikingdutchman.com

Yacu Amu Rafting

If you've never tried whitewater rafting before, or even if you have had the pleasure, Yacu Amu Rafting will provide an adventure that you'll never forget. Yacu Amu trips run the gamut, from week-long stays with prearranged activities to simple day trips. Professional tour guides will instruct you in the proper etiquette, safety rules, etc. After a thorough tutorial, you're on your way! Whether you're bumping down the Blanco River or being tossed around on the Toachi, you are bound to have a good time. The company also provides fresh meals during the day to refuel adventurers. End the long day by scribbling in the tour guide's "blah blah book," where weary adventurers recap their day along the river. Check out the company's website to choose exactly which excursion is perfect for you. Shyris N34-40 and Republica de El Salvador, Tapia Building, Office 104, Tel: 02-246-1511/1512, URL: www.yacuamu.com. Updated: Jan 08, 2013.

Opuntia Eco Journeys

Contrary to all the hype and fuss over cruises, Opuntia aims to organize a well-rounded experience that's based around taking in the wildlife, nature and adventure that's to be found in land-based tours of the islands. The moments you do spend in the water will only involve either going from island to island quickly or checking out the wildlife below with snorkeling, rather than spending it on a cruise. As added karma, Opuntia is also recognized by the Rainforest Alliance as a sustainable tour operator. Their guides are top-notch and the tours are meant to give you a thorough experience of the Galapagos islands and its highlights, rather than just a passing visit which cruise-based tours are prone to giving. Manuel Sotomayor E17-105 and Flores Jijón Tel: 1-800-217-9414, URL: www.opuntiagalapagostours.com. Updated: Jan 08, 2013.

Andean Discovery !

Experts in putting together your Andean "dream trip," Andean Discovery sets out to take care of all the logistics involved in arranging an itinerary for you and filling your time in Ecuador (or even Peru). Their interest and devotion in taking you off the beaten path is what makes them quite exceptional, showing you places many others rarely get to see. Their itineraries can also convert just about any set of variables (budget, interests, schedule, group size, etc.) into an unforgettable and solid experience. The guides are well-trained English speakers and will be there to offer you a safe and memorable experience as well. Tel: 1-800-893-0916, E-mail: info@andeandiscovery.com, URL: www.andeandiscovery.com. Updated: Jan 08, 2013.

Galapagos Travel Center

The Galapagos Travel Center is perhaps one of the best places to reserve your Galápagos cruise due to having one of the widest selection of boats and highly-competitive prices available on the GalapagosIslands.com website. Its website is highly informative and useful for trip planning, and its British-lead staff have an excellent reputation. The GTC

QUITO

office is at a new location right off of Plaza Foch in the Mariscal. Mariscal Foch E-612 and Reina Victoria, Tel: 02-602-0851, URL: www.galapagosislands.com.

Gulliver Expeditions

Gulliver Traveloffers a wide range of options for exploring this beautiful country, from guided vehicle tours to extreme outdoor pursuits such as mountain biking, horseback riding, hiking and climbing in the Avenue of the Volcanoes. Ecuador has much to offer its visitors: very diverse climatic zones spread over a relatively small area easily accessible from Quito, diverse indigenous populations, impressive historic city centers and excellent safety conditions. Every Gulliver tour offers high-quality, personalized service, competitive prices, high standards in safety procedures, and professional, qualified guides. Juan León Mera N24-156 and Calama, Tel: 02-252-9297, URL: www.gulliver.com.ec. Updated: Jan 08, 2013.

La Mariscal

The Mariscal neighborhood of Quito, or "Gringolandia" as it has come to be known, is the main tourist hub of Quito. It runs from Parque El Ejido in the south up to Avenida Orellana in the north, and is centered around the roads Juan Leon Mera and Reina Victoria. Most of Quito's budget hostels are located here, as well as every tourist service you could possibly want.

For the tech-savvy travelers, Mariscal has many Internet cafés offering speedy connections and Skype. The neighborhood also offers other basic services like banks, laundromats and mini-marts. Most<bold>Quito travel agencies also have their offices in Mariscal, so it's a good place to find a tour, whether you're looking for an international or domestic flight from Quito, a Galápagos cruise, an Amazon lodge stay or an Andean hiking adventure. Quality and prices vary a lot, so be sure to shop around before making any final decision.

In La Mariscal, you will also find the city's best selection of international restaurants and nightlife, all concentrated within a few blocks. It is a good place to meet up with friends and hop around from place to place. The Mariscal is also home to some of the best artisan markets in Quito. Updated: Mar 13, 2013.

La Mariscal Services

While other areas of Quito, such as Centro Histórico and the New Town, offer many services -- supermarkets, laundry, internet and banking -- La Mariscal has the most concentrated and easiest to access number of resources.

While these services may cost a bit more (they're used to foreigners arriving with a different concept of what qualifies as 'expensive'), the convenience is tough to beat. There are laundry and internet services in many hostels (ask when you book a room), though it's also easy to find them on various Mariscal streets (look anywhere around the plaza at Reina Victoria and Foch).

As far as supermarkets go, La Mariscal has an abundance of small corner store (*tiendas*), usually found near Juan Leon Mera and José Calama. If you're in need of a fully stocked supermarket, just walk up Lizardo Garcia (east of 6 de Diciembre) to 12 de Octubre and you can't miss the large red and white sign indicating Supermaxi, Quito's main grocery chain. Updated: Mar 11, 2013.

MONEY

Banks open from 9a.m. to 5pm. and remain closed on weekends.

ATM

On Reina Victoria (between Calama and Foch)

Banco de Guayaquil

Av. Amazonas N22-147 and Veintimlla

Banco del Pacifico

Av. Amazonas, between Carrion and Veintimilla

Producambios

Ave. Amazonas 350 and Vicente Ramon Roca

Western Union

Near the corner of Mariscal Foch and Colon (with DHL)

Casas de cambio specifically deal with international money, so if you didn't manage to change what you needed to at the airport (or gotten enough cash via machine) you can find a couple around the neighborhood (search down Amazonas).

QUITO

KEEPING IN TOUCH

Internet Cafes are ubiquitous in the Mariscal, and you can find a couple on every other block; specifically along Amazonas Ave. Although they all charge under $2 an hour, the quality of the hardware and connection speed vary from place to place.

If you find one cafe that doesn't offer satisfactory service, there is probably an alternative right down the street.

DHL Express

Colon 1333, between Amazonas and Foch, Tel: 1-800-345-345, URL: http://www.dhl.com.ec/en.html, Price relative: Budget, Open Hours From: 8:30a.m., Open Hours To: 7:00p.m, Day Closed: Sundays. Updated: Mar 11, 2013.

Correos Del Ecuador

Ecuador's Official Postal Service that's actually quite reliable in sending mail and/or packages in and around the country, as well as internationally (United States, Canada, Australia, Brazil). Colon and Reina Victoria, Torres almagro, Tel: 02-250-8980, URL: http://www.correosdelecuador.com.ec/index.htm, Open Hours From: 8:00 a.m. to 6:00 p.m. Updated: Mar 11, 2013.

MEDICAL
Pharmacy's

Av Colon 1310 y Foch, Tel: 02-222-2278, URL: http://www.pharmacys.com.ec, Open Hours From: 8:00a.m. to 9:00p.m. Updated: Mar 11, 2013.

TOURISM
The South American Explorers Club

The Quito branch of the South American Explorers' Club is a lively hub. It has a lot to offer to both travelers and ex-pats, and is a great place to meet people. For travelers, the club is an excellent source for maps, guidebooks and general up-to-date safety and travel information. Regular weeknight events include pub quizzes, Spanish and cooking classes.

The club also regularly organizes good-value beach or hiking excursions. Club members get discounts on all of this, plus cheaper deals in many bars, restaurants and tour agencies in Ecuador. Jorge Washington E8-64 and Leonidas Plaza, Tel: 02-222-5228, E-mail: quitoclub@saexplorers.org, URL: www.saexplorers.org. Updated: Mar 08, 2013.

Quito Turismo

For information about Quito and Ecuador in general, the knowledgeable and friendly staff here at Galeria Ecuador Gourmet will be sure to help you out. Reina Victoria and Cordero, Tel: 02-255-1566. Updated: Mar 08, 2013.

Things to See and Do In La Mariscal

The Mariscal is also home to some of the best artisan markets in Quito: one that is near Parque El Ejido, one that is on Jorge Washington between Juan León Mera and Reina Victora, and one that takes place in Plaza Foch on Saturdays.

* Parque El Ejido
* Mercado Artesanal de La Mariscal ♩
* Plaza Foch
* Museo Nacional

Refer to www.vivatravelguides.com for more information.

La Mariscal Lodging

BUDGET
Hostal Posada Del Maple

(ROOMS: $20-36) Located alongside busy streets, this hostel is a dream for every tired traveler: clean, nicely decorated rooms, hot water, helpful staff, and a cozy/inviting atmosphere. It has a common room that comes with cable TV, a mini-library to exchange books, a garden to chill-out, a well-equipped kitchen, and a living room with a fireplace. Additionally it provides Internet access, telephone boxes, a safety box and free luggage storage. For security reasons, the front door is always locked and come late-evening, you'll have to ring/knock to come in.

The staff is extremely friendly and will help you out whenever it can. Because the hostel is quite popular among travelers, it's best to try to arrange and reserve a room in advance. The hostel regularly offers discounts during the off season (March, April and May) and for students, SAE members and longer stays; be sure to ask when making a reservation. Juan Rodriguez E8 - 49 and 6 de Diciembre, Tel: 02-290-7367, Fax: 02-290-6367, E-mail: admin@posadadelmaple.com, URL: www.posadadelmaple.com. Updated: Jan 09, 2013.

QUITO

The Magic Bean Hotel

(ROOMS: $14.50-30) This hostel is not the best value in town, but dorm rooms (which sleep three or four people) are clean, the beds are comfortable, and there are big lockers in each room for you to store your stuff. There's also a great American-style restaurant/café below, which sometimes hosts live music. The central location is convenient for the Mariscal's best bars, clubs and restaurants—though it can get a bit noisy at night when music from numerous locations filters through the windows until well into the early hours. Mariscal Foch E5-08 and Juan Leon Mera, Tel: 02-256-6181/290-6105, E-mail: info@magicbeanquito.com, URL: www.magicbeanquito.com.
Updated: Jan 09, 2013.

Hostal Backpackers' Inn

(ROOMS: $7-24) This charming little hostel is located right in the heart of the bustling Mariscal, still manages to be quiet. It is clean and has comfortable beds. The well-equipped kitchen is for communal use and is one of the better ones you will find among hostels in Quito. Juan Rodriguez 748 and Diego de Almagro, La Mariscal, Tel: 02-250-9669, E-mail: info@backpackersinn.net, URL: www.backpackersinn.net.
Updated: Jan 09, 2013.

MID-RANGE

La Casa Sol 🔔

(ROOMS: $39-99) A quaint, homey hostel on a side street away from most of the noise of the Mariscal, La Casa Sol has comfortable rooms, a couple of cozy sitting areas, a book exchange, a fireplace and a peaceful central courtyard. With a strong emphasis on native culture, decorations create a uniquely Ecuadorian atmosphere. Cultural events the last Friday of every month add to this. The 24-hour café boasts that it has some of the best coffee in Ecuador. Calama 127 and Av. 6 de Diciembre, Tel: 02-223-0798, Fax: 02-222-3383, E-mail: info@lacasasol.com, URL: www.lacasasol.com.
Updated: Jan 09, 2013.

Antinea Apart-Hotel

(ROOMS: $42-134) Declared a cultural heritage site, this charming and unique French hotel is located in the very heart of Quito. Antinea offers spacious rooms, suites and furnished apartments, all decorated with good taste and class, making it a popular home away from home for leisure and business travelers alike. Antinea is located close to the city's best restaurants, bars, and shops, and is situated only 15 minutes from both Quito's historic center and the airport. All rooms have WiFi access. Ask about their extended stay and/or corporate discounts. Juan Rodríguez E8-20 and Diego de Almagro, Tel: 02-250-6838, Fax: 02-250-4404, E-mail: info@hotelantinea.com, URL: www.hotelantinea.com.
Updated: Jan 09, 2013.

HIGH-END

Nü House

(ROOMS: $95-189) The swankiest of newcomers in the area, walking into this boutique hotel makes you feel like you could be in a trendy high-class hotel anywhere in the world. Shiny elevators take you to rooms and suites with modern red and white décor, flat-screen TVs and mini-bars. This place screams posh down to the fancy shampoos and loofahs in marble-tiled bathrooms. If this is your style, you might also check out its sister restaurant and club, Q Café to the right toward Foch Plaza, and The Loft to the left. All three are owned by the same, and guests of the hotel receive a 10 percent discount at the others. Mariscal Foch E6-12 and Reina Victoria, Tel: 02-255-7845, E-mail: reservas@nuhousehotels.com, URL: www.nuhousehotels.com.
Updated: Jan 09, 2013.

Hotel La Rábida

(ROOMS: $61-93) This small, Anglo/Italian-owned boutique hotel has a clean, colonial feel with friendly service, great food and lots of personal touches that make it unique. It is one of only a few hotels in Quito awarded with the *Distintivo Q*, a certificate of quality and sustainable tourism. Hostal de La Rábida is an old traditional house recently restored into a first-class South American boutique hotel.

It offers guests the gracious atmosphere and style of a beautiful home located in the heart of Quito, near most places of historical and tourist interest as well as restaurants, banks, travel agencies and shops. With only 11 charming and tastefully decorated rooms, Hostal de la Rábida is a very special hotel in which to enjoy your stay in Quito. La Rábida 227 and Santa Maria, Tel: 02-222-1720/2169, E-mail: info@hostalrabida.com, URL: www.hostalrabida.com.
Updated: Jan 09, 2013.

QUITO

JW Marriott Hotel Quito

(ROOMS: $189-1,500) The newest of Quito's luxury international hotels, the JW Marriott Quito is a gigantic, modern pyramid in the northern end of La Mariscal. With spacious, sunny and elegantly decorated rooms with excellent city and mountain views, two excellent restaurants, a tropical pool area that will make you forget you are in the middle of a polluted city, and relaxing common areas including an indoor waterfall, the Marriott is well-worth the price for travelers desiring a luxurious stay. Each of the over 250 rooms has safes, cable TV, data ports and minibars, and some also have in-room hot tubs. Av. Orellana 1172 and Av. Amazonas, Tel: 02-297-2000, Fax: 02-297-2050, E-mail: businesscenter.quito@marriothotels.com, URL:www.marriott.com/hotels/travel/uiodt-jw-marriott-quito.

Hilton Colón Ecuador

(ROOMS: $179-329) The Hilton Colón is one of Quito's older international luxury chains and it is beginning to show its age. Nonetheless, it is a beautiful hotel with extensive amenities and great city views. Located in the southern end of La Mariscal, right in front of Parque el Ejido, home to a weekend outdoor market with crafts from all over Ecuador, the Hilton Colón is a blockish concrete structure. Services include a small but modern gym and heated outdoor pool. Two restaurants downstairs offer ample buffets and spacious seating areas. Av. Amazonas N19-14 and Av. Patria, Tel: 02-256-1333, Fax: 02-256-3903, E-mail: reservations.quito@hiltoncolon.com /frontdesk.quito@hiltoncolon.com, URL: www.hiltoncolon.com. Updated: Jan 09, 2013.

La Mariscal Restaurants

Finding a place to eat is no problem in La Mariscal—it's deciding where to go that can be a challenge. Whether you're in the mood for a hearty steak, spicy Mexican food, sushi or traditional Ecuadorian fare, this area is prepared to appease your gastronomical cravings with a wide-array of culinary pickings down every block.

Entrée prices range across the board, as you can just as easily get a cheap almuerzo or burger and fries combo somewhere as you can enjoy a fancy sit-down meal. Either way, La Mariscal's offerings are accessible and abundant; plan to grab a bite here while you're in Quito.
Updated: January 18, 2013

ECUADORIAN
Achiote !

(ENTREES: $15-25) Specializes in preparing exquisite Ecuadorian plates that you simply cannot miss out on if you're staying in Quito. Located on the fringe of the Mariscal's bustling nightlife (but still within it's borders) the restaurant presents a haven of sorts for those interested enjoying a night out, minus the rowdiness that's typical of that neighborhood at night. Serving a range of typical dishes all the way from seafood to delicacies of the highlands (including guinea pig!), Achiote provides your palette with an abundance of choices.

The appetizers come in small or large portions so you can easily sample a number of items on the menu. The services on top of it all is delightful, with a near perfect command of English and an extensive knowledge regarding everything that's on the menu. Juan Rodriguez 282 and Reina Victoria, Tel: 02-250-1743, E-mail: lcastro@achiote.com.ec, URL: http://achiote.com.ec.
Updated: Mar 11, 2013.

C.A.C.T.U.S.

(ENTREES: $5-20) In a neighborhood filled with pizzerias, Chinese restaurants and shawarma joints, C.A.C.T.U.S. serves authentic, honest-to-goodness Ecuadorian food. Specializing in the traditional cuisine of the Sierra's indigenous population, the restaurant cooks up delicious *llapingachos*, tasty trout, and a number of bean, corn, *cuy* and vegetable salads. The restaurant is tiny and the atmosphere is intimate, with groups of friends crowded around the small tables drinking beer and cocktails. On especially festive nights, the patrons have been known to engage in some traditional Otavalo-style dancing. Carrión, between Av. Amazonas and 9 de Octubre, Tel: 02-254-9591.
Updated: Jan 16, 2013.

Fried Bananas !

(ENTREES: $5-15) Fried Bananas Restaurant & Cafe is small, off the beaten track, and what some might call "cute" thanks to its ambiance. What really steals the show however, is the combination of simplicity and imagination in their plates as they serve up some incredibly delightful Ecuadorian cuisine. From avocado cream to shrimp bathed in wonderful sauces, spaghetti with saffron or some incredibly tender beef, Fried Bananas does its name justice by getting you to its glorious desert via some wonderful entrees

QUITO

along the way. Cozy and with prices much lower than one would expect given the elegant atmosphere, you can't pass up coming here at least once. Open Monday to Saturday, 12 p.m. to 9 p.m. Mariscal Foch E4-150 and Amazonas, Tel: 02-223-5208 / 09-970-7695, E-mail: info@newfriedbananas.com. Updated: Mar 13, 2013.

ARGENTINIAN
El Rincón del Gaucho

(ENTREES: $20-25) This Argentinean steakhouse has huge portions of excellent steak cooked on a charcoal grill on the premises. Try the *parrillada* (BBQ platter) to share in a group; it's served on a mini grill that keeps your meat warm. The service is great. A good wine selection is another plus. Diego de Almagro 422, between Lizardo García and Calama, Tel: 02-254-7846/222-3782, E-mail: info@rincondelgaucho.net, URL: www.rincondelgaucho.net.
Updated: Jan 16, 2013

ASIAN
Uncle Ho's

(ENTREES: $7-10) Uncle Ho's brings Vietnamese food to Quito in a fun, casual atmosphere. The owner is part-Vietnamese and unlike most of the Asian food in Quito, the food is very authentic. The restaurant combines delicately flavored, mouth-watering food with friendly, though slow, service. For a real taste of Vietnam, slurp on the *pho*, which is a Hanoi-style beef noodle soup.

Other options include summer rolls, coconut curry chicken, lemongrass beef kebabs over a rice or noodle plate, and sea bass in lime and chili sauce. Finish up with a round of stuffed fried bananas, flambéed at your table. *Que rico!* José Calama E8-40 and Diego de Almagro, Tel: 02-511-4030, E-mail: kevinheehee@gmail.com, URL: http://unclehos.com.
Updated: Jan 16, 2013

CAFES
Kallari

($3-6) Kallari is a community-owned coffee shop and crafts shop owned by an association of Quechua communities in the Napo province, mostly from the Amazon Rainforest. Organic coffee and organic chocolate in brownies and hot chocolate accompany tasty snacks. Wilson E4-266 and Juan Leon Mera, Tel: 02-223-6009, URL: www.kallari.com. Updated: Jan 18, 2013.

Este Café

($4-8) Lovers of coffee shouldn't pass up a quick glimpse at the gourmet drinks on offer at Este Café. Whether you settle into one of the colorful couches with a frozen Oreo cappuccino, soak up some funky break beats over a steaming cup of chai, or peruse the book exchange with a Baileys iced latte, it's easy to chill at this artsy coffee spot. The drinks selection is varied and impressive, ranging from wholesome natural juices to wicked hot chocolates with marshmallows or cheese, to a variety of caipiriñhas with a twist. The mix of traditional Ecuadorian and international food choices also makes Café Este a popular haunt for students, travelers and businessmen with eccentric ties. Be sure to catch one of Café Este's monthly exhibitions featuring the works of Ecuadorian artists or one of its regular live music and theater performances. Flyers and information about what else is on in Quito are also available. Juan León Mera n23-94 and Wilson, Tel: 02-254-2488, E-mail: eventos@estecafe.com, URL: www.estecafe.com.

Coffee Tam Plaza Foch

($10-15) With four branches in the Mariscal, Coffee Tam has become a neighborhood institution. Coffee Tam Plaza Foch is THE spot for people-watching and pre-game drinks, or catching a fútbol match or late-night bite on the always-hopping plaza. A slew of outdoor tables are always full of a mixed gringo/Ecuadorian crowd clamoring to be heard over the pulsing pop and electronic music. Drinks are reasonably priced (there's a different 2-for-1 cocktail every day); its overpriced food is pretty varied and comes in big portions. Mariscal Foch and Reina Victoria, Plaza Foch, Tel: 02-252-6957.

CUBAN
La Bodeguita de Cuba

(ENTREES: $10-15) A classy restaurant-come-bar, this place serves excellent food, accompanied by live Cuban music most nights. On Thursday to Saturday nights, it stays open until 2 a.m., when different live bands play to a packed room. Drinks are fairly expensive, but you pay for the atmosphere. Varadero, which is next door, is run by the same owners and also has live music on Friday and Saturday nights, and appeals to a more mature clientele. Reina Victoria N26-105 and La Pinta (next to Varadero), Tel: 02-254-2476, E-mail: evarcuba@yahoo.com. Updated: Jan 09, 2013

FRENCH
Crêpes de París
(ENTREES: $3-5) This cozy restaurant in the Mariscal specializes in French food, especially, as its name hints, in crepes. It is a bit pricey for Quito, but in reality a value compared to French restaurants in other countries. The food is very good but the service is not always great. If you are craving French food, this is an excellent option in Quito. José Calama 362.
Updated: Jan 18, 2013

INDIAN
The Great India Restaurant ♪
(ENTREES: $3.50-8) Situated in the buzzing café thoroughfare of Calle Calama, The Great India Restaurant holds its own in the Mariscal restaurant scene as a longtime favorite haunt whose cheap and authentic Indian food lure a stream of budget diners, both local and foreign. Simple and low-key in its setting, the restaurant is brightened up by bustling student crowds and the occasional woman adorning colorful saris. For vegetarians, The Great India Restaurant is heavenly, with the menu arranged by the separation of meat and veggie dishes. There is a wide range of curry dishes, with meat options of beef, chicken and goat. All meals are accompanied by rice or naan bread. Smaller appetites can order pakoda, shwarma or falafel. It is also popular for its bargain beer combo specials. It is also one of the only restaurants in town reliably open on Sundays. Calama E4-54, between Juan Leon Mera and Amazonas, Tel: 02-223-8269, Cel: 09-9418-0183.
Updated: Jan 09, 2013

ITALIAN
Cosa Nostra ♪
(PIZZAS: $10-14) What some proclaim to be one the best italian pizzerias in all of Quito, Cosa Nostra is a restuarant that accurately hits the the bullseye when it comes to delicious and authentic Italian cuisine. Attracting foreigners and locals alike, this pizzeria offers dozens of thin-crust, brick-oven pizzas with lots of typical and gourmet toppings to choose from. Cosa Nostra also offers a variety of homemade pastas such as ravioli, gnocchi and lasagna. The place has an near perfect balance across price, quality, charisma and service - including a "buongiorno!" from the owner when you walk in through the door (sometimes, not always!). The restaurant only uses high-quality ingredients and also incorporates local products, including organic tomatoes and cheese from Cayambe. With an ambiance that's incredibly relaxed and classy, Cosa Nostra is a gem lying right near the heart of La Mariscal that you shouldn't pass up on. Baquerizo Moreno E7-86 and Diego de Almagro, Tel: 02-252-7145, E-mail: pizzeria.cosanostra@yahoo.com.
Updated: Mar 13, 2013

INTERNATIONAL
Crepes and Waffles
(ENTREES: $8-12) This Colombian chain is found in several locations around Quito and has reliably tasty food that comes in good-sized portions. The waffles are not meant to be breakfast, but rather dessert; they are piled high with ice cream, whipped cream, nutella, fruit and more. Crepes are served with sweet or salty fillings and are full of flavor. The salads are gigantic and delicious, while the pita sandwiches are stuffed with a number of combinations of veggie and meat options.

The atmosphere is casual, almost diner-style, but attracts a gringo and classy Ecuadorian crowd. If for nothing else, stop by for a scoop or two of Crepe and Waffles' delicious ice cream, which is served in either a cup or homemade waffle cone! This is the main restaurant in La Mariscal, but there are also locations in the Quicentro and El Jardin malls. Rábida N26-249 and Francisco de Orellana, Tel: 02-250-0658, E-mail: servicioalcliente@crepesywaffles-ec.com / smosquera@crepesywaffles-ec.com, URL: www.crepesywaffles.com.ec.
Updated: Jan 09, 2013

La Boca del Lobo ♪
(ENTREES: $12-25) Featuring a brightly lit, colorfully painted glass-encased patio with funky chandeliers, hanging bird cages, and faux renaissance portraits, La Boca del Lobo sticks out as the most flamboyant joint in the Mariscal's somewhat low-key gringo scene. It's no surprise, then, that La Boca del Lobo is also gay-friendly, and you'll find Quito's "beautiful people" here mixed in with upper-scale gringo tourists. With a huge menu of Mediterranean-fusion appetizers and entrées and a long list of fruity cocktails all made with Absolut Vodka, La Boca del Lobo is the kind of place you can lounge in for hours. Calama 284 and Reina Victoria, Tel: 02-223-8123/254-5500, E-mail: eventos@labocadellobo.com.ec, URL: www.labocadellobo.com.ec.
Updated: Jan 09, 2013.

QUITO

The Magic Bean

(ENTREES: $5-14) From the "Have a nice day" sign by the bar to the huge pancakes served for breakfast, there's nothing Ecuadorian about this place. Unless you're seeking an authentic dining experience, you're unlikely to be disappointed. The cozy patio café is always packed with travelers so it's a great place to meet people. All the dishes on the huge menu are delicious; the smoothies are most definitely a must! Some menu options include omelettes, French toast and huevos rancheros for breakfast, and salads, sandwiches, burgers and chicken kebabs for lunch or dinner. Mariscal Foch E5-08 and Juan León Mera; also Portugal E9-106 and República del Salvador, Tel: 02-256-6181, Fax: 593-2-290-6105, E-mail: info@magicbeanquito.com.
Updated: Jan 09, 2013.

MEXICAN
Red Hot Chili Peppers

(ENTREES: $7.50-11) Red Hot Chili Peppers is a great Tex-Mex restaurant with the best fajitas in Quito and possibly the best margaritas in Ecuador. Right in the heart of the Mariscal, this place's flavors and portions are American style: full of taste and huge portions for reasonable prices. All dishes can also be served vegetarian. Mariscal Foch E4-314 and Juan Leon Mera, Tel: 02-255-7575, Cel: 09-8552-3548, E-mail: fierro.fabian@gmail.com.
Updated: Jan 17, 2013.

MIDDLE EASTERN
Balbeek ❗

(ENTREES: $12-25) For a taste of authentic Lebanese cuisine, Balbeek is where it's at. If you're not familiar with Lebanese food, rest assured that the delightful owner will take care of any questions you have, as he himself takes your order. Beware however, for he might take over ordering for you if you allow him to! This can (and will) rack up the bill considerably.

Portions are on the smaller side for appetizers specifically, given that the idea is to order a variety of things to taste and sample. There are main courses however, for those desiring larger portions of food, but these are considerably more expensive. Arabic dancing is featured on Thursday nights! 6 de Diciembre N23-103 and Wilson. Quito, Ecuador, Tel: 02-255-2766, E-mail: info@restaurantbaalbek.com, URL: www.restaurantbaalbek.com.
Updated: Mar 07, 2013.

El Arabe

(ENTREES: $5-8) Despite a newly remodeled interior that gives it a more middle-eastern ambiance, El Arabe has always been on track with the authenticity of its warm and filling meals. In addition to offering exotic cuisine, El Arabe is actually a restaurant that caters to the vegetarian-scene quite well; all in all, it offers a nice change of pace beginning with its wonderful hummus all the way to the filling shawarma's they serve up. Reina Victoria 627 and Carrion, Tel: 02-549-414.
Updated: Mar 12, 2013

PUBS
Finn McCool's

(ENTREES: $7-10) Finn McCool's is one of the the few places in Quito where many travelers are likely to feel at home. European and North American sporting events are regularly shown, and there's a free pool table, great drinks, and excellent pub food, including Irish stew, bangers and mash, and fish and chips. Finn McCool's is a great place to meet fellow travelers, expats and Ecuadorians, and this Irish pub often has DJs on weekends and hosts the city's best St. Patty's Day party every year. Diego de Almagro N24-64 and Joaquin Pinto, Tel: 02-252-1780, E-mail: info@irishpubquito.com, URL: www.irishpubquito.com.
Updated: Jan 09, 2013

Turtle's Head

(ENTREES: $5-10) An excellent Scottish-owned pub in Quito's Mariscal district and one of the only spots in Quito to get home-brewed beer. Three varieties of micro-brewed beers are for sale from the on-site brewery, which provide a nice break from the national beers. The Turtle's Head also has great hamburgers and snacks, along with pool, darts and foosball. The pub is very British in look and feel, enhanced by cartoon strips from the adult comic Viz, that are displayed on the walls and in the toilets. There is also a new Turtle's Head in Cumbaya near Quito. La Niña 626 and Juan León Mera, Tel: 02-256-5544, E-mail: tthquito@hotmail.com.
Updated: Jan 09, 2013.

SEAFOOD
La Canoa Manabita

(ENTREES: $4-6) By far one of the most overlooked holes in wall in the Mariscal area, La Canoa Manabita is easy to miss, but unjustifiably so. Offering incredibly delicious plates from the coast, ranging anywhere

from fried and breaded fish to yummy ceviches, La Canoa Manabita is an oasis for seafood lovers in the city that want an authentic taste of the delicious plates that the coast of Ecuador has to offer, all for a cheap price too.
Updated: Mar 12, 2013.

VEGETARIAN

El Maple
(ENTREES: $3-7) El Maple serves up a variety of vegetarian and even entirely vegan dishes. It's a simple and convinient little place located in la Mariscal that serves up their meals rather quickly too, specifically their executive lunch specials (appetizer, soup, entree, dessert and juice) which cost a mere $3-5. With food that's always fresh and flavorful, it's hard to go wrong here, especially if your a vegan or vegetarian. Joaquin Pinto E7-68 and Diego de Almagro, Tel: 02-229-0000, URL: http://www.elmaple.com. Updated: Mar 13, 2013.

La Mariscal Nightlife

The Mariscal is undoubtedly Quito's nightlife hot spot. With an overwhelming number of bars and clubs on every street, this is definitely the best place to head to on Friday and Saturday nights (sometimes Tuesdays, Wednesdays, and Thursdays as well). Despite its name, Gringolandia is the place to go out for quiteños just as much, if not more, than backpackers. Technically all bars in the Mariscal area must close by 2 a.m., in accordance with a law passed a few years ago. However, many stay open until three, or later if they think no one's looking. There are also a number of "clubs", which open later, often until 6 or 7am.
Updated: Mar 07, 2013.

Bungalow 6 ♪
(COVER: $5-10 for men, FREE for women on most nights) Bungalow 6 is the most famous club in Quito among expats and visitors, and odds are that at some point you will find yourself on its crowded dance floors, in its lounge or leaning over its pool tables. Bungalow's playlist is dominated by last year's Top 40 hits and reggaeton, while the clientele is dominated by gringos and the Ecuadorians who would like to pick them up. The meat market atmosphere is amplified on Wednesdays, Ladies' Night, when the place is opened only to women from 8-10 p.m. After plying the girls with free drinks for two hours, the staff opens up the doors to men, who charge in like bulls stampeding

through the streets of Pamplona. Corner of José Calama and Diego de Almagro, E-mail: bungalow6disco@gmail.com.
Updated: Jan 17, 2013

Strawberry Fields Forever ♪
(Drinks: $4-10) If you love the Beatles and Classic Rock, you'll love Strawberry Fields. If you're not looking carefully, you might miss it. Strawberry Fields is tucked away next to the popular No Bar. Take a seat in the cozy alcove in the back, and rock out to the amazing playlist, which includes songs by the fab four and their peers. Drinks are named after the best of the Beatles, from their signature Strawberry Fields margarita to the eclectic Octupus's Garden. Be sure to check out the Yellow Submarine-themed restroom, and chat up the friendly, young owners, who are usually sitting by the bar. Strawberry Fields Forever also has another location in La Floresta (Gonzalez Suárez 171 and 12 de Octubre). Calama E5-27 and Juan Leon Mera, Tel: 09-9903-1592.
Updated: Jan 18, 2013.

Cherusker
(DRINKS: $4-10) Cherusker is the first German brew pub in Ecuador, and it offers a variety of German craft beer at reasonable prices. Beer options range from wheat beer (Hafeweizen) to dark stout beer and can be sampled in a few different sizes. You can accompany your pint with typical German food, including bratwurst and currywurst. Cherusker's ambiance is friendly and comfortable, with lounge-type seating indoors as well as tables outdoors for a beer garden atmosphere. Monday-Thursday 3 p.m.-midnight, Friday-Saturday 3 p.m.-2 a.m. Closed Sundays. Joaquin Pinto E7-85 and Diego de Almagro, Tel: 02-601-2144, URL: www.facebook.com/CheruskerCerveceriaAlemana.
Updated: Jan 17, 2013

No Bar
(COVEr: $5) Hot, sweaty and crowded, this place appeals almost exclusively to the very young and the very drunk. The Ecuadorian to foreigner ratio is about 50-50, mainly aged between 16 and 25, who come for the cheap drinks and the school disco/meat market atmosphere. The music is a mix of Latin and western chart cheese. It could be anywhere in the world, but if you want to dance the night away and forget that you're in Ecuador, it might be the place for you. Calama y Juan León Mera, Tel: 02-254-5145.
Updated: Mar 13, 2013

QUITO

Fragola Fusion Hookah Lounge

(DRINKS: $4-6) Definitely not providing the fastest service in the world, what La Fragola lacks in speed it makes up for in atmosphere. The hip red and yellow décor is certainly a draw for this sweet little night spot on always-happening Calama Street in the heart of La Mariscal. This is a prime spot for people-watching, as this bar and restaurant is perched on the second floor, with a great view of the night's activities below. The all-you-can-drink deal for $10.99 for three hours of mojitos, caipirinhas, vodka tonics, and Cuba libres is another draw for those looking to get drunk, as are the hookahs. Calama E5-10, between Reina Victoria and Juan León Mera, Tel: 02-255-6159, E-mail: mongosgrill@gmail.com.
Updated: Jan 17, 2013.

Centro Histórico (Old Town)

The Centro Histórico (also known as the Old Town) is Quito's extensive colonial center that was built over the ashes of what was once a major part of the Inca empire.

One of the first areas to be named a World Heritage Site by the United Nations in 1978, Old Town will send you across centuries of history as you stroll down its cobblestone streets and alleyways, filled by local residents and *vendedores ambulantes* (street vendors).

At the beginning of the 20th century, Quito fit within the boundaries of this entire neighborhood. Today however - following decades of expansion - it's only a small piece of the entire city but still undoubtedly the most iconic one. Filled with a rich past, it's here that some of Ecuador's most famous battles and executions took place in the plazas, only to be replaced now by the much more peaceful but lively bustle of residents, tourists, businessmen, street vendors, and protesters. Not to mention - all the noisy cars and buses that wind through its single-lane streets.

Once considered dangerous, Old Town has drastically changed over the past few years. Beggars and pushy merchants have dwindled in numbers, the façades of old buildings have been repainted, streets and the plazas are better illuminated at night now, and the Trole and Ecovia have managed to cut down on bus traffic and fumes. Most significant is the fact that the police force is a much stronger presence now, notably helping deter pickpockets and other criminals. It's still advised to be cautious and discreet though, as the streets tend to fill up quickly with locals during lunch-time and at the end of the day, and tourists are still a bit of an oddity in this area of Quito.

For some extra fun, veer off from the guided tour and spend some quality time in the plazas or side streets that feature exquisite colonial architecture and winding pathways that open up into lovely courtyards.
Updated: Feb 28, 2013.

Centro Histórico Services

TOURISM
Quito Turismo
For information about Quito and Ecuador in general, the knowledgeable and friendly staff here will be sure to help you out. They offer flyers, maps and tour-bus tickets. On the corner of Venezuela and Espejo, Tel: 02-257 0786, E-mail: info@quito-turismo.com.
Updated: Mar 11, 2013.

MONEY
Banco de Pichincha
Guayaquil, between Olmedo and Manabi. Tel: 02-295-5700, Open Hours From: 08:30 a.m. to 5:00 p.m., Monday-Friday, Days Closed: Sundays but open Saturdays from 9:00 a.m. to 1:00 p.m..
Updated: Mar 11, 2013.

MEDICAL
Farmacias SanaSana (Pharmacy)
Venezuela N1-84 and Bolivar, Tel: 02-396-8500, Open Hours From: 9:00a.m., Open Hours To: 5:00p.m..
Updated: Mar 11, 2013.

SHOPPING
Tianguez Gift Shop
The Tianguez Gift Shop supports the entrepreneurial spirit of Ecuador. There are handmade crafts from around 350 groups and individuals in the country; from Panama Hats to blow guns, precolombian ceramics, tapestries and Tigua paintings. Aspiring to pay fair prices to the original artists, you will find the prices here higher than most outdoor markets, however the variety and quality is exceptional. Plaza de San Francisco cuenca y sucre under the church's atrium, Tel: 593-2-257-0233 / 593-2-954-326, E-mail: administracion@sinchisacha.org, URL: www.tienguez.org /www.sinchisacha.org/ www.mindalae.com.
Updated: Jun 15, 2012.

QUITO

Things To See and Do in the Old Town

You will need more than one afternoon to see and do all that Quito's Centro Histórico has to offer. The hilly cobblestone streets take you back to the era of the Spanish Empire, with large central plazas, sprawling green parks, beautiful colonial buildings and elaborate Catholic churches. With so much to gaze at, you might find yourself just wandering through the pleasant neighborhood without setting foot inside one of the historic buildings. When you do, however, you will be instantly amazed. Check out the gold ornamented Iglesia de La Compañia, or wander through the President's Palace in Plaza Grande. Pay a visit one of Centro Histórico's many interesting museums, with exhibits on colonial and indigenous art, military memorabilia, and relics that chart the country's checkered history from pre-Inca times to the present. Even if you are sleeping in another part of Quito, it is worth your while to spend time embracing one of Ecuador's most historic areas.

Quito's historic center takes you back to the era of the Spanish Empire, with its beautiful colonial buildings and elaborate churches such as the Monasterio de San Francisco and the Compañia de Jesus. There are also several interesting museums in this area that house colonial and indigenous art, military memorabilia and relics that chart the country's checkered history from pre-Inca times to the present.
Updated: Jan 21, 2013.

Los Coches de La Colonia: Horse-Drawn Carriage Tours

What better way to enjoy the colonial center of Quito than in the preferred method of transportation of a century ago, a horse and buggy! Quito's colonial founders would be surprised to hop into one of these carriages as soon as the MP3 player starts bumping, the headlights flick on and the high-tech brakes kick in.

The tour is about 15 minutes long and runs from near the Plaza de la Independencia (Plaza Grande) to the Plaza de San Francisco and back. Go after dark when the cathedrals are lit up, traffic is less horrendous, and the cool breeze will require snuggling to stay warm! Ca. García Moreno, between Ca. Espejo and Sucre, Tel: 099-030 3216.
Updated: Jan 24, 2013.

Centro Histórico Lodging

BUDGET

Casa Bambú

(DORMS: $7, ROOMS: $25) Casa Bambu is one of Quito's best values with clean dorm rooms and shared rooms. This small hotel is full of character and homey touches. The lounges are spacious and have comfy couches, flowering plants, and a collection of books, games and DVDs for guests to use. Its several outdoor patios provide excellent views of Quito. We recommend you take a cab when you first arrive, as the hotel is located up a steep hill not conducive to luggage. It's just a block from several main bus lines, so transportation isn't a problem once you stash the heavy stuff. Casa Bambu also locations in Mindo and Canoa. Solano E527 and Av. Colombia (up a steep hill from the southernmost corner of Parque el Ejido), Tel: 02-222-6738, E-mail: hotelbambuecuador@hotmail.com, URL: www.hotelbambuecuador.com/pages/casaquito.html.
Updated: Jan 08, 2013.

Hostel Revolution Quito

($8.50-25 per person) Hostel Revolution Quito is a cool backpacker hostel in the Old Town created by and for backpackers who want to socialize, take in the historical sights and culture, exchange info, and go out and have a great time. The hostel is located in a renovated colonial-type house with wooden floors and decorative plaster ceilings, and has a bar, lounge, shared kitchen and rooftop terrace with great views. It is within walking distance of most of the city's historical sites: colonial houses, plazas, museums, churches and monuments. Hostel Revolution can also help with arranging volunteering, Spanish lessons or work teaching English. Los Rios N13-11 and Julio Castro, Tel: 02-254-6458, E-mail: stay@hostelrevolutionquito.com, URL: www.hostelrevolutionquito.com.
Updated: Jan 09, 2013.

MID-RANGE

Hotel Viena Internacional

($24-76 per person) This hotel is popular with Ecuadorian and foreign visitors alike. Although it is set in an old, colonial building, the interior is modern and clean. Rooms are fairly standard and look out onto the central patio. Some, however, are quite dark. All have private bathrooms with new, fully functioning fittings. The hotel is centrally located

and provides a good launching point for seeing the major sights of Quito's historic center. The staff is friendly and willing to answer any queries. Ca. Flores 600 and Chile (corner), Tel: 02-295-4860, Fax: 02-295-4633, E-mail: reservas@hotelvienaint.com, URL: www.hotelvienaint.com.
Updated: Jan 09, 2013.

Hotel San Francisco de Quito

(ROOMS: $27-58) San Francisco de Quito offers simple, clean rooms in a very central part of the Old Town. Many sights are within easy walking distance. The hotel is located on the second and third floors of a pleasant inner courtyard. All rooms are equipped with private bathrooms, a telephone and television. Decorations are sparse, although the dark wood furniture is aesthetically pleasing. Rooms on the third floor are very quiet, with high ceilings, although you might consider bringing a sleeping mask given the skylights. Note also that hot water and water pressure can take a while to pass through the pipes on the upper level. The price includes free internet and breakfast at the restaurant downstairs, including bread, tea or coffee, and eggs (fruit salad costs 1 dollar extra). The hotel has taken serious safety precautions; a guard monitors the entrance, and you must be buzzed in through a wrought-iron gate. However, since Quito can be dangerous, if arriving late, take a taxi and make sure the driver stops right outside the entrance and have him stay until someone lets you in. Sucre 217 y Guayaquil, Tel: 02228-7758, URL: www.sanfranciscodequito.com.ec.
Updated: May 18, 2013.

HIGH-END

Patio Andaluz ♪

(ROOMS: $200-250) Patio Andaluz is located in the heart of the Centro Histórico in an over 400-year-old-house that was once owned by the first president of Ecuador, Juan José Flores. The hotel was renovated almost a decade ago but retains its classic colonial style. The rooms are beautiful, with hardwood floors and views onto the courtyard. You can play chess on handcrafted tables overlooking the courtyard, relax in the hammocks, read magazines and books in English and Spanish in the peaceful Guayasamin Lounge, or spend your free time in the sauna and fitness room in the back. Some guests have complained about the lack of ventilation, as the only windows in rooms look out onto the indoor courtyard. There is

also an on-site restaurant and gift shop with local artisan crafts. Ask about package deals, which include all meals and tours around the Centro and to featured museums. Av. García Moreno N6-52, between Olmedo and Mejia, Tel: 02-228-0830, Fax: 02-228-8690, E-mail: info@hotelpatioandaluz.com, URL: www.hotelpatioandaluz.com.
Updated: Jan 09, 2013

Hotel Plaza Grande

(ROOMS: $500-2,000) Located in the heart of Quito's Old Town, Hotel Plaza Grande is surrounded by fascinating historical sights, including the Presidential Palace. This luxury hotel offers 15 suites including Royal, Plaza View and Presidential options. All rooms have air conditioning, VIP treatment and many additional premium amenities. Other services include 24-hour room service, spa and fitness facilities, and meeting facilities. Fine dining is available at three restaurants as well as a variety of entertainment. If your budget can't accommodate these extravagances, show up with a smart appearance and a polite demeanor and the staff will be happy to invite you on a free tour of the elegant facilities. The fourth floor balcony offers an unbeatable view of the Plaza Grande below. Take a moment to absorb the hustle and bustle of the square, while a rose-filled fountain trickles gently beside you. To your right, you'll get a great view of the Presidential Palace. Ca. García Moreno N5-16 and Chile, Tel: 02-2-251-0777, Fax: 02-251-0800, E-mail: recepcion@plazagrandequito.com, URL: www.plazagrandequito.com.
Updated: Jan 09, 2013.

Centro Histórico Restaurants

The Centro Histórico offers everything from elegant restaurants with traditional live music, dress codes and waiters in tuxedos, to small locally owned places that sell cheap fixed-price lunches for under $2. In the last few years, several international restaurants have opened, especially in the area around Plaza de la Independencia (Plaza Grande). There are also quite a few fast food joints. La Ronda is lined with cafés and restaurants that sell canelazo (warm drink made with sugar cane alcohol, fruits and cinnamon), empanadas and other local specialties like *seco de chivo* and *guatita*.

Theatrum Restaurant

(ENTREES: $14-20) Located on the second floor of the historic Teatro Nacional Sucre, the Theatrum Restaurant is a must-see while in the Centro Histórico. With its soaring ceilings and muted décor, it is a fancy atmosphere befitting an equally posh menu. With offerings such as baby Ecuadorian banana with warm chocolate soup and rabbit risotto, travelers are infused with a feeling of international cuisine made with Ecudorian ingredients. Don't be afraid to splurge when it comes to Theatrum. The restaurant even offers free transportation when you make a lunch or dinner reservation online, so be sure to take advantage of this offer. Ca. Manabí, between Guayaquil and Flores, 2nd floor of Teatro Nacional Sucre, Tel: 02-257-1011/228-9669, E-mail: reservas@theatrum.com.ec, URL: www.theatrum.com.ec.

Café Mosaico

(ENTREES: $7-20) Ecuador goes international at this lively restaurant and café, perched high above the city, having one of the best restaurant views in Quito! Originally from New York, the owners clearly packed their stylish city instincts and gastronomical intuition. Café Mosaico offers an extensive menu, including sandwiches, salads, burgers, Ecuadorian specialties and Greek dishes. The food is wide-ranged but overpriced and nothing to write home about. However, the amazing view is really the selling point here (and what you truly pay for), so it is still worthwhile to come for a meal, dessert, coffee or glass of wine. Manuel Samaniego N8-95 and Anteparra, Itchimbia, Tel: 02-254-2871, Fax: 593-2-254-2871, E-mail: cafe@cafemosaico.com.ec / julia_charpentier@hotmail.com, URL: www.cafemosaico.com.ec. Updated: Jan 09, 2013.

Vista Hermosa

(ENTREES: $11-30) As its name suggests, Vista Hermosa's (Gorgeous View) biggest selling point is its spectacular 360-degree view of Quito from its romantic roof terrace. Located on the sixth floor of a colonial building, Vista Hermosa has a simple but slightly pricey menu featuring Ecuadorian plates, pizzas, and meat and seafood mains, in addition to a full bar list. Come and enjoy a bowl of *locro de papas* (traditional potato soup topped with cheese and avocado), *seco de chivo* (goat stew), or *corvina en salsa de mariscos* (sea bass in seafood sauce) while gazing out over Centro Histórico's colonial building tops. Ca. Mejía 453 and García Moreno, Tel: 02-295-1401, E-mail: info@vistahermosa.com.ec, URL: http://vistahermosa.com.ec. Updated: Jan 18, 2013.

Hasta la Vuelta Señor

(ENTREES: $8-15) Set in the Mediterranean courtyard of Edificio Arzobispal facing the cathedral in the Plaza de la Independencia. The location is ideal and the atmosphere is warm and inviting. Hasta la Vuelta feaures traditional Quiteño dishes. You can definitely find a slightly less sanitary version of the same fare for a much cheaper price in dozens of cafes in this same area. The atmosphere is what makes this restaurant special. Calle Chile OE-422 and Venezuela, Palacio Arzobispal, third floor, Tel: 02-258-0887/5812, E-mail: reservas@hastalavuelta.com, URL: http://www.hastalavuelta.com.

Mea Culpa

(ENTREES: $15-23) This lovely and spacious restaurant on the second floor of the Edificio Arzobispal on the northern side of the Plaza de la Independencia (Plaza Grande) has a wide selection of Mediterranean food, featuring seafood and an extensive tapas menu. Chile and Venezuela, Palacio Arzobispal, Plaza de Independencia, Tel: 02-295-1190, E-mail: reservaciones@meaculpa.com.ec, URL: www.meaculpa.com.ec. Updated: Jan 09, 2013.

El Cafeto

(DRINKS: $2-6) This small and open-air café serves deliciously rich coffee, made from 100 percent organic Ecuadorian beans. In addition to buying coffee, take-home bags of coffee beans can be bought for a reasonable $8. Food is basic, with a small selection of breakfast, sandwiches and cake. Still, you're here for the genuinely delicious coffee, which is hard to come by in Quito. For a quiet escape, head up to the second-floor balcony, which offers people-watching views of the street below. Daily 8 a.m.-7:15 p.m. Ca. Chile 930 and Flores, Tel: 02-257-2921, URL: www.elcafeto.com. Updated: Jan 24, 2013.

Tianguez Café

(ENTREES: $8 and up) Set right in the Plaza de San Francisco, this is the perfect spot to try out some traditional Ecuadorian dishes in one of the most traditional colonial plazas in the Old Town. Its also a great place to relax, sip a cappuccino and people-watch. Try the *plato típico*, with *mote* (Andean white corn), *maduro frito* (fried plantain), *llapingacho* (a type of cheesy potato pancake), fresh avocado, lettuce and tomato, and your choice of chicken or *fritada* (fried pork bits). The restaurant—which is also connected to a

QUITO

small gift shop/museum in a cave-like structure underneath the church—is named after the Nahuatl word for market. Before the Spanish arrived, the plaza was used as a market for tribes from all over Ecuador. When the Spanish constructed the church between 1536 and 1580 over the ruins of an Inca palace, the market continued for centuries more. Today, besides the items for sale at the Tianguez Café and gift shop, pretty much only wares for purchase are shoe shines and newspapers. Plaza de San Francisco, under the San Francisco Monastery, Tel: 02-257-0233, E-mail: tianguez_reservas@hotmail.com / administracion@sinchisacha.org, URL: www.tianguez.org.

Govindas
(Set Lunch: $2.50) Vegetarians can get inexpensive meals at Govindas, located within the Hare Krishna's Academia Vaisnava in Quito's colonial center. At this restaurant, meals are presented cafeteria-style, with a choice of the day's well-seasoned offerings, including brown rice. The three-course meal includes soup, main dish, with plenty of sides and dessert, as well as tea or a fresh juice. Dining is in the main front room, or the small courtyard in back. Academia Vaisnava also has evening classes in vegetarian cooking, yoga and other topics, and a bakery-shop. Esmeraldas Oe3-119 and Venezuela, Tel: 02-295-7849.
Updated: Jan 09, 2013.

Heladería San Agustin
Featuring the delicious helados de paila, ceviche, traditional food and pastries, the Heladería San Agustín has been making the same excellent dishes for an unbelievable 140 plus years and has never used preservatives or artificial coloring! You can't leave without trying the helado de paila (ice cream that tastes more like sorbet). The owner is almost always on-site and will happily recommend her favorite dishes, or tell you some of Quito's history, as seen from the doorway of this classic café. Ca. Guayaquil N5-59 and Mejía, Tel: 02-228-5082, Cel: 09-8351-4580, E-mail: heladeriasanagustin@yahoo.com. Updated: Jan 24, 2013.

Pim's
(ENTREES: $17-25) Pim's provides an elegant view of the city from the inside and out. Despite its spacious two-level dining area inside and plenty of outdoor seating with space heaters, reservations are highly recommended, especially for weekends. With an extensive menu that starts with a page of Quichua vocab translated into Spanish and English, you may be surprised that the most recommended dish is the hamburger! There are five different steak preparations, seafood, pork, salads and a few traditional dishes. On Sundays there is only an all-day buffet for a set price. Gral. Aymerich, Top of El Panecillo or Parque Itchimbía Palacio de Cristal, Calle Iquique, Tel: 02-317-0878, E-mail: reservacionespanecillo@grupopims.com, URL: www.grupopims.com.
Updated: Jan 09, 2013.

La Floresta
Located east of La Mariscal, La Floresta is a more residential and less touristy district. Nonetheless, it's a neighborhood that still offers a wide variety of mid-range to luxury hotels as well as many of the city's trendiest restaurants, cafés and bars; and not to mention - Quito's only independent movie theater 'Ocho y Medio'. It's core is on 12 de Octubre and Coruña (Plaza Artigas roundabout) near the Swissotel and "The Strip" of apartments-with-wonderful-views that is Gonzales Suarez.
Updated: Mar 13, 2013.

Things To See and Do in La Floresta

Cine Ocho y Medio (Indie Movie Theater)
(TICKETS: $4.80) Ocho y Medio is Quito's only independent movie theater and is a great spot to catch a flick. Located east of the Swisshotel in the La Floresta neighborhood, the artsy film spot has two comfy rooms (one with throw pillows in front of the screen) to view movies and is teamed up with the trendy and delicious La Cafetina Galería Restorán out front, where you can grab a bite to eat or a drink before or after the showing. Ocho y Medio screens indie and second-run films and documentaries from around the globe in a variety of languages (with Spanish or English subtitles), and hosts film festivals and the occasional live theater, music or dance show. Valladolid N24-353 and Vizcaya, URL: www.ochoymedio.net.
Updated: Jan 22, 2013.

El Mercado De La Floresta
Just down and around the block from the Swissotel, you'll find some incredibly cheap groceries for sale at the outdoor and indoor

market of La Floresta. Search amidst foods, flowers, vegetables, or meats to find what you need and barter for how much you believe its worth! Arriving earlier gets your fresher goods, and cheaper prices as well. Open everyday except Sundays, 7 a.m. to 1 p.m. Galavis Street, between Isabel La Catolica and Andalucia.
Updated: Mar 13, 2013.

La Floresta Lodging

Accommodations run the gamut in La Floresta, with budget hostels existing side-by-side fancy hotels practically. Hostels here are typically cozy bunkhouses that start at $10/person.

In La Floresta you'll also find theSwissotel (Quito's most expensive hotel) with room prices starting at well over $200. It's just a short walk fromLa Mariscal, but the two neighborhoods are worlds apart given that you're less likely to be running into tourists, and you'll be avoiding the nightly noise and chaos as well.

BUDGET
Hotel Folklore ♪
(ROOMS: $29-49) Hotel Folklore is a colorfully decorated, intimate hotel. The rooms include a private bath and a home-cooked breakfast served every morning in its pleasant dining room. You're even welcome to use the kitchen to whip up a specialty from your home country!

It is located close enough to the Mariscal area to be close to the action but far enough to be quiet. Madrid E13-93 and Pontevedra, Tel: 02-255-4621, Cel: 09-8927-2700, Fax: 02-255-4621, E-mail: reservaciones@folklorehotel.com.
Updated: Jan 09, 2013.

Casona de Mario
($12-14 per person) Hostal La Casona de Mario is a quaint home with a spacious garden, two community kitchens and two comfortable lounges. All bathrooms are shared, and rooms are spacious and clean with lots of natural light; most have private balconies.

The Internet cafe a few doors down gives guests a 10 percent discount on Internet and international phone calls. Andalucía 213 and Galicia, two blocks east of 12 de Octubre, Tel: 02-254-4036, Fax: 02-223-0129, E-mail: lacasona@casonademario.com.
Updated: Jan 09, 2013.

MID-RANGE
Hostal Sur
(ROOMS: $25-64) A larger house in a quiet neighborhood in La Floresta, Hostal Sur has comfortable, if slightly overpriced, rooms. The rooms are basic, with no frills, but all have private bathrooms and cable TV. Its good service is one of the major perks of this family-run hotel; the staff is friendly and helpful, and has a working relationship with travel agencies nearby if you want to plan day trips near Quito or overnight adventures in other parts of Ecuador. There is a computer in the common area with Internet for hostel guests to use, but it has an hourly cost. Francisco Salazar 134-E10 and Tamayo (corner), Tel: 02-255-8086, E-mail: jparedesguz@gmail.com.

Aleida's Hostal
($12-25 per person) Aleida's Hostal has recently opened in the laid-back neighborhood of La Floresta. It is a restored private residence with great views of Quito and a pretty garden where you can drink complimentary coffee. The staff speaks English and can help arrange trips and/or tours to several locations in Quito and the surrounding areas. Rooms come with either private or shared bathrooms. Andalucia 559 and Francisco Salazar, Tel: 02-223-4570, E-mail: info@aleidashostal.com.ec, URL: www.aleidashostal.com.ec.
Updated: Jan 09, 2013.

HIGH-END
Hotel Quito
(ROOMS: $57-80) Hotel Quito is a large luxury hotel in La Floresta with some of the best views over the city and the valleys to the east. The hotel offers all of the services one would expect of an international chain, but charges a much lower price. The exterior is somewhat obtrusive and outdated, but inside, the hotel feels spacious, comfortable and clean. The outdoor pool is a highlight; like the rooms and rooftop restaurant, the pool offers excellent views. If you feel like exercising, there also tennis courts, playing fields and walking trails, among other options. Most rooms feature a balcony with a view, and all of them have WiFi, cable TV and room service. The rooftop restaurant, El Techo del Mundo, is a definite benefit and is worth a visit even if you aren't staying at the hotel. Gonzales Suarez N27-142, Tel: 02-254-4600, Fax: 02-3964911, E-mail: reservaciones@hotelquito.com, URL: www.hotelquito.com.
Updated: Jan 09, 2013.

QUITO

Casa Aliso ♪

(ROOMS: $110-135) Casa Aliso is a beautifully preserved private residence, with plenty of furnishings and colors to keep the senses pleased. The hotel is actually a renovated and heartily decorated home, with 10 rooms to spare and garden out back, offering travelers the luxury of spending their time in an ambiance that feels more like a friend's home than it does a mere place to rest, really. With tonnes of character, decor and excellent service here to keep your spirits lifted, the hotel goes the extra mile by providing its guests with its scrumptious meals over at its restaurant. Given all this, it's hard to go wrong with Casa Aliso. Francisco Salazar E 12-137 y Toledo, Tel: 02-252-8062, info@casaaliso.com, URL: www.casaaliso.com. Updated: Aug 1, 2012

Swissotel

(ROOMS: $230-500) Undoubtedly one of Quito's most elegant hotels, the Swissotel has full facilities, including a lovely outdoor pool and spa area with beautiful views of the city and nearby Pichincha and Cotopaxi volcanoes. Most of the rooms are spacious, over-sized suites catering to upper-class business customers and travelers willing (and able) to spend almost double that of other high-end hotels in Quito. The hotel has six exquisite restaurants that can cater to any palate. Av. 12 de Octubre 1820 and Cordero, Tel: 02-256-7600/7128, URL: www.swissotel.com/hotels/quito.
Updated: Jan 09, 2013.

La Floresta Restaurants

Some of Quito's finest restaurants can be found in the La Floresta neighborhood, most of which are concentrated on Avenida Isabel La Católica, Avenida Coruña, Avenida Whymper and Avenida 12 de Octubre. Restaurants in La Floresta tend to be high-end and cater to a clientele to match, so you will find sleek atmospheres, elegant food and elevated prices here. Excellent French, Chinese, Japanese, Peruvian, Italian and Ecuadorian cuisine can all be enjoyed in this neighborhood. La Floresta is also home to one of Quito's most popular universities so there are also more casual restaurants and bars to check out here as well.

ECUADORIAN AND LATIN AMERICAN
El Pobre Diablo ♪

(ENTREES: $7.50-15) El Pobre Diablo is a well-decorated jazz bar, popular with artsy intellectuals and local bohemian types. Live music lights the place up most Wednesday, Thursday and Saturday nights, with jazz and soft Cuban beats on other nights. Its food is pricier than local norms, but dishes are decent and the atmosphere more than makes up for the extra cents. You can order a portion of fried yucca, empanadas, or a meat-and-cheese plate to pick at as you drink and enjoy the music, or a full-on main course. It also has a set lunch menu on weekdays for $7, which includes a soup, entree with a side, dessert and juice. When there is a live show, there is usually a cover of $6.50-8. Drinks are also very expensive here, especially compared to other Quito bars. Av. Isabel La Católica N24-274 and Francisco Galavis (corner), one block south of Swissotel on Isabel La Católica, Tel: 02-223-5194/222-5397, E-mail: eventos@elpobrediablo.com, URL: www.elpobrediablo.com.
Updated: Jan 09, 2013.

Barlovento

(ENTREES: $10-15) Barlovento is an elegant place to try Ecuadorian cuisine. Guests can lounge on the outdoor terrace or, for a more upscale feel, sit on the upper floor, which has live music on select days. The menu includes empanadas and soup for lighter appetites, as well as hearty entrees. Main dishes include local favorites such as *fritada* (fried pork), *seco de chivo* (goat stew with rice), and a variety of *ceviches* (cold seafood broth marinated with lime, onion and tomato). 12 de Octubre N27-09 and Orellana, Tel: 02-222-4683, URL: www.grupobarlovento.com.
Updated: Jan 09, 2013.

Restaurante La Choza

(ENTREES: $10-12) La Choza has all the classic Ecuadorian and Quiteño dishes. It is easy to construct a vegetarian dish with *llapingachos* (cheesy potato pancakes), *mote tostado* (different preparations of Andean corn), cheese-filled empanadas and more. There are also several meat and fish dishes which are excellent. 12 de Octubre N24-551 y Cordero, Tel: 593-2-250-7901 / 2230839, E-mail: info@lachozaec.com, URL: www.lachozaec.com.
Updated: Jan 3, 2013.

ASIAN
Formosa ♪

(ENTREES: $3-6.50) Sitting quietly two blocks off the main avenue of 12 de Octubre, and just behind the Swiss Hotel, is this quaint little hole in the wall which at midday is bustling inside. Serving meals consisting solely of vegetarian food, Formosa boasts a daily buffet fit for the ravenous, and serves you a selection of 3-4 items of your choice from a variety of options - all for an incredibly cheap price ($3-4, including juice and soup). There are à la carte plates and entrees that you can order for a bit of a higher price as well, but whatever you do, don't miss out on their tasty tofu! Andalucia and Luis Cordero. Updated: Mar 13, 2013.

Noe Sushi

(ENTREES: $6-34) Sushi lovers rejoice when they discover Noe Sushi Bar, which serves a mix of high-quality traditional and special rolls (many of which can also be ordered as half rolls), sashimi, and combination plates. Even if you don't like sushi, there are some satisfying Asian mains on the menu, such as grilled beef in ginger sauce, udon noodles with prawns and tempura veggies, and chicken teriyaki. Top it all off with a dessert like guanábana meringue or Toblerone cheesecake. Noe Sushi has several locations in Quito: in the shopping centers Quicentro, El Jardin and Plaza Las Américas, and in La Floresta; it also has a restaurant in Cumbayá in Plaza Cumbayá. In Quito, the La Floresta location has the nicest ambiance. Isabel La Católica 24 and Coruña, Tel: 02-395-5400, URL: www.noesushibar.com. Updated: Jan 18, 2013.

FRENCH
Chez Jerome Restaurant

(ENTREES: $15-30) This French cuisine in town combines a bit of Ecuadorian culture with the most classic French cuisine. The restaurant is in a remarkable and magical location with a very comfortable ambience, as well as decent prices. Whymper N30-96 y Coruña, Sector La Paz, Tel: 02-223-4067, E-mail: secretaria@chezjeromerestaurante. com / chezjero@uio.satnet.net, URL: www. chezjeromerestaurante.com. Updated: Jan 09, 2013.

ITALIAN
La Briciola

(ENTREES: $4-8) This Italian-owned restaurant located in a quiet neighborhood in La Floresta is a perennial favorite and great value for your money. Service is friendly, the food is delicious and the prices are very reasonable. There aren't many choices for vegetarians though; non-meat eaters will be limited to salads and plain pasta dishes. Toledo 1255 and Luis Cordero, Tel: 02-254-7138, URL: www.labriciolaquito.com.

SEAFOOD
Segundo Muelle

(ENTREES: $11.50-20) Excellent Peruvian food comes in tiny portions at the sleek Segundo Muelle, one of Quito's finest restaurants. Although your pocketbook may not thank you when the check arrives, your palate certainly will. Prepare your taste buds with a fruit-infused *pisco* sour followed by the *ceviche mixto en salsa de tres ajís* (mixed ceviche made with three different chilis), a *tacu tacu*, or tortellini filled with crab and ricotta. Although heavy in seafood, the menu has a few different beef and pasta options as well. Segundo Muelle has restaurants in Peru, Panama and Spain, with two locations in Quito: one in La Floresta and the other in Quicentro shopping. Av. Isabel La Católica N24-883 and Gangotena, Tel: 02-222-6548, Cel: 09-9846-9287, E-mail: quito@segundomuelle.com, URL: www.segundomuelle. com. Updated: Jan 09, 2013.

La Jaiba

(ENTREES: $8-18) A restaurant with over 37 years of tradition in Quito, La Jaiba's menu contains a fantastic selection of seafood—all served by an attentive staff. Staying true to the claim that their ingredients "slept in the sea yesterday," the food is extremely fresh and tasty, making it worth the price. Av. Coruña and San Ignacio, Tel: 02-254-3887, E-mail: xponcem42@andinanet.net, URL: www.restaurantelajaiba.com. Updated: Jan 09, 2013.

Guápulo

Located behind Hotel Quito, the neighborhood of Guápulo runs down the winding cobblestone Camino de Orellana, from Gonzalez Suárez to Calle de los Conquistadores, the main road out of Quito, and to the neighboring suburbs of the Tumbaco Valley. Guápulo is nestled more or less on the side of a large hill, between Bellavista, an affluent residential area to the north, and the affordable yet trendy, La Floresta to the south.

Often considered Quito's artsy, bohemian neighborhood, Guápulo is home to many local artists, hip expats and a couple of hipster cafés/bars. These cafés lie in the middle of the neighborhood, halfway up the road from the famed Iglesia de Guápulo. This 15th-century church, built in honor of the Virgin of Guadalupe, is undoubtedly the focal point of this enchanting area, and combined with the

QUITO

stucco mountainside homes, towering palm trees, and cobblestone streets, it creates a picturesque remembrance of old Spain. Updated: Jan 18, 2013.

Things To See and Do in Guápulo

While Guápulo is small and somewhat hidden beneath the posh Avenida de Gónzalez Suárez, the bohemian neighborhood is worth the trip. You can begin walking from the Mirador de Guápulo, a restaurant and lookout point, which by day offers local *artesanía* to tour buses that stop to see the sprawling green valley below and by night pumps out live music and a full menu of Ecuadorian fare. Take the stairs (as long as there's still daylight), as the view is unbeatable. At the bottom of the stairs, you'll hit a small *tienda* (shop), which is a perfect place to grab water or a snack for the rest of your walk.

As you head down the winding Camino de Orellana, you'll pass five or so small cafés, most open for dinner. There are a couple more *tiendas* along the way; one has Internet and a phone booth for national or international calls. At the bottom of the great hill is the Iglesia de Guápulo, a gorgeous sanctuary with a museum and monastery inside. There are also park benches for relaxing in this church square below, which you will want to take advantage of before making the long hike back up. Updated: Jan 18, 2013.

Museo "Fray Antonio Rodríguez" de Guápulo

(ADMISSION: $1.50) Museo "Fray Antonio Rodríguez" de Guápulo is housed inside the Iglesia de Guápulo. A history lesson along with a tour of the sanctuary can be arranged. Small religious momentos can be purchased in the museum shop, from posters of the Last Supper to silver rosaries; compared to other religious paraphernalia in town, the prices are cheap and the variety is plenty. Tel: 02-256-5652/254-1858. Updated: Jan 09, 2013.

Guápulo Restaurants

Cafe Arte Guápulo
(ENTREES: $6-7) With hot chocolate, hot wine, hot canelazo, and giant drip candles on the tables, Cafe Arte Guápulo is a good place to warm up on chilly Quito nights. This funky spot is home to a friendly kitty, and the red walls are covered in old music

posters and sketches as well as drawings by local artists and café patrons. Come on the weekend, when the usually laid-back café and outdoor patio fill up with a crowd of hipsters and hippies. Café Guápulo sometimes has live music and other events, and has hosted events by big-name bands like Manu Chao in the past. Monday-Thursday 6 p.m.-midnight, Friday-Saturday 6 p.m.- 2 a.m. Closed Sundays. Camino de Orellana N27-492, Tel: 02-513-2424, URL: www.facebook.com/cafe-arteguapulo. Updated: Jan 22, 2013.

Mirador de Guápulo
(ENTREES: $4-8) Mirador de Guápulo specializes in traditional Ecuadorian dishes like *fritada* (fried pork platter), *sanduches de pernil* (pulled pork sandwiches), *empanadas* (turnovers) and much more. This small restaurant and bar has live music Wednesday-Saturday evenings starting around 8 p.m. As a part of the Sinchi Sacha Foundation, the Mirador de Guápulo highlights traditional Ecuadorian food, culture, music and artifacts along with the museum in the same building. Even if you aren't interested in learning anything new, Mirador de Guápulo is a beautiful spot you shouldn't miss with excellent views and rooftop seating with space heaters. Rafael León Larrea and Pasaje Stubel, behind Hotel Quito, Tel: 02-256-0364. URL: www.miradordeguapulo.com. Updated: Jan 09, 2013.

Pizzeria Ananké
(PIZZAS: $5-10) A small converted bungalow that feels more like a hipster's home than a restaurant, Ananké has a stunning view of Guápulo from its upstairs outdoor patio. This artsy dive specializes in inexpensive, delicious homemade wood-oven pizzas and calzones. The menu also includes an array of appetizers and mixed drinks, including a fresh watermelon vodka cocktail. If you're lucky to drop in at the right time, they have live music playing every so often. Camino de Orellana 781, Tel: 02-255-1421, Cel: 09-9561-3074, E-mail: anankepizzeria@hotmail.com.
Updated: Jan 09, 2013.

Guayaquil

4 meters   2,350,000   04

Guayaquil used to be a place to avoid with little to offer tourists, but Ecuador's largest city and commercial hub now has more than enough to keep you busy for a couple of days. The 3km-long riverside Malecón is a triumph of local organization, mixing cultural and recreational attractions; the bars and art galleries of the regenerated Las Peñas district are ideal for a stroll in the evening and there are plenty of museums as well as extravagant malls to cool off. If you're travelling along the coast or en route to the Galapagos it's convenient to stop over here, but keep things in perspective: as much as Guayaquil has improved in recent years, the oppressive heat could certainly affect your enjoyment and the city remains dangerous in certain places, particularly at night. Luckily, though, the main tourist areas are very safe and well-patrolled. The Malecon is especially safe.

Getting To and Away from Guayaquil

Along with Quito, Guayaquil is one of Ecuador's two major transport hubs, both nationally and internationally. From here it is possible to get to almost anywhere in the country. Even if you don't plan on visiting the country's largest city, you may find yourself passing through the bus station or airport.The new airport and renovated bus station are both conveniently located in the north of the city, just a few blocks from each other, making connections between air and land transport extremely easy. Much to the locals' pride, these two new facilities give Guayaquil a definite edge over Quito at present.

BY AIR

José Joaquín de Olmedo International Airport
Guayaquil's Simón Bolívar Airport closed in 2006 when it was replaced by the brand new José Joaquín de Olmedo International Airport (GYE), named after Guayaquil's first mayor. This terminal is the "Best Airport in Latin America and the Caribbean," according to Business Week Maga-

zine, an accolade it's won several times. The clean, well-organized, and airport is located five kilometers (3 mi, $4 taxi ride), north of the city center, right next to the old airport building. A modern stone and glass building houses both the Domestic and International Terminals, from where it is possible to fly to destinations all across Ecuador (including the Galápagos), in addition to international destinations in Europe and North and South America.

BY BUS

Terminal Terrestre Guayaquil
Along with a new airport, Guayaquil has also just acquired a brand new bus terminal, just north of the airport (Av. Benjamín Rosales and Av. de las Américas, Tel: 04-213-0166 & 7 Ext. 1 / www.terminalterrestreguayaquil.com). The new bus station is clean, relatively hassle-free and contains a pleasant shopping mall, the Outlet Shopping Center. From the Terminal Terrestre, buses run to destinations all across the country, as well as some international destinations, such as Lima, Peru. Purchase your ticket at the offices located downstairs before heading upstairs to find your bus. Regular buses make the eight-hour journey to Quito, the five-hour trip to Cuenca and the 3.5-hour journey up the coast to Montañita.
Updated: Feb 21, 2013.

Getting Around Guayaquil
Because of the heat, you won't want to walk around Guayaquil for very long. There are three options for getting around: public bus, Metrovia or taxi. The public buses ($0.25) are variable in quality and the system is chaotic and confusing, so if it's anything more than a simple, short journey then you're better off avoiding them. The new Metrovia system was modeled on Quito's and is a good way of getting from the bus terminal to downtown.

Avoid rush hour though, when it is jam-packed. Taxis are never in short supply in Guayaquil but few use their meters and will usually try to overcharge foreigners. Most taxi rides around the city should be $2-4. Always negotiate in advance, never take unmarked cabs (very dangerous) and take extra care at night. Many hotels and restaurants will have cards of private taxi companies, which tend to be safer and more reliable. Note that the standard of driving is notori-

GUAYAQUIL

ously bad in Guayaquil so take extra care when crossing the road and check the taxi has a seatbelt before getting in.

Car Rentals in Guayaquil

To rent a car in Guayaquil, all you need is a valid drivers license from your home country. Some companies require you be at least 25, others ask for a security deposit, sometimes as much as $2000 in the form of a hold on your credit card.
Updated: Jul 15, 2012.

Guayaquil Tours

Guayaquil cannot rival Quito in terms of quantity of travel agencies but if you're stopping here, there are plenty of reputable companies to arrange tours to the Galapagos, jungle and elsewhere in Ecuador. The following list is a selection rather than a comprehensive list.

Amazonas

Cdla. Entre Ríos, Av. Río Guayas and Calle Primera, Mz. X1 S, 04-283-1251. www.viajesamazonas.com.

Canodros

Urb. Santa Leonor, Mz 5, Solar 10, Vía al Terminal Terrestre, 04-228-5711. www.canodros.com .

Cetitur

9 de Octubre 109 and Malecón, Piso 1, 04-232-5299. www.cetitur.com.

Dream Kapture

Alborada, Doceava Etapa, Juan Sixto Bernal, Manzana 02, Villa 2104-224-2909. www.dreamkapture.com.

Ecoventura

Miraflores, Av Central 300A, 04-283-9390, www.ecoventura.com.

Galasam

Gran Pasaje building, bottom floor, 9 de Octubre 424 and Cordova, 04-230-4488, www.galasam.com.ec.
Updated: Feb 21, 2013.

Guayaquil Vision

This company specializes in quick and inexpensive open-top bus tours, which are a great way to see several parts of the city. The tour company offers three regular routes, with different levels of amenities and services: the Scenic City Tour, Grand Guayaquil Tour and Noche de Fiesta Tour. Av. de las

Américas # 406, Centro de Convenciones de Guayaquil, Centro Empresarial Of. 11, Tel: 04-228-0732 / 04-230-0744 ext 114 / 098-906-4033, E-mail: info@guayaquilvision.com, URL: www.guayaquilvision.com.
Updated: Feb 21, 2013.

Things To See and Do in Guayaquil

Malecón 2000

The multi-million dollar Malecón 2000 project was begun by former Mayor León Febrés Cordero in the late 1990s and is an astonishing achievement. This 3km public space is by far the biggest attraction in the city for tourists. The cool breezes off the river and the watchful eye of security guards make the Malecón the most relaxing place to spend time in Guayaquil. The obvious starting point is La Plaza Cívica at the end of 9 de Octubre. The highlight is La Rotonda, a statue depicting a famous meeting of South America's two most prominent liberators, José de San Martín and Simón Bolívar. This semicircular monument is spectacular at night. South of La Rotonda are towers dedicated to the four elements, the Guayaquil Yacht Club and the Moorish Clock Tower, constructed in 1931. Just down from the clock tower is the Henry Morgan, a replica of a seventeenth-century pirate ship. A one-hour trip on the river costs $5 (afternoons and evenings only, late-night trips at weekends). South of this is the shopping area. It's bland and mainly sells modern items rather artisan wares but it's a good place to escape the heat. On the other side is an outdoor food court with countless cheap restaurants serving fast food and traditional Ecuadorian specialities, notably seafood. Further south is the quietest part of Malecón at Plaza Olmedo, named after the city's first mayor and beyond that a small artisans' market.

North of La Rotonda is a large children's play area leading to a beautifully laid out set of botanical gardens with more than three hundred species of plants and trees. This is one of the highlights of Malecón so it's worth getting lost in the greenery and stopping for a drink at Aroma Café. Above the gardens are 32 transparent panels with the names of more than 48,000 citizens who contributed to the Malecón project. North of the botanical gardens is the new Museo Guayaquil en La Historia (open 10am–6.30pm daily; $2.50), which packs a history of the city from pre-historic times to the present into 14 dioramas. Above the museum is one of South America' only IMAX cinemas with a 180-degree screen. It's a unique but somewhat disorientating experience.

At the far north end of Malecón, just below Las Peñas, is the impressive Museo Antropológico y de Arte Contemporáneo (MAAC) (04-230-9383 Tues–Sun 9am–5pm. Free entrance), which has an exhibition on ancient history and a huge collection of pre-Columbian ceramics as well as modern art. If you're not visiting the mountains but want to stock up on handicrafts and indigenous clothes, head a couple of blocks in from the north end of Malecón along Calle Loja to the huge, enclosed Mercado Artesanal. Prices are higher than in the Sierra so haggle away.

Further information about Malecón can be obtained from the Fundación Malecón's office in Sargento Vargas 116 and Av. Olmedo, Tel: 593-4-252-4530 / 4211, URL: www.malecon2000.com.
Updated: Feb 21, 2013.

Malecón del Salado
As if the huge Malecón 2000 project weren't enough, it now has a junior version at the opposite end of 9 de Octubre. The Malecón del Salado is named after the tributary of the river Guayas that it straddles. Citizens used to bathe here in the 19th century but it's far too dirty nowadays. However, the pleasant walkway, which undulates up and down bridges, makes for a pleasant stroll and if you work up an appetite there is a cluster of good seafood restaurants at the end.
Updated: Feb 21, 2013.

Las Peñas and Cerro Santa Ana
The north end of Malecón blends conveniently into the colorful artistic district of Las Peñas. This area has been completely regenerated in recent years and is almost as impressive an achievement as Malecón itself. It's a relaxing place to hang out during the day but best enjoyed in the evening when the steep climb up 444 steps is more comfortable and can be broken up by visits into the many welcoming cafes, bars and restaurants. At the top is an open-air museum Museo El Fortín del Santa Ana which has original cannons and replicas of Spanish galleons. There is also a small chapel and replica lighthouse at the top of the hill, but the main attraction is the fabulous view over the city and Guayas estuary. An alternative to climbing the hill is

to walk around to the right from the foot of the steps along the cobbled street of Numa Pompillo Llona, named after the Guayaco who wrote Ecuador's national anthem. There are several art galleries and one of the city's most interesting bars – La Paleta. Further on, the old district blends into the modern Puerto Santa Ana, which is already impressive but as yet incomplete. In addition to the shops and cafes lining the riverside, there will soon be an extensive marina overlooked by luxury apartments. Updated: Feb 21, 2013.

Guayaquil City Center
Beyond Malecón and Las Peñas, the center of Guayaquil is a bit hit and miss with the heat and heavy traffic often marring your sightseeing experience. The center is also sadly lacking in historic architecture, the legacy of several devastating fires, notably in 1896. However, there are a couple of attractions that you shouldn't miss. Top of the list is the small Parque Seminario, most commonly known as the Parque de las Iguanas. If you're on your way to the Galapagos, this will be an amusing hors d'oeuvre and if you're not, it's certainly a memorable experience to get up close and personal with these lethargic creatures. The iguanas lounge around on the grass and in the trees, remarkably unconcerned by the crowds of people. There's also a small pool filled with turtles. The park is dominated by the monument to liberator Simón Bolívar on horseback at its center and the huge white Neo-Gothic Cathedral, rebuilt in 1948, towering over the west side of the square. Between the park and Malecon there is a pleasant square, Plaza de la Administración, surrounded by the elegant buildings of the local municipal government. North along Pedro Carbo will take you to another attractive square, Plaza San Francisco, dominated by the church of the same name and a statue of Pedro Carbo on top of a large fountain.

One block to the south-west of Parque de las Iguanas is the Museo Municipal (Sucre and Chile, Tues–Sat 9am–5pm; free). This is the oldest museum in Ecuador, it's still the city's best and as it's free, what do you lose to? The Pre-Hispanic room hosts a collection of fossils, including the tooth of a mastodon, dating back ten thousand years. There are also sculptures from Ecuador's oldest civilization, the Valdivia, and a huge Manteña funeral urn. Upstairs is a room of portraits of Ecuadorian presidents and a small exhibi-

GUAYAQUIL

tion of modern art. There are five shrunken heads on display in a closed room upstairs, which can only be viewed on a guided tour. Free English-speaking tours are available on request.
Updated: Feb 21, 2013.

General Cemetery and Flower Market

Guayaquil's General Cemetery is among the most elaborate in the Americas. The grounds include neo-classical architecture and sculpture from noted Spanish and Italian artists of the 20th century. Each turn through the labyrinth of mausoleums brings more surprises, such as marble angels weeping or standing over the decorated graves. You can also see Guayaquil's Masonic influence in the nooks and crannies of the cemetery.

The lavish decoration and expensive materials of the tombs on one side of the General Cemetery are a sharp contrast to the wooden crosses on the western side of the hill, where the almost vertical graves seem to have been piled one on top of the other. The west side is where those unable to afford a niche in a cement mausoleum buried their relatives during the night. At the main entrance is the grandiose tomb of Victor Emilio Estrada, a banker and former President of the Republic. Legend says that he made a pact with the devil, exchanging his soul for wealth and power. As a result, his spirit is not at peace and wanders the nearby streets at night. Taxi drivers tell ghost stories in which one of them picks up a man who is walking alone and the passenger then asks to be dropped off at the cemetery entrance, near his tomb.

The flower market is in front of this main entrance, where Calle Machala meets Julián Coronel. The main entrance is next to the "salones de velorio," the place where the families of the deceased mourn for 24 hours before crossing the footbridge to the cemetery. Note that robberies have been reported so do not travel to the cemetery alone and avoid it completely after dark. Julián Coronel and Machala.
Updated: Apr 16, 2013.

Guayaquil Historical Park

Guayaquil historical park is a great place to go if you want to learn more about the city's history and the culture of the coastal region. The park is separated into three main sections: the wildlife zone, the urban architecture zone and the traditions zone. The wild-

life zone consists of elevated paths through natural mangroves. You pass enclosures of animals such as tapir, caiman, deer, sloths, toucans and monkeys. The urban architecture zone has reconstructions of houses and a church from the 19th and early 20th century. The traditions zone gives a glimpse of what life is like in rural parts of the coast, where people continue to live in bamboo homes. This area also includes the "Granja urbana solidaria" program, which promotes communities and families working together to grow healthy produce and curative plants.

The highlight is the boisterous programme of theatrical performances at weekends. Even those who do not understand Spanish will enjoy the spectacle of these lively shows, which reenact traditions and legends from 100 years ago. Characters range from cacao plantation owners to a French-educated Ecuadorian heiress to a hoofed devil disguised as a gentleman. When you're done with the show, the kiosk at the 'peasant's house' offers a variety of tasty traditional snacks. The park is 20 minutes from the city center across the bridge. There are occasional buses from the Terminal but it's easier to take a taxi ($5). Km 1 1/2 Vía a Samborondón, Av. Esmeraldas (junto a Cdla. Entre Ríos), Tel: 04-283-5356/2958, URL: www.parquehistorico.gob. ec.
Updated: Feb 21, 2013.

Cerro Blanco

Cerro Blanco is a protected forest that's easily accessible by bus and is a great day trip from Guayaquil. Visitors can take advantage of a self-guided tour along the two trails, or request a trained guide for a more educational experience. Administered by the Fundación Pro-Bosque, Cerro Blanco protects a section of dry forest that is a biodiversity hotspot. There are more than 500 vascular species of plants and one of the highlights is seeing the ceibo or kapol trees up-close: their green, human-like trunks seem to come right out of a Dr. Seuss book.

The park is located on the edge of a city that has three million inhabitants and harbors populations of jaguar, ocelot, agouti, peccary and other mammals. Birdwatchers will be excited by the opportunity to see mora, with more than 200 species, of which 20 are endemic. The forest is home to a dozen endangered bird species, including the Guayaquil subspecies of the great green macaw (locally called the "papagayo de Guayaquil").

For those looking to stay a while, there is a camping and picnic area with flush toilets, showers and cooking grills. Alternatively, you can enjoy the comfort of a two-bedroom sustainably built cabin. If you're interested in volunteering at the forest, contact the very helpful director of the foundation, Eric Horstman. To get here from Guayaquil, catch a Salinas bus from the terminal and ask to be dropped off. It takes about 20 minutes. Km 16 off the Guayaquil-Salinas highway, Tel: 593-4-287-4947, E-mail: bosqueprotector@yahoo.com.
Updated: Apr 16, 2013.

Guayaquil Lodging

Guayaquilis still not a very popular destination with budget travelers, probably because decent cheap or mid-range accommodation is less abundant than in Quito or Cuenca. There are plenty of high-class hotels to blow your budget. With a handful of in-house restaurants and even a beauty parlor, one Guayaquil hotel where you can really pamper yourself isHotel Oro Verde. Rooms at this chain hotel start around $130 per night.

In the mid-range, Guayaquil accommodations tend to cost between $40-60. Places to stay in this range are called 'guest houses' or 'hostals' instead of hotels, even though they are much more classy establishments than the backpacker hostels most travelers are accustomed to. Hostal Linda has marble floors and elegant furnishings, while the more homeyTangara Guest House has peaceful gardens and a shared kitchen.

Your options are fewer if you're shorter of cash when in Guayaquil. Hostels such asHostal Manso are more like a boutique hotel than a place where backpackers flock. Hostal Manso has a bar and decently designed rooms, as far as Ecuadorian standards go. Prices start around $25 per night.

Note that it's best to avoid the cheapest hotels or Guayaquil hostels in the center of town because many are seedy, unfriendly 'motels,' frequented by locals for secret amorous encounters. The following budget options do not fit into this category.
Updated: Jun 30, 2013.

BUDGET
Dreamkapture Inn
($11-40 per person) Guayaquil is sadly lacking in good-quality budget accommodation

but Dreamkapture, located in a northern suburb Alborada, is a notable exception It's a few miles from the city center but secure, well-maintained and good value for the price. Choose from dorms, rooms with shared bath up to more comfortable rooms with air conditioning and private bath. There is a small waterfall and pool, hammocks to relax in and a small travel agency. and tourism information desk. The manager is American and very helpful. Alborada Doceava Etapa, Calle Juan Sixto Bernal, Manzana 02, Villa 21, Tel: 04-224-2909, E-mail: info@dreamkapture.com, URL: www.dreamkapture.com.
Updated: Feb 20, 2013.

Hostal Manso
(ROOMS: $12-90) Boutique hotels are very hard to find in Guayaquil and you could easily miss Hostal Manso. It's small front door is snuggled into a large block opposite Malecón. Venture up the stairs and you'll find a welcoming slice of Arabia. The maroon décor of the lounge, the seating on cushions and the hammocks in the bar all make for an eclectic mix of originality. The rooms are individually colored and designed (in descending order of price) amber, white, orange, blue, green and pink. The best rooms have private bath and air conditioning, and the cheapest do not. Don't come here expecting to get luxury though; you are paying for the atmosphere and original designs rather than for extra comfort. There are regular theatrical and musical performances in the lounge area and the rooms are closed every three months when the hotel is converted into an Arabian-style bazaar. Malecon 1406 and Aguirre, upper floor., Tel: 04-252-6644, E-mail: reservas@manso.ec, URL: www.manso.ec.
Updated: Feb 20, 2013.

Ecovita
(CAMPING: $22 per day) Ecovita is an organic farm camping site located in Pallatanga, two hours from Guayaquil, promoting projects geared toward community efforts and raising awareness about conservation. The name "ecovita" itself means "ecological life," fitting for a place dedicated to agrotourism and environmental education. Comfortable tents are equipped with mattresses and bug nets, and there are several simple double rooms with baths. Lots of areas for relaxing and play with hammocks, a natural pool, volley ball court, soccer field, pool and ping pong tables, mountain bikes, and even go-kart racing. Pallatanga-Panamericana

GUAYAQUIL

Sur, Km 139 Guayaquil - Riobamba road., Tel: 04-288-8196 - 099-908-5226 / 099-730-0558, E-mail: ecovita@vivecovita.com / info@vivecovita.com, URL: www.vivecovita.com.
Updated: Feb 20, 2013.

Hotel Andaluz

(ROOMS: $25-34) Located just a few blocks from Malecón and 9 de Octubre, the elegantly designed Hotel Andaluz is perhaps the best mid-range deal for travelers who want to be in the middle of everything in downtown Guayaquil. The hotel provides all of the basic amenities: private bath with hot water, air conditioning, and a living room area with leather sofas and TV. One of the hotel's highlights is its garden-like roof terrace. Decoration is simple with a splash of Ecuadorian art. Rooms off the street may be best for those sensitive to noise, since the hotel is located in a rather busy area. Baquerizo Moreno 840 and Junín, Tel: 04-230-5796, Fax: 04-231-1057, E-mail: hotel_andaluz@yahoo.com, URL: www.hotelandaluz-ec.com.
Updated: Feb 20, 2013.

MID-RANGE
Hotel Rizzo

(ROOMS: $40-73) It's not as endearing inside as Andaluz but Hotel Rizzo's position is perfect, right on Parque de las Iguanas. The rooms are well-appointed, some have small balconies and others overlook the park. Downstairs there's a good if slightly pricey café Jambelí which serves set menus for breakfast, lunch and dinner. Clemente Ballén 319 and Chile, Corner., Tel: 04-601-7500, E-mail: reservas@rizzohotel.com, URL: www.rizzohotel.homestead.com/principal.html.
Updated: Feb 21, 2013.

Tangara Guest House

(ROOMS: $40-60) Located in a residential area on the outskirts of downtown, the Tangara Guest House offers a homely hostel atmosphere not easily found in Guayaquil. The communal kitchen and gardens make for a pleasant extended visit. The guesthouse owners also run a tour agency. Breakfast included. Ciudadela Bolivariana, block "F" house 1. Manuela Sáenz & O'Leary streets., Tel: 04-228-2828and9 / 04-228-4445 / 098-129-5186, E-mail: tangara@gye.satnet.net / reservastangara@cablemodem.com.ec / aperroneg@gmail.com, URL: www.tangara-ecuador.com.

Hotel Las Peñas

(ROOMS: $60-90) Hotel Las Peñas, located above the bakery "Panadería California" and just one block from Av. 9 de Octubre, is a nice mid-range option if you want a comfortable place to stay. Rooms have a hotel-chain feel to them without the hefty price. They come with private bath, air conditioning, mini-bar, cable TV, telephone and room service. Laundry and private shuttle service are also available. Light sleepers might want to request an inside room to avoid Guayaquil's street noise. Breakfast is included. Escobedo 1215 between Av. 9 de Octubre and Vélez, Tel: 04-232-3355, E-mail: ventas@hlpgye.ec, URL: www.hlpgye.ec.
Updated: Feb 20, 2013.

Hotel La Fontana

(ROOMS: $45-56) Situated in Guayaquil's downtown banking district (a.k.a. "a well-guarded area") just three blocks from Malecón 2000 and one block from 9 de Octubre, Hotel La Fontana is the best located hotel in its price range and its boutique style is a breath of fresh air from the mundane chain hotels. Rooms have air conditioning, private bath with hot water, cable TV and a telephone. On the corner of Francisco de P. Icaza and General Córdova, Tel: 04-230-7230, E-mail: gerencia@lafontana-ecuador.com, URL: www.lafontana-ecuador.com.
Updated: Feb 20, 2013.

Hotel Suites Guayaquil

(ROOMS: $49-56) Hotel Suites Guayaquil is located in the center, near Malecon del Salado. They are comfortable suites ideal for people looking for more privacy and independence than a hotel can offer. Prices include tax and Internet is free. Airport pick up is also included, just call Mario to set an arrival time. There is a sister hotel located next to the airport. 305, 3rd. Av and 8th St. Cdla. Ferroviaria (railway, near Guayaquil Malecón of El Salado, Tel: 04-239-1120 / 04-239-8305 / 04-220-8089 / 098-624-4077 / 099-961-6161 / 099-768-9186 / 099-791-1246, E-mail: info@suitesguayaquil.com, URL: www.SuitesGuayaquil.com.
Updated: Feb 20, 2013.

HIGH-END
Hampton Inn Guayaquil-Downtown

(ROOMS: $110) Boasting 95 rooms and a 24-hour business center, the Hampton Inn Guayaquil-Downtown offers all the necessities for business or pleasure. Dining options

inside the hotel include Japanese cuisine at the Bonsai Sushi Bar, a la carte lunch and dinner at the Kafe Boulevard Restaurant and a gourmet deli and French bakery at the Deli Boulevard. This family-friendly hotel offers babysitting services, cribs and family package deals. Included in the price of the room are a breakfast buffet, airport shuttle, use of the spa and fitness center, lap pool, Jacuzzi, sauna, valet parking and free WiFi anywhere on the property. Av. 9 de Octobre 432 and Baquerizo Moreno, Tel: 04-256-6700, Fax: 04-256-6427, URL: www.guayaquil.hamptoninn.com
Updated: Feb 20, 2013.

Hotel Oro Verde

(ROOMS: $130) Centrally located and only 10 minutes from the airport, the Oro Verde is a plush choice for those with money to burn. This chain hotel boasts spotless well-furnished rooms, complete with cable TV, Internet, radio, telephone, safe and mini-bar. A couple of days at this hotel would give you just enough time to try out the numerous eateries in the building: El Patio, the Gourmet Deli, La Fondue, Bar El Capitan and the Gourmet Restaurant. The culinary choices are varied enough to satisfy almost anyone's palate and the buffet breakfast is a delicious way to start the day. Aside from eating, you can get pampered in the beauty parlor or head to Oro Fit, the place to work off that heavy breakfast or lunch. Other services include 24-hour room service, laundry, dry cleaning, currency exchange, airport transfer, valet parking and limousine service. A sister hotel is located in Manta. 9 de Octobre and Garcia Moreno, Tel: 04-232-7999, Fax: 04-232-9350, E-mail: reservas_gye@oroverdehotels.com / ventas_gye@oroverdehotels.com / ov_gye@oroverdehotels.com, URL: www.oroverdeguayaquil.com.
Updated: Feb 20, 2013.

Mansion Del Rio Boutique Hotel

(ROOMS: $109-125) We are located in the Barrio Las Peñas, important center of tourism development and one of the most representative traditional neighborhoods of the city of Guayaquil, Mansion del Rio Boutique Hotel provides pleasant space. All of our rooms are decorated with an antique European style, enabling our customers to have the experience of live in the 20th century with the comforts of the present time, making our rooms and suites unique in the city with a splendid view of the river Guayas. Enjoy a friendly atmosphere full of art and delicious Ecuadorian and international food with excellent wines in our restaurant. 120, Numa Pompilio Llona St., Las Peñas neighborhood, next to Puerto Santa Ana, in front of Guayas River., Tel: 04-256-6044 / 04-256-5827 / 04-256-5983 / 04-230-3576, E-mail: reservas@mansiondelrio-ec.com, URL: www.mansiondelrio-ec.com.
Updated: Feb 20, 2013.

Grand Hotel, Guayaquil

(ROOMS: $98-110) The ageing concrete of Grand Hotel Guayaquil looks very uninviting from the outside but inside it lives up to its name, featuring a spacious reception area and excellent service. Centrally located, it's convenient for the city sights and a great place to indulge for a day or two. Activities include splashing in the pool, relaxing in the sauna, massage or working out in the rooftop gym. Rooms are tastefully decorated and have cable TV, telephones, internet connection, hair dryers, radio alarms and in-room coffee machines (always a nice perk). For a bite to eat, head to La Pepa de Oro, the 24-hour coffee shop; alternatives are the 1822 Restaurant, the Turtle Bar and the Barbecue Restaurant. Boyaca between Clemente Ballen and 10 de Agosto, Tel: 04-232-9690, Fax: 04-232-7251, E-mail: reservas@grandhotelguayaquil.com / info@grandhotelguayaquil.com, URL: www.grandhotelguayaquil.com.
Updated: Feb 22, 2013.

Unipark Hotel

(ROOMS: $89-200) Convenient for a leisurely stroll to the Malecón, this upscale hotel is owned by the Oro Verde chain. Smack in the middle of the central commercial district, the hotel is spread across two towers accommodating 139 rooms, including wheelchair accessible room options. The hotel has several restaurants including the UniCafé, UniBar, the Uni Deli and the Sushi Bar, the latter of which has an all-you-can-eat promotion on Wednesdays. Rooms are comfortable, well-serviced and include telephone, voice mail, cable TV, mini-bar, Internet, hair dryer and safe. Airport transfers are available. There is also a small shopping center next door with Banco de Guayaquil ATM. This is a good option for families as the hotel can offer a babysitting service on request. Clemente ballen 406 between Chile and Chimborazo, Tel: 04-232-7100, E-mail: unipark@oroverdehotels.com, URL: www.uniparkhotel.com.

GUAYAQUIL

Sol de Oriente

(ROOMS: $93-111) This is a simple, yet sleek hotel whose various oriental inspirations make it stand out against other characterless hotels in the area. Its 56 rooms come equipped with air conditioning, cable TV, WiFi, and a mini-fridge. Hotel Sol del Oriente has four event rooms that can accommodate anywhere between 40 and 180 guests. The hotel has various dining options, including the Great Wall, which serves international fare, and the Oriental Corner, the in-house breakfast buffet. For a tranquil end to the day, visit the hotel's spa. Those wanting to test out their vocal chords can head to the on-site karaoke bar. There's also an Internet café, international phone booths, printers and other technical support. The hotel can also set up airport transfers. On the corner of Aguirre and Escobedo., Tel: 04-232-5500 / 04-232-8150, E-mail: info@hotelsoloriente.com, URL: www.hotelsoloriente.com.
Updated: Feb 20, 2013.

Hotel City Plaza

($85-135) The newest addition to Guayaquil's top-range accommodation is a modern, sleek business-like hotel. It's a touch more economical than the city's grander options but the rooms are still immaculately presented and the service attentive. Boyaca 922 and V. Manuel Rendon, Tel: 04-230-9209, E-mail: operaciones@hotelcityplaza.com.ec / reservas@hotelcityplaza.com.ec, URL: www.hotelcityplaza.com.ec.
Updated: Feb 20, 2013.

Guayaquil Restaurants and Nightlife

Finding somewhere to eat in Guayaquil is not as relaxed an experience as in Ecuador's more tourist-friendly cities. Many of the restaurants in the center are either bog-standard or else overpriced, attached to high-class hotels. However, look hard enough and you will find some very appealing options. Away from the center, head up to Las Peñas for the most relaxed evening experience or, alternatively, to the northern district of Urdesa, which has plenty of good restaurants along the main street Victor Emilio Estrada.

After dinner, Las Peñas has plenty of bars to have go and have civilized drink. Alternatively, if you want something more raucous, head to la Zona Rosa along Rocafuerte between Roca Rodriguez and Juan Montalvo, but don't stray from the main street and take a taxi back to your hotel when your night is over.

La Pepa de Oro

(ENTREES: $3-9) With service 24/7, The Grand Hotel's La Pepa de Oro is the perfect place to safely grab a bite in Guayaquil if you arrive into town late. Choices range from typical coastal dishes like sea bass ceviche to American options such as a club sandwich. Only a few blocks from the Malecón, it also makes a refreshing stop while taking a walking tour of the downtown area on a sunny Guayaquil afternoon. On Thursday, Friday and Saturday nights, meals are accompanied by traditional "pasillo"music. The menu is in English and includes a brief history of the Ecuadorian Cacao Boom that inspired the restaurant's décor. Boyaca between Clemente Ballen and 10 de Agosto, Tel: 04-232-9690, URL: www.grandhotelguayaquil.com.
Updated: Feb 21, 2013.

La Parrilla del Ñato

La Parrilla del Ñato is an enticing restaurant for meat lovers who want to indulge in a barbecue. Most people come for the parrillada (grilled meats), but be careful when ordering from the untranslated menu and make sure that if you ask for "morcilla" or "chinchulín" that you are ready to eat blood sausage or intestines. Eating with a vegetarian? The ravioli in a rich, four-cheese sauce is a great option and the pizza is also popular. If there is any room left after dinner, try one of the desserts such as a coconut flan (queso de coco) or an after-dinner drink from the bar. This local chain of restaurants is extremely popular at weekends and there's a large restaurant on Victor Emilio Estrada in Urdesa a couple of miles north of the center. Luque 104 and Pichincha (corner), Tel: 04-232-1649.
Updated: Feb 25, 2013.

Sweet and Coffee

Many Guayacos like to pretend they live in Miami, so it's no surprise that this chain has been a huge success in recent years. Large slices of walnut cake, chocolate Oreo cheesecake and lime meringue pie can be accompanied by a frothy vanilla latte or an iced coffee drink. You pay more than most other coffee places, but the quality cannot be questioned. If you want to eat something more authentically Ecuadorian, try an humita (steamed mashed corn with cheese). Malecón 2000, Galería C.

GUAYAQUIL

Updated: Apr 20, 2013.

Menestras del Negro

(ENTREES: $3 and up) Menestras del Negro may seem like a strange, even offensive name ("The Black Guy's Beans" just does not translate well into English), but in Ecuador "El Negro" is often considered an endearing nickname. What the restaurant's name tries to inspire is that they know what they are doing when it comes to making beans.

"Arroz con menestra" (Red beans or lentils and rice) is one of the most common dishes on the Ecuadorian coast. It can be eaten with just a few "patacones" (fried plantain wedges) or more frequently it is also accompanied by thin, well-cooked slices of beef, chicken, or pork. This is a fast-food restaurant, so prices are fairly low, though ordering the same thing at a hole-in-the-wall restaurant around the corner might be almost half the price. On the corner of Malecón and Sucre streets.

Updated: Feb 21, 2013.

Frutabar

(ENTREES: $5-10) Frutabar feels like a piece of Montañita has been transplanted to the big city. Instead of waves crashing, you might catch a view of the Guayas River slowly drifting by, but surfboards converted into tables definitely recall the beach. This café serves light fare like turkey sandwiches and humitas but the highlight is the selection of large batidos (milkshakes). Flavors range from strawberry and peach to coconut and mango or you can create your own. For an extra kick, try the borojó—a dark-brown, endemic fruit paste locally known as an aphrodisiac. Estrada 608 between Las Monjas and Ficus. Tel. 04-288-0255- CENTRO Malecón 514 between Tomás Martinez and Imbabura. Tel. 04-230-0743- SUR C.C. Centro Sur. Chile between el Oro and Azuay. Tel. 04-244-402, URL: www.frutabar.com.

Updated: Feb 25, 2013.

Aroma Café

(ENTREES: $5-10) To break up a hot day of sightseeing, it's hard to beat the location of this open-air restaurant, nestled in the cool, shaded atmosphere of the botanical gardens of Malecón. The café serves a wide range of Ecuadorian meat and seafood specialities, all cooked to perfection and well-presented. If you're not that hungry, it's great for snacks, desserts and of course a wide selection of coffee. Jardines de Malecón 2000, Tel: 04-239-1328, E-mail: aromacafe01@yahoo. com, URL: www.actiweb.es/aromacafegquil.

Artur's Café

(ENTREES: $10) Wander up to the right along Numa Pompillo in Las Peñas to find this dramatically located café/restaurant perched over the river. The open windows make for a fresh, breezy experience and the menu offers all the Ecuadorian staples but it's also good for a quiet drink. Evenings only. Numa Pompillo Llona 127, Las Peñas, Tel: 04-231-2230 / 256-1017, E-mail: arturscafe@hotmail.com / info@arturscafe.com, URL: www.arturscafe.com.

Updated: Feb 25, 2013.

Chapus

This rustic, wooden bar is one of the oldest in the northern district of Urdesa. You can have a quiet drink upstairs early in the evening or shake it up on the dancefloor downstairs later on. It gets very busy at weekends and you're guaranteed a fun, raucous evening. There is usually a cover charge for men at weekends. Victor Emilio Estrada (Las Monjas), Urdesa.

Updated: Feb 25, 2013.

Diva Nicotina

(ADMISSION: $5-7) At the bottom of the steps of Las Peñas, this bar is either quiet or heaving, depending on the live music offering, which is its main attraction. The management are quite selective about who plays here and acts mainly play original songs, so for a entrance charge of $5-7 you can catch some great live music - from Cuban Habanera to jazz. The bar is stocked with every liquor imaginable and they specialize in cigars if you want to puff away while you listen. Moran de Buitron (Malecon), Las Peñas, Price description: Admission: $5-7.

Updated: Feb 25, 2013.

Hotel Oro Verde

Guayaquil's top hotel also hosts many of its best restaurants. Choose from French haute cuisine at Le Gourmet, Ecuadorian specialities at El Patio, Swiss dishes including the obligatory cheese fondue at Le Fondue, and cakes and pastries at Le Gourmet Deli. None of it is cheap, but that's precisely the point – you splash out on something special. Le Gourmet is probably the pick of the bunch. 9 de Octubre and Garcia Moreno, Tel: 04-232-7999, URL: www.oroverdeguayaquil.com.

Las 3 Canastas

(ENTREES: $2.50-4) This Guayaquil institution has a few branches dotted about the

city. It's a colorful, informal café specializing in pastries, fruit salads, ice creams and of course traditional Ecuadorian specialities. You get big portions and it's half the price of many of its rivals in the center. There's a smaller café on the corner of Pedro Carbo and Clemente Ballen between Parque de las Iguanas and Malecon. Panama and Junin.
Updated: Apr 16, 2013.

La Española

If your standard hotel breakfast hasn't quite hit the spot then head to this spotless Spanish bakery. It's a cool escape from the city's heat with reasonable prices and friendly service. It has a wide selection of delicious cakes, pastries and sandwiches so is also a good option for a light lunch or treat. Junin and Boyaca.
Updated: Apr 16, 2013.

La Paleta

You wouldn't happen upon this place by accident, hidden mid-way up Numa Pompillo in Las Peñas, but you should certainly make a beeline for it because it's one of the most interesting bars in Guayaquil. It epitomizes the Bohemian, artistic atmosphere of Las Peñas with an eclectic, colorful décor, low ceilings, nooks and crannies, and a wide-ranging menu of cocktails and tapas. Guayaquil's creative crowd head here and if you're not in Guayaquil for long, this is one place you shouldn't miss. Note that although it's not open-air (like other bars in Las Peñas)and as a result it gets quite smoky later on. Open 8 p.m.-3 a.m. Numa Pompillo Llona 174, Tel: 04-231-2329.
Updated: Feb 25, 2013.

!!!!!

Index

INDEX

INDEX

INDEX

—GALÁPAGOS SPECIES LIST—

Galápagos Species List

This is a general checklist to some of the most commonly seen species in the Galápagos. There are many species in the islands that are not listed here. Spanish names are given in parentheses. For an exhaustive list of just about every species ever seen in the Islands, see the Charles Darwin Research Station's web site: http://www.darwinfoundation.org/english/

FLORA

Thus far, over 1300 vascular plant species have been registered in the Galápagos. Most are introduced species. In addition, there are hundreds of types of lichens, molds, fungi and other flora.

Beach and Shore

☐ Arrayancillo
☐ Beach Morning Glory
☐ Black Mangrove (mangle negro)
☐ Button Mangrove (mangle botón)
☐ Red Mangrove (mangle)
☐ Saltbush (monte salado)
☐ Sea Purslane
☐ White Mangrove (mangle blanco)

Cactuses

☐ Candelabra cactus (candelabro)
☐ Lava Cactus (cacto de lava)
☐ Opuntia, Prickly Pear (cacto gigante)
—There are 14 varieties of Opuntia in the islands.

Inland Plants and Trees

☐ Acacia, Thorn Tree (acacia)
☐ Espino (espino)
☐ Galápagos Passion Flower
☐ Galápagos Rock Purslane
☐ Glorybower (rodilla del caballo)
☐ Guayabillo
☐ Manzanillo, Poison Apple (manzanillo)
☐ Mesquite (algarrobo)
☐ Palo Santo, Incense Tree (palo santo endémico)
☐ Scalesia (escalesia)
—In total, 22 varieties of Scalesia grow in Galápagos.
☐ Yellow Cordia, Glue Bush (muyuyu)

FAUNA

Amphibians

No amphibian species are native to Galápagos. These are introduced species:

Toad (sapo)
Frog (rana de árbol)

Reptiles

In addition to these species, there are some geckos and other reptiles native or endemic to the Islands.

☐ East Pacific Green Turtle (tortuga verde)
☐ Galapagos Land Iguana (iguana terrestre de Galápagos)
☐ Giant Tortoise (tortuga gigante)
—There are 11 surviving species of Geochelone, each restricted to an island or region of island.
☐ Lava Lizard (lagartija de lava)
—There are 7 subspecies of lava lizard.
☐ Marine Iguana (iguana marina)
☐ Galápagos Snake (culebra de Galápagos)

Mammals

Of the 56 mammal species recorded in the Galápagos, only 16 are native or endemic. Others are migratory visitors or introduced animals. Most are marine animals. There were once several species of rice rat native to Galapagos, but they are almost extinct and now only rarely seen.

☐ Bryde's Whale (ballena de Bryde)
☐ Common Dolphin (delfín común de hocico corto)
☐ Risso's Dolphin (delfín de Risso)
☐ Orca, Killer Whale (orca)
☐ Bottle-nose Dolphin (delfín nariz de botella)
☐ Galapagos Fur Seal (lobo marino de dos pelos)
☐ Galapagos Sealion (lobo marino de un pelo)

Fish

The waters around Galápagos are teeming with life, and there are hundreds of fish and marine invertebrate species that make the

WILDLIFE CHECKLIST

island waters their home.Here are just a few of the more commonly seen ones:

- ❑ Galápagos Garden Eel (anguila jardín de Galápagos)
- ❑ Moray Eel(morena)
- ❑ Zebra Moray (morena cebra)
- ❑ Speckled Moray (morena pintita)
- ❑ Pacific Machete (chiro)
- ❑ King Angelfish (pez bandera)
- ❑ Panamic Sergeant Major (banderita)
- ❑ Giant Damselfish (jaqueta gigante)
- ❑ Yellowtail Damselfish (jaqueto amarillo)
- ❑ White-Tail Damselfish (damisela cola blanca del norte)
- ❑ Yellowtail Surgeonfish (pez cirujano)
- ❑ Moorish Idol (ídolo moro)
- ❑ Sabertooth Blenny (diente sable)
- ❑ Mexican Hogfish (vieja de piedra)
- ❑ Harlequin Wrasse (vieja mulata)
- ❑ Wounded Wrasse (señorita herida)
- ❑ Chameleon Wrasse (doncella san pedrano)
- ❑ Spinster Wrasse (doncella solterona)
- ❑ Azure Parrotfish (loro chato)
- ❑ Bumphead Parrotfish (loro jorobado)
- ❑ Bicolor Parrotfish (loro violáceo)
- ❑ Blacktip Cardinalfish (cardenal punta negra)
- ❑ Tailspot Cardinalfish (cardenal pintado)
- ❑ Barberfish (mariposa barbero)
- ❑ Hieroglyphic Hawkfish (carabalí)
- ❑ Leather Bass (caga leche)
- ❑ Flag Cabrilla Grouper (cabrilla piedrera)
- ❑ Creolefish (gringo)
- ❑ Pacific Spotted Scorpionfish (brujo)
- ❑ Ocean Sunfish (mola mola)
- ❑ Guineafowl Puffer (tamboril negro)

SHARKS AND RAYS

- ❑ Galápagos Shark (tiburón de Galápagos)
- ❑ Blacktip Shark (tiburón macuira)
- ❑ Whitetip Reef Shark (tiburón coralero ñato)
- ❑ Scalloped Hammerhead (tiburón martillo)
- ❑ Whale Shark (tiburón ballena)

- ❑ Whiptail Stingray (raya batana)
- ❑ Longtail Stingray (raya coluda)
- ❑ Giant Manta (manta voladora)
- ❑ Spotted Eagle Ray (chucho pintado)
- ❑ Golden Cow Ray (gavilán negro)

MARINE INVERTEBRATES

This extensive group of animals includes mollusks, worms, sea urchins, sea cucumbers, corals, sponges and a whole host of underwater creatures.

- ❑ Galapagos Hermit Crab (cangrejo hermitaño, punta anaranjada)
- ❑ Ghost Crab (cangrejo fantasma)
- ❑ Giant Galápagos Chiton (quitón gigante de Galápagos)
- ❑ Green Sea Urchin (erizo verde)
- ❑ Variegated shore crab, Hairy Rock Crab (Cangrejito de roca)
- ❑ Pencil-spined Sea Urchin (erizo lapicero)
- ❑ Pink Coralline Algae (alga incrustante)
- ❑ Red Algae (alga roja)
- ❑ Sally Lightfoot Crab (zayapa)
- ❑ Sea Cucumber (pepino del mar)

Birds

Some 200 species of birds have been recorded in the Galápagos Islands, of which 56 are endemic or native.

LAND BIRDS

Finches:

- ❑ Mangrove Finch (pinzón de manglar)
- ❑ Woodpecker Finch (pinzón carpintero, artesano)
- ❑ Small Tree Finch (pinzón arboreo pequeño)
- ❑ Medium Tree Finch (pinzón arboreo mediano)
- ❑ Large Tree Finch (pinzón arboreo grande)
- ❑ Warbler Finch (pinzón cantor)
- ❑ Large Cactus Finch (pinzón de cactus grande)
- ❑ Sharp-beaked Ground Finch (pinzón vampiro)
- ❑ Medium Ground Finch (pinzón tierrero mediano)
- ❑ Small Ground Finch (pinzón tierrero pequeño)
- ❑ Large Ground Finch (pinzón tierrero grande)
- ❑ Cactus Finch (pinzón de cactus)
- ❑ Vegetarian Finch (pinzón vegetariano)

- ❑ Galapagos Dove (paloma de Galápagos)
- ❑ Smooth-billed Ani (garrapatero)
- ❑ Galapagos Hawk (gavilán de Galápagos)
- ❑ Galapagos Martin (golondrina de Galápagos)
- ❑ Española Mockingbird (cucuve de Española)
- ❑ San Cristóbal Mockingbird (cucuve de San Cristóbal)
- ❑ Galapagos Mockingbird

(cucuve de Galápagos)
- ☐ Floreana Mockingbird
(cucuve de Floreana)
- ☐ Yellow Warbler (canario María)
- ☐ Vermilion Flycatcher (pájaro brujo)
- ☐ Galápagos Flycatcher (papamoscas)
- ☐ Short-eared Owl (lechuza de campo)
- ☐ Barn Owl (lechuza de campanario)
- ☐ Galapagos Rail (pachay)

- ☐ Elliot's Storm Petrel
(golondrina de Elliot)
- ☐ Wedge-rumped (Galapagos)
Storm Petrel (golondrina de
tormenta de Galápagos)
- ☐ Galápagos Petrel (petrel de Galápagos)
- ☐ Galapagos Shearwater
(pufino de Galápagos)
- ☐ Galapagos Penguin (pingüino
de Galápagos)

WATERFOWL
- ☐ White-cheeked Pintail (patillo)
- ☐ Great Egret (garza blanca)
- ☐ Great Blue Heron (garza morena)
- ☐ Cattle Egret (garza bueyera)
- ☐ Striated Heron (garza de lava)
- ☐ Snowy Egret (garcita blanca
- ☐ Yellow-crowned Night Heron
(garza nocturna huaque)
- ☐ Common Gallinule
(Moorhen) (gallinula)
- ☐ Greater Flamingo (flamenco)
- ☐ Pied Billed Grebe (sormomujo)

SHORE BIRDS
- ☐ Ruddy Turnstone (vuelve piedras)
- ☐ Semipalmated Plover (chorlitejo)
- ☐ American Oystercatcher
(ostrero, cangrejero)
- ☐ Black-necked Stilt (tero real)
- ☐ Spotted Sandpiper (correlino)
- ☐ Sanderling (playero común)
- ☐ Least Sandpiper (playero enano)
- ☐ Willet (playero aliblanco)
- ☐ Wandering Tattler (errante)
- ☐ Whimbrel (zarapito)

SEA BIRDS
- ☐ Swallow-tailed Gull (gaviota
cola bifurcada)
- ☐ Lava Gull (gaviota de lava)
- ☐ Brown Noddy (gaviotín
de cabeza blanca)
- ☐ Magnificent Frigatebird (fragata real)
- ☐ Great Frigatebird (fragata común)
- ☐ Brown Pelican (pelícano café)
- ☐ Red-billed Tropicbird (pájaro tropical)
- ☐ Flightless Cormorant
(cormorán no volador)
- ☐ Nazca (White) Booby
(piquero de nazca)
- ☐ Blue-footed Booby (piquero
patas azules)
- ☐ Red-footed Booby (piquero patas rojas)
- ☐ Waved Albatross (albatros
de Galápagos)

WILDLIFE CHECKLIST

Amazon,
yasuni National Park.
∘Napo wildlife Centre?

CPSIA information can be obtained
at www.ICGtesting.com
Printed in the USA
BVHW04s0957100418
512972BV00020B/333/P